T0353345

Strategic IT Governance and Alignment in Business Settings

Steven De Haes
Antwerp Management School, University of Antwerp, Belgium

Wim Van Grembergen
Antwerp Management School, University of Antwerp, Belgium

A volume in the Advances in Business Information Systems and Analytics (ABISA) Book Series

www.igi-global.com

Published in the United States of America by
    IGI Global
    Business Science Reference (an imprint of IGI Global)
    701 E. Chocolate Avenue
    Hershey PA 17033
    Tel: 717-533-8845
    Fax: 717-533-8661
    E-mail: cust@igi-global.com
    Web site: http://www.igi-global.com

Library of Congress Cataloging-in-Publication Data

Names: Haes, Steven de, editor. | Van Grembergen, Wim, 1947- editor.
Title: Strategic IT governance and alignment in business settings / Steven De
  Haes and Wim van Grembergen, editors.
Description: Hershey : Business Science Reference, [2017] | Series: Advances
  in business information systems and analytics | Includes bibliographical
  references and index.
Identifiers: LCCN 2016028043| ISBN 9781522508618 | ISBN 9781522508625
Subjects: LCSH: Information technology--Management.
Classification: LCC HD30.2 .S7884 2016 | DDC 004.068/4--dc23 LC record available at https://
lccn.loc.gov/2016028043

This book is published in the IGI Global book series Advances in Business Information Systems and Analytics (ABISA) (ISSN: 2327-3275; eISSN: 2327-3283)

British Cataloguing in Publication Data
A Cataloguing in Publication record for this book is available from the British Library.

Advances in Business Information Systems and Analytics (ABISA) Book Series

ISSN: 2327-3275
EISSN: 2327-3283

MISSION

The successful development and management of information systems and business analytics is crucial to the success of an organization. New technological developments and methods for data analysis have allowed organizations to not only improve their processes and allow for greater productivity, but have also provided businesses with a venue through which to cut costs, plan for the future, and maintain competitive advantage in the information age.

The **Advances in Business Information Systems and Analytics (ABISA) Book Series** aims to present diverse and timely research in the development, deployment, and management of business information systems and business analytics for continued organizational development and improved business value.

COVERAGE

- Algorithms
- Information Logistics
- Decision Support Systems
- Geo-BIS
- Business Information Security
- Business Models
- Legal information systems
- Management information systems
- Forecasting
- Big Data

IGI Global is currently accepting manuscripts for publication within this series. To submit a proposal for a volume in this series, please contact our Acquisition Editors at Acquisitions@igi-global.com or visit: http://www.igi-global.com/publish/.

Titles in this Series

For a list of additional titles in this series, please visit: www.igi-global.com

Data Envelopment Analysis and Effective Performance Assessment
Farhad Hossein Zadeh Lotfi (Islamic Azad University, Iran) Seyed Esmaeil Najafi (Islamic Azad University, Iran) and Hamed Nozari (Islamic Azad University, Iran)
Business Science Reference • copyright 2017 • 365pp • H/C (ISBN: 9781522505969) • US $160.00 (our price)

Enterprise Big Data Engineering, Analytics, and Management
Martin Atzmueller (University of Kassel, Germany) Samia Oussena (University of West London, UK) and Thomas Roth-Berghofer (University of West London, UK)
Business Science Reference • copyright 2016 • 272pp • H/C (ISBN: 9781522502937) • US $205.00 (our price)

Automated Enterprise Systems for Maximizing Business Performance
Petraq Papajorgji (Canadian Institute of Technology, Albania) François Pinet (National Research Institute of Science and Technology for Environment and Agriculture, France) Alaine Margarete Guimarães (State University of Ponta Grossa, Brazil) and Jason Papathanasiou (University of Macedonia, Greece)
Business Science Reference • copyright 2016 • 312pp • H/C (ISBN: 9781466688414) • US $200.00 (our price)

Improving Organizational Effectiveness with Enterprise Information Systems
João Eduardo Varajão (University of Minho, Portugal) Maria Manuela Cruz-Cunha (Polytechnic Institute of Cávado and Ave, Portugal) and Ricardo Martinho (Polytechnic Institute of Leiria, Portugal & CINTESIS - Center for Research in Health Technologies and Information Systems, Portugal)
Business Science Reference • copyright 2015 • 318pp • H/C (ISBN: 9781466683686) • US $195.00 (our price)

Strategic Utilization of Information Systems in Small Business
M. Gordon Hunter (The University of Lethbridge, Canada)
Business Science Reference • copyright 2015 • 418pp • H/C (ISBN: 9781466687080) • US $195.00 (our price)

Enterprise Management Strategies in the Era of Cloud Computing
N. Raghavendra Rao (FINAIT Consultancy Services, India)
Business Science Reference • copyright 2015 • 359pp • H/C (ISBN: 9781466683396) • US $210.00 (our price)

www.igi-global.com

701 E. Chocolate Ave., Hershey, PA 17033
Order online at www.igi-global.com or call 717-533-8845 x100
To place a standing order for titles released in this series,
contact: cust@igi-global.com
Mon-Fri 8:00 am - 5:00 pm (est) or fax 24 hours a day 717-533-8661

Editorial Advisory Board

Table of Contents

Chapter 9

Michael Clarke, The Open University, UK
Jon G. Hall, The Open University, UK
Lucia Rapanotti, The Open University, UK

Detailed Table of Contents

Chapter 1
A Business Case Process for IT-Enabled Investments: Its Perceived
Effectiveness from a Practitioner Perspective 1

> Kim Maes, Antwerp Management School, University of Antwerp,
>   Belgium
> Steven De Haes, Antwerp Management School, University of Antwerp,
>   Belgium
> Wim Van Grembergen, Antwerp Management School, University of
>   Antwerp, Belgium

Many organisations perform an adequate job in order to build a sound justification for their decision-making on IT enabled investments. It is recognised that developing a detailed business case is an essential step in order to realise the value potential of IT enabled investments. However, many business cases are often disregarded after the investment approval. Such an attitude towards business case use might be risky. Moreover, several advantages attributed to business cases could only be achieved if they are used continuously throughout the investment life cycle. It is suggested that the latter approach would be more capable to enable benefit realisation and increase the investment success. According to some scholars, a rational transformation is therefore required in which the perspective on business cases shifts from document thinking to process thinking. This study presents an interesting part of the exploration of a process perspective on business cases. Prior research has been helpful to explore individual practices that could support a continuous business case approach and to develop a conceptual model for a business case process. As an important step to increase the validity of the conceptual model and business case practices, the present study investigates through what practices the business case process can be effective in order to enable well-founded investment decision-making and to ultimately increase investment success? Therefore, the article has a threefold aim: (1) to obtain a validated list of business case practices and definitions, (2) to understand the practices' perceived effectiveness / ease of implementation, and (3) to identify a minimum set of key business case practices. In order to achieve these objectives, a group of academic and practitioner experts participated in a Delphi study and validated in total 31 business case practices, of which the majority was perceived as highly effective to support the objectives of a business case process. The paper ends with an exploration of the practical application of business case process practices in the context of COBIT 5, as an instance of a widely used practitioner's framework.

Chapter 2

Ruben Pereira, ISCTE - Instituto Universitário de Lisboa, Portugal
Miguel Mira da Silva, Universidade Nova de Lisboa, Portugal
Luís Velez Lapão, Universidade Nova de Lisboa, Portugal

The pervasive use of technology in organizations to address the increased services complexity has created a critical dependency on Information Technology (IT) that calls to a specific focus on IT Governance (ITG). However, determining the right ITG mechanisms remains a complex endeavor. This paper uses Design Science Research and proposes an exploratory research by analyzing ITG case studies to elicit possible ITG mechanisms patterns. Six interviews were performed in Portuguese healthcare services organizations to assess the ITG practices. Our goal is to build some theories (ITG mechanisms patterns), which we believe will guide healthcare services organizations about the advisable ITG mechanisms given their specific context. We also intend to elicit conclusions regarding the most relevant ITG mechanisms for Portuguese healthcare services organizations. Additionally, a comparison is made with the financial industry to identify improvement opportunities. We finish our work with limitations, contribution and future work.

Chapter 3

François Bergeron, Université du Québec, Canada
Anne-Marie Croteau, Concordia University, Canada
Sylvestre Uwizeyemungu, Université du Québec à Trois-Rivières,
    Canada
Louis Raymond, Université du Québec à Trois-Rivières, Canada

The need to effectively manage IT resources such that they enhance the business value of firms makes IT Governance (ITG) an important issue for both IS researchers and practitioners. The purpose of this paper is to build a conceptual framework for ITG in small and Medium-Sized Enterprises (SMEs). The authors first analyze the main theories applied in ITG research, and confront them with the specificities of SMEs. The authors then highlight the limits of those theories in SMEs context and discuss adaptations needed or alternative theories in such context. The resulting framework is then applied to generate a set of six research propositions on ITG in SMEs.

Chapter 4
Business/IT Alignment in Two-Sided Markets: A COBIT 5 Analysis for
Yannick Bartens, University of Hamburg, Germany
Hashim Iqbal Chunpir, German Climate Computing Centre, Germany
Frederik Schulte, University of Hamburg, Germany
Stefan Voß, University of Hamburg, Germany

Business/IT alignment can be considered a key challenge in IT governance and becomes especially important in IT-heavy and internet based business models. Recent discussions express the need for a bi-directional paradigm for internet based business models. IT governance frameworks support business/IT alignment but mostly follow a business-driven alignment paradigm. We identify characteristics of internet based business models and use the case of streaming to examine how the IT governance framework COBIT 5 can integrate these characteristics under consideration of a bi-directional business/IT alignment process. We reveal that requirements for streaming business models may not be fully covered by the framework. Based on a structural description of internet based business models and the COBIT 5 Goal Cascade, we explain these specific requirements and propose a possible integration of a bottom-up alignment. With this work we provide guidance in the challenge of business/IT alignment for internet based business models and show pathways for IT governance frameworks to better support a bi-directional alignment.

Chapter 5
Aligning Information Systems and Technology with Benefit Management
Jorge Gomes, Instituto Superior de Economia e Gestão, Portugal &
Universidade de Lisboa, Portugal
Mário Romão, Instituto Superior de Economia e Gestão, Portugal &
Universidade de Lisboa, Portugal

Investments in Information Systems and Technology (IS/IT) have not always generated the business value or the financial revenue that should be expected. Some authors argue that the result of those studies that related investments in IS/IT to increased organisational performance over the last thirty years were far from true. Others say that the amount spent on IS/IT and business success has no direct connection. The relationship between IS/IT and performance is widely discussed, but is little understood. Organizations today need to deliver more complex products and demanding services in a better, faster, and cheaper way. The challenges that companies address today require enterprise-wide solutions that call for an integrated approach and the effective management of organizational resources in order to achieve business objectives. Benefits Management (BM) approach proposes a continuous mapping of the benefits of IS/IT investments, implementing and monitoring intermediate results. Balanced Scorecard (BSC) is an innovative approach that considers the financial and non-financial perspectives in determining the performance level of an organization. Not only does it represent a measurement tool, but it is also a multi-dimensional system of performance management which focusses on the alignment of all business initiatives with the strategy. In this paper, the authors propose a link between these two approaches to improve the management of business benefits and to ensure that actions taken along the investment life-cycle lead to foreseen benefits realization. The goal of this integration is to propose a framework that combines the "best of" the both methods. A key issue of this combination lies in the fact that all involved stakeholders must understand more clearly what is required, what is realistically expected, and what is possible to achieve from these investments.

Chapter 6

The call for Business and IT Alignment (BITA) is an everlasting and increasing concern for today's enterprises. BITA is no longer just a technical or local concern. Instead we need to embrace various dimensions in the concept of BITA, for instance strategic, structural, social and cultural. In addition to this, the development of concepts like Digital Innovation (DI), Internet of Things (IoT), Cyber Physical Systems (CPS) has further challenged the success of BITA. As one approach to deal with the multi-dimensional BITA problem and to move the BITA positions forward, Enterprise Modeling (EM) has been acknowledged as a helpful practice. Particularly, EM provides the opportunity to facilitate the creation of integrated models that capture and represent different focal areas of an enterprise, and allows representing the numerous points of view of the key stakeholders. In order to consider the points of view of different stakeholders and create a shared understanding between them the participative character of EM sessions can play an important role. This chapter presents various challenges that EM practitioners face during participative EM sessions, and a number of recommendations that can help to overcome these challenges.

IT Business Value (ITBV) research generally proposes that various "good" IT governance and management practices influence positively IT performance. Yet, this claim has proved hard to verify with empirical data. In this study we first identified and analyzed factors that are seen to influence IT deployment success, then hypothesized about the relationships among and between these factors and finally integrated the hypotheses into a research model. We then empirically evaluated the hypotheses and the entire research model. The consistency of IT investments as the response to the cyclical behavior of the economy is a novel factor introduced in this study to the ITBV research. Special attention was also placed on the perceived importance of IT to business, business-IT alignment and IT management. We used survey data of 212 responses collected from CxOs during an economic recession to test the hypotheses and the model for path coefficients and indirect effects. Empirical results confirmed that all research model factors influenced positively IT deployment success. Moreover, high values in the perceived importance of IT, business-IT alignment and the quality of IT management were discovered to be antecedents to the consistency of IT investments, and when that was achieved, the impact was positive on IT deployment success.

Information Technology (IT) governance is known to play a vital role in the corporate governance in terms of the accountability of the organization's Board of Executives to determine that organization's IT promotes to attain the goals and objectives of the organization, through employing various specific methods, processes and procedures for communication and relationship. In addition, IT governance focuses on how IT is delivering value, controlling risks, managing resources and increase performance. The aim of this work is to analyse IT governance practices used in Abu Dhabi public sector. It employs a quantitative research approach to accomplish the goals of this study. The outcomes of this work refer to important findings such as that most known and recommended international standards and IT frameworks as well as non-IT frameworks are employed by the Abu Dhabi public sector. The known frameworks and standards include ISO 9001, ITILv3, ISO 27001, ISO 20000, PMBOK, BSC, and COBIT respectively, are used as per public entities' needs to enhance the performance of public sector organizations and to comply with local, federal and governmental regulations. This work recommends many plans and best practices that can be employed by both IT governance Board and IT practitioners to leverage IT assets and improve IT governance. Ultimately, the enforcement of such recommended measures in the organizations will result in decreasing overall operational cost as well as enhancing service quality, IT governance effectiveness and interoperability between government bodies.

Chapter 9

Michael Clarke, The Open University, UK
Jon G. Hall, The Open University, UK
Lucia Rapanotti, The Open University, UK

Enterprise Architecture (EA) has been portrayed as one of the cornerstones of modern IT Governance, with increasing numbers of organisations formally recognising an EA function and adopting EA frameworks such as TOGAF (The Open Group Architectural Framework). Many claims have been made of the benefits of EA, yet little is known as to what organisations actually do or evidence of the benefits they accrue through EA. In this paper we report on the results of a small scale survey painting a snapshot of recent EA practice in large UK organisations across the private and public sectors. A key insight from the survey is that, in practice, EA appears to have a greater effect on business-IT alignment than on technological choices.

Preface

Information Technology (IT) has become crucial in the support, sustainability and growth of enterprises. Previously, governing boards and senior management executives could delegate, ignore or avoid IT decisions. In most sectors and industries, such attitudes are now impossible, as enterprises are increasingly completely dependent on IT for survival and growth. Given this centrality of IT for enterprise risk management and value generation, a specific focus on Enterprise Governance of IT (EGIT) has arisen over the past two decades.

Within the University of Antwerp and Antwerp Management School, we have been executing and stimulating applied research in this domain for more than 15 years. We established the IT Alignment and Governance Research Institute in 2003 (www.antwerpmanagementschool.be/itag) to organize and disseminate our research and launched the International Journal on IT/Business Alignment and Governance (www.igi-global.com/IJITBAG) in 2010 for further build an international ecosystem in this research area. The International Journal of IT/Business Alignment and Governance (IJITBAG) focuses on management and governance issues within the IT-related business domain. The emphasis is on how organizations enable both businesses and IT people to execute their responsibilities in support of business/IT alignment and the creation of business value from IT-enabled investments. This journal distributes leading research that is both academically executed and relevant for practice in the professional IT and business community. The journal encourages practice-oriented research papers from academics, case studies, and reflective papers from practitioners. Both quantitative and qualitative research papers are welcome, and special attention is given to explorative research reports that leverage innovate research methodologies to explore new insights in the practitioners' field and theory.

With this manuscript, we want to highlight some of the research that was published in the journal in the period 2013, 2014 and 2015. Authors were asked to improve and update their work with new empirical findings, insights and discussions that they have obtained after publishing their original work in the journal. These enhanced manuscripts are now collected and published in this edited book.

The target audience for this book is threefold:

- Researchers and academics in the field of enterprise governance of IT and alignment, who are interested in new advances in this research area.
- Master students, for whom this textbook can be used in courses typical on IT strategy, Enterprise Governance of IT, IT management, IT processes, IT and business architecture, IT assurance/audit, information systems management, etc.
- Executive students in business schools, for MBA type of courses where IT strategy or IT management modules are addressed.
- Practitioners in the field, both business and IT managers, who are seeking research based fundamentals and practical implementation issues related to it in the domain of Enterprise Governance of IT.

We hope that with this book, we can contribute to further developing the knowledge domain of Enterprise Governance of IT. This book is one of the outcomes of our work within the University of Antwerp – Antwerp Management School – IT Alignment and Governance (ITAG) Research Institute and we would like to thank all business managers, IT managers, audit and control professionals, academics and colleagues who shared their experiences with us during our teaching, research and advisory activities.

Steven De Haes
Antwerp Management School, University of Antwerp, Belgium

Wim Van Grembergen
Antwerp Management School, University of Antwerp, Belgium

Chapter 1
A Business Case Process for IT–Enabled Investments:
Its Perceived Effectiveness from a Practitioner Perspective

Kim Maes
Antwerp Management School, University of Antwerp, Belgium

Steven De Haes
Antwerp Management School, University of Antwerp, Belgium

Wim Van Grembergen
Antwerp Management School, University of Antwerp, Belgium

ABSTRACT

Many organisations perform an adequate job in order to build a sound justification for their decision-making on IT enabled investments. It is recognised that developing a detailed business case is an essential step in order to realise the value potential of IT enabled investments. However, many business cases are often disregarded after the investment approval. Such an attitude towards business case use might be risky. Moreover, several advantages attributed to business cases could only be achieved if they are used continuously throughout the investment life cycle. It is suggested that the latter approach would be more capable to enable benefit realisation and increase the investment success. According to some scholars, a rational transformation is therefore required in which the perspective on business cases shifts from

DOI: 10.4018/978-1-5225-0861-8.ch001

document thinking to process thinking. This study presents an interesting part of the exploration of a process perspective on business cases. Prior research has been helpful to explore individual practices that could support a continuous business case approach and to develop a conceptual model for a business case process. As an important step to increase the validity of the conceptual model and business case practices, the present study investigates through what practices the business case process can be effective in order to enable well-founded investment decision-making and to ultimately increase investment success? Therefore, the article has a threefold aim: (1) to obtain a validated list of business case practices and definitions, (2) to understand the practices' perceived effectiveness / ease of implementation, and (3) to identify a minimum set of key business case practices. In order to achieve these objectives, a group of academic and practitioner experts participated in a Delphi study and validated in total 31 business case practices, of which the majority was perceived as highly effective to support the objectives of a business case process. The paper ends with an exploration of the practical application of business case process practices in the context of COBIT 5, as an instance of a widely used practitioner's framework.

1. INTRODUCTION

Business investments enabled by Information technology (IT) are consistently recognised as investments that hold the highest potential for value creation (Weill & Ross, 2009). The research group Gartner forecasts a stable growth of four per cent per year on IT spending (Gartner, 2013). De Haes and Van Grembergen (2013, p60) state however that "a common and critical dilemma confronting enterprises today is how to ensure that they realise value from their large-scale investments in IT and IT-enabled change." The development of a detailed business case is perceived to be an essential step in the pursuit of value creation from IT enabled investments (Swanton & Draper, 2010; Ward, Daniel, & Peppard, 2008). Yet, many business cases are developed solely in order to acquire a formal approval for the investment and to obtain funding; after which they are disregarded, gather dust on a shelf or are lost on someone's hard disk (Davenport, Harris, De Long, & Jacobson, 2001; Franken, Edwards, & Lambert, 2009; Witman & Ryan, 2010). Some scholars attribute various risks to such an attitude (Avison, Gregor, & Wilson, 2006; S. Brown & Eisenhardt, 1997), while others argue that several advantages of a sound business case come only to the surface if it is adequately used during and after investment implementation (Al-Mudimigh, Zairi, Al-Mashari, & others, 2001; D. Brown & Lockett, 2004; Jeffrey & Leliveld, 2004; Law & Ngai, 2007; Luftman & McLean,

2004; Smith, McKeen, Cranston, & Benson, 2010). In order to realise these advantages, Franken et al. (2009) emphasise that a business case should become a living document that is frequently updated and matures during the entire investment life cycle. This requires a rational transformation on business case use in which people should shift from document thinking to process thinking.

Prior exploratory research in literature and day-to-day operations enabled the identification of multiple individual practices supporting business case use throughout the investment life cycle (Maes, De Haes, & Van Grembergen, 2013, 2014; Maes, Van Grembergen, & De Haes, 2013). Taking a process perspective, the individual practices have been structured into a conceptual model that is developed in line with the process theory (Janowicz, Kenis, & Oerlemans, 2005; Van de Ven, 1992). Hence, the individual business case practices can be employed in order to operationalise the conceptual model of the business case process. As an important step to increase the validity of the business case process model, the present study investigates *through what practices the business case process model can be effective in order to enable well-founded investment decision-making and to ultimately increase investment success?* Therefore, the article has three objectives:

1. To obtain a validated list of business case practices and definitions,
2. To understand the practices' perceived effectiveness / ease of implementation,
3. To identify a minimum set of key business case practices.

These objectives will be achieved by way of a Delphi study in which a group of academic and practitioner experts has been consulted. They validated in total 31 business case practices, of which the majority was perceived as highly effective to support the overall aim of a business case process. The paper ends with an exploration of the practical application of business case process practices in the context of COBIT 5, as an instance of a widely used practitioners framework.

2. CONCEPTUAL MODEL

In academic literature on IT and management, a business case is generally defined as a formal document that provides a structured overview of information about a potential investment. The information enclosed in the business case can be limited to the basic costs, benefits and risks (Hsiao, 2008), or an enriched version may include the identified actions necessary to implement changes and realise benefits along with a benefit realisation plan (Krell & Matook, 2009; Ward & Daniel, 2006). The overall goal of a business case is consistently described as to enable well-founded business decisions to make, let proceed or stop the investment (ITGI, 2008; Post,

1992). Various advantages attributed to business cases result from its continuous use. Business cases can help to monitor the investment progress, budget and risks, while regularly updating a business case increases the likelihood of responding adequately to changes in the investment context (D. Brown & Lockett, 2004; Smith et al., 2010). After the investment has been delivered, it can help to evaluate its contribution and success (Jeffrey & Leliveld, 2004; Luftman & McLean, 2004). Such a disciplined approach increases the use and adoption of the information system (IS) and is fundamental to benefit realisation (Al-Mudimigh et al., 2001; Law & Ngai, 2007). Moreover, frequently developing and continuously using a business case is one of the major success factors for an investment and a source of a competitive advantage (Altinkemer, Ozcelik, & Ozdemir, 2011; Krell & Matook, 2009).

Taking a process perspective on business case use, we assume that such a process can help to transform the static business case document into a dynamic, living document, as suggested by Franken et al. (2009). A common definition of a business process is provided by Davenport and Short (1990, p14): "a business process is a set of logically related tasks performed to achieve a defined business outcome." Building on this definition, we define a business case process as a set of logically related practices that affect a business case and supports continuous business case use with the intent to enable well-founded investment decision-making and to ultimately increase investment success. A business case process runs in parallel with an investment life cycle, presented through a simplified three phase-perspective by Hitt, Wu and Zhou (2002): before, during and after implementation. The conceptual model, displayed in Figure 1, presents a business case process consisting of three distinct but consecutive phases supported by an accommodating layer. These four components constitute together the business case process model and each component is defined in Table 1.

Figure 1. The business case process aligned with an investment life cycle

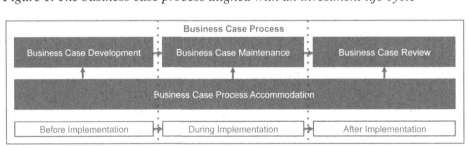

Table 1. Definition of the business case process model components

Component	Definition: A Set of Logically Related Practices to…
Business Case Development	Identify relevant investment information that is integrated in a structured way with adequate and objective argumentation, in order to provide a rationale and justification of the initial investment idea.
Business Case Maintenance	Monitor whether the investment is implemented in accordance with the business case (e.g. objectives, changes, costs), and to update the business case with the prevailing reality (e.g. assumptions, risks).
Business Case Review	Monitor benefit realisation resulting from the utilisation of products and services, and to facilitate the evaluation of the overall investment success.
Business Case Process Accommodation	Facilitate an adequate execution of the business case process adjusted to the investment and organisational context.

3. RESEARCH METHODOLOGY

Building on prior exploratory research that helped to identify individual business case practices and to develop the conceptual business case process model, this study employs a Delphi study in order to achieve the above mentioned research objectives. A Delphi study lends itself well to validate the exploratory findings through the experience of international academic and practitioner experts (Nakatsu & Iacovou, 2009). It structures a group communication process in which experts can individually give their opinion on complex phenomena without needing a face-to-face meeting (Linstone, Turoff, & Helmer, 1975; Taylor-Powell, 2002). In line with academic colleagues (Dalkey, 1969; Nakatsu & Iacovou, 2009; Okoli & Pawlowski, 2004), the Delphi study was performed through a multi-round procedure as presented in Figure 2. After a preliminary phase in which quality experts were selected, objec-

Figure 2. Multi-round Delphi study procedure

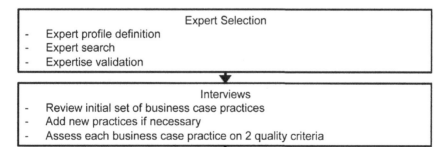

tive 1 was achieved through individual interviews with a small expert group. Two consecutive survey rounds dealt with objective 2 and 3. Each step was executed through an online survey platform.

3.1. Expert Selection

The Delphi study preparation starts with the development of expert profiles for academics and practitioners, and a search for them through multiple networks. The validity of a Delphi study is largely determined by the selection of quality experts (Taylor-Powell, 2002) and we therefore identified qualified experts based on a set of minimum qualifications (Nakatsu & Iacovou, 2009; Schmidt, Lyytinen, Keil, & Cule, 2001). For instance, among other criteria the working experience and expertise level in business case related topics respectively had to account for at least 10 years and good knowledge respectively. In total, 8 experts were individually interviewed and 24 experts participated in the two survey rounds. The background information and expertise level of the 24 experts is shown in Figure 3

3.2. Interviews

As a second step in the Delphi study procedure, interviews were organised to review the quality of the initial set of 54 business case practices in order to obtain a validated list of business case practices and definitions (objective 1). In line with the Delphi study philosophy, the interviews were performed individually without participant

Figure 3. Background information

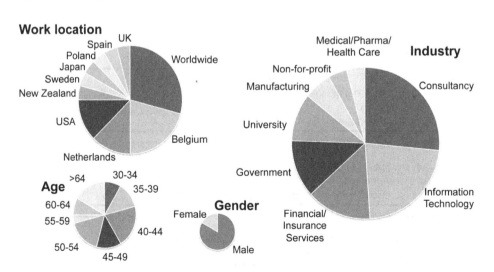

interaction. The interviews started with a structured questionnaire, which was pretested by academic researchers and practitioners, including closed and open-ended questions (Bryman, 2012). The closed questions assessed the practices and definitions through a 5-point Likert-scale (very low to very high) on 2 quality criteria: clarity (robustness and comprehensibility) and relevance (appropriateness to business case usage). The open-ended questions gave the experts the opportunity to provide feedback on individual practices, and to make suggestions to add new practices or to delete others. We followed up on the questionnaire by email to discuss their answers in order to get a deeper understanding of their opinion. We systematically analysed and discussed the quantitative and qualitative responses and updated the list with business case practices.

3.3. Survey Round 1 and 2

In survey round 1 and 2, we aimed to understand the usability of the business case practices (objective 2), and to identify a minimum set of key business case practices (objective 3). Both questionnaires included a clear description of the business case process model and its components to structure the list with business case practices. The experts needed to score each practice on 2 usability criteria, similarly on a 5-point Likert-scale (very low to very high): perceived effectiveness (contribution to the overall objective of the business case process) and perceived ease of implementation (e.g. based on impact, cost, effort). Furthermore, we asked them to provide the top 10 most important business case practices, taking into account their personal experience and their previous scores assigned to perceived effectiveness and perceived ease of implementation. Round 2 was organised to let the experts re-evaluate their own scores attributed in round 1 and to reconsider their top 10 ranking of most important business case practices. We presented the expert's previous individual score/rank, the group average score/rank and the delta between both ranks. The objective of such a reiteration is to achieve a higher level of consensus among the experts. The consensus was measured by the Kendall's W coefficient of concordance for the top 10 ranking (Schmidt, 1997) and we adhered to Van den Heede, Clarke, Vleugels and Aiken (2007) for the effectiveness and ease of implementation questions. The reiteration process of scoring and ranking was performed until we reached one of the following stopping criteria (Okoli & Pawlowski, 2004):

1. A high level of concordance is achieved (Kendall W above 0,7 or average Likert-scale consensus above 0,7 on 'perceived effectiveness'),
2. A third survey round is finished according to our initial promise,
3. The mean rankings for two successive rounds does not show great difference.

Eventually, we reached two stopping criteria in round 2.

The first criterion was reached because the average consensus level on perceived effectiveness scored 0,76 in round 2. The Kendall W coefficient on the other hand did not reach the stopping level. Although the coefficient increased between round 1 and 2 from 0,10 to 0,26, this score is low indicating that a weak consensus has been achieved on which practices are most important. This low consensus can be explained by two reasons. First, determining which practice will be most important is different for dependent and independent practices. Some Delphi studies are performed for independent practices or factors where an expert must determine which practice or factor will be most important or risky (De Haes & Van Grembergen, 2008; Schmidt et al., 2001). In this study however, experts needed to rank practices that can be employed in a sequential manner, i.e. they are dependent upon each other. We assume that some experts have reasoned that therefore the starting practices will be more important, because if one starts from a questionable basis then the next practices are of lesser importance. While other experts might have focused on which practices are indeed the most important if all will be executed anyways. Second, we consider that the investment context could have a substantial impact on which business case practice is perceived to be the most important. Some experts might have reasoned from a different perspective. As we stopped based on criterion 1, the second criterion was not reached. The third criterion was also realised because the top 10 most important business case practices included no new practices in round 2 and no substantial shifts could be ascertained between round 1 and 2. Due to a tied 10th and 11th rank, the final top 10 includes 11 practices (see Table 3).

Table 3. Minimum set of key business case practices

Top 10 Business Case Practices	Total Times Mentioned	Total Score	Total Rank
BCD02 Capturing business drivers	18	136	1
BCD09 Identifying investment benefits	18	135	2
BCD07 Identifying investment objectives	16	127	3
BCD03 Identifying stakeholder expectations	16	119	4
BCD01 Capturing investment vision	12	79	5
BCD10 Identifying investment costs	12	74	6
BCD14 Evaluating cost/benefit analysis	11	66	7
BCD11 Identifying investment risks	14	65	8
BCPA07 Ensuring communication and involvement with stakeholders	11	48	9
BCD05 Identifying investment scope	10	38	10
BCD12 Developing benefits realisation plan	7	38	10

4. FINDINGS AND INTERPRETATIONS

4.1. Interviews: Validation of Initial Set Business Case Practices

The interviews provided much quantitative and qualitative data, which we systematically analysed and discussed in order to achieve the first objective. The list with business case practices was eventually reduced from 54 initially identified practices to 31 validated practices based on two principles. First, practices had to be focused and easy to comprehend so we merged several practices while others were split, and all definitions were drastically shortened to increase the comprehensibility. Second, practices had to focus on business case usage so we removed practices that were more closely related to project management and other operational issues. We also structured the business case practices through the process model. Table 2 shows the validated list of practices with their respective definitions, and an individual code that links them to a specific process model component (as explained before).

4.2. Survey Round 1 and 2: Score and Rank Business Case Practices

Figure 4. shows the consensus level between experts regarding effectiveness and ease of implementation by providing the percentage of experts that rated 4 or 5 (on a scale of 5) for these questions. In total, we see that above 90 per cent of the experts perceive BCD03, BCD07 and BCPA07 as highly effective, reaching the cut-off level of very high consensus (Schmidt, 1997). More than 80 per cent of the experts perceive 12 practices as highly effective, and 23 practices are within the cut-off consensus level that more than 70 per cent of the experts perceive them as highly effective (grey rectangle in Figure 4). Eight practices do not reach the 70 per cent consensus level.

In general, we observe that stakeholders attention is found to be highly effective: 'Identifying stakeholder expectations' (BCD03) and 'Ensuring communication and involvement with stakeholders' (BCPA07) is positioned within the top 3 of highly effective practices, and reach a very high level of consensus among experts. This does not come as a surprise as various academics have stressed before on the importance of stakeholder involvement and commitment (Davenport, Harris, & Shapiro, 2010; Sherif & Vinze, 2002; Smith et al., 2010). Another set of practices that are perceived to be highly effective deals with what the investment wants to realise. One expert clarifies: "It is of utmost importance to (1) know exactly what problem you want to solve, (2) understand how this will be solved, and (3) obtain and maintain the desire to achieve this." Although the latter refers mostly to the importance

Table 2. Validated list of business case practices and their respective definitions

Code	A Business Case Is Developed by…	Definition
BCD01	Capturing investment vision	Capture the investment vision and establish the appropriate investment context.
BCD02	Capturing business drivers	Capture the business challenges and opportunities that drive the investment and how they contribute to the achievement of the organisational strategy.
BCD03	Identifying stakeholder expectations	Identify the stakeholders' expectations, needs and requirements in terms of delivered benefits.
BCD04	Identifying technology opportunities	Identify proven and emerging technologies that support the business drivers and may realise the investment objectives.
BCD05	Identifying investment scope	Identify what will be done in the investment and what not, and explain why.
BCD06	Identifying investment assumptions	Identify realistic assumptions and their logic for business drivers, investment objectives, investment solution(s), benefits, and costs.
BCD07	Identifying investment objectives	Identify and categorise what objectives the investment should achieve.
BCD08	Identifying investment solution(s)	Identify what organisational and technological changes are required, design one or more alternative investment solutions and implementation scenarios, and assign change owners.
BCD09	Identifying investment benefits	Identify and categorise what benefits will be created by the investment based on relevant evidence, define their explicit measures and assign benefit owners.
BCD10	Identifying investment costs	Identify and categorise what costs will be created by the investment based on relevant evidence, and define their explicit measures.
BCD11	Identifying investment risks	Identify and evaluate the impact and probability of investment risks and critical success factors, and determine preferred solutions to take a proactive approach.
BCD12	Developing benefits realisation plan	Develop a structured plan on when each benefit will be realised, in relevant phases and with appropriate consideration of organisational factors.
BCD13	Evaluating investment feasibility and viability	Evaluate the feasibility and viability of each alternative investment solution.
BCD14	Evaluating cost/benefit analysis	Capture identified investment costs and benefits with measures and values, and evaluate cost/benefit analysis to support the financial argumentation.
Code	Maintained by…	Definition
BCM01	Monitoring business case relevance	Monitor the business drivers, objectives and assumptions, and control whether they are still relevant and realistic.
BCM02	Monitoring investment scope	Monitor the investment scope and realisation of changes, and control whether it is still in line with the business case relevance.

continued on following page

Table 2. Continued

BCM03	Monitoring investment costs	Monitor whether the investment costs are consumed according to the scope and identified changes.
BCM04	Monitoring investment risks	Monitor the investment risks and evaluate their impact on the business case.
BCM05	Updating business case to react adequately	Update the business case frequently based on business case monitoring and identify adequate actions.
Code	**Reviewed by…**	**Definition**
BCR01	Identifying objective evaluation criteria	Identify and communicate objective criteria with predefined weighting that help to evaluate the investment effectiveness and efficiency.
BCR02	Evaluating investment effectiveness	Monitor benefits realisation, and evaluate the contribution of investment objectives and changes.
BCR03	Evaluating investment efficiency	Evaluate the effort and costs that were consumed to realise the investment.
Code	**A Business Case Process Accommodated by…**	**Definition**
BCPA01	Establishing adaptable business case approach	Establish an adaptable business case approach according to investment and accept a growing maturation and granularity through its development and usage.
BCPA02	Establishing business case templates, training and guidance	Establish standard business case templates and tools, and accommodate training and guidance on what constitute business case practices and how to employ them adequately.
BCPA03	Establishing maximum objectivity in business case usage	Maximise objectivity to support well-founded and comparable decision-making without influence from politics, lobbying or institutional powers.
BCPA04	Establishing simple and dynamic business case usage	Describe and employ business case practices and its content in a simple, straightforward and dynamic manner to encourage their usage.
BCPA05	Establishing business case practices as standard approach	Establish and evangelise business case practices as a standard way of working.
BCPA06	Ensuring business case practice improvements	Ensure business case practice improvements further through experience and continuous learning.
BCPA07	Ensuring communication and involvement with stakeholders	Ensure clear communication and active involvement with all stakeholders in order to gain insight, commitment and ownership.
BCPA08	Ensuring stakeholder confirmation	Ensure formal confirmation from relevant stakeholders on the (updated) business case to increase their commitment.
BCPA09	Evaluating business case regularly	Evaluate all business case documents in order to make well-founded decisions to approve, let proceed or stop the investment.

Figure 4. Background information of the final 24 experts

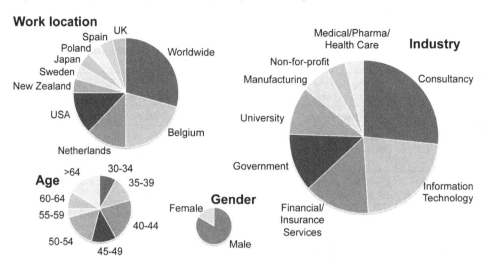

of stakeholder attention and involvement, the other two can directly be linked to BCD01, BCD02, BCD05, and BCD07. Indeed, the development of a business case should start from these fundamental practices (Ward et al., 2008).

The consensus levels on perceived ease of implementation are much lower and many experts attributed a score of 3 to several practices (moderate easiness). This demonstrates that experts have great difficulty to agree on their ease of implementation. Very low consensus levels on ease of implementation were achieved for 25 practices. In Figure 5, the light grey bars for these practices do not reach the 30 per cent consensus level indicated by the vertical black line. In other words, experts reached a high consensus level (>70%) that these 25 practices are difficult or moderately easy to implement. This finding should not come as a surprise as many organisations still struggle with business case usage (Jeffrey & Leliveld, 2004; Taudes, Feurstein, & Mild, 2000).

If we perform an analysis on the consensus levels per business case process component, we observe that the BCM component has achieved highest consensus on its effectiveness, closely followed by those in the BCD component (see Figure 6). The consensus level for BCPA practices is still within the high consensus cut-off level (>70%), while only 64% of the experts perceive BCR practices as effective. Although all four components receive a low to very low consensus rate on perceived ease of implementation, again practices from the BCM component achieve the highest rate. Hence, we might reason that organisations will achieve the highest return on effort when they implement the practices from the BCM component. Following up on the relevance of the business case is certainly important (Al-Mudimigh

Figure 5. Consensus levels on perceived effectiveness and perceived ease of implementation of business case practices (based on score 4 and 5 on Likert-scale)

et al., 2001), because the business drivers and objectives can be impacted by a shift in market, organisational or technological issues. If an organisation wants to understand how it needs to react on these changes, this impact should be investigated. In case a dramatic change threatens the business case relevance, one should reassess the fundamental assumptions and perform a new cost-benefit analysis (Flynn, Pan, Keil, & Mähring, 2009; Iacovou & Dexter, 2004). We think experts perceive the effectiveness of these BCM practices as high as they possess the ability to have a direct impact on last-minute changes and to contribute greatly to the effects of ongoing investment-decision-making.

The lowest return might be expected from practices in the BCR component, as they score lowest on both effectiveness and ease of implementation. Potentially, experts have reasoned that the job is done by then and that these practices have no direct impact anymore on the final result. This is however not entirely true, because

13

Figure 6. Average consensus levels on perceived effectiveness and perceived ease of implementation of business case practices per process model component

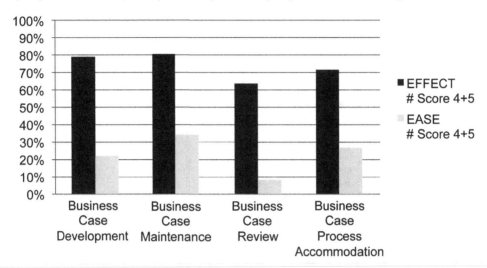

'Monitoring benefit realisation' is included in BCR02 and believed to be critical after the resulting products and services from the investment have officially been launched (Iacovou & Dexter, 2004). With regard to the second objective of this paper, we conclude that a great discrepancy can be found between how effective most business case practices are perceived to be and the perception of their ease of implementation. This contrast signals an important urge to investigate how these practices can be (better) implemented in the future.

The third objective of this study was to identify a minimum set of key business case practices. Experts were therefore asked to rank the ten most important practices from 1 to 10, taking into account their personal experience and their previous scores assigned to perceived effectiveness and ease of implementation. Although the ranking exercise is limited by a weak agreement among experts (low Kendall W score of 0,26) on the top 10, as we explained before, this might be affected by the chronological dependence among individual practices. We are thus not able to deduce strong conclusions on what are the most important practices. Yet, if we compare the results of the top 10 ranking with the set of practices that received a high consensus on perceived effectiveness, we observe that 10 out of 11 top 10 ranked practices achieved consensus by 79 per cent of the experts or more. Table 3 presents the 11 practices ranked in the top 10 (11 practices were included due to a tied 10th and 11th rank), where practices that reached a high consensus level on perceived effectiveness are indicated in grey. The table also shows the number of times a practice was mentioned in the top 10 (total times mentioned) and the total ranking score (e.g. if a practice is ranked 1st, it receives 10 points).

Only 'Identify investment costs' (BCD10) did not reach the 70 per cent cut-off level of high consensus on perceived effectiveness (scoring 63 per cent). This finding surprises us as many scholars in literature emphasise the importance of identifying the investment costs in detail (Franken et al., 2009). According to Ward et al. (2008, p. 9), "a complete business case must obviously include all costs." The authors say that it should be relatively easy to calculate the direct IT costs, but people have much more difficulty with estimating the costs associated with business and organisational changes. The underestimation of costs can have a dramatic impact on budget overruns and on ultimate value contribution. Combining these claims from literature with its 6th rank in the top 10 ranking, we might argue that this practice can be perceived as necessary in the business case process. Especially, since 'Monitoring investment costs' (BCM03) is perceived as effective by 83 per cent of the experts, we consider the identification of investment costs as necessary to effectively execute BCM03.

5. LINKING THE BUSINESS CASE PROCESS AND GENERAL PRACTITIONER FRAMEWORKS: THE COBIT 5 CASE

This article discusses the expert view on how a business case process can be valuable. In other words, through what business case practices the business case process can be effective in order to support well-founded investment decision-making and to increase the investment success. In the context of the COBIT 5 Enabling Processes (ISACA, 2012), an instance of a widely used practitioners framework, we see various opportunities for the business case process model and its individual practices. This paper will focus on two enabling processes as an example that is shown in Table 4: 'Manage Innovation' (APO04) and 'Manage Programmes & Projects' (BAI01).

First, the process 'Manage Innovation' (APO04) helps an organisation to be on the outlook for innovation opportunities and to plan how they can benefit from innovation in relation to business needs. The business case practices BCD02 and BCD04 can be of direct help by identifying technology opportunities and capturing the business drivers of these opportunities in relation to the enterprise environment (APO04.02 'Maintain an understanding of the enterprise environment' / APO04.03 'Monitor and scan the technology environment'). In order to understand how the organisation can benefit from these technology enabled innovations, it can employ BCD09 and BCD12 to assess the potential of emerging technologies and innovation ideas (APO04.04). While BCD09 helps with the identification of the anticipated benefits, practice BCD12 will outline when these benefits should be realised. Practices from the BCM component can be of specific value for management practice

Table 4. Mapping diagram of business case practices to two enabling processes of COBIT 5

	Manage Innovation (APO04)	Manage Programmes and Projects (BAI01)
BCD01 Capturing investment vision		
BCD02 Capturing business drivers	APO04.02	
BCD03 Identifying stakeholder expectations		BAI01.03
BCD04 Identifying technology opportunities	APO04.03	
BCD05 Identifying investment scope		
BCD06 Identifying investment assumptions		
BCD07 Identifying investment objectives		
BCD08 Identifying investment solution(s)		
BCD09 Identifying investment benefits	APO04.04	
BCD10 Identifying investment costs		
BCD11 Identifying investment risks		BAI01.10
BCD12 Developing benefit realisation plan	APO04.04	BAI01.02
BCD13 Evaluating investment feasibility and viability		
BCD14 Evaluating cost/benefit analysis		
BCM01 Monitoring business case relevance	APO04.06	BAI01.06
BCM02 Monitoring investment scope	APO04.06	BAI01.06
BCM03 Monitoring investment costs	APO04.06	
BCM04 Monitoring investment risks	APO04.06	BAI01.10
BCM05 Updating business case to react adequately	APO04.06	BAI01.02
BCR01 Identifying objective evaluation criteria		BAI01.11
BCR02 Evaluating investment effectiveness		BAI01.11
BCR03 Evaluating investment efficiency		BAI01.11
BCPA01 Establishing adaptable business case approach		
BCPA02 Establishing business case templates, training and guidance		
BCPA03 Establishing maximum objectivity in business case usage		
BCPA04 Establishing simple and dynamic business case usage		
BCPA05 Establishing business case practices as standard approach		
BCPA06 Ensuring business case practice improvements		
BCPA07 Ensuring communication and involvement with stakeholders		BAI01.03
BCPA08 Ensuring stakeholder confirmation		BAI01.02 BAI01.03
BCPA09 Evaluating business case regularly		

APO04.06 by monitoring "the implementation and use of emerging technologies and innovations during integration, adoption and for the full economic life cycle to ensure that the promised benefits are realised" (ISACA, 2012, p72).

Second, the process 'Manage Programmes & Projects' (BAI01) covers the entire investment life cycle of a programme/project, so we argue that multiple practices spread across the business case process can be of importance. As a practice to develop and accommodate the business case process, stakeholder inclusion is perceived to be highly effective in order to achieve a desirable investment outcome (supporting BAI01.03 Manage stakeholder engagement). As part of the management practice BAI01.02 (Initiate a programme), confirmation should be achieved from stakeholders on their active participation as sponsor or member of the programme board or committee. The development of a benefit realisation plan (BCD12) and the continuous act of reviewing and updating the business case (BCM05 / BCPA09) is also foreseen in this management practice (BAI01.02). In addition, we would advise the use of practices BCM01 and BCM02 to evaluate whether the investment is still in line with the drivers and objectives, and on track with the implementation of the required changes (BAI01.06 Monitor, control and report on the programme outcomes). The practices BCR01, BCR02 and BCR03 on the other hand help to evaluate the investment contributions against predefined review criteria (BAI01.11 Monitor and control projects). The management of programme and project risks (BAI01.10) can be safeguarded by way of the business case practices to identify and monitor the investments risks (BCD11 / BCM04). These two examples demonstrate that the business case process and its individual practices can be of use in parallel with the execution of some enabling processes from COBIT 5.

6. CONCLUSION AND FUTURE RESEARCH

As an important step to increase the validity of the business case process model, the present study investigated *through what practices the business case process model can be effective in order to enable well-founded investment decision-making and to ultimately increase investment success?* The findings show that a validated set of 31 business case practices and definitions has been obtained (objective 1). The Delphi study additionally provided us with a better understanding of the perceived effectiveness and perceived ease of implementation of these business case practices (objective 2); and with the identification of a minimum set of key business case practices (objective 3).

As a subset of business case practices, especially those practices that focus on stakeholder inclusion and the specification of 'what the investment wants to achieve' are considered to be of utmost importance. In many study fields, stakeholder management and stakeholder involvement is seen as critical for the success of an invest-ment, whether this includes an IT enabled project, a business change program, or a large organisational transformation. For instance, according to Matthews (2004) an important step in an investment project "is to start contacting internal and external stakeholders to discuss the business implications of such a system. By lining up internal support behind the program (hopefully on both economic and environmen-tal grounds), a stronger and broader business case can be developed and presented to management." A clear definition of what the investment wants to achieve is an equally essential part of the business case process. Beatty and Gordon (1991) argue that "without a business case containing clear targets, progress is difficult to moni-tor and evaluate, and evangelists set their own targets." Similar observations can be found in the top 10 rank of most important business case practices as well as in the two enabling processes of the COBIT 5 framework through the management practices APO04.02, BAI01.03, APO04.03. This cross validation makes a strong argument to spend sufficient time and effort on:

1.   Clearly defining what the investment should realise, and
2.   How stakeholders can be involved throughout the investment life cycle.

The findings also show a noticeable gap between the effectiveness and ease of implementation of business case practices. This finding is quite problematic since experts are convinced that organisations will have enormous difficulties with the implementation of the business case practices. This calls for future research that focuses on how these practices could be implemented. If we would be able to gain a better understanding on the applicability of business case practices, organisations can directly benefit from the dispersion of this knowledge. Organisations should be closely involved in the next steps of this research, so it can be investigated why the practices are difficult to implement. In this study experts have reasoned that it would be difficult, yet the observation and reasoning of organisations may differ. If organisations have the knowledge and skills to continuously employ a business case, they would appreciate the advantages it can bring to their investment success.

The paper ended with an exploration of the practical application of business case process practices in the context of COBIT 5, as an instance of a widely used practi-tioners framework. Organisations do not need to start with the implementation of all 31 business case practices, but they can start with those practices that are considered to be most effective by experts. Organisations that have already implemented COBIT 5 can benefit from the link between our business case practices and the COBIT 5 enabling processes as described in the discussion section. This study was executed within the context of large for-profit organisations, but it would be interesting to undertake future research on the applicability of the business case process and practices in other environments. For instance, small and medium sized companies or governments might need other or more focused practices in their specific context. The latter could also be related to the investigation of the perceived effectiveness and ease of implementation of business case practices. It would be very interesting to explore how this perception and experience may vary between different types of investments and organisational contexts.

ACKNOWLEDGMENT

The authors would like to thank the international experts who took the time to participate in the Delphi study and to share their experiences and suggestions. Our research has been funded by a Ph.D. grant of the Belgian Agency for Innovation by Science and Technology.

REFERENCES

Al-Mudimigh, A., Zairi, M., & Al-Mashari, M. et al. (2001). ERP software implementation: An integrative framework. *European Journal of Information Systems*, *10*(4), 216–226. doi:10.1057/palgrave.ejis.3000406

Altinkemer, K., Ozcelik, Y., & Ozdemir, Z. (2011). Productivity and Performance Effects of Business Process Reengineering: A Firm-Level Analysis. *Journal of Management Information Systems*, *27*(4), 129–162. doi:10.2753/MIS0742-1222270405

Avison, D., Gregor, S., & Wilson, D. (2006). Managerial IT unconsciousness. *Communications of the ACM*, *49*(7), 89–93. doi:10.1145/1139922.1139923

Beatty, C., & Gordon, J. (1991). Preaching the Gospel: The Evangelists of New Technology. *California Management Review*, *33*(3), 73–94. doi:10.2307/41166662

Brown, D., & Lockett, N. (2004). Potential of critical e-applications for engaging SMEs in e-business: A provider perspective. *European Journal of Information Systems*, *13*(1), 21–34. doi:10.1057/palgrave.ejis.3000480

Brown, S., & Eisenhardt, K. (1997). The art of continuous change: Linking complexity theory and time-paced evolution in relentlessly shifting organizations. *Administrative Science Quarterly*, *42*(1), 1–34. doi:10.2307/2393807

Bryman, A. (2012). *Social Research Methods*. Oxford University Press.

Dalkey, N. (1969).*The Delphi Method: An Experimental Study of Group Opinion (No. RM-5888-PR)*. The Rand Corporation.

Davenport, T., Harris, J., De Long, D., & Jacobson, A. (2001). Data to Knowledge to Results: Building an Analytic Capability. *California Management Review*, *43*(2), 117–138. doi:10.2307/41166078

Davenport, T., Harris, J., & Shapiro, J. (2010). Competing on Talent Analytics. *Harvard Business Review*, *88*(10), 52–58. PMID:20929194

Davenport, T., & Short, J. (1990). The New Industrial Engineering: Information Technology and Business Process Redesign. *Sloan Management Review*, *31*(4), 11–27.

De Haes, S., & Van Grembergen, W. (2008). An exploratory study into the design of an IT governance minimum baseline through Delphi research. *Communications of the Association for Information Systems*, *22*, 443–458.

De Haes, S., & Van Grembergen, W. (2013). Improving enterprise governance of IT in a major airline: a teaching case. *Journal of Information Technology Teaching Cases*.

Flynn, D., Pan, G., Keil, M., & Mähring, M. (2009). De-escalating IT projects: The DMM model. *Communications of the ACM*, *52*(10), 131–134. doi:10.1145/1562764.1562797

Franken, A., Edwards, C., & Lambert, R. (2009). Executing Strategic Change: Understanding the Critical Management Elements That Lead to Success. *California Management Review*, *51*(3), 49–73. doi:10.2307/41166493

Gartner. (2013, September 26). *Gartner Worldwide IT Spending Forecast*. Retrieved December 6, 2013, from http://www.gartner.com/technology/research/it-spending-forecast/

Hitt, L., Wu, D., & Zhou, X. (2002). Investment in enterprise resource planning: Business impact and productivity measures. *Journal of Management Information Systems*, *19*(1), 71–98.

Hsiao, R. (2008). Knowledge sharing in a global professional service firm. *MIS Quarterly Executive*, *7*(3), 399–412.

Iacovou, C., & Dexter, A. (2004). Turning Around Runaway Information Technology Projects. *California Management Review*, *46*(4), 68–88. doi:10.2307/41166275

ISACA. (2012). *COBIT 5 Enabling Processes*. ISACA.

ITGI. (2008). *Enterprise Value: Governance of IT Investments: The Business Case*. IT Governance Institute. Retrieved from www.isaca.org

Janowicz, M., Kenis, P., & Oerlemans, L. (2005). *Promises and pitfalls of studying process patterns of networks*. Unpublished manuscript, Tilburg University, Netherlands.

Jeffrey, M., & Leliveld, I. (2004). Best practices in IT portfolio. *MIT Sloan Management Review*, *45*(3), 41–49.

Krell, K., & Matook, S. (2009). Competitive advantage from mandatory investments: An empirical study of Australian firms. *The Journal of Strategic Information Systems*, *18*(1), 31–45. doi:10.1016/j.jsis.2008.12.001

Law, C., & Ngai, E. (2007). ERP systems adoption: An exploratory study of the organizational factors and impacts of ERP success. *Information & Management*, *44*(4), 418–432. doi:10.1016/j.im.2007.03.004

Linstone, H., Turoff, M., & Helmer, O. (1975). The Delphi method: Techniques and applications. Addison-Wesley Publishing Company.

Luftman, J., & McLean, E. (2004). Key issues for IT executives. *MIS Quarterly Executive*, *3*(2), 89–104.

Maes, K., De Haes, S., & Van Grembergen, W. (2013). Investigating a Process Approach on Business Cases: An Exploratory Case Study at Barco. *International Journal of IT/Business Alignment and Governance*, *4*(2), 37–53.

Maes, K., De Haes, S., & Van Grembergen, W. (2014). An Expert View on Business Case Usage: A Delphi Study. In *Proceedings of the European Conference on Information Management and Evaluation*.

Maes, K., Van Grembergen, S., & De Haes, S. (2013). Identifying Multiple Dimensions of a Business Case: A Systematic Literature Review. *The Electronic Journal Information Systems Evaluation*, *16*(4), 302–314.

Matthews, H. (2004). Thinking Outside "the Box": Designing a Packaging Take-Back System. *California Management Review*, *46*(2), 105–119. doi:10.2307/41166213

Nakatsu, R., & Iacovou, C. (2009). A comparative study of important risk factors involved in offshore and domestic outsourcing of software development projects: A two-panel Delphi study. *Information & Management*, *46*(1), 57–68. doi:10.1016/j.im.2008.11.005

Okoli, C., & Pawlowski, S. (2004). The Delphi method as a research tool: An example, design considerations and applications. *Information & Management, 42*(1), 15–29. doi:10.1016/j.im.2003.11.002

Post, B. (1992). A Business Case Framework for Group Support Technology. *Journal of Management Information Systems, 9*(3), 7–26. doi:10.1080/07421222. 1992.11517965

Schmidt, R. (1997). Managing Delphi Surveys Using Nonparametric Statistical Techniques. *Decision Sciences, 28*(3), 763–774. doi:10.1111/j.1540-5915.1997. tb01330.x

Schmidt, R., Lyytinen, K., Keil, M., & Cule, P. (2001). Identifying software project risks: An international Delphi study. *Journal of Management Information Systems, 17*(4), 5–36.

Sherif, K., & Vinze, A. (2002). Domain engineering for developing software repositories: A case study. *Decision Support Systems, 33*(1), 55–69. doi:10.1016/ S0167-9236(01)00130-0

Smith, H., McKeen, J., Cranston, C., & Benson, M. (2010). Investment Spend Optimization: A New Approach to IT Investment at BMO Financial Group. *MIS Quarterly Executive, 9*(2), 65–81.

Swanton, B., & Draper, L. (2010). *How do you expect to get value from ERP if you don't measure it?* AMR Research.

Taudes, A., Feurstein, M., & Mild, A. (2000). Options Analysis of Software Platform Decisions: A Case Study. *Management Information Systems Quarterly, 24*(2), 227–243. doi:10.2307/3250937

Taylor-Powell, E. (2002). *Quick Tips Collecting Group Data: Delphi Technique.* University of Wisconsin. Retrieved from http://www.uwex.edu/ces/pdande/resources/pdf/Tipsheet4.pdf

Van de Ven, A. (1992). Suggestions for studying strategy process: A research note. *Strategic Management Journal, 13*(5), 169–188. doi:10.1002/smj.4250131013

Van den Heede, K., Clarke, S., Vleugels, A., & Aiken, L. (2007). International experts' perspectives on the state of the nurse staffing and patient outcomes literature. *Journal of Nursing Scholarship, 39*(4), 290–297. doi:10.1111/j.1547-5069.2007.00183.x PMID:18021127

Ward, J., & Daniel, E. (2006). *Benefits management: delivering value from IS and IT investments.* Wiley.

Ward, J., Daniel, E., & Peppard, J. (2008). Building better business cases for IT investments. *MIS Quarterly Executive*, *7*(1), 1–15.

Weill, P., & Ross, J. (2009). *IT Savvy: What Top Executives Must Know to Go from Pain to Gain*. Harvard Business Press Books.

Witman, P., & Ryan, T. (2010). Think big for reuse. *Communications of the ACM*, *53*(1), 142–147. doi:10.1145/1629175.1629209

Chapter 2
IT Governance Maturity Patterns in Portuguese Healthcare

Ruben Pereira
ISCTE - Instituto Universitário de Lisboa, Portugal

Miguel Mira da Silva
Universidade Nova de Lisboa, Portugal

Luís Velez Lapão
Universidade Nova de Lisboa, Portugal

ABSTRACT

The pervasive use of technology in organizations to address the increased services complexity has created a critical dependency on Information Technology (IT) that calls to a specific focus on IT Governance (ITG). However, determining the right ITG mechanisms remains a complex endeavor. This paper uses Design Science Research and proposes an exploratory research by analyzing ITG case studies to elicit possible ITG mechanisms patterns. Six interviews were performed in Portuguese healthcare services organizations to assess the ITG practices. Our goal is to build some theories (ITG mechanisms patterns), which we believe will guide healthcare services organizations about the advisable ITG mechanisms given their specific context. We also intend to elicit conclusions regarding the most relevant ITG mechanisms for Portuguese healthcare services organizations. Additionally, a comparison is made with the financial industry to identify improvement opportunities. We finish our work with limitations, contribution and future work.

DOI: 10.4018/978-1-5225-0861-8.ch002

INTRODUCTION

Information Technology (IT) has become crucial to the support, sustainability and growth of most businesses (Law & Ngai, 2005; Quershil, 2009; De Haes et al, 2015). IT not only has the potential to support existing business strategies, but also to shape new strategies (Guldentops, 2003; Henderson & Venkatraman, 1993). In this mindset, IT is considered a core element in most business models (Bartens et al, 2015) and becomes a relevant success factor for survival, prosperity and an opportunity to differentiate in order to achieve competitive advantage (Grembergen & De Haes, 2009).

Additionally, the pervasive use of technology has created a critical dependency on IT that calls for a specific focus on IT Governance (ITG) (De Haes & Grembergen, 2008; Grembergen et al, 2003). Prior research has demonstrated an important relationship between ITG and business-IT alignment (De Haes et al, 2010).

ITG defines the necessary mechanisms as a means of rationalizing, directing and coordinating an organization's IT-related decision making to ensure the present and future business/IT alignment objectives (Park et al., 2006; Gerrard, 2009; Weill & Ross, 2004).

These ITG mechanisms are expected to support IT-related decisions, actions and assets that are more tightly aligned with an organization's strategic and tactical intentions. However, good ITG is no longer a "nice to have", but a "must have" (Pereira & Mira da Silva, 2012). Proper ITG can contribute to higher returns on assets at a time when businesses are increasing their technology investment (Webb et al, 2006). Gartner states that ITG was recognized as a CIO top-10 issue for more than five years and has risen in priority between 2007 and 2009 (Gerrard, 2009).

A mixture of structures, processes and relational mechanisms exists (Grembergen et al, 2003). It is known that enterprises which have addressed properly ITG have actively implemented a set of ITG mechanisms that encourage behaviors consistent with the organization's mission, strategy, values, norms, and culture (Weill, 2004).

When designing ITG, it is important to recognize that it is contingent upon a variety of sometimes conflicting internal and external factors. Determining the right mechanisms for each organization is therefore a complex endeavor (Grembergen et al, 2003). It requires commitment from both the enterprise leadership and professionals as ITG implies continuous scrutiny.

Recent studies have identified some ITG problems as the inconsistencies and incongruities about the ITG mechanisms (Almeida et al, 2013) or the lack of consensus about ITG definition (Pereira & Mira da Silva, 2012). However, little research can be found on how organizations can effectively implement ITG (De Haes & Grembergen, 2008a; Lapão et al, 2009).

Our research aims at analyzing several ITG case studies (CSs) and elicits some ITG mechanisms patterns. Such patterns solve "real world" problems because they capture and allow for the reuse of experiences of best practice in a specific professional domain (Schadewizt & Timothy, 2007). The patterns result from one or more ITG practices.

These patterns should not be seen as cookbook recipes to be followed by organizations when implementing ITG. They should be seen as a roadmap for guidance about the most relevant ITG mechanisms to implement given a specific organizational context.

The definition of minimum baselines has been proposed as a way to help organizations in ITG implementation (Bartens et al, 2015).

The main motivation for this paper was De Haes and Grembergen (2008a) paper suggesting that more research is needed to address the ITG mechanisms implementation in different contexts. The paper has the following structure: Introduction (1), Research Methodology (2), Related Work (3), Case Studies Analysis (4), Evaluation (5), Lessons Learned (6), and finally Conclusion (7).

RESEARCH METHODOLOGY

The Design Science Research (DSR) methodology was used for two main reasons: first, this study focus on ITG which is highly related with information systems (IS) domain and DSR began growing in popularity for use in scholarly investigations in IS (Osterle et al, 2011); second, current ITG solutions has been pointed out as too complex (Pereira and Mira da Silva, 2012) and DSR is suitable to capture the complexity of the topic (Schermann et al, 2009).

From the four types of artifacts produced by DSR (constructs, models, methods and instantiations) we will focus on the first two, constructs and models. Constructs are necessary to describe certain aspects of a problem domain and allowing for the development of the research project's terminology (Schermann et al, 2009) while models use constructs to represent a real world situation, the design problem and the solution space (Simon, 1996).

The constructs that we propose are the domain definition, the ITG mechanisms and the ITG Factors identification. The model we propose is the definition of healthcare ITG patterns taking into account the integration of the constructs.

As advised by March and Smith (1995), the research methodology applied follows the two processes of DSR in IS: build and evaluate. Our approach can be seen in Table 1.

To identify the ITG mechanisms and factors an extensive literature review (LR) was performed by analyzing the most relevant research in the field. In order to

Table 1. Research methodology

Build		Evaluate
Constructs definitions • Domain definition • ITG Mechanisms • ITG Factors	Model Construction • Integrate constructs and define ITG patterns	Evaluation • Interviews • Literature Review • Comparison

elicit the ITG in healthcare patterns several published ITG case studies were analized.

The LR started with a conception of the topic and a definition of key terms in order to derive meaningful search terms (Vom Broke et al, 2009). We have started by looking into journals' articles. We have also looked into some of the most known communities, as IEEE and ACM, where we searched for terms as "IT Governance", "IT Governance mechanisms", "IT case study", and finally "IT Governance factors". In these processes we enhanced the queries by adding synonyms or abbreviations.

RELATED WORK

An effective review creates a firm foundation for advancing knowledge. It makes theory development easier, closes areas where there is a plethora of research, and uncovers areas where research is needed (Webster & Watson, 2002). In this section we are going to present the state of the art of the main issues of our research.

First we describe our proposal composed by three artefacts: ITG factors, ITG mechanism and ITG mechanisms patterns. These factors were used to capture the context of the organizations while the mechanisms were used to assess the ITG implementation in the organization. Finally, the patterns were created based on similar approaches founded in the data elicited from the several CSs.

ITG Factors

Determining the appropriate ITG mechanisms is a complex endeavor and one should be aware that what strategically works for one organization does not necessarily work for another (Patel, 2003). This means that some factors may influence the successfulness of ITG implementation. Therefore, it is necessary to look in the literature for such factors.

Three significant studies (Weill, 2004; Pereira and Mira da Silva, 2012a; Sambamurthy and Zmud, 1999) were found. The first approach is provided by Pereira and

Mira da Silva (2012a) which identified the following set of factors: Culture, Ethic, Industry, IT Strategy, Maturity, Regional Differences, Size, Structure and Trust.

The second approach can be seen in Sambamurthy and Zmud study (1999) and the factors provided are: Overall Governance mode, Firm size, Diversification mode, Diversification breadth, Exploitation strategy for scope economies and Line IT knowledge.

The third approach is provided by Weil (2004) and the factors are as follows: Strategic and performance goals, Organizational structure, Governance experience, Size and diversity and Industry and regional differences.

After analyzing these three approaches, we decided to use the first approach since it encompasses several factors presented in the other two approaches and is the most recent one.

The ITG factors will not be presented here; readers can see it on the original article (Pereira and Mira da silva, 2012a).

ITG Mechanisms

ITG can be deployed using a mixture of various structures, processes and relational mechanisms (De Haes & Grembergen, 2004).

The Structure Mechanisms can be defined as the organizational units and roles, responsible for making IT decisions. Some examples of such mechanisms are committees, executive teams and business/ IT relationship managers (Grembergen & De Haes, 2008; Weill & Ross, 2004).

The Processes Mechanisms are formal processes for ensuring that daily behaviors are consistent with IT policies and provide input back to decisions. These mechanisms include IT investment proposal, architecture exception processes, Strategic Information System Planning, chargebacks, among others (Grembergen & De Haes, 2008; Weill & Ross, 2004).

Finally, the Relational Mechanisms complete the ITG framework and are paramount for attaining and sustaining business-IT alignment, even when the appropriate structures and processes are in place. For attaining and sustaining business-IT alignment, mechanisms like announcements, advocates, channels and education efforts are used (De Haes & Grembergen, 2008; Ribbers et al, 2002; Weill & Ross, 2005).

The ITG mechanisms research was overviewed. The most detailed ones regarding ITG mechanisms are (Almeida et al, 2013; Grembergen & De Haes, 2008; Weill and Ross, 2004; Peterson, 2003). However, after a detailed analysis the Almeida's study (Almeida et al, 2013) was considered the most complete one. It is grounded on an extensive LR, tries to solve some inconsistencies among the ITG mechanisms and provides a complete list of ITG mechanisms. Plus, it is also the most recent study (2012) encompassing all the other mentioned researches.

We have adopted the list of ITG mechanisms (46) provided by this research. It should be noted that all the mechanisms could be considered as general to any organizations' context.

Unfortunately, again due to space limitations, we cannot provide the definition of all the mechanisms, therefore, we forward the readers to the original article (Almeida et al, 2013).

As suggested by Van Grembergen's definition (Grembergen & De Haes, 2008), ITG is located at multiple layers within the organization: at a strategic level where the board is involved, at a management level within the C-suite layer and finally at the operational level with IT and business management. This implies that all these levels, business as well as IT, need to be involved in the IT governance process and they have to understand their individual roles and responsibilities within the framework.

Based on the definition of the ITG mechanisms (Almeida et al, 2013) and the definition of the different layers (Grembergen & De Haes, 2008) we mapped both (Figure 1). A 3x3 matrix was draw, where the columns are the different layers and the rows are the different type of ITG mechanisms (Figure 1). We then fill the cells with the ITG mechanisms that match both definitions (column and row).

ITG Patterns

Few papers have focused on any kind of ITG patterns elicitation, only three were found in the literature.

The first approach is provided by Weill and Ross (2004). This research addressed large enterprises and a wide range of industries, where the authors want to understand how the different domains of ITG (in this case, IT principles, IT architecture, IT infrastructure, Business applications needs and IT investment and prioritization) are governed.

This study tries to depict the styles of governance (from a more decentralized to a more centralized style) used by top performers to decide what major IT decisions must be made.

Other approach is by De Haes and Grembergen (2008a), which provides a minimum baseline of ITG practices that organizations at least should have. The researchers focused on Belgian financial services organizations with headcounts ranging from 100 to more than 1000 employees. The authors alert to the need for more research on this.

The last research is provided by Pereira (2014). This research addresses the examination of several CSs from where the authors extract a set of ITG patterns and then they perform some interviews in order to evaluate the ITG patterns. The authors alert to the need of more similar researches.

Figure 1. ITG mechanisms vs organizational layers

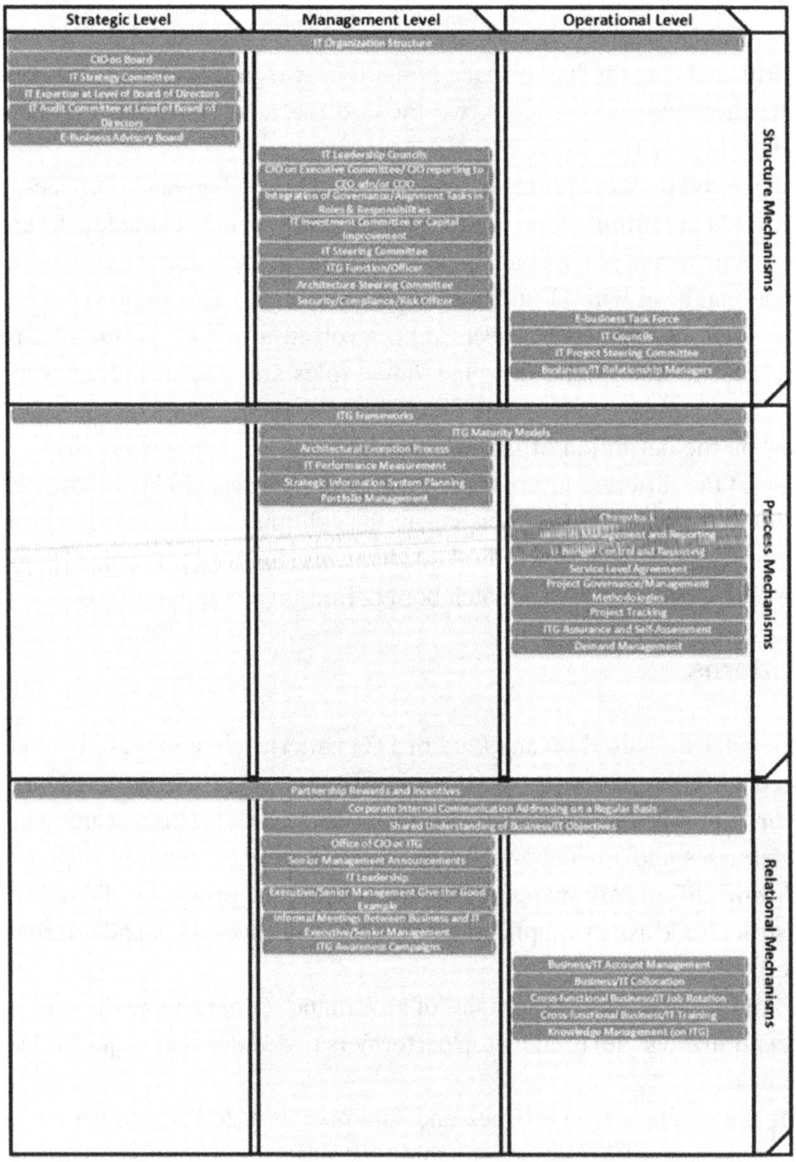

It becomes clear that this is a topic that requires further investigation and we did it in the next sections.

ANALYSIS OF THE CASE STUDIES

After the identification of the ITG factors and mechanisms, we have selected 50 CSs published in scientific conferences proceedings, journals and books. Besides few ITG CSs among the literature, many of them lack a lot of crucial information. The CSs were selected according to the ITG information richness. Therefore, several CSs were dropped during the selection process.

For space limitation and since our focus will be on the healthcare industry, we only provide the references on this industry CSs: 10 (Wilkin & Riddet, 2008), 38, 39, 40, 41, 42, 43, and 44 (Herrera & Giraldo, 2012).

All the information gathered from the 50 CSs regarding both the ITG mechanisms and the ITG factors can be seen in Table 2 and Table 3.

In Table 2 was adopted the following symbols: if the mechanism does not exist, the cell is empty; when the mechanism is partially implemented or there is some evidence that it is used, the cell is filled with "❨"; when the mechanism is totally implemented, we use "●"

Regarding Table 3, we use painted cells to indicate by which factors each organization is characterized. When all the cells regarding a certain ITG factor are empty, it means there was no evidence of it.

We must also clarify that we decided to call "Gulf" to the following group of countries: Bahrain, Kuwait, Oman, Qatar, Saudi Arabia and the United Arab Emirates.

All the patterns were manually elicited by the authors without the help of any specific algorithm or any other method. As a result, the authors had to be very careful about unclear mechanisms references.

It should be noted that in Table 3 we are not considering the information about ethic, maturity and trust since there were several gaps in the analyzed ITG CSs regarding these factors. Such gap of information forced us to exclude these factors from the patterns' elicitation. Moreover, since we will evaluate the patterns by interviewing CIOs in Portuguese organizations we also excluded the regional differences factor because none Portuguese CS were found among the literature.

The elicited patterns can be seen in Table 4. For space limitations, only the patterns able to be validated by our interviews were leveraged.

A brief explanation of how the patterns were elicited from each CS is also advisable. For example, this sentence (CS1 (Grembergen & De Haes, 2008)): "Service level agreements (SLAs) are put in place to guarantee that every piece of the IT puzzle knows exactly its role and responsibility in particular situations", we understand that they are considering the "Service Level Agreement" mechanism.

Another example is (CS15 (Wittenburg & Matthes, 2007)): "The main purpose of the portfolio management is to identify those project proposals, which should be

Table 2a. ITG mechanisms 1-25

ITG Mechanisms		Case Studies																								
		1	2	3	4	5	6	7	8	9	10	11	12	13	14	15	16	17	18	19	20	21	22	23	24	25
Structure																										
1	Integration of governance /alignment tasks in roles and responsibilities	●	▪	▪	●	●	●	●						●	●		●	●	●		●	●			●	
2	IT strategy committee	●	●	●		●													●	●	●	●	●		●	
3	IT steering Committee	●	●	●			●	●	●		●				●		▪	●	●	●	●	●	●		●	●
4	CIO on Board			●		●			●								●	●				●			●	
5	IT councils	●	●	●					●														●		●	
6	IT leadership councils		●			●				●					●		●				●	●			●	
7	E-business advisory board	▪																●								
8	E-business task force					●			●	●																
9	IT project steering committee	●	●	●	●	●	●	●	●						●	●	●	●	●	●	●	●	●	●	●	●
10	IT organization structure	●	●	●	●	●	●	●			●				●		●	●	▪	●	●	●	●	●	●	
11	IT expertise at level of board of directors	▪		●	●	●				▪					●			●	●	●	●	●				
12	IT audit committee at level of board of directors	▪			▪	▪												●								
13	CIO on executive committee/CIO reporting to CEO and/or COO	●	●				●	●			●							●			●				●	●
14	ITG function/officer					●		●										▪			●					
15	Security/Compliance/Risk officer								●						●											
16	Architecture steering committee							●							●							●			●	
17	IT investment committee or capital improvement																									●
18	Business/IT relationship managers	●	●	●		●	●	●							●	●			●		●					●
Process																										
19	IT performance measurement	●	▪	●	●	●	●	●	●			●			●		●	●	●	●		●			●	
20	Strategic Information System Planning	▪	●	●	●	●	●	▪	▪	●	●		●		●		●	●	●	●			●			
21	Frameworks ITG	●	●	●	●	●	▪		●	●	●	●	●	▪	●				●	●						●
22	Service Level Agreement	●	●	●	●	●	●	●		●	●					●	●					●			●	
23	Portfolio management	●	●	●	●	●	●	●	●	●	●		●			●						●	●	●	●	●

Table 2a. Continued

	ITG Mechanisms	1	2	3	4	5	6	7	8	9	10	11	12	13	14	15	16	17	18	19	20	21	22	23	24	25
24	Project Governance/Management methodologies																									●
25	Chargeback	●		▾	●			●															●		●	
26	ITG assurance and self-assessment																●							●		
27	IT budget control and reporting	●	●	●	●	●	●	●	●		●				●	●	●	●	●	●	●	●	●		●	
28	Project Tracking	●	●	●	●	●	●	●	●	●	●	●			●	●	●		●	●	●	●	●	●	●	●
29	ITG Maturity Models	●	●	●	●	●	●	●	●	●					●	●	●		●	●						
30	Demand management							●									●		●							
31	Architectural exception process							●								▾							●		▾	
32	Benefit management and reporting					●			●		●														●	
	Relational																									
33	Partnership rewards and incentives	●			●	●	●				●							●			●					
34	Business/IT collocation	●	●	●	●																					
35	Shared understanding of business/IT objectives	●	▾	●	▾	▾	●								▾	▾		●	●	●		●				●
36	Cross-functional business/IT training	●	▾			▾														●						
37	Cross-functional business/IT job rotation	●	▾	▾	●	●	●																			
38	ITG awareness campaigns	●	●	●	●	●	▾				●				●	●		●		●	●		●			
39	Corporate internal communication addressing on a regular basis	●	●			●					●								▾							
40	IT leadership			●			●				●					●		●	●	●	●				●	
41	Informal meeting between business/IT executive/senior management	▾					●																			
42	Executive/Senior management give the good example	●																							●	
43	Business/IT account management	●	●	●		●																●		●		●
44	Knowledge management (on ITG)	●	▾			●		●			●					●		●		●						●
45	Senior management announcements																					●		●		
46	Office of CIO or ITG				●	●		●												●	●					

Table 2b. ITG mechanisms 26-50

ITG Mechanisms	26	27	28	29	30	31	32	33	34	35	36	37	38	39	40	41	42	43	44	45	46	47	48	49	50
Case Studies																									
Structure																									
1 Integration of governance / alignment tasks in roles and responsibilities	•						•	-	-				-	-	-					•	•	•	•	•	•
2 IT strategy committee																				•					
3 IT steering Committee	•	•	•	•	•											-	-	-	•	•					
4 CIO on Board			-																	•	•				
5 IT councils	•	•	•			•															•				
6 IT leadership councils			•	•			•						•								•				•
7 E-business advisory board																									•
8 E-business task force													-												
9 IT project steering committee					•	•	•					•					•			•	•	•			•
10 IT organization structure	•	•	•	•	•	•		•	•	•	•	•	•	•	•		•	•	•	•	•	•	•	•	•
11 IT expertise at level of board of directors																						•			
12 IT audit committee at level of board of directors																									
13 CIO on executive committee/CIO reporting to CEO and/or COO	•		•	•	•			•		•	•	•		•	•			•			•	•	•	•	•
14 ITG function/officer														•	•										
15 Security/Compliance/Risk officer																									
16 Architecture steering committee			•								•	•	•	•	•		•	•		•			•		
17 IT investment committee or capital improvement									•	•	•	•		•	•										
18 Business/IT relationship managers	•	•	•	•	•		•	•	•	•	•	•							•						
Process																									
19 IT performance measurement					•		•	•	•					•						•					-
20 Strategic Information System Planning		•																		•	-	-	-	-	-
21 Frameworks ITG							•													•					

ITG Mechanisms		26	27	28	29	30	31	32	33	34	35	36	37	38	39	40	41	42	43	44	45	46	47	48	49	50
																		Case Studies							
22	Service Level Agreement	•					•		•	•	•	•	•	•	•								•	•		•
23	Portfolio management		•	•			•		•	•	•	•	•	•	•	•	•	•	•	•						
24	Project Governance/Management methodologies						•	-	•	•	•	-	•	•	•	•	•	•	•	•						-
25	Chargeback	•					•																		-	
26	ITG assurance and self-assessment																									
27	IT budget control and reporting			•																						
28	Project Tracking			•		•	•	-			•	-								•	•	•	•	•	•	
29	ITG Maturity Models																									
30	Demand management																									
31	Architectural exception process	•		•			•		•		-	-	•	•	•	•										
32	Benefit management and reporting						•		•		•	-	-		•	•				•	•					
	Relational																									
33	Partnership rewards and incentives	•						•	•													-	•	•	•	•
34	Business/IT collocation																				•	•				
35	Shared understanding of business/IT objectives	•		•				•	•	-		•					•	•			•	•	•	•	•	•
36	Cross-functional business/IT training		-																		•	•	•	•	•	
37	Cross-functional business/IT job rotation																				•		•	•		
38	ITG awareness campaigns	•	•																		•					-
39	Corporate internal communication addressing on a regular basis																									
40	IT leadership	•	•	•			-																			
41	Informal meeting between business/IT executive/senior management																				•	•	•	•	•	•
42	Executive/Senior management give the good example							-																		
43	Business/IT account management	•			•	•			•	•	•	•	•							•						
44	Knowledge management (on ITG)		•		•		•																		•	
45	Senior management announcements						-																			
46	Office of CIO or ITG						•																			

35

Table 3a. ITG factors 1-25

ITG Factors	Case Studies																								
	1	2	3	4	5	6	7	8	9	10	11	12	13	14	15	16	17	18	19	20	21	22	23	24	25
Industry																									
Airline											x	x	x												
Automotive															x						x				
Chemical					x																				
Education																x	x	x	x						
Financial/ Banking/ Insurance	x	x	x	x			x	x						x						x		x		x	
Government																							x		
Healthcare / Healthcare Services										x															
Infrastructure Services																									
Intergovernmental																									
Pharmaceutical Laboratories																									
Retail																									x
Steel Producer						x																			
Telecommunications																									
Transport																									
Utility									x																
Size																									
Large	x	x	x	x	x	x	x	x	x	x	x	x	x	x	x	x	x	x	x	x	x	x	x	x	x
SME																									

continued on following page

36

Table 3a. Continued

ITG Factors	Case Studies																								
	1	2	3	4	5	6	7	8	9	10	11	12	13	14	15	16	17	18	19	20	21	22	23	24	25
Structure																									
Centralized		x			x	x										x			x						x
Decentralized																									
Federal	x		x	x			x			x					x		x	x		x	x	x	x	x	
Culture																									
The contest model					x					x							x	x				x	x	x	x
The organization as a family								x												x	x				
The network model														x											
The pyramidal organization									x		x	x	x												
The Solar system	x		x	x		x																			
The well-oiled machine															x										
Strategy																									
IT for comprehensiveness														x											
IT for efficiency	x	x	x	x	x	x	x	x		x				x	x	x	x	x			x	x	x	x	x
IT for flexibility	x		x	x			x							x						x	x	x	x	x	

Table 3b. ITG factors 26-50

ITG Factors	Case Studies																								
	26	27	28	29	30	31	32	33	34	35	36	37	38	39	40	41	42	43	44	45	46	47	48	49	50
Industry																									
Airline																									
Automotive																									
Chemical																									
Education																									
Financial/ Banking/ Insurance			x			x																			
Government													x	x	x	x	x	x		x	x	x	x	x	x
Healthcare / Healthcare Services																			x						
Infrastructure Services							x																		
Intergovernmental		x										x													
Pharmaceutical Laboratories								x	x	x	x														
Retail																									
Steel Producer					x																				
Telecommunications				x																					
Transport					x																				
Utility	x																								
Size																									
Large	x	x	x	x		x	x	x		x	x	x	x	x	x	x	x	x	x	x				x	x
SME									x												x	x	x		

continued on following page

Table 3b. Continued

ITG Factors	Case Studies																								
	26	27	28	29	30	31	32	33	34	35	36	37	38	39	40	41	42	43	44	45	46	47	48	49	50
Structure																									
Centralized	x				x															x	x	x	x	x	
Decentralized																									x
Federal		x	x	x		x		x	x	x	x	x	x	x	x	x	x	x	x						
Culture																									
The contest model	x		x	x		x																			
The organization as a family																									
The network model																									
The pyramidal organization					x			x	x	x	x	x	x	x	x	x	x	x	x						
The Solar system																									
The well-oiled machine					x																				x
Strategy																									
IT for comprehensiveness					x																				
IT for efficiency	x	x	x			x	x	x	x	x	x	x	x	x	x	x	x	x	x	x	x	x	x	x	
IT for flexibility	x	x		x		x	x	x	x	x	x	x	x		x			x	x	x	x	x	x	x	

39

Table 4. ITG mechanisms patterns elicited

1	Large enterprises use the following mechanisms: 10, 23
2	Large enterprises with "IT for Efficiency" Strategy use the following mechanisms: 10, 23
3	Large enterprises with "The Pyramidal Organization" Culture and IT for Efficiency" Strategy use the following mechanisms: 10, 23
4	Large enterprises with "The Pyramidal organization" Culture and "IT for Flexibility" Strategy use the following mechanisms: 10, 23

accomplished and are finally stated as approved", which clearly shows us that the "Portfolio Management" mechanism was implemented.

These patterns cannot be seen as cookbook recipes to be followed by healthcare organizations when implementing ITG. On the contrary, they should be seen as guidance about which can be the most relevant ITG mechanisms to implement given a specific organizational context.

Table 5. Interviewees' information

	Experience	Size	Structure	Regional Differences	Culture	Strategy
1	24 years	Large [1000-2000]	Centralized	Portugal	The pyramidal organization	IT for Efficiency IT for Flexibility
2	20 years	Large [1000-2000]	Centralized	Portugal	The pyramidal organization	IT for Efficiency
3	25 years	Large [3000-4000]	Centralized	Portugal	The pyramidal organization	IT for Efficiency
4	15 years	Large [2000-3000]	Centralized	Portugal	The pyramidal organization	IT for Efficiency IT for Flexibility
5	28 years	Large [4000-5000]	Centralized	Portugal	The pyramidal organization	IT for Efficiency IT for Flexibility
6	18 years	Large [1000-2000]	Centralized	Portugal	The pyramidal organization	IT for Efficiency

EVALUATION

We performed an exhaustive LR since a review of prior, relevant literature is an essential feature of any academic project. An effective review creates a firm foundation for advancing knowledge, makes theory development easier, closes areas where there is a plethora of research, and uncovers areas where research is needed (Webster & Watson, 2002). To review articles is critical to strengthen IS as a field of study. When proposing a new study or a new theory, researchers should ensure the validity of the study and reliability of the results by making use of quality literature to serve as the foundation of their research.

From the previous CSs analysis, we elicited a set of ITG mechanisms patterns compatible with healthcare organizations, namely Hospitals. In order to elicit the patterns we focused only in CSs from both central and regional hospitals. The elicited patterns can be seen as our theory.

In order to validate our artifacts, besides the complete LR, we also performed six qualitative interviews in six Portuguese healthcare organizations. The interviewees were IT experts from those organizations, with managing responsibilities, with several years of experience on IT (Table 5). We used semi-structured interviews.

In spite of not having a large number of interviews, we decided to use a qualitative approach instead of a quantitative one. As we can see the interviewees have a lot of experience in the IT area that can be exploited. The interviews were conducted by two of the authors over a period of one month. Each session lasted from 1 to 2 hours and was transcribed into digital data for analysis (Table 6).

To support and lead the interviews, a questionnaire was designed with both open-response questions and close-response questions about the ITG factors (Table 5) and the ITG mechanisms (Table 6). Furthermore, clarifications regarding the various concepts used by the respondents were sought during the conversation, so that later these descriptions could be examined and matched to the more standard designations.

In Table 6 we present the data collected from the six interviews (columns) performed. Each main column has 3 sub-columns, which correspond to a specific answer to the questionnaire. The "U" portrays the ITG mechanisms used in the organization. The "E" represents how effective the mechanism under the interviewees' viewpoint (from 0, not effective at all, up to 5, highly effective). Finally, the "D" represents how difficult is the implementation of the mechanisms according to the interviewees' viewpoint (from 0, not difficult at all, up to 5, extremely difficult).

A fourth and last question was also present on the questionnaire. We asked the interviewees to choose the ten most important mechanisms. Grey cells represent these choices over the columns.

Table 6. Interviews

	1			2			3			4			5			6			Sum	
	U	E	D	U	E	D	U	E	D	U	E	D	U	E	D	U	E	D	E	D
Structure Mechanisms																				
IT organization structure	●	5	3	●	5	1	●	5	2	●	5	0	●	5	4	●	5	2	30	12
Business/IT relationship managers	●	5	3	●	5	4	●	5	2	●	5	5	●	5	0		4	4	29	18
Integration of governance/alignment tasks in roles & responsibilities	●	5	4	▼	4	2	●	5	4	●	4	3	●	5	3	●	5	1	28	17
Security/Compliance/Risk officer	●	5	4	●	5	5	●	5	3	●	5	4	●	5	3		4	2	29	21
IT project steering committee	▼	5	3	▼	3	4	●	5	3	●	5	2	●	5	3		4	4	27	19
IT expertise at level of board of directors	●	5	4	●	5	3	●	4	3		5	5	▼	5	0		2	5	26	20
IT councils	●	5	3		4	4	●	4	3	●	5	3		5	4		3	3	26	20
IT steering Committee	●	4	3		5	4	▼	3	4		5	2	●	5	3		3	4	25	20
IT strategy committee		4	5		5	3	●	5	4	●	5	1	▼	4	4		3	5	26	22
IT audit committee at level of board of directors	▼	4	4	▼	4	4	●	3	4	●	5	3	▼	2	3		5	4	23	22
IT investment committee or capital improvement		3	4		5	3	●	2	4		4	1		5	4		2	4	21	20
Architecture steering committee		4	4		3	5		3	3		4	3	●	3	3	●	4	3	21	21
CIO on executive committee/CIO reporting to CEO and/or COO	▼	5	3	▼	5	4	●	2	4	▼	1	2	▼	2	2		1	4	16	17
E-business task force		4	5		4	4		2	4		4	2		3	5		4	4	21	24
E-business advisory board		4	5		5	4		2	4		3	4		3	5		5	4	22	26
ITG function/officer		3	5		3	4		4	1	●	5	4	▼	4	3		1	4	20	25
CIO on Board		4	5		5	5		5	3		2	5		3	4		1	3	20	25
IT leadership councils								n/a												
Processes Mechanisms																				
Average																			22,9	20,5
Demand management	●	5	2	●	5	4	●	5	4	●	4	1	●	5	0	●	5	4	29	15
Service Level Agreement	●	5	4	▼	4	5	●	5	4	●	5	3	●	5	2	●	5	2	29	20
Architectural exception process	▼	4	4	●	3	2	●	5	1	●	4	2	●	5	5	●	5	3	26	17
IT budget control and reporting		5	2	▼	4	3	●	5	3	●	4	1	●	4	3		2	3	24	15

continued on following page

Table 6. Continued

	1			2			3			4			5			6			Sum	
	U	E	D	U	E	D	U	E	D	U	E	D	U	E	D	U	E	D	E	D
Project Tracking		4	4	●	5	4	●	5	2	●	4	3	●	5	3	●	5	4	28	20
Strategic Information System Planning	▼	5	4	●	5	4		4	5	●	5	4	●	5	0		4	4	28	21
ITG assurance and self-assessment	●	5	3		4	4		4	4	●	4	3	●	5	2		4	3	26	19
Portfolio management	●	5	3	●	5	3		4		▼	3	3	▼	5	2		4	3	26	19
Frameworks ITG		4	4	▼	4	4		5		▼	5	2	●	5	3		5	3	28	22
Chargeback		5	5		4	5		4	4	●	4	2	●	5	2		4	5	26	23
Project governance/management methodologies		5	4		4	5		4	4		4	5	●	5	3		4	4	26	25
Benefits Management and Reporting	▼	4	5	▼	5	4		4	4		3	3		5	3		4	4	25	24
IT Performance Measurement (E.g. IT BSC)		4	4		3	4		4	5	●	5	4	●	3	3		4	4	23	24
ITG Maturity Models		4	5		4			3	4		4	3		2	3		5	4	21	24
Average																			26,1	20,6
Relational Mechanisms																				
Informal meeting between business and IT executive/senior management	●	4	3	●	4	1	●	5	2	●	3	1	●	5	0	●	4	2	25	9
Corporate internal communication addressing on a regular basis	●	5	2	●	4	4	●	5	3	●	4	1	●	5	0		5	2	28	12
Executive/Senior management give the good example	●	5	5	●	5	1		5	5	●	4	1	●	5	1		5	1	29	14
Business/IT collocation	●	5	3	●	5	2	●	5	3	●	5	4	●	5	3		5	2	30	17
Senior management announcements	●	4	4	●	5	2		4	2	●	4	1	●	5	3		5	1	27	14
IT leadership	●	5	2	●	4	3		5	5	●	4	4	●	5	1		5	2	28	17
Cross-functional business/IT training	▼	5	5		5	3	●	5	2		4	4	●	5	0		3	3	27	17
Business/IT account management	●	5	4	●	4	3	●	5	2		4	5		5	2		4	4	27	20
Office of CIO or ITG		3	4		4	5		3	1		4	1	▼	5	1		4	4	23	16
Partnership rewards and incentives	●	4	5		5	5		5	5		5	1	●	5	5		5	2	29	23
Shared understanding of business/IT objectives		5	4	▼	5	2		4	4		4	4	▼	3	3		3	4	27	21
Knowledge management (on ITG)		4	4		5	4		4	5		4	2	▼	3	3		5	3	25	20
ITG awareness campaigns		5	4		3	5		4	5		4	2	●	4	4		5	5	25	24
Cross-functional business/IT job rotation		4	5	▼	4	5	▼	4	5		3	3		3	3		2	4	20	25
Average																			26,4	17,8

The last two columns of Table 6 are the sum of the "E" columns and the sum of the "D" columns. These numbers are important because we ordered the lines regarding the difference between the effectiveness and the difficulty to reflect somehow the relevance of the mechanisms. The first criterion was sum "E" minus sum "D" where the largest difference wins. When the difference was equal the major sum "E" prevails. When equal sum "E" also exists we chose the most used mechanism to prevail. We also marked with red the mechanisms used by all the organizations.

We have also evaluated our research by comparing the most relevant mechanisms used by Portuguese healthcare organizations with the ITG patterns proposed by Pereira and Mira da Silva for Portuguese financial services (Pereira et al, 2014).

At Table 4 we present the four patterns that were elicited from Table 2 and Table 3 in order to be compared with the interviews' results.

After the analysis we concluded that patterns 1, 2 and 3 were not confirmed by the interviews. Pattern 4 was impossible to compare since none of the interviewed organizations adopt the "IT for Flexibility" strategy. During the comparison we considered the "❨" as a positive match.

In Table 7 we can see the comparison between Pereira (2014) ITG patterns, the chosen mechanisms of the interviewees, and the most relevant mechanisms according the sum "E" minus sum "D". Cells in grey represent a match between at least two of them. All the mechanisms in the grey cells are the minimum baseline mechanisms proposed for healthcare services.

LESSONS LEARNED

From the IT CSs analysis (Table 2 and Table 3) we conclude that a lot of information regarding ITG mechanisms is missing, a problem already identified and under study (Pereira et al, 2013). However, a lot of information regarding the mechanisms was elicited. Some mechanisms appear to be more used such as "IT Organizational structure", "Demand Management", or "Business/IT Collocation".

Regarding the factors, several points must be stated:

- Unfortunately giving the few or none IT CSs performed in Portugal we do not have much information about regional differences;
- All the analyzed organizations (Hospitals) are large because large organizations are more available to be targeted of a CS;
- The majority of the CSs are Federal; and
- None CSs use IT for Comprehensiveness as IT strategy;

Table 7. ITG mechanisms comparison

Financial ITG Patterns (Pereira et al, 2014)	Interviews (Healthcare)	Sum "E" minus Sum "D"
Business/IT relationship managers	Business/IT relationship managers	Business/IT relationship managers
IT leadership	IT leadership	IT leadership
IT organization structure	IT organization structure	IT organization structure
IT strategy committee	IT strategy committee	
Service Level Agreement	Service Level Agreement	
IT project steering committee		
CIO on Board		
Portfolio management		
IT budget control and reporting		
Partnership rewards and incentives		
Frameworks ITG		
	Integration of governance/ alignment tasks in roles & responsibilities	Integration of governance/alignment tasks in roles & responsibilities
	Security/Compliance/Risk officer	
	Strategic Information System Planning	
		Informal meeting between business and IT executive/senior management
		Corporate internal communication addressing on a regular basis
		Executive/Senior management give the good example
		Demand Management
		Business/IT collocation
		Senior management announcements

Interviews were very productive and insightful. A lot of useful information was collected. From the average numbers we can conclude that relational mechanisms seem to be the easiest to implement and also the more effective when implemented. Probably for this reason relational mechanisms are the most common among all the organizations interviewed.

Table 8. Financial industry versus healthcare industry

	Most Relevant Mechanisms			Efficiency			Difficulty		
	Structure	Process	Relational	Structure	Process	Relational	Structure	Process	Relational
Financial Industry	46.7%	40%	13.3%	23.6	24.6	22.0	17.7	23.1	20.4
Healthcare Industry	41.7%	28.3%	30%	22.9	26.1	26.4	20.5	20.6	17.8

Each interviewee had to choose the 10 most important mechanisms. From a universe of 60 possible choices (10 per interview), 25 (41.7%) were structure mechanisms while 18 (30%) were relational mechanisms and 17 (28.3%) were process mechanisms.

The CSs analysis shows that there are a set of ITG mechanisms which are comprehensively implemented by organizations. So far four ITG mechanisms patterns were elicited, each according to a specific organizational context characterized by the selected factors. There is the perception that the adoption of the ITG mechanisms follows the need to overcome increased processes complexity, but not in a systematic way.

Some information regarding the comparison between financial industry (Pereira et al, 2014) and healthcare industry is presented in Table 8. We can easily conclude that there are several differences between both industries, as for example:

- Relational mechanisms are the less relevant for financial industry and process mechanisms for healthcare industry;
- Relational mechanisms are the less efficient for financial industry while for healthcare industry are structure mechanisms;
- Process mechanisms are the most efficient mechanisms for financial industry while for healthcare industry are the relational mechanisms; and
- Structure mechanisms are the less difficult to implement in financial industry while in healthcare industry are the relational mechanism;

There are also some similarities between both industries:

- Process mechanisms are the most difficult to implement for both industries; and
- Structure mechanisms are the most relevant for both industries.

Figure 2. Assessing business-IT alignment maturity
Luftman, 2000.

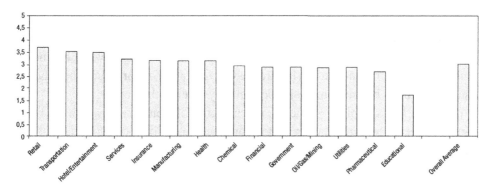

CONCLUSION

The aim of this paper was to elicit some ITG mechanisms patterns for healthcare organizations through IT CSs reading and analysis, as well as the identification of the minimum baseline mechanisms for Portuguese healthcare organizations. Moreover, this research intended to present the differences regarding ITG patterns between the financial and healthcare industries. The conclusion is organized according these two main goals.

Regarding the patterns, the global evaluation is negative. From four possible patterns presented in Table 4, none were confirmed. The authors argue that more Healthcare case studies should be considered in the future, as well as more interviews.

Regarding the minimum baseline mechanisms several conclusions can be withdraw. First, there are five common mechanisms shared between Portuguese financial services organizations and Portuguese healthcare organizations. Three of the common mechanisms have a great effectiveness/difficulty ratio.

Another mechanism with a good effectiveness/difficulty ratio was selected by Portuguese healthcare organizations: "Integration of governance/alignment tasks in roles & responsibilities".

Few mechanisms (4) remain without any match. We can conclude that healthcare industry is nearly to use almost all the ITG mechanisms. On the other side we must say that the usefulness of the remained ITG mechanisms still being unknown. We cannot conclude anything about them with rigor but they must certainly be studied in the future.

The financial industry appears to be more complete regarding ITG mechanisms adoption and implementation. This situation can be due to the fact that the financial industry was the first industry to use IT intensively and as such is already more mature in these domains. This situation allows that good practices in govern IT in this sector are widespread all over the world.

Based on the relevance of ITG for business growth and sustainability (De Haes et al, 2015) as well as on the importance of the ITG mechanisms to achieve a good business-IT alignment (Bartens et al, 2015) and yet on the average level of business-IT alignment of some industries (Figure 2), we can state that Portuguese healthcare industry seems to be under to desirable maturity level of this topic.

If we pick for example the structure mechanism "CIO on Board" which has been pointed in recent research has an important mechanism for organizational performance and then we look to Table 6, we can exemplify the low maturity of Portuguese healthcare industry. This confirms the results from a previous study done a decade ago (Lapão, 2007). Despite such fact may not be a completely surprise since some recent research has reported that less than 20 percent of corporate boards worldwide has directors with technology expertise (Valentine, 2015). Yet, stills a proof of low ITG maturity.

Once the healthcare industry adopts a patient-centric perspective it will be pushed to make a more comprehensive use of IT, leading to a more mature use of ITG.

We are aware that not much information about the organizations and the interviewees is provided. However, on one side Portugal is a small country and is easy to identify the organization when all the information is provided. On the other side, healthcare organizations are very cautious about their information and therefore we had to exclude some information to fulfill the required confidentiality of the data collected.

Of course our research has some limitations as well. The chosen factors are not static and other factors can be considered in the future as well. Plus, ethic, maturity and trust should be further detailed for a more comprehensive analysis. Finally, despite the difficulty to find good IT CSs in the literature, more CSs may be considered in the future.

Another limitation is the information collected from the IT CSs. Given the problem already identified on the field (Pereira et al, 2013) about the lack of rigor among IT CSs that inhibit the generalization. It must be stated that the information collected is under authors' interpretation.

While this research for validity reasons is focused on Portuguese healthcare industry only, and despite the comparison with Pereira and Mira da Silva paper about the financial industry (Pereira et al, 2014) it can be expected that many conclusions might apply to other sectors and factors. Future research, focusing on other sectors and factors could support this assumption.

REFERENCES

Almeida, R., Pereira, R., & Mira da Silva, M. (2013). IT Governance Mechanisms: A Literature Review. In J.F. Cunha, M. Snene, & H. Nóvoa, (Eds.), *International Conference in Exploring Services Science 1.3* (vol. 143, pp. 186-199). Berlin, Germany: Springer-Verlag. doi:10.1007/978-3-642-36356-6_14

De Haes, S., & Grembergen, W. (2004). IT Governance and Its Mechanisms. *Information Systems Control Journal, 1.*

De Haes, S., & Grembergen, W. (2008). Analysing the Relationship Between IT Governance and Business/IT Alignment Maturity.*Proceedings of the 41st Hawaii International Conference on System Sciences*, 428. doi:10.1109/HICSS.2008.66

De Haes, S., & Grembergen, W. (2008a). An exploratory study into the design of an IT Governance minimum baseline through Delphi research. *Communications of the Association for Information Systems, 22*, 24.

Gerrard, M. (2009). *IT Governance, a Flawed Concept: It's Time for Business Change Governance*. Stamford: Gartner Research.

Grembergen, W., & De Haes, S. (2008). *Implementing Information Technology Governance: Models, Practices, and Cases*. Hershey, PA: IGI Publishing. doi:10.4018/978-1-59904-924-3

Grembergen, W., & De Haes, S. (2009). *Enterprise Governance of Information Technology: Achieving Strategic Alignment and Value*. Heidelberg, Germany: Springer-Verlag.

Grembergen, W., De Haes, S., & Guldentops, E. (2003). Structures, Processes and Relational Mechanisms for IT Governance. In W. Grembergen (Ed.), *Strategies for information technology governance* (pp. 1–36). Hershey, PA: IGI Publishing.

Guldentops, E. (2003). Governing information technology through COBIT. In W. Grembergen (Ed.), *Strategies for information technology governance* (pp. 269–309). Hershey, PA: IGI Publishing.

Henderson, J.C., & Venkatraman, N. (1993). Strategic alignment: leveraging information technology for transforming organizations. *IBM Systems Journal, 38*(2-3), 472-484.

Herrera, A., & Giraldo, O. (2012). IT Governance State of Art in the Colombian Health Sector Enterprises. In J. Varajão, M. M. Cruz-Cunha, & A. Trigo (Eds.), *Organizational Integration of Enterprise Systems and Resources: Advancements and Applications* (pp. 332–353). Hershey, PA: IGI Publishing. doi:10.4018/978-1-4666-1764-3.ch019

Lapão, L. V. (2007). Survey on the status of the hospital information systems in Portugal. *Methods of Information in Medicine*, *46*(4), 493–499. PMID:17694246

Lapão, L.V., & Rebuge, A., Mira da silva, M., & Gomes, R. (2009). ITIL Assessment in a healthcare environment: The role of IT governance at Hospital São Sebastião. *Studies in Health Technology and Informatics*, *150*, 76–80. PMID:19745270

Law, C., & Ngai, E. (2005). IT Business Value Research: A Critical Review and Research Agenda. *International Journal of Enterprise Information Systems*, *1*(3), 35–55. doi:10.4018/jeis.2005070103

March, S., & Smith, G. (1995). Design and Natural Science Research on Information Technology. *Decision Support Systems*, *15*(4), 251–266. doi:10.1016/0167-9236(94)00041-2

Osterle, H., Becker, J., Frank, U., Hess, T., Karagiannis, D., Krcmar, H., & Sinz, E. J. et al. (2011). Memorandum on Design-Oriented Information Systems Research. *European Journal of Information Systems*, *20*(1), 7–10. doi:10.1057/ejis.2010.55

Patel, N. V. (2003). An emerging strategy for e-business IT Governance. In W. Grembergen (Ed.), *Strategies for Information Technology Governance* (pp. 81–98). Hershey, PA: IGI Publishing.

Pereira, R., Almeida, R., & Mira da Silva, M. (2013). How to Generalize an Information Technology Case Study. In J. vom Brocke, R. Hekkala, S. Ram, & M. Rossi (Eds.), *8th International Conference on Design Science Research in Information Systems and Technology* (vol. 7939, pp. 150-164). Berlin, Germany: Springer-Verlag. doi:10.1007/978-3-642-38827-9_11

Pereira, R., Almeida, R., & Mira da Silva, M. (2014). *IT Governance Patterns in the Portuguese Financial Industry*. 47th Hawaii International Conference on System Sciences, Hawaii, HI. doi:10.1109/HICSS.2014.541

Pereira, R., & Mira da Silva, M. (2012). Designing a new Integrated IT Governance and IT Management Framework Based on Both Scientific and Practitioner Viewpoint. *International Journal of Enterprise Information Systems*, *8*(4), 1–43. doi:10.4018/jeis.2012100101

Pereira, R., & Mira da Silva, M. (2012a). Towards an Integrated IT Governance and IT Management Framework.*Proceedings of the 16th International Enterprise Distributed Object Computing Conference*. doi:10.1109/EDOC.2012.30

Peterson, R. (2003). Integration Strategies and Tactics for Information Technology Governance. In W. Grembergen (Ed.), *Strategies for information technology governance* (pp. 37–80). Hershey, PA: IGI Publishing.

Quershil, S., Kamal, M., & Wolcott, P. (2009). Information Technology Interventions for Growth and Competitiveness in Micro-Enterprises. *International Journal of E-Business Research*, 5(1), 117–140. doi:10.4018/jebr.2009010106

Ribbers, P., Peterson, R., & Parker, M. (2002). Designing Information Technology Governance Processes: Diagnosing Contemporary Practices and Competing Theories.*Proceedings of the 35th Hawaii International Conference on System Sciences*. doi:10.1109/HICSS.2002.994351

Sambamurthy, V., & Zmud, R. W. (1999). Arrangements for Information Technology Governance: A theory of multiple contingencies. *Management Information Systems Quarterly*, 23(2), 261–290. doi:10.2307/249754

Schadewizt, N., & Timothy, J. (2007). Comparing Inductive and Deductive Methodologies for Design Patterns Identification and Articulation.*Proceedings of the International Design Research Conference*.

Schermann, M., B'Ohmann, T., & Krcmar, H. (2009). Explicating Design Theories with Conceptual Models: Towards a Theoretical Role of Reference Models. In J. Becker, H. Krcmar, & B. Niehaves (Eds.), Wissenschaftstheorie (pp. 175-194). Heidelberg, Germany: Springer Berlin.

Simon, H. A. (1996). *The Sciences of the Artificial*. MIT Press.

Vom Brocke, J., Simons, A., Niehaves, B., Reimer, K., Plattfaut, R., & Cleven, A. (2009). Reconstructing the Giant: On the importance of Rigour in Documenting the Literature Search Process.*Proceedings of the 17th European Conference On Information System*.

Webb, P., Pollard, C., & Ridley, G. (2006). Attempting to Define IT Governance: Wisdom or Folly? *Proceedings of the 39th Hawaii International Conference on System Science*. doi:10.1109/HICSS.2006.68

Webster, J., & Watson, R. T. (2002). Analyzing the past to prepare for the future: Writing a Literature Review. *Management Information Systems Quarterly*, 26(2), xiii–xxiii.

Weill, P. (2004). Don't Just Lead, Govern: How Top-Performing Firms Govern IT. *Management Information Systems Quarterly Executive*, *3*(1), 1–17.

Weill, P., & Ross, J. (2004). *IT Governance: How Top Performers Manage IT Decision Rights for Superior Results*. Boston: Harvard Business School Press.

Weill, P., & Ross, J. (2005). A matrix approach to designing IT Governance. *Sloan Management Review*, *46*(2).

Wilkin, C. L., & Riddet, J. L. (2008) Issues for IT Governance in a Large Not-for-Profit Organization: A Case Study.*Proceedings of the International MCETECH Conference on e-Technologies*. doi:10.1109/MCETECH.2008.24

Wittenburg A. & Matthes, F. (2007). Building an integrated IT governance platform at the BMW Group. *International Journal Business Process Integration and Management, 2*(4).

Chapter 3
A Framework for Research on Information Technology Governance in SMEs

François Bergeron
Université du Québec, Canada

Anne-Marie Croteau
Concordia University, Canada

Sylvestre Uwizeyemungu
Université du Québec à Trois-Rivières, Canada

Louis Raymond
Université du Québec à Trois-Rivières, Canada

ABSTRACT

The need to effectively manage IT resources such that they enhance the business value of firms makes IT Governance (ITG) an important issue for both IS researchers and practitioners. The purpose of this paper is to build a conceptual framework for ITG in small and Medium-Sized Enterprises (SMEs). The authors first analyze the main theories applied in ITG research, and confront them with the specificities of SMEs. The authors then highlight the limits of those theories in SMEs context and discuss adaptations needed or alternative theories in such context. The resulting framework is then applied to generate a set of six research propositions on ITG in SMEs.

DOI: 10.4018/978-1-5225-0861-8.ch003

1. INTRODUCTION

Given that some organizations achieve higher performance with their IT investments while others fail to do so (Gattiker & Goodhue, 2004), the issue that matters now is to know under which conditions organizations create value from their IT (Kohli & Grover, 2008).

It has been argued that IT governance (ITG), which "is about controlling the strategic impact of IT and its value delivery to the business" (Zarvić et al., 2012, p. 543) can make the difference (Nfuka, & Rusu, 2011; Devos, et al., 2012; Wilkin, 2012). The need to effectively manage IT resources so that they can enhance the business value of firms makes of ITG an important issue and yet an uneasy task (Weill & Ross, 2004; Van Grembergen & De Haes, 2010). Indeed, the most important IT challenges faced by organizations now and in the future are less related to technology than to governance (Nfuka, & Rusu, 2011).

The literature related to ITG in particular, and to corporate governance (CG) in general, has mobilized and proposed different theories and frameworks to explain the mechanisms of governance. However, most of those theories and frameworks are often criticized as being more appropriate for large enterprises (LEs) and less for small and medium-sized enterprises (SMEs), hence the call for revisiting existing theories and frameworks or for proposing alternative ones with in mind the specific realities of SMEs (Banham & He, 2010). This call is important, all the more so that studies on ITG in SMEs are rather rare (Vogt et al., 2011; Alves et al., 2013). This paucity of studies does not mean, however, that ITG does not exist in the context of SMEs. Previous studies have shown that SMEs use IT in their basic activities and are expanding IT usage in more advanced processes (Raymond & Croteau, 2006; Mardikyan, 2010; Ruivo, Oliveira & Neto, 2012; Sila & Dobni, 2012). As IT users, SMEs have to find ways to allocate IT-related responsibilities and to ensure IT-business alignment for increased business value, brief ways to practice ITG (Luftman et al., 2010). Given the important consequences IT can have on growth and survival of SMEs in a competitive market, we argue that ITG for SMEs is a necessity and must be researched.

The purpose of this theoretical study is to develop a framework for research on IT governance in SMEs. To do so, we proceed in three phases. First, we analyze theories generally applied in ITG literature with in mind the specificities of SMEs, and we bring out salient limits of these theories with regards to the realities of SMEs. Second, we identify adaptations necessary to these theories to account for the SME's realities, and alternative theories better suited to its context. Third, building on the results of the precedent analysis we propose a conceptual framework for ITG in SMEs and related propositions that can be used as hypotheses for future research.

2. THEORETICAL AND EMPIRICAL BACKGROUND

In the literature, corporate governance (CG) is generally conceptualized with reference to the rights and responsibilities of different stakeholders in the firm, to the relationships among stakeholders with regards to the decision-making process, resolution of possible conflicts, and control of organizational resources, and to the means for setting corporate objectives and monitoring performance (Turlea et al., 2010). The OECD has proposed the following definition of CG which seems to have gained widespread popularity (Mason & O'Mahony, 2008): "a set of relationships between a company's management, its board, its shareholders and other stakeholders [that] provides the structure through which the objectives of the company are set, and the means of attaining those objectives and monitoring performance are determined" (p. 32).

ITG has emerged since the 1990s as a conceptualization of steering the use of IT within a company (Zarvić et al., 2012). It is now acknowledged that ITG is the responsibility of top management and an integral part of corporate governance (De Haes et al., 2013). This view is integrated in frameworks such as CoBIT 5 that establish good practices for ITG.

Definitions of ITG in the literature refer implicitly to the principal-agent problem which is central in the dominant agency theory in CG literature. In this perspective, a parallel is made between the alignment of executives' decisions to the owners' interests in CG and the alignment of IT management practices to the firm's needs in ITG. We define ITG as follows: ITG, a responsibility of top-management and an integral part of corporate governance, encompasses the decision rights and the accountability framework for encouraging desirable behavior in the use of IT, and ensuring that IT goals and objectives are realized in an efficient and effective manner (De Haes et al., 2013).

2.1 SMEs' Specificity Regarding Corporate Governance and IT Governance

Early previous studies have pointed out SMEs' specificities (Jennings & Beaver, 1997; Raymond, Bergeron, & Rivard, 1998; Torrès, & Julien, 2005). Blili and Raymond (1993) grouped these specificities in five categories: environmental, organizational, decisional, psycho-sociological, and informational. Generally speaking, SMEs operate in local markets and exert little control over their environment, they rather bank on their flexibility to adapt to changing conditions in environment; they count on limited resources, financial and human, and they are characterized by a simple organic structure, developed around interests/abilities of key employees, and by a centralized management; their decision-making and strategic formulation processes are intuitive, adaptive, and short-term oriented; they are in almost all aspects overwhelmingly dominated by the owner-managers who cumulate the roles of entrepreneurship, ownership, and management; their internal and external information systems are generally simple and informal.

The specificity assumption of SMEs should, however, be cautiously considered. At least two cautions should be heeded. First, the statement of the specificities of SMEs does not mean that the group of SMEs is homogenous. The heterogeneity inside this group is a deep-seated phenomenon in the small business research field (Torrès & Julien, 2005). With regard to ITG for example, one would assume that SMEs pertaining to different categories such as local, transition, and world-class SMEs which are characterized by different IT adoption patterns (Raymond and Croteau, 2006) would adopt different ITG mechanisms.

As second caution, the assumption of specificity should not be transformed into a universal principle (such as *all SMEs are specific*) ignoring that "[a] small business may sometimes not be, or no longer be, specific" (Torrès & Julien, 2005, p. 360). Indeed, in some contexts, referred to as "denaturing contexts", the very characteristics that found the specificity of SMEs tend to disappear, giving place to an "anti-small business", that is a firm that, without growing in size, takes on all or most of the opposite features of small businesses (Messeghem, 2003; Torrès & Julien, 2005). These authors, considering the denaturing potential of some contexts, plead for a contingent approach to SMEs specificity. This is exactly what have done Brouard and Di Vito (2008) by putting SMEs with multiple external shareholders on the same footing as (big) public companies with widespread shareholding, considering that agency conflicts in both situations would be similar.

Does the specificity of SMEs hold in the context of CG and ITG respectively? Can a SME embrace CG and ITG mechanisms and then keep the distinctive features of SMEs? At first sight, CG and ITG would appear counterintuitive for SMEs, in such they push for more structuring, planning, and formalization. Acknowledging this fact, we propose a framework for research on ITG that takes into account the specificities of SMEs, showing that there would be ITG mechanisms that are compatible with the SME's nature. In this research we use the OECD definition of a SME which is any firm that falls under the upper limit of 250 employees, in both manufacturing and service sectors (OECD, 2005).

2.2 Theories Applied in Corporate Governance and IT Governance Research

Different theories applied into CG research have been applied in ITG research as well. The theories discussed in this study results from a literature review we conducted. We do not pretend in the completeness of the list of existing theories; nevertheless, we believe that the main and most referred to theories are covered. The main theories are agency theory, stakeholder theory, power perspective, stewardship theory, resource dependency theory, network governance theory, institutional theory, upper echelon theory, institutional trust theory (Al Mamun, Yasser, & Rahman, 2013).

In the following sub-sections we briefly present each theory and succinctly analyze its specific application in ITG empirical studies and its level of suitability to SMEs' realities. We begin with those that seem less applicable to ITG in the context of SMEs.

Agency Theory

This theory is the overwhelmingly dominant school of thought both in academic research and practice (Mason & O'Mahony, 2008). It focuses on problems arising from separation of ownership and control (Uhlaner et al., 2007). It embraces a narrow, shareholder-centric view of CG, which reflects the traditional finance paradigm of shareholder value maximization as the main (if not the sole) goal of corporate management (Turlea, et al., 2010). Following agency theory reasoning, studies in ITG have analyzed the relationships between ownership and control structures of the firm and the IT performance (Karake, 1995; Ferguson et al., 2013).

The problem of applying this reasoning in the context of SMEs, at least as it has been applied in ITG in LEs is threefold. First, this reasoning is based on the principal / agent problems that are less likely to happen in SMEs due to the overlapping of management and ownership in those firms (Banham & He, 2010; Brunninge et al., 2007). Second, structures that are referred to in proposed governance mechanisms inadequately mirror the ones found in LEs as if SMEs were just scaled down LEs (Uhlaner et al., 2007). Third, due to the small size of SMEs, the information asymmetry is very low (Brouard & Di Vito, 2008). Information asymmetry is at the basis of opportunistic behaviors that agency theory-related governance mechanisms seek to thwart. Therefore we consider that agency theory does not apply well to SMEs.

Stakeholder Theory

While agency theory focuses on the sole dual relationship between managers and shareholders, the stakeholder theory broadens constituencies, adding to managers and shareholders other groups of actors that may have a direct or indirect stake at the firm's operations (Talaulicar, 2010; Abraham, 2012). Stakeholder theory is inherently inscribed into ITG. Many ITG definitions "explicitly or implicitly refer to stakeholders either as ends of or as contributors to the ITG activities" (Messabia, & Elbekkali, 2010, p. 981).

The stakeholder theory has been criticized as a perspective that can lead SMEs to implement policies with sub-optimal outcomes (Abor, & Adjasi, 2007; Abor & Biekpe, 2007). The pursuit of divergent stakeholders' interests such as environmental versus financial is less of an issue in SMEs than in LEs. As a "definitive stakeholder", the SME owner-manager is the most salient among all stakeholders, that is, the one whose claims will be given priority in ITG (Mitchell et al., 1997). Therefore the stakeholder theory does not apply so well to the reality of SMEs with regards to ITG.

Power Perspective

The power perspective is used in corporate governance to analyze potential conflicts of interests that may arise among different stakeholders, notably among executives, directors, and shareholders (Chen, 2007). With regard to ITG, this perspective is referred to analyze the relative influence of IT function comparatively to the influence of other business units in IT-related decision processes (Xue et al., 2008; Weill & Ross, 2005).

The potential conflicts opposing executives, directors, and shareholders that are at the core of the power perspective theory (Daily et al., 2003) are less likely to be observed in SMEs. Thus, this theory does not capture well the reality of SMEs with regards to ITG. The above theories that we assess as less applicable to ITG in SMEs are summarized in Table 1.

Among alternative theories that can be mobilized to study ITG in SMEs, we propose the following ones as more appropriate: stewardship theory, resources dependency theory, network governance theory, institutional theory, upper echelon

Table 1. Theories with lower applicability to IT governance in SMEs

Theories	Key Issues with Regard to ITG Mechanisms in SMEs	Reasons Why Lower Applicability to SMEs
Agency theory	Relationship management with external IT partners	• Principal / Agent problems less likely (Brunninge, et al., 2007; Banham & He, 2010) • Reference to unlikely structures (van Gils, 2005) • Low information asymmetry (Brouard & Di Vito, 2008)
Stakeholder theory	Predominant role of owner-manager	Suboptimal outcomes (Abor, & Adjasi, 2007; Banham & He, 2010)
Power perspective	Predominant role of owner-manager	Lower levels of power playing (Fiegener et al., 2004)

theory, and institutional trust theory (Brunninge et al., 2007; Devos et al., 2012). Here are their key characteristics and why they seem more applicable to ITG for SMEs. They are summarized in Table 2.

Stewardship Theory

This theory is based on an assumption opposite to the agency theory's premise of opportunistic behavior as inherent to human nature. According to the stewardship theory, managers are naturally trustworthy, and seek to be good stewards of the corporate assets (Uhlaner et al., 2007; Nicholson & Kiel, 2007; Del Baldo, 2012). With regard to ITG specifically, the stewardship theory may be more consistent with the nature of ITG because the managers' interests are perfectly aligned with the shareholders' interests, thanks to the overlapping of ownership and control in most SMEs (McGinnis et al., 2004; Brunninge et al., 2007).

Table 2. Theories with higher applicability to IT governance in SMEs

Theories	Key Issues with Regard to ITG Mechanisms	Reasons Why Higher Applicability to SMEs
Stewardship theory	• No need for agency-based control mechanisms • Empowerment of owner-managers and key employees	Convergence of ownership and management (Brunninge, et al., 2007)
Resource dependency theory	• Role of IT external partners • Role of outside and independent directors	Limited internal resources (Devos et al., 2012)
Network governance theory	• Pressures from partners to conform • Support from the network	• Pressure to formalize the network structure • Pressure to implement controls • Pressure to improve IT knowledge and communication • Need for partners' support
Institutional theory	Institutional pressures towards ITG mechanisms adoption	• Pressures towards IT innovations adoption from the SME's networks (MacGregor, 2004; Raymond et al., 2012) • Little capacity of SMEs to resist to pressures
Upper echelon theory	• IT-related roles and responsibilities for owner-manager • IT champion among key employees	• Predominance of owner-managers (Brunninge et al., 2007; Napoli, 2012) • Important role of key employees (Brunninge et al., 2007; Napoli, 2012)
Institutional trust theory	Moderating effect of institutional trust between SME and external IT partner on the adoption of ITG mechanisms.	• Partnership based on trust (Devos et al., 2012) • Limited resources for agency-based controls implementation (Huang et al., 2010)

Resource Dependency Theory

This theory is used in CG to explain the role of board of directors as a link to access to further resources available in the firm's environment (Nicholson & Kiel, 2007). Board members extend the reach of an organization in its environment, and provide it with access to resources that would otherwise be out of reach or expensive (Daily et al., 2003). Research in this area focuses on the size and the composition of the boards as they may reflect the extent of exposure to external environments networks and access to various resources (Jackling & Johl, 2009). The resource-dependency theory can be and has been specifically applied to ITG (Rasheed & Geiger, 2001; Xue et al., 2008). The resource-dependency theory fits well to the context of SMEs, particularly because most SMEs depend on external IT expertise (Devos et al., 2012).

Network Governance Theory

This theory involves a select, persistent and structured set of private firms and non-profit agencies engaged in creating, manufacturing or distributing products or services, based on implicit and open-ended contracts designed to adapt to their environmental specificities and to coordinate and safeguard exchanges (adapted from Jones et al., 1997). Based on the network governance theory, research on interorganizational ITG unveiled the two profiles of interorganizational ITG: contractual and consensual (Croteau et al., 2013). These profiles take into account the ITG structure, the process followed to make decisions, and the roles of participants involved in setting and promoting interorganizational mechanisms (Croteau & Bergeron, 2009). Given the more informal structure of SMEs, they have a lower number of hierarchical levels, a lower ratio of managers/employees and they are at an earlier level (state) of interorganizational ITG maturity (Barthon & Jepsen, 1997; Croteau & Bergeron, 2009). It is therefore expected that SMEs will have a more informal and flatter interorganizational ITG structure, will be more dependent upon partners as to the choice and obligation of IT control processes, and the interorganizational participants to ITG will be less in number yet more involved into their IT-related decisions and actions. It is thus expected that the more a SME is involved in external networks, the more it will implement ITG mechanisms. It will be under pressure to conform itself to its partners' practices and will rely on the network capacity to compensate for its lack of internal resources and capabilities (Xiaobao et al., 2013).

Institutional Theory

This theory considers that organizations are not just economic systems motivated by the pursuit of economic efficiency and performance, but are also social and cultural systems that seek to gain legitimacy in their environment by adjusting themselves to regulations, norms and values (Al Mamun et al., 2013; DiMaggio & Powell, 1983). Institutional theory acknowledges the influence of an organization's environment on its IT structures and practices. More precisely, the intensity of institutional pressures will affect the IT department power, and will influence an organization's ITG patterns (Xue et al., 2008). Moreover, due to their size and to their limited resources, SMEs may be more influenced by their environment than LEs. Hence the institutional theory seems be suitable for analyzing the adoption of ITG practices in the SME's context (MacGregor, 2004; Mohnnak, 2007; Islamoglu & Liebenau, 2007; Raymond et al., 2012).

Upper Echelon Theory

According to upper echelon theory, the characteristics of top-level managers play a crucial role in determining the strategic organizational outcomes and processes (Hambrick & Mason, 1984). The small size and the structural flexibility of SMEs intensify the involvement of top managers in almost all of the firm's activities, and their influence is thus stronger than it can be in LEs (Brunninge et al., 2007). The upper echelon theory offers new theoretical lens through which ITG mechanisms in SMEs can be analyzed. The focus shifts from agency-related levels of analysis (ownership structure, board of directors, incentive compensation) towards the SME's top management team (or key employees). The upper echelon theory has been mainly used to analyze the strategic changes in SMEs (Brunninge et al., 2007; Napoli, 2012), but it is quite appropriate for ITG as well. The values, norms, backgrounds, and interests of top-level managers of SMEs may explain their readiness and their predisposition to adopt certain forms of ITG mechanisms and to reject others.

Institutional Trust Theory

This theory is an interesting alternative theoretical perspective to agency theory and it is suitable to the context of SMEs as well. Instead of relying on agency-based control mechanisms to deter opportunistic behavior in IT collaboration relationships, SMEs may develop a partnership based on trust, which "can be seen as a coordinating mechanism, based on shared moral values and norms" (Devos et al., 2012, p. 210). Trust reduces the need to resort to structured controls, such as steering committees, management guidelines, policies and procedures, or to comprehensive outcome-based contracts, for which SMEs may not be well-equipped to deal with given their financial constraints and their limited capabilities in terms of internal IT-related human resources (Huang et al., 2010).

3. CONCEPTUAL FRAMEWORK

The preceding analysis shows that when analyzing ITG in SMEs, we need to take into account theories that are more appropriate for SMEs. Building on such theories as discussed in the precedent section, we propose a framework for research on ITG in SMEs with the corresponding supportive theories by constructs, as illustrated in Figure 1.

In this framework, the SME's owner-manager and key (internal) employees are the main actors. The inclusion of the SME's owner-manager characteristics in the conceptual framework of ITG in SMEs is based on the stewardship theory and the upper echelon theory, which both acknowledge the SME's owner-manager's tight grip on any major organizational activities and decisions. Besides, the primary role played by owner-managers in the context of SMEs is unanimously acknowledged in the small business literature.

The inclusion of the SME's key employees is based on the stewardship theory and the upper echelon theory as well: key employees' influence is inversely proportional to the size of their organization, so the role of key employees in any major decisions would be greater in SMEs than in LEs. Shared values, beliefs and norms of both the owner-manager and the key employees are based on the institutional theory.

Figure 1. Framework for research on IT governance in SMEs

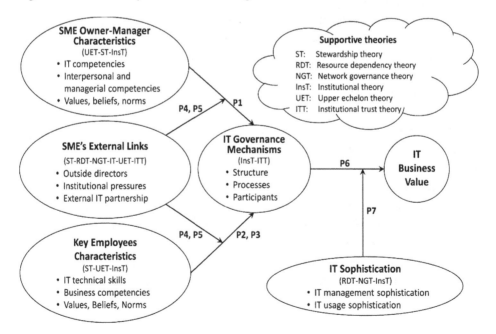

The proposed framework also assumes that in their decision with regard to ITG mechanisms, the SME's owner-manager and key employees will be to some extent influenced by its external links. This assumption is based concurrently on the resource-dependency theory, the network governance theory, the institutional theory, and the institutional trust theory. In accordance with the resource-dependency theory and network governance theory, the access to external resources through either independent and outside directors or IT external partners would influence the SME's owner-manager and key employees with respect to their ITG decisions.

The network governance theory and the literature on interorganizational governance of IT suggest that governance mechanisms related to structure, processes and participants lead to higher competitive advantage or IT business value. The network governance theory also suggests that SMEs involved in networks are likely to be influenced by their business partners in adopting ITG mechanisms. According to institutional theory, mimetic, normative, and coercive pressures would be exerted on the SME's main actors towards the implementation of the same ITG mechanisms adopted by organizations evolving in the SME's environment. As for the theory of institutional trust, it allows to take into account the moderating effect of trust between a SME and its IT external partners on the level of ITG mechanisms implementation: high levels of trust reduce the need for owner-managers and key employees to implement agency theory-inspired ITG mechanisms.

So, the proposed conceptual framework is essentially composed of six groups of factors. At the framework's core, there is the group of IT governance mechanisms. The adoption of such mechanisms by a SME is deemed to be directly or indirectly determined by three groups of factors: the SME's owner-manager's characteristics, its key employees' characteristics and the SME's external links. The SME's IT business value, as the outcome of its adoption of ITG mechanisms, constitutes the next element in the framework (discussed later in the section on the consequences of ITG mechanisms). The firm's IT sophistication constitutes the last exogenous element, and is meant to assure the presence of the IT function and the "IT artifact" within the conceptual framework (Orlikowski & Iacono, 2001; Akhlaghpour et al., 2013) (discussed later in the section on the moderating role of this element in the relationship between ITG mechanisms and IT business value).

3.1 IT Governance Mechanisms in SMEs

Having its roots in the network governance theory (Jones, 1997; Barthon et al., 1997), ITG and interorganizational ITG generally classifies ITG mechanisms into three dimensions: structures, processes, and participants (Croteau & Bergeron, 2009; Croteau et al., 2013; Ko & Fink, 2010). Sometimes, participants is also referred to as relational mechanisms (De Haes & Van Grembergen, 2006; Wilkin, 2012; Mohamed

& Singh, 2012). The structure dimension emphasizes control and coordination and refers to the organization of IT function, to its roles and responsibilities, brief, to the formal and rational units and mechanisms put in place to carry out IT-related decisions and activities in organizations; structure refers to the locus of authority with regards to IT decision-making, in other words it determines who act and with which resources (Croteau & Bergeron, 2009). The processes dimension emphasizes control and sustainable capability, and refers to tools, techniques, frameworks or standards combined to ensure IT-business strategic alignment and to track IT performance achievements. The participants dimension refers to the persons at various levels and functions who take part in leadership, training and sharing, who actively participate, collaborate, communicate, and get involved in order to disseminate IT-related policies, principles and outcomes. ITG would be even more important in a network or interorganizational environment due to the partners requirements in terms of a minimum threshold of quality, uniformity and reciprocity of IT mechanisms needed to create value for all network members. In this situation, the network strength is as high as the weakest of its link. Much adaptation will therefore have to be made to SMEs specificities.

Some highly-formalized ITG mechanisms are less suitable to rather organic and loosely structured SMEs (Jennings & Beaver, 1997). Basic ITG mechanisms are likely to be found in SMEs. These ITG mechanisms are not necessarily denaturing. Structure-related ITG mechanisms such as CIO on board and IT steering committee (De Haes & Van Grembergen, 2006) are less likely to be in place in SMEs, as their structural ITG capability is likely to be assumed by the owner-manager. Clear IT-related roles and responsibilities of the owner-manager are thus necessary as structural governance mechanism in this case (Wilkin, 2012). Instead of the formal CIO function, a SME is likely to rely on an IT champion, a much more informal role and yet a very important one for its IT-related activities (Pollard, 2003). SMEs may also rely on external expertise to compensate their lack of expertise internally. The IT champion will play a determinant role in the relationship between a SME and its IT external expert.

For process-related mechanisms such as externally developed standards, tools, techniques, or frameworks like COBIT, ITIL, ISO17799 which are highly formalized and certification oriented, SMEs are not either well equipped (Ko & Fink, 2010). Without necessary resorting to highly developed tools, SMEs have to find ways to align their IT projects to their strategic business and to track IT business value creation. Otherwise, overwhelmed by operational imperatives as they tend to be, SMEs may lose sight of long term and strategic imperatives in their IT decision-making. So, one would consider IT strategic alignment and IT performance tracking as key process-related ITG mechanisms in SMEs.

As for participants, relational mechanisms such as business/IT co-location and active participation and collaboration between key stakeholders do not need to be formally implemented in SMEs as they are naturally evident in such context (Wilkin, 2012). However, for an effective collaboration between participants (Peterson, 2004), people involved in ITG need to develop mutual understanding which can be reached through IT training, and proper communication for developing awareness and understanding of business/IT objectives.

3.2 Antecedents of IT Governance Mechanisms

In our framework, the adoption of ITG mechanisms is directly determined by both SME owner-manager's characteristics and key employees' characteristics, and indirectly affected by SME's external links. In other words, the relationship between, on one hand the owner-manager's characteristics and the key employees' characteristics, and on the other hand the adoption of ITG mechanisms is moderated by the SME's external links.

SME's Owner-Manager

Studies on SMEs have acknowledged the central role of the entrepreneur or owner-manager in shaping the firm. As the principal stakeholder concurrently assuming multiple roles, he/she is involved in almost if not all major decisions that affect the firm for better or worse. His/her characteristics will then be determinant. Banking on previous studies, we put these characteristics in three main categories: IT-related competencies (Caldeira & Ward, 2003; Wainwright et al., 2005; Scupola, 2008; Cragg et al., 2011), interpersonal and managerial competencies (Kraemmergaard & Rose, 2002; Bassellier & Benbasat, 2004) and personal values, beliefs, and norms (Ramdani, et al., 2009; Del Baldo, 2012).

IT-related competencies of an owner-manager are important in that they will shape not only his/her understanding of opportunities of IT usage in business activities, but also his or her expectations with regards to how IT activities should be managed. These understanding and expectations will lead to the IT adoption decision, and more important, to the creation of facilitating conditions for the actual IT implementation and use (Scupola, 2008). ITG mechanisms can be viewed as facilitating conditions meant to leverage IT for achieving business goals.

Interpersonal and managerial competencies will help the owner-manager to effectively communicate his/her vision of ITG mechanisms, motivate and get employees to adhere to that vision, overcome change resistance, and meet the scope, time, and goal objectives throughout the implementation phases of ITG mechanisms. Adapting Kraemmergaard and Rose's (2002) and Bassellier and Benbasat's (2004) definitions to the context of ITG, we retain leadership, interpersonal communication, human resource, change management, and project management as part of interpersonal and managerial competencies.

Another determinant factor that would sway an owner-manager's decision in favor or not of ITG mechanisms adoption is the level of compatibility between these mechanisms and his/her values, beliefs, and norms. The notion of compatibility, which refers to the perception of consistence of an innovation (ITG mechanisms in this case) with regards to values, experiences, beliefs, and needs of would-be adopters, is important, especially in small firms (Ramdani et al., 2009). Owner-managers will obviously willingly push for adoption of ITG mechanisms that are compatible with their values, beliefs, and norms. Considering the precedent considerations, the following proposition can be stated:

P1: Greater competencies (IT-related, interpersonal and managerial) of the SME's owner-manager and higher levels of perceived compatibility of his/her values, beliefs, and norms with ITG mechanisms will positively influence the implementation of ITG mechanisms in a SME.

SME's Key Employees

Notwithstanding the key role of the entrepreneur or the owner-manager in all major decisions, key employees' influence in SMEs is likely to be paramount. This major influence stems from the fact that small firms tend to be structured around key employees' abilities and interests (Jennings & Beaver, 1997). It is also due to the small size and organizational flexibility of SMEs (Brunninge et al., 2007) that do not restrict key employees in narrowly-defined roles. The paramount influence of the SMEs' key employees is in line with the upper echelon theory (Hambrick & Mason, 1984). The characteristics of a SME's key employees have to be taken into consideration in order to understand the adoption of ITG mechanisms in the firm. Based on previous studies (Kraemmergaard & Rose, 2002; Bassellier et al., 2003), these characteristics are grouped into three main categories:

1.   IT technical skills,
2.   Business competencies, and
3.   Values, beliefs, and norms.

At the level of key employees, IT technical skills required are more than a certain level of comfort with IT as is the case for owner-manager's IT knowledge. IT technical skills of key employees are a reflection of their IT-related explicit knowledge with regards to technology, applications, system development, IT management, access to IT knowledge. IT technical skills also include their IT-related tacit knowledge, that is experience in IT projects and experience in the management of IT (Bassellier et al., 2003). While owner-manager's IT knowledge play a role in the decision to adopt IT, IT technical skills at the key employees level are indispensable for the actual implementation and effective use of IT (Raymond et al., 2012). We would here assume the same pattern applies to ITG mechanisms adoption and implementation.

So, for this study we define business competencies of key employees as the knowledge and skills of key employees of a SME related to their understanding the business domain and the specific organizational context. The business domain-specific competencies refer to the knowledge of the production system of a firm's industry, the ability to recognize the firm's challenges and opportunities, including the potential of IT leverage for enhancing business processes. The organization-specific competencies are about the acute acquaintance of the firm's functioning (e.g. power distribution, structures), specificities (e.g. culture and history), and partnership. Key employees with stronger business competencies (business domain-specific and organizational-specific) are more likely to better understand the potential of IT usage in business activities and the necessity to adopt ITG mechanisms for achieving higher IT business value.

As in the case of owner-managers, values, beliefs, and norms of key employees of a SME will affect ITG mechanisms adoption. Shared cognitive characteristics (such as values, beliefs, and norms) will be conducive to consensus among team members which in turn will facilitate the introduction of strategic change in SMEs (Brunninge et al., 2007). This can be seen as a positive factor for ITG mechanisms adoption. But according to institutional trust theory, shared values and norms may reduce the need of formalized mechanisms (Devos et al., 2012). So, we would argue that shared values, beliefs, and norms among the SME's key employees will accelerate the process of ITG mechanisms adoption (pace) while reducing the diversity of ITG mechanisms adopted. We would also argue that the SME's key employees will favor the adoption of ITG mechanisms they deem compatible with their values, beliefs, and norms over others deemed less compatible. From the above developments, the two following propositions can be stated:

P2: Greater competencies (IT technical skills, business competencies) of the SME's key employees and higher levels of perceived compatibility of their values, beliefs, and norms with ITG mechanisms will positively influence the implementation of ITG mechanisms in a SME.

P3: The more the values, beliefs, and norms are shared among a SME's key employees, the more easily a SME will adopt and implement ITG mechanisms (quick pace), and the less diversified ITG mechanisms will be.

SME's External Links

In SMEs, decisions are mainly made by the owner-manager assisted by key employees. However, in their decision-making process, they may be swayed one way or another by external stakeholders. Following the literature review, we retained four sources of influence that can affect the decision to adopt ITG mechanisms: outside and independent directors, institutional pressures, IT external partnership and the network members.

We have already underscored that, in most SMEs, board of directors are either inexistent or purely formal, or sometimes used to serve the owner-manager's purposes (Fiegener et al., 2004; van Gils, 2005; Brouard & Di Vito, 2008). Yet, in accordance with the resource-dependency theory, having a board on which sit a number of external directors increases a firm's exposure to external environment networks and its convenient access to valuable resources (Jackling & Johl, 2009). The latter's independence vis-à-vis the owner-manager (and key employees) gives them much more latitude in their supervision role of the firm's management. So, SMEs are compelled to adopt boards with a great number of outside and independent directors (Abor & Adjasi, 2007). This would prevent them from developing "a myopic and narrow view" that stalls change (Brunninge et al., 2007, p. 299). Outside and independent directors would influence owner-managers and key employees towards ITG mechanisms adoption.

Institutional theory posits that changes in organizations are determined more by external or environmental pressures than "rational" decisions by internal actors (owner-managers and key employees) (DiMaggio & Powell, 1983). In accordance with the institutional perspective, it has been found that the diffusion of corporate social responsibilities in SMEs is linked to the extent at which these SMEs are embedded in a network of local socio-economic institutions (Del Baldo, 2012). Similarly, a SME's network ties will play a role in deciding the owner-manager and key employees to embrace ITG mechanisms that are in place in other organizations within the network. Besides, inter-organizational exchanges entail task and function interdependence that requires a great deal of coordination (Croteau & Bergeron, 2009). Challenges related to the coordination of business partners which are more or less different with regard to various organizational aspects (strategy, processes, structure, IT infrastructure and architecture) incite each other to put in place governance mechanisms (Croteau & Bergeron, 2009). In the same vein, compared to the local SMEs, world-class SMEs would need more ITG mechanisms due to their being involved in more extended networks (Raymond & Croteau, 2006).

It is almost a truism to say that most SMEs lack internal IT expertise. To compensate this, they mainly rely on IT external expertise. Somehow, this dependence put a SME in a situation of inter-organizational ITG. Studying profiles of interorganizational ITG, Croteau et al. (2013) proposed a continuum with at one end the contractual profile, and at the other, the consensual profile: in contractual profiles, "organizations are involved in a legal relationship with their outsourcers", while consensual profiles are characterized by "a collaborative and cooperative approach" (p. 36). Potential opportunistic behaviors are fought mainly through the formalization of commitments in contractual profiles, and through mutual trust in consensual profiles. Contractual profiles are consistent with agency theory according to which, as previously stated, a SME would adopt ITG mechanisms to deter opportunistic behavior from the external expert. We have seen however, in accordance with the theory of institutional trust, that some SMEs, ill-equipped for developing structured controls or outcome-based contracts, will instead seek a partnership based on trust (Devos et al., 2012). So, an external partnership based on trust will reduce the need to resort to formalized ITG mechanisms in SMEs. All of these considerations related to the SME's external links lead to the following propositions:

P4: A SME's external links through outside and independent directors, networks, and IT partners will positively influence the owner-manager's and key employees' decision to adopt ITG mechanisms.

P5: The higher the level of institutional trust between a SME and its IT external partner, the less its owner-manager and key employees will be swayed towards ITG mechanisms adoption.

3.3 Consequences of IT Governance Mechanisms

It has been suggested that there may be a positive correlation between ITG mechanisms and different organizational performance measures as captured into Kaplan and Norton's balanced scorecard framework (Mohamed & Singh, 2012). Bradley et al. (2012) have established that ITG has a positive impact on different measures of hospital performance. The underlying assumption is that effective ITG would enhance IT impacts on the organizational performance.

The idea that the ultimate effectiveness of ITG mechanisms adopted in organizations should be appreciated in terms of IT contribution to business value (IT business value) seems to be a largely shared understanding in ITG literature (Zarvić et al., 2012). IT business value is defined as "the organizational performance impacts of information technology at both the intermediate process level and the organization-wide level, and comprising both efficiency impacts and competitive impacts'' (Melville et al., 2004, p. 287). More precisely, Weill and Ross (2005) suggested assessing the ITG effectiveness against the achievement of four IT-enabled organizational objectives: "cost-effectiveness, asset utilization, business growth and business flexibility" (p. 26).

As the effectiveness of IT initiatives and investments is one of the priorities of ITG (Bradley et al., 2012), any failure with regards to IT initiatives hints to the failure of ITG. For example, failure of outsourced information systems may be seen as a failure of ITG (Devos et al., 2012). In the same way, the under-exploitation of IT business value in SMEs can be blamed on weaknesses of their ITG (Wilkin, 2012). Even a weak interorganizational ITG can lead to disastrous results in terms of competitiveness. So, the adoption of ITG mechanisms may have a positive impact on IT business value in SMEs, hence the following proposition:

P6: The adoption of ITG mechanisms in a SME will positively influence its IT business value.

3.4 Moderating Effect of IT Sophistication on IT Governance Mechanisms

The evolution of the strategic role of IT in SMEs, and thus the increasing need for IT governance, is closely linked to the *IT sophistication* of these firms, that is, to the way they manage and use IT in order to gain business value from their investment in the IT function and in IT artifacts (Philip & Booth, 2001; Bradley et al., 2012). IT sophistication was first defined, conceptualized and operationalized by Raymond, Paré and Bergeron (1995), this concept being later employed by other researchers (Chwelos et al., 2001; Paré & Sicotte, 2001; Pflughoest et al., 2003). IT sophistication "refers to the nature, complexity, and interdependence of the management and use of IT within an organization" (Raymond et al., 2011, p. 205). Now, the strategic role of IT sophistication in SMEs can best be understood by the extent to which the management and usage of IT by these firms are "aligned" with their strategic objectives (Dutot et al., 2014).

The form of IT governance adopted by an organization is one the key attributes used by researchers to characterize its IT function (Weill & Ross; 2005). Thus, forms of governance are differentiated by the extent to which the IT function is held accountable for the development of IT-enabled organizational capabilities (Reich & Nelson 2003), and for the ensuing contribution to organizational agility, innovation and IT business value (Guillemette and Paré, 2012). From a governance standpoint, the sophistication of the SMEs' IT function would thus affect the outcomes produced by ITG mechanisms such as the roles and responsibilities assigned to their owner-managers, external IT partners and key users with regard to IT-related issues and IT investments (Sambamurthy & Zmud, 1999). This presumed role of IT sophistication would be further supported by the resource dependence, network governance and institutional theories in particular, upon which "ideal" IT management and governance profiles can be founded (Ross, 2003; Willcocks et al., 2006). The delineation of such profiles would then imply that improvements in the SMEs' IT business value brought about by their increasing adoption of ITG mechanisms would be greater in firms whose level of IT sophistication is higher, that is, whose actual IT management and governance profile shows greater alignment or "fit" (Bergeron et al., 2004). The ITG research framework's final proposition follows:

P7: The greater the SME's IT sophistication, the greater the positive influence of its adoption of ITG mechanisms upon its IT business value.

Note that this last research proposition is based on the view of the SME's IT function as a moderator of its IT governance, moderation being conceptualised as the interaction between IT sophistication and ITG mechanisms (Baron & Kenney 1986). Thus, in line with Bharadwaj et al.'s (1995) perspective of IT alignment and with Venkatraman's (1989) "fit as moderation" perspective, IT sophistication is deemed to positively moderate the relationship between ITG mechanisms and IT business value.

3.5 Control Variables: The Firm's Size, Age, and Sector of Activity

We previously underscored the necessity of carefully considering the heterogeneous nature of SMEs. All of these enterprises share some particularities, but they may also present some differences due to their size (very small-, small-, medium-sized), industry sector, or their age. All these factors are taken into account in the proposed research framework as control variables.

The size of firms (in terms of the number of employees or in terms of revenues) is generally positively associated with the adoption of innovations (Ko et al., 2008; Pekovic, 2010). More precisely, in the field of ITG, it has been advanced that there may be a positive correlation between the firm's size and ITG effectiveness (Mohamed & Singh, 2012). The same authors posit that organizations operating in information intensive sectors or in sectors characterized by high levels of uncertainty are more likely to effectively implement ITG mechanisms than organizations in less information intensive sectors, or in less uncertain environments. The firm's age can also explain differences between SMEs with regard to ITG mechanisms adoption. After reporting mixed results in literature on this topic, Mohamed & Singh (2012) formulate the hypothesis that a firm's age would be negatively correlated with ITG effectiveness.

4. CONCLUSION

Theories and frameworks generally referred to in the field of CG in general, and in ITG in particular, have mainly been developed in the context of large enterprises. In this study we analyzed the main theories applied in CG and ITG research, and confronted them with the specificities of SMEs. This exercise allowed us to highlight the limits of these theories in the SME's context, and to discuss adaptations needed or alternative theories in such context. Building on these developments, we then proposed a conceptual framework of ITG in SMEs.

We have shown that the mainstream agency theory does not fare well when applied in the context of SMEs. So, the proposed ITG research framework is based on a combination of alternative theories: upper echelon theory, stakeholder theory, resource-dependence theory, the network governance theory, institutional theory, and the theory of institutional trust. In accordance with the now abundant literature on SMEs, the conceptual framework acknowledges the central role played by the owner-manager in all major decisions of the firm. In accordance with the upper echelon theory, the role of the SME's key employees (or the top-management team) is also acknowledged in the conceptual framework proposed. Together, resource-dependency theory, the network governance theory, the institutional theory and the theory of institutional trust have been referred to for propositions related to the role of the SME's external links in its decision towards ITG mechanisms adoption.

In taking the SME's specificities into account, we followed the previous research recommendation that size is one of the contingencies that must be heeded when designing a mix of structures, processes, and relational mechanisms for an ITG research framework (Pollard, 2003). The seven propositions presented in this study may thus serve as initial hypotheses for empirical verification. This theoretical study is a first step in our research. In the next step, case studies will be conducted to refine the conceptual framework, followed by a survey to test the framework.

REFERENCES

Abor, J., & Adjasi, C. K. D. (2007). Corporate governance and the small and medium enterprises sector: Theory and implications. *Corporate Governance*, 7(2), 111–122. doi:10.1108/14720700710739769

Abor, J., & Biekpe, N. (2007). Corporate governance, ownership structure and performance of SMEs in Ghana: Implications for financing opportunities. *Corporate Governance*, 7(3), 288–300. doi:10.1108/14720700710756562

Abraham, S. E. (2012). Information technology, an enabler in corporate governance. *Corporate Governance, 12*(3), 281–291. doi:10.1108/14720701211234555

Akhlaghpour, S., Wu, J., Lapointe, L., & Pinsonneault, A. (2013). The ongoing quest for the IT artifact: Looking back, moving forward. *Journal of Information Technology, 28*(S2), 150–166. doi:10.1057/jit.2013.10

Al Mamun, A., Yasser, Q. R., & Rahman, M. A. (2013). A discussion of the suitability of only one vs. more than one theory for depicting corporate governance. *Modern Economy, 4*(1), 37–48. doi:10.4236/me.2013.41005

Alves, C. R. C., Riekstin, A. C., Carvalho, T. C. M. B., & Vidal, A. G. R. (2013). IT governance frameworks: A literature review of Brazilian publications. *Proceedings of the International Conference on Information Resources Management* (CONF-IRM).

Banham, H., & He, Y. (2010). SME governance: Converging definitions and expanding expectations. *International Business & Economics Research Journal, 9*(2), 77–82.

Baron, R. M., & Kenny, D. A. (1986). The moderator mediator variable distinction in social psychological research: Conceptual, strategic, and statistical considerations. *Journal of Personality and Social Psychology, 51*(6), 1173–1182. doi:10.1037/0022-3514.51.6.1173 PMID:3806354

Barthon, P., & Jepsen, B. (1997). How time affects transaction costs and relational governance in the distribution channel: A review and research proposition. *Management Research News, 20*(6), 14–29. doi:10.1108/eb028566

Bassellier, G., & Benbasat, I. (2004). Business competence of information technology professionals: Conceptual development and influence on IT-business partnership. *Management Information Systems Quarterly, 28*(4), 673–694.

Bassellier, G., Benbasat, I., & Reich, B. H. (2003). The influence of business managers' IT competence on championing IT. *Information Systems Research, 14*(4), 317–336. doi:10.1287/isre.14.4.317.24899

Bergeron, F., Raymond, L., & Rivard, S. (2004). Ideal patterns of strategic alignment and business performance. *Information & Management, 41*(8), 1003–1020. doi:10.1016/j.im.2003.10.004

Bharadwaj, A. S., Bharadwaj, S. G., & Konsynski, B. R. 1995. The moderator role of information technology in firm performance: A conceptual model and research propositions. *Proceedings of the Sixteenth International Conference on Information Systems*.

Blili, S., & Raymond, L. (1993). Information technology: Threats and opportunities for small and medium-sized enterprises. *International Journal of Information Management, 13*(6), 439–448. doi:10.1016/0268-4012(93)90060-H

Bradley, R. V., Byrd, T. A., Pridmore, J. L., Thrasher, E., Pratt, R. M., & Mbarika, V. W. (2012). An empirical examination of antecedents and consequences of IT governance in US hospitals. *Journal of Information Technology, 27*(2), 156–177. doi:10.1057/jit.2012.3

Brouard, F., & Di Vito, J. (2008). Identification des mécanismes de gouvernance applicables aux PME. *9ème Congrès International Francophone en Entrepreneuriat et PME*. Université Louvain-La-Neuve.

Brunninge, O., Nordqvist, M., & Wiklund, J. (2007). Corporate governance and strategic change in SMEs: The effects of ownership, board composition and top management teams. *Small Business Economics, 29*(3), 295–308. doi:10.1007/s11187-006-9021-2

Caldeira, M. M., & Ward, J. M. (2003). Using resource-based theory to interpret the successful adoption and use of information systems and technology in manufacturing small and medium sized enterprises. *European Journal of Information Systems, 12*(2), 127–141. doi:10.1057/palgrave.ejis.3000454

Chen, D. (2007). The behavioral consequences of CEO-board trust and power relationships in corporate governance. *Business Renaissance Quarterly, 2*(4), 59–75.

Chwelos, P., Benbasat, I., & Dexter, A. S. (2001). Research report: Empirical test of an EDI adoption model. *Information Systems Research, 12*(3), 304–321. doi:10.1287/isre.12.3.304.9708

Cragg, P., Caldeira, M., & Ward, J. (2011). Organizational information systems competences in small and medium-sized enterprises. *Information & Management, 48*(8), 353–363. doi:10.1016/j.im.2011.08.003

Croteau, A.-M., & Bergeron, F. (2009). Interorganizational governance of information technology. *42nd Hawaii International Conference on System Sciences*.

Croteau, A.-M., Bergeron, F., & Dubsky, J. (2013). Contractual and consensual profiles for an interorganizational governance of information technology. *International Business Research, 6*(9), 30–43. doi:10.5539/ibr.v6n9p30

Daily, C. M., Dalton, D. R., & Cannella, A. A. Jr. (2003). Corporate governance: Decades of dialogue and data. *Academy of Management Review, 28*(3), 371–382.

De Haes, S., & Van Grembergen, W. (2006). Information technology governance best practices in Belgian organizations. *39th Hawaii International Conference on System Sciences.*

De Haes, S., Van Grembergen, W., & Debreceny, R. S. (2013). COBIT 5 and enterprise governance of information technology: Building blocks and research opportunities. *Journal of Information Systems, 27*(1), 307–324. doi:10.2308/isys-50422

Del Baldo, M. (2012). Corporate social responsibility and corporate governance in Italian SMEs: The experience of some spirited businesses. *Journal of Management & Governance, 16*(1), 1–36. doi:10.1007/s10997-009-9127-4

Devos, J., Van Landeghem, H., & Deschoolmeester, D. (2012). Rethinking IT governance for SMEs. *Industrial Management & Data Systems, 112*(2), 206–223. doi:10.1108/02635571211204263

DiMaggio, P. J., & Powell, W. W. (1983). The iron cage re-visited: Institutional isomorphism and collective rationality in organizational fields. *American Sociological Review, 48*(2), 147–160. doi:10.2307/2095101

Dutot, V., Bergeron, F., & Raymond, L. (2014). Information management for the internationalization of SMEs: An exploratory study based on a strategic alignment perspective. *International Journal of Information Management, 34*(5), 672–681. doi:10.1016/j.ijinfomgt.2014.06.006

Ferguson, C., Green, P., Vaswani, R., & Wu, G. (2013). Determinants of effective information technology governance. *International Journal of Auditing, 17*(1), 75–99. doi:10.1111/j.1099-1123.2012.00458.x

Fiegener, M. K., Brown, B. M., Dreux, D. R., & Dennis, W. J. (2004). CEO stakes and board composition in small private firms. *Entrepreneurship Theory and Practice, 28*(4), 5–24.

Gattiker, T. F., & Goodhue, D. L. (2004). Understanding the local-level costs and benefits of ERP through organizational information processing theory. *Information & Management, 41*(4), 431–443. doi:10.1016/S0378-7206(03)00082-X

Guillemette, M. G., & Paré, G. (2012). Towards a new theory of the contribution of the IT function in organizations. *Management Information Systems Quarterly, 36*(2), 529–551.

Hambrick, D. C., & Mason, P. A. (1984). Upper echelons: The organization as a reflection of its top managers. *Academy of Management Review, 9*(2), 193–206.

Huang, R., Zmud, R. W., & Price, R. L. (2010). Influencing the effectiveness of IT governance practices through steering committees and communication policies. *European Journal of Information Systems, 19*(3), 288–302. doi:10.1057/ejis.2010.16

Islamoglu, M., & Liebenau, J. (2007). Information technology, transaction costs and governance structures: Integrating an institutional approach. *Journal of Information Technology, 22*(3), 275–283. doi:10.1057/palgrave.jit.2000107

Jackling, B., & Johl, S. (2009). Board structure and firm performance: Evidence from India's top companies. *Corporate Governance, 17*(4), 492–509. doi:10.1111/j.1467-8683.2009.00760.x

Jennings, P., & Beaver, G. (1997). The performance and competitive advantage of small firms: A management perspective. *International Small Business Journal, 15*(2), 63–75. doi:10.1177/0266242697152004

Jones, C., Hesterly, W. S., & Borgatti, S. (1997). A general theory of network governance: Exchange conditions, and social mechanisms. *Academy of Management Review, 22*(4), 911–945.

Karake, Z. A. (1995). Information technology performance: Agency and upper echelon theories. *Management Decision, 33*(9), 30–37. doi:10.1108/00251749510098964

Ko, D., & Fink, D. (2010). Information technology governance: An evaluation of the theory-practice gap. *Corporate Governance, 10*(5), 662–674. doi:10.1108/14720701011085616

Ko, E., Kim, S. H., Kim, M., & Woo, J. Y. (2008). Organizational characteristics and the CRM adoption process. *Journal of Business Research, 61*(1), 65–74. doi:10.1016/j.jbusres.2006.05.011

Kohli, R., & Grover, V. (2008). Business value of IT: An essay on expanding research directions to keep up with the times. *Journal of the Association for Information Systems, 9*(1), 23–39.

Kraemmergaard, P., & Rose, J. (2002). Managerial competences for ERP journeys. *Information Systems Frontiers, 4*(2), 199–211. doi:10.1023/A:1016054904008

Luftman, J., Ben-Zvi, T., Dwivedi, R., & Rigoni, E. H. (2010). IT governance: An alignment maturity perspective. *International Journal of IT/Business Alignment and Governance, 1*(2), 13–25.

MacGregor, R. C. (2004). Factors associated with formal networking in regional small business: Some findings from a study of Swedish SMEs. *Journal of Small Business and Enterprise Development, 11*(1), 60–74. doi:10.1108/14626000410519100

Mardikyan, S. (2010). Analyzing the usage of IT in SMEs. *Communications of the IBIMA*, 1-10.

Mason, M., & O'Mahony, J. (2008). Post-traditional Corporate Governance. *Journal of Corporate Citizenship, 31*(31), 31–44. doi:10.9774/GLEAF.4700.2008.au.00007

McGinnis, S. K., Pumphrey, L., Trimmer, K., & Wiggins, C. (2004). Sustaining and extending organization strategy via information technology governance.*37th Annual Hawaii International Conference on System Sciences*. doi:10.1109/HICSS.2004.1265390

Melville, N., Kraemer, K., & Gurbaxani, V. (2004). Information technology and organizational performance: An integrative model of IT business value. *Management Information Systems Quarterly, 28*(2), 283–322.

Messabia, N., & Elbekkali, A. (2010). Information technology governance: A stakeholder approach, *An Enterprise Odyssey. International Conference Proceedings*.

Messeghem, K. (2003). Strategic entrepreneurship and managerial activities in SMEs. *International Small Business Journal, 21*(2), 197–212. doi:10.1177/0266242603021002004

Mitchell, R. K., Agle, B. R., & Wood, D. J. (1997). Toward a theory of stakeholder identification and salience: Defining the principle of who and what really counts. *Academy of Management Review, 22*(4), 853–886.

Mohamed, N., & Singh, J. K. G. (2012). A conceptual framework for information technology governance effectiveness in private organizations. *Information Management & Computer Security, 20*(2), 88–106. doi:10.1108/09685221211235616

Mohnnak, K. (2007). Innovation networks and capability building in the Australian high-technology SMEs. *European Journal of Innovation Management, 10*(2), 236–251. doi:10.1108/14601060710745279

Napoli, F. (2012). The effects of corporate governance processes of strategy change and value creation in small- or medium-sized firms: A study of family-owned firms in Italy. *International Journal of Management, 29*(3), 232–260.

Nfuka, E. N., & Rusu, L. (2011). The effect of critical success factors on IT governance performance. *Industrial Management & Data Systems, 111*(9), 1418–1448. doi:10.1108/02635571111182773

Nicholson, G. J., & Kiel, G. C. (2007). Can directors impact performance? A case-based test of three theories of corporate governance. *Corporate Governance, 15*(4), 585–608. doi:10.1111/j.1467-8683.2007.00590.x

OECD. (Ed.). (2005). *SME and Entrepreneurship Outlook*. Paris: OECD.

Orlikowski, W. J., & Iacono, C. S. (2001). Research commentary: Desperately seeking the "IT" in IT research - A call to theorizing the IT artifact. *Information Systems Research, 12*(2), 121–134. doi:10.1287/isre.12.2.121.9700

Paré, G., & Sicotte, C. (2001). Information technology sophistication in health care: An instrument validation study among Canadian hospitals. *International Journal of Medical Informatics, 63*(3), 205–223. doi:10.1016/S1386-5056(01)00178-2 PMID:11502433

Pekovic, S. (2010). The determinants of ISO 9000 certification: A comparison of the manufacturing and service sectors. *Journal of Economic Issues, 44*(4), 895–914. doi:10.2753/JEI0021-3624440403

Peterson, R. (2004). Crafting information technology governance. *Information Systems Management, 21*(4), 7–22. doi:10.1201/1078/44705.21.4.20040901/84183.2

Pflughoest, K. A., Ramamurthy, K., Soofi, E. S., Yasai-Ardekani, M., & Zahedi, F. (2003). Multiple conceptualizations of small business Web use and benefit. *Decision Sciences, 34*(3), 467–512. doi:10.1111/j.1540-5414.2003.02539.x

Philip, G., & Booth, M. E. (2001). A new six 'S' framework on the relationship between the role of information systems (IS) and competencies in 'IS' management. *Journal of Business Research, 51*(3), 233–247. doi:10.1016/S0148-2963(99)00051-X

Pollard, C. (2003). Exploring continued and discontinued use of IT: A case study of OptionFinder, a group support system. *Group Decision and Negotiation, 12*(3), 171–193. doi:10.1023/A:1023314606762

Ramdani, B., Kawalek, P., & Lorenzo, O. (2009). Knowledge management and enterprise systems adoption by SMEs: Predicting SMEs' adoption of enterprise systems. *Journal of Enterprise Information Management, 22*(1/2), 10–24. doi:10.1108/17410390910922796

Rasheed, H. S., & Geiger, S. W. (2001). Determinants of governance structure for the electronic value chain: Resource dependency and transaction costs perspectives. *The Journal of Business Strategy, 18*(2), 159–176.

Rau, K. G. (2004). Effective governance of IT: Design objectives, roles, and relationships. *Information Systems Management, 21*(4), 35–42. doi:10.1201/1078/447 05.21.4.20040901/84185.4

Raymond, L., Bergeron, F., & Rivard, S. (1998). Determinants of business process reengineering success in small and large enterprises: An empirical study in the Canadian context. *Journal of Small Business Management, 36*(1), 72–85.

Raymond, L., & Croteau, A.-M. (2006). Enabling the strategic development of SMEs through advanced manufacturing systems: A configurational perspective. *Industrial Management & Data Systems, 106*(7), 1012–1032. doi:10.1108/02635570610688904

Raymond, L., Croteau, A.-M., & Bergeron, F. (2011). The strategic role of IT as an antecedent to the IT sophistication and IT performance of manufacturing SMEs. *International Journal on Advances in Systems and Measurements, 4*(3&4), 203–211.

Raymond, L., Paré, G., & Bergeron, F. (1995). Matching information technology and organizational structure: Implications for performance. *European Journal of Information Systems, 4*(1), 3–16. doi:10.1057/ejis.1995.2

Raymond, L., Uwizeyemungu, S., Bergeron, F., & Gauvin, S. (2012). A framework for research on e-learning assimilation in SMEs: A strategic perspective. *European Journal of Training and Development, 36*(6), 592–613. doi:10.1108/03090591211245503

Reich, B. H., & Nelson, K. M. (2003). In their own words: CIO visions about the future of in-house IT organizations. *The Data Base for Advances in Information Systems, 34*(4), 28–44. doi:10.1145/957758.957763

Ross, J. W. (2003). Creating a strategic IT architecture competency: Learning in stages. *MIS Quarterly Executive, 2*(1), 31–43.

Ruivo, P., Oliveira, T., & Neto, M. (2012). ERP use and value: Portuguese and Spanish SMEs. *Industrial Management & Data Systems, 112*(7), 1008–1025. doi:10.1108/02635571211254998

Sambamurthy, V., & Zmud, R. W. (1999). Arrangements for information technology governance: A theory of multiple contingencies. *Management Information Systems Quarterly, 23*(2), 261–290. doi:10.2307/249754

Scupola, A. (2008). Conceptualizing competences in e-services adoption and assimilation in SMEs. *Journal of Electronic Commerce in Organizations, 6*(2), 78–91. doi:10.4018/jeco.2008040105

Sila, I., & Dobni, D. (2012). Patterns of B2B e-commerce usage in SMEs. *Industrial Management & Data Systems, 112*(8), 1255–1271. doi:10.1108/02635571211264654

Talaulicar, T. (2010). The concept of the balanced company and its implications for corporate governance. *Society and Business Review, 5*(3), 232–244. doi:10.1108/17465681011079464

Torrès, O., & Julien, P.-A. (2005). Specificity and denaturing of small business. *International Small Business Journal, 23*(4), 355–377. doi:10.1177/0266242605054049

Turlea, E., Mocanu, M., & Radu, C. (2010). Corporate governance in the banking industry. *Accounting and Management Information Systems, 9*(3), 379–402.

Uhlaner, L., Wright, M., & Huse, M. (2007). Private firms and corporate governance: An integrated economic and management perspective. *Small Business Economics, 29*(3), 225–241. doi:10.1007/s11187-006-9032-z

van Gils, A. (2005). Management and governance in Dutch SMEs. *European Management Journal, 23*(5), 583–589. doi:10.1016/j.emj.2005.09.013

Van Grembergen, W., & De Haes, S. (2010). A research journey into enterprise governance of IT, business/IT alignment and value creation. *International Journal of IT/Business Alignment and Governance, 1*(1), 1–13. doi:10.4018/jitbag.2010120401

Venkatraman, N. (1989). The concept of fit in strategy research: Toward verbal and statistical correspondence. *Academy of Management Review, 14*(3), 423–444

Vogt, M., Küller, P., Hertweck, D., & Hales, K. (2011). Adapting IT governance frameworks using domain specific requirements methods: Examples from small & medium enterprises and emergency management. *Proceedings of the 17th Americas Conference on Information Systems.*

Wainwright, D., Green, G., Mitchell, E., & Yarrow, D. (2005). Towards a framework for benchmarking ICT practice, competence and performance in small firms. *Performance Measurement and Metrics, 6*(1), 39–52. doi:10.1108/14678040510588580

Weill, P., & Ross, J. (2005). A matrixed approach to designing IT governance. *Sloan Management Review, 46*(2), 26–34.

Weill, P., & Ross, J. W. (Eds.). (2004). *IT governance: How top performers manage IT decision rights for superior results.* Boston: Harvard Business School Press.

Wilkin, C. L. (2012). The role of IT governance practices in creating business value in SMEs. *Journal of Organizational and End User Computing, 24*(2), 1–17. doi:10.4018/joeuc.2012040101

Wilkin, C. L., Campbell, J., & Moore, S. (2013). Creating value through governing IT deployment in a public/private-sector inter-organizational context: A human agency perspective. *European Journal of Information Systems, 22*(5), 498–511. doi:10.1057/ejis.2012.21

Willcocks, L., Feeny, D., & Olson, N. (2006). Implementing core IS capabilities: Feeny-Willcocks IT governance and management framework revisited. *European Management Journal*, *24*(1), 28–37. doi:10.1016/j.emj.2005.12.005

Xiaobao, P., Wei, S., & Yuzhen, D. (2013). Framework of open innovation in SMEs in an emerging economy: Firm characteristics, network openness, and network information. *International Journal of Technology Management*, *62*(2-4), 223–250. doi:10.1504/IJTM.2013.055142

Xue, Y., Liang, H., & Boulton, W. R. (2008). Information technology governance in information technology investment decision processes: The impact of investment characteristics, external environment, and internal context. *Management Information Systems Quarterly*, *32*(1), 67–96.

Zarvić, N., Stolze, C., Boehm, M., & Thomas, O. (2012). Dependency-based IT Governance practices in inter-organizational collaborations: A graph-driven elaboration. *International Journal of Information Management*, *32*(6), 541–549. doi:10.1016/j.ijinfomgt.2012.03.004

Chapter 4
Business/IT Alignment in Two-Sided Markets:
A COBIT 5 Analysis for Media Streaming Business Models

Yannick Bartens
University of Hamburg, Germany

Hashim Iqbal Chunpir
German Climate Computing Centre, Germany

Frederik Schulte
University of Hamburg, Germany

Stefan Voß
University of Hamburg, Germany

ABSTRACT

Business/IT alignment can be considered a key challenge in IT governance and becomes especially important in IT-heavy and internet based business models. Recent discussions express the need for a bi-directional paradigm for internet based business models. IT governance frameworks support business/IT alignment but mostly follow a business-driven alignment paradigm. We identify characteristics of internet based business models and use the case of streaming to examine how the IT governance framework COBIT 5 can integrate these characteristics under consideration of a bi-directional business/IT alignment process. We reveal that requirements for streaming business models may not be fully covered by the framework. Based on

DOI: 10.4018/978-1-5225-0861-8.ch004

a structural description of internet based business models and the COBIT 5 Goal Cascade, we explain these specific requirements and propose a possible integration of a bottom-up alignment. With this work we provide guidance in the challenge of business/IT alignment for internet based business models and show pathways for IT governance frameworks to better support a bi-directional alignment.

1. INTRODUCTION

Due to the recent growth rates of internet based business and e-commerce worldwide (IDC, 2009), internet based business models have become an important part of the worldwide economy that have transformed brick and mortar business into internet based business (Dutta & Biren, 2001; Fingar & Aronica, 2001) or enabled the creation of novel, purely internet based businesses. This market transformation process usually either involves drastic changes from previous strategies, as often seen, e.g., in the newspaper industry (Smith, Binns, & Tushman, 2010) or enforces new business strategies to be developed (Eisenmann, Parker, & Van Alstyne, 2006; Smith et al., 2010), as, e.g., seen in media streaming business models. Occasionally this also comes under the umbrella of new buzz words like digital transformation (Patel & McCarthy, 2012) and digital transition (McFadden, 2012). Recognizing the nature of internet based business models and the foundation of their business base, a pervasive influence of information technology (IT) is observable throughout the whole organization (Evans & Wurster, 1996). In addition, they mostly act in two sided market (Armstrong, 2006) environments, serving multiple classes of customers, requiring another shift in strategy (Eisenmann et al., 2006).

In recent years the concept of IT governance represents a well-discussed set of concepts for ensuring the 'optimal' utilization of IT for the benefit of a business (De Haes & Van Grembergen, 2005; Iskandar & Salleh, 2010; Lainhart, 2001; Weill & Ross, 2004). With regard to its worldwide and cross-industry spread, COBIT constitutes a popular framework for addressing the challenges of IT governance in a holistic manner. COBIT 5 emphasizes a generic approach, aiming to be customizable into any specific field of application for all kinds of enterprises (ISACA, 2012a). As the core of the COBIT 5 framework, the Goals Cascade transfers the generic stakeholder needs into business and IT-related goals, leading off into processes as well as activities, giving a suitable base for our investigation.

Internet based business models inherit a combination of unique characteristics that demonstrate current challenges for IT governance (Breuer, 2004). While customer and success orientation are deeply associated with each other, and a recurring issue in business model approaches, they entail the reversal of the causal chain of requirements in internet based business models. Furthermore, these characteristics embrace two sided market situations and require unique considerations in order to be successful. Contrary to popular concepts, as depicted by the top-down business/ IT alignment approach in COBIT 5, the requirements of internet based business models in two sided markets can emerge out of the business operations and be defined by the customer. An example is the business cooperation of T-Mobile and Spotify Inc., where the satisfactory needs of customers implied the adoption of both business models (Oestreich, 2012).

In this paper, while extending Bartens et al. (2014a), we focus on the characteristics of internet based business models in two sided markets and their representation within the COBIT 5 framework. Here, the requirements of a bi-directional business/ IT alignment can be observed and exhibited in a very distinct and comprehensible manner. After a brief literature review on internet based business models in two sided markets, IT governance and IT governance frameworks in Section 2, we investigate the degree of representation of internet based business requirements in two sided markets and possible gaps within the framework, following the 'COBIT 5 Goals Cascade', in order to achieve a basic understanding. Thus, we consolidate the characteristics of these business models and their success factors in Section 3 and examine their appropriate representation in COBIT 5 in Section 4. Consecutively, in Section 5, we give a brief excursion on internet based business models in two sided markets and introduce the case of media streaming. After that we outline how these business characteristics influence the business/IT alignment and perform a detailed analysis of Cobit 5 for media streaming business models in Section 6. Finally, Section 7 gives conclusions and an outlook on future work.

2. LITERATURE REVIEW

2.1. Two Sided Markets and Internet Based Business Models

Two sided markets depict a specific market situation, which usually integrates two (or more) participants/agents, which are interacting over a platform offered by depicting an intermediary. Via this platform exchange transactions are processed (Armstrong, 2006; Hildebrand, 2011; Osterwalder, 2010; Rochet & Tirole, 2003, 2004). Two sided markets are naturally strongly associated with advertising related or implying business models (Hildebrand, 2011; Lin, Li, & Whinston, 2011; Osterwalder, 2010; Rysman, 2009; Schmidtke, 2006). The main challenge for operating a business model as the intermediary is seen in successful revenue generation (Schmidtke, 2006). These revenues by the intermediary are either to be generated directly, e.g. via subscription based pricing (Rysman, 2009), or indirectly, as often seen in online or e-business based environments (Hildebrand, 2011; Osterwalder, 2010; Rysman, 2009).

Our postulation of the term 'internet based business model' relays on the combination of classical e-business models, as well as the concept of two sided markets, in which these business models operate. We introduce this term, since the established term of e-business models, from our point of view, does not consider the role of two sided markets to a suitable extent. In this sense we focus on the current environment with its broad group of social networking sites, online newspapers, online startup companies, market places and so on.

The foundation for our considerations is set by e-business models, in which internet technology and its economic adaption in the form of e-business are combined. Early approaches did not differentiate between e-business and e-commerce (Timmers, 1999), where today there is a clear distinction being made (Wirtz, 2013). E-commerce nowadays represents a manifestation of e-business. Assuming this point of view, the definition of e-business describes all concepts of utilization of information technology under the premise of optimizing internal and external value-adding business activities. In this context, e-commerce depicts the execution of transaction processes over digital networks (Romm & Sudweeks, 1998).

The common idea of looking at business activities as business models dates back to the beginning of the last century (Wirtz, 2011). First approaches were based on management theory and, over time, highly influenced either by strategy or organization theory orientation. Apart from that, by the mid 1970s another approach evolved: The concept of information systems opened a whole new approach, far away from management theory. Therefore, business models are inheriting a strong historic relatedness to e-business.

One key characteristic is represented by the importance of indirect revenue streams, which on the other hand, as aforementioned, are pervasive throughout two sided market situations.

Where e-business models and their characteristics feature strong correlations to IT governance, this effect becomes even more evident when e-business models operate in two sided markets ("internet based business models"), since now the market environment is also correlated. As stated by Patel (Patel, 2002, 2004), the particularities of e-business models, entail implications and distinct exceptions on the governance process. The main argument concerns the emergence of technologies and requirements

Under the given circumstances it becomes clear, that the influence of technology has to be managed in an appropriate way. According to Patel (Patel, 2002, 2004), this enforces a "radical re-direction" and extension of generic IT governance. Agile (re-)alignments of the business, customer-centricity and handling of the aforesaid integration of IT are the main drivers. This is encompassed by the term of "emergent organizations." In addition internet technologies are described as fluid (Patel, 2002).

The general approach of the alignment of business and IT, as given by many authors (Henderson & Venkatraman, 1993; Kearns & Sabherwal, 2007), inhibits shortcomings leading to an unsuitable match for usage or adoption in e-business models (Patel, 2002, 2004).

2.2. IT Governance and Business IT/Alignment

The growing influence of information technology on business operations makes the control of IT inevitable. Failure entails negative implications in terms of substantial financial or legal risks. For more than a decade, the concept of IT governance, or as it has been recently re-branded: 'Enterprise governance of IT' (EGIT), is being adopted by companies to address this challenge. This paper acknowledges and adopts the sense of the term 'Enterprise Governance of IT' while continuously using IT governance for its description.

While a broad range of definitions on IT governance are proposed in the academic literature, we adopt those influenced by the IT Governance Institute and Van Grembergen (see (Van Grembergen & De Haes, 2009), pg. 3): Enterprise Governance of IT is "an integral part of corporate governance and addresses the definition and implementation of processes, structures and relational mechanisms in the organization that enable both business and IT people to execute their responsibilities in support of business/IT alignment and the creation of business value from IT-enabled business investments."

Business/IT alignment can be briefly described in the sense that the "ultimate goal of IT governance is achieving strategic alignment between the business and IT to make sure that money spent in IT is delivering value for the business" (De Haes & Van Grembergen, 2005; Henderson & Venkatraman, 1993).

2.3. IT Governance Frameworks

Since the beginning of the IT governance movement, numerous frameworks and standards have been released. Often these publications resemble a collection of best practices, approved by their originating context (Goeken & Alter, 2009). Most are common in their structured body. Another similarity is given by their aim: They describe goals, processes and organizational aspects of IT management and control (Hevner, March, Park, & Ram, 2004; Van Grembergen, De Haes, & Guldentops, 2004). Well known examples are the IT Infrastructure Library (ITIL), COBIT, Capability Maturity Model Integration as well as several proprietary ones. Today a remarkable set of standards and frameworks for guidance and implementation of IT governance can be found.

By now the COBIT framework can be considered an accepted standard in theory and in practice across all industries or even the de facto standard (Soomro & Hesson, 2012). The framework, updated to version 5 in April 2012 (ISACA, 2014), represents a generic, comprehensive and perceived as complex (Bartens et al., 2014, 2015) catalogue of practice-proven best practices for understanding and implementation of IT governance.

The publication of COBIT 5 achieves the aforementioned alignment of business and IT via the linkage of generic sets of goals. These goals are derived from the needs of enterprise's stakeholders and are cascaded ('COBIT 5 Goals Cascade') from the level of enterprise goals to IT-related goals until the enabler level is reached. The process layer, as the most important enabler, consists of 37 processes organized into five domains. The 'Evaluate, Monitor and Direct' domain (EDM) offers overall governance tasks, representing the now integrated ISO/IEC 38500 standard. The remaining four domains are based on the Plan-Build-Run-Monitor schematics. 'Align, Plan and Organise' (APO) comprises planning tasks; 'Build, Acquire and Implement' (BAI) consists of functions for systems and organizational development, implementation and acquisition of assets; 'Deliver, Service and Support' (DSS) services operations, delivery and incident management; and 'Measure, Evaluate and Assess' covers continual improvement, internal control and compliance.

3. CHARACTERISTICS OF INTERNET BASED BUSINESS MODELS WITH RELEVANCE FOR IT GOVERNANCE

Internet business and classic business models can be distinguished with a characteristics analysis (Liu, Wu, Yu, & Lei, 2010). Below we analyze these characteristics.

3.1. Characteristics

Characteristics of internet based business models are widely spread. Notably, single characteristics are not unique to internet based business models.

3.1.1. Technology Driven Alignment

The large influence of IT and the accompanying focus on it is well discussed. Likewise, it can be considered as common knowledge. Technology in general, and in particular the Internet, can be considered as the foundation of internet based business models. This extreme dependency requires high availability, reliability and capacities (Patel, 2002). Differences in technology standards have to be managed and, in case of border crossing operations and multinational companies, regional aspects and restrictions have to be kept in mind. Above all, security issues have to be considered, not only to ensure proper operations, but also to build trust on the customer side. Many important and quite recent challenges arise in the form of management of new technologies, which might entail major groundbreaking differences compared to previous approaches. These technologies may be related to leapfrogging decisions but also as disruptive technologies, which have to be observed carefully and eventually incorporated quickly. It becomes evident that in e-business a fusion of business and IT is necessary, as it is in other classes of business models. In literature, a linkage between business and IT is often stipulated and by now thoroughly represented (De Haes & Van Grembergen, 2005). It is commonly referred to as "fusion of business and IT" or "business/IT alignment."

Due to the technological drive, change and alignment requirements emerge from operations mainly influenced by customer needs and behavior (Langer & Yorks, 2013). This encompasses bottom-up alignment in addition to established top-down approaches, as they currently dominate alignment concepts in generic IT governance (Chen, 2008). In the context of technology driven alignment, all identified characteristics develop strong potential for bottom-up inputs. Although being focused on service-oriented architectures, Chen emphasizes the importance of different approaches on business/IT alignment including top-down and bottom-up (Chen, 2008). This is best shown in his example on outlining bottom-up introduction of new services. One could argue that considering both paradigms together somewhat depicts a bi-directional approach.

3.1.2. Universal Convergence

Besides observing IT as key influence on business operations the tendency to universal convergence can be found in three areas. These areas are technology, offered goods and services as well as hybrid business models. All of these are caused by the attempt to satisfy customer requirements and wishes (Orr, 2000).

In terms of technology, rapid development and changes are the main reason for the steadily growing convergence. This can be shown in the recent evolutions in the smartphone and mobile market. Offered goods and services are seemingly influenced by the efforts of the network participants on focusing on inherent key competencies while integrating the offerings of external service providers. Lastly, the development of hybrid business models can be observed in the restructuring of a company's value stream when combining online business with brick and mortar stores.

3.1.3. Network Orientation

In the literature, network orientation within internet based business models depicts another key characteristic (Breuer, 2004). This exemplifies the usage of the given opportunities offered by internet technology. Still, contemplation is not exclusively focused on networking technologies. Yet general business networks with diverse relationships, primarily exchange-centered, are perceptible. Many reasons for the network orientation can be found. For instance, the focus on key competencies induces companies to source services from network partners. In addition, higher customer expectations and focus on competencies call for integrated solutions which can often only be accomplished by smart sourcing (Wirtz, 2013). Likewise, network orientation raises the flexibility of a company due to the possibility of offering certain solutions without being forced to stockpile all elements.

3.1.4. Exchange of Digital Goods

Another internet-based distinction is given by the exchange of digital goods as part of business transactions (Madureira et al., 2011; McFadden, 2012; Mahadevan, 2000; Timmers, 1999). Exchange is mainly conducted over digital networks. Therefore, often products and services are provided as digital goods. Replication of issues is cost efficient and done easily without any loss in quality. Though, certain technical or legal steps have to be considered to prevent unauthorized reproduction. Again, security ensures reliability of transactions and revenue, but also reassures the customer. At this juncture the IT architecture and service management come into focus, while the portfolio management sets business wide decisions and implicates operational influence.

3.1.5. Indirect Revenue Streams

Often indirect revenue streams are used to support or even represent the main revenue stream (Breuer, 2004). Indirect revenue streams are present when not only the main service but ancillary services are commercialized. Common examples are the display of advertisements or services or the disposition of user profiles. Historically, companies chose this way of revenue generation to slowly introduce users to the new way of business associated with online business (Timmers, 1999). Users became accustomed to free of charge services, resulting in a low willingness to pay. Furthermore, negative side effects of the actions of ancillary services commercialization are often ignored. Either way direct or indirect, IT strategy and IT service management is given the role of designing the main revenue stream and ensuring business profits.

3.1.6. Highly Dynamic Environment

Internet based business models are subject to a highly dynamic environment. Overall, e-business can be considered a highly competitive sector. Companies are required to keep up with the pace of technology changes as well as adjust to changing customer needs. Companies operating under these circumstances are described as emergent organizations (Patel, 2002). Through the low entrance barriers and easy to copy business functions, growth rates are steadily increasing, resulting in even higher competition (Kalakota & Robinson, 2001).

Reconsidering the high influence of IT on the business models themselves, disruptive technologies, e.g., cloud computing or smartphones, play an overwhelmingly important role. Yet for e-business companies, generally the adoption and integration of new technologies is easier to accomplish than the readjustment of their business model to the quick change in behavior and satisfactory needs of customers.

3.1.7. Compliance Requirements

Overarching the business model and its operations, external laws and regulations have an influence and provide restrictions and requirements (Pathak, 2003). On top of sector-independent regulations as for IT and business in general, specific other policies for e-business apply (Harkness & Green, 2004). Tangible examples are on the one hand PCI-DSS for regulated credit card-based transactions, where key contributors are Visa and MasterCard/Maestro and on the other hand country-specific data privacy and protection acts, e.g., the EU Data Protection Directive as well as the FTC Fair Information Practice.

3.2. Success Factors

There are a number of success factors for internet based business models, which mostly evolve out of the context of the aforementioned characteristics or can be considered their successful transformation (Booz, Allen & Hamilton, 2000).

3.2.1. ePricing

The successful participation and management of ePricing represents a major success factor (Asdemir, 2004). Since the operation is technology based, management of operations is dependent and relates to its mechanisms. Pricing as a superior strategic and tactical management task has to be provided with required information and suitable tools for participating in ePricing environments. Hence major input is demanded from IT architecture and internal services. Though, IT strategy and portfolio management need to support ePricing on a higher level.

3.2.2. Individualized Products and Services

Individualized offerings are dependent on corresponding process and organizational design (Timmers, 1999). A company being capable of providing such products and services usually meets the discussed characteristics and successfully positions itself within the areas of tension of network orientation, universal convergence trends, the dynamic environment and possibly digital goods exchange and suitable revenue streams (Booz, Allen & Hamilton, 2000; Liu et al., 2010). In this particular case, all IT governance domains are called to support the fulfillment of this challenge – if intended. IT sourcing as service management in combination with strategy (here IT and business strategy) are responsible for building an adequate base for a capable product/service portfolio.

3.2.3. 1-to-1 Marketing/Community Building

1-to-1 marketing as well as community building (Biggs, 2000; Darby, Jones, & Madani, 2003; Portuese, 2006) are going hand in hand with the trend of universal convergence and the implications of indirect revenue streams. On top of that the highly dynamic environment sets the direction. Trust, satisfaction and involvement are the drivers.

The strategic decision to comply with the requirements for actions is more or less self-imposed, though the operational implementation has to be well managed and executed. In particular, service management and design is pivotal to satisfy customer needs, whilst other domains of IT governance set the general direction at a higher level.

4. ANALYSIS AND FINDINGS

In this section we present findings regarding the representation of e-business model's characteristics and success factors within the COBIT 5 framework. The description is process oriented.

- **Research Approach:** The applied research methodology is based around the collection of detailed information regarding the central aspects of each characteristic and success factor, including a broad group of various sources. As seen in the previous sections, as our first step we focused on the collocation of characteristics and success factors. In a second step the condensed aspects are guided down the COBIT 5 Goals Cascade, starting from the high level Stakeholder needs, beyond enterprise and IT-related Goals down into the most specific Process Goals, Practices and Activities. While taking the generic approach of COBIT into account, the degree of representation of all characteristics and success factor is investigated (Bartens et al., 2014a) resulting in a suitable overview (as an example see the tables in Section 6.2). The degree of representation is measured by assessing and matching the elements of identified characteristics and success factors onto the corresponding goals (on all layers), processes and activities along the COBIT 5 Goals Cascade. In addition we illustrate mismatches between COBIT 5 and our findings for each characteristic and success factor before we condense these in the following section. In this paper the term mismatch defines gaps, missing elements or links and differences between e-business requirements and the contents of COBIT 5. Gaps are mostly represented by the level of specificity versus generality, missing elements/links result from distinct e-business peculiarities, while differences are inhered from procedural or organizational circumstances in e-business.

The analysis process is commenced on the superior level of enterprise goals. Here the first relevant links to the peculiarities of indirect revenue streams and the aspect of ancillary services commercialization can be found. Major interconnections are found in four enterprise goals. Therefore, these enterprise goals cascaded along the COBIT 5 Goals Cascade via the mapping of enterprise goals and IT-related goals (see Appendix B of the Enabling processes document (ISACA, 2012b)). Again, a set of the most relevant goals are chosen. Consequently another iteration of mapping is carried out, this time (see Appendix C), with the aim of identifying the most relevant processes. In this case the results are a group of eight processes. Lastly and on the final and most specific layer, the process descriptions and partly the corresponding activities are consulted and an examination regarding possible mismatches is conducted.

Analyzing the relevant aspects of indirect revenue streams and their impact on IT governance, it is obvious that customer behavior represents a risk requiring an unforeseen severity. Generally, for all aspects strong interactions with EDM and the APO domain (in particular APO01, 02, 03) are evident. Other alignment, planning or organization processes will be consulted according to the requirements related to the IT management.

- **Analysis of Technology Driven Alignment:** Generally when operating internet based business models, there is a profound focus on operating reliably.

This is related to the foundation on primarily one technology and the inherent dependency. Therefore, besides the general technological focus, availability has a pronounced importance (BAI04).

The overall business operations have to be embedded within adequate settings. The EDM domain, as well as strategic surroundings, provides good guidance and a generic representation of e-business model characteristics. Furthermore, processes for innovation/agility as well as supporting information for targeted decisions are important. Technological requirements regarding the described compliance to relevant standards are to be seen in BAI0I, BAI03.

COBIT achieves cohesion via linking enterprise goals to IT-related goals and operationalizing them through the given reference processes (ISACA, 2012a, 2012b, 2012c). This shows that COBIT is exclusively focusing the alignment of business and IT in a top-down approach. Overall bottom-up benefits and risks (as evolving from customer needs in e-business) are not represented in COBIT. This becomes particularly tangible when consulting the Goals Cascade, the external stakeholder questions (see (ISACA, 2012a), Figure 7) or when reflecting the principle of separating governance from management in combination with an end-to-end coverage of the enterprise. On a finer scale, indicators are given when analyzing the process descriptions and their linkages via inputs/outputs as well as the mappings enclosed within the framework.

However, in e-business, the observable fusion can rather be rephrased as a merger. In certain parts of operations functions, processes and responsibilities merge into a dynamic and fluent bundling (Cochran, 2010; Kalakota & Robinson, 2001; Patel, 2002) in order to achieve an extraordinary degree of agility, and fulfill upcoming desires in a timely manner. This merger contradicts the general approach as given by many frameworks, i.e., a clear distinction between business and IT cannot be made (Langer & Yorks, 2013). Apart from that, the huge influence and importance of the customer creates a major challenge. Requirements, change requests and innovations relevant for the well-being of a company, arise from the bottom up (Chen, 2008; Kalakota & Robinson, 2001; Kooper, Maes, & Lindgreen, 2011; Langer & Yorks, 2013; Mirza & Chan, 2004; Schepers, Iacob, & Van Eck, 2008). In this realm of business models, the customer, not the business, issues requirements. In COBIT, the business side is enabled to designate requirements, which are to be fulfilled by IT. Recognizing our findings, we see a main difference to the approach invoked by the process definitions and descriptions of COBIT. Especially innovation monitoring lacks the direct influence of the customer as needed in adequate consumerization handling – in COBIT 5, 'groups of experts' are to be consulted instead of the customer himself (see (ISACA, 2012b) pg. 71, APO04.03 activities 3/4). When combining these two prerequisites, bottom-up requirements by the customer (Chen,

2008; Langer & Yorks, 2013) clash into merged and 'de-distinctioned' business/ IT processes and functions (Cochran, 2010; Kalakota & Robinson, 2001). It could be stated that this discharges the order of generic structures and responsibilities of COBIT by inversing the causal chain. In conclusion, the combination of these two key findings unveils a mismatch in COBIT 5.

- **Universal Convergence:** In terms of tackling the upcoming challenges of universal convergence, innovation management (APO04) and change handling (BAI05, BAI06) must be emphasized and well represented in the framework. Hybrid business models lie in the responsibility of enterprise management and are not exclusively part of IT Governance. Still, strategic IT-aspects are to be found in the APO domain as well as in the IT-related goal of meeting the business requirements (07) and providing adequate systems (08, 12). Additionally, when integrating foreign services into their own value chain, business requirements have to be met again, as well as sourcing and supplier management (APO10) thoughtfully executed. The strong focus on customer needs, behavior and ingrowing requirements to perform and stay successful is perfectly observable and exemplified with disruptive technologies – representing general trends of convergence.
- **Network Orientation:** Network participation has to be understood as a measure to offer a portfolio of competitive products and services as a result of customer orientation (enterprise goals 2, 6). These business management decisions drag along major requirements for sourcing-related issues, within the business just as on the customer side (APO08, 09, 10). On the other hand, business requirements are influenced by customer preferences (as described before) and thus play a substantial role. The desired flexibility increases the need for agility and capability of performing changes quickly.
- **Exchange of Digital Goods:** As the base for distribution of digital goods, adequate systems have to be provided (BAI03). The handling of digital goods entails fundamental differences for business operations with tangible goods. In a second step, risks, security and availability issues have to be considered. Future risks, requirements and innovations have to be evaluated in advance and with forethought. The management of costs per transaction can be considered either strategically (partial APO05) or part of budgeting (APO06) and optimization of operative factors (APO08, 09 and BAI01, 02, 03). A special focus must also be put on the restriction of unauthorized replication (for instance digital rights management).
- **Indirect Revenue Streams:** On top of the main portion as elaborated in the example, ancillary services commercialization brings up a variety of compliance requirements in the remaining case of utilization of user data/profiles.

The aforementioned requirements depend on the kind and extent of which user data is utilized, and the sovereign territory in which collection or commercialization is made use of (IT-related goal 02 and connected processes).

Taking another look at the elaborated example, innovation processes and user behavior go hand in hand, but imply preceding business management directions and decisions. It has to be emphasized that here, as in the whole realm of internet based business models, the (end) user becomes main recipient of provided services.

- **Highly Dynamic Environment:** Again, innovation management has to be emphasized. Considering the previous factors and aspects, technology orientation, competition and customer influence emerge into a complex group of requirements, especially when considering the business model and the market situation/environment as two complexity drivers (Lin et al., 2011; Smith et al., 2010). These requirements ask for an extraordinary way of adapting the business to trends, technologies and behavior. Quick adaption and adjustments of the business model are necessary. This falls also in the business management domain as well as EDM and related activities.
- **Compliance Requirements:** Following the COBIT 5 approach and goals cascade, the management of compliance and regulatory requirements are represented in a sophisticated way. Due to the holistic integration of their outreaches in the EDM domain and APO01, 02, 03, a clear guidance is given.
- **ePricing:** In ePricing initiatives, the right combination of information and adequate systems is mandatory. For both, COBIT 5 provides generic processes covering the required actions and connected setting. These can be found in BAI01, 02, 03 and 08. They are derived from the enterprise goals 02 and 06.
- **Individualized Products and Services:** As a combination or result of the previous aspects within universal convergence, network orientation and the dynamic environment a suitable coverage in the COBIT framework is given. Additionally, the suitable design of the responsible processes and systems can be related to BAI01, 02, 03, and on a superior level in the management of service levels (APO09). If needed, even management of suppliers (APO10) and quality (APO11) can be addressed.
- **1-to-1 Marketing/Community Building:** As proclaimed in the aspect description, this characteristic can be considered in line with the enterprise goal of a customer-oriented service culture. Following the Goals Cascade, connections to the management of relationships (APO08) and human resources (APO07) are recognizable. Besides those well-tended relations and trained employees, available information and appropriate systems/infrastructure are needed.

- **Internet Based Business Model Representation in COBIT 5:** As a result, regarding the generic structure of COBIT 5, all relevant aspects are fully represented in the framework. However, when taking the in-depth research and analysis of internet based business models and their characteristics into account, a group of mismatches is identified which will be elaborated and condensed in the next section. It becomes highly evident that in e-business the alignment of business and IT is enriched by an additional direction/approach, namely bottom-up. As exhibited by means of the example, COBIT 5 is not taking this need for a bi-directional approach into account.

5. STRUCTURE OF INTERNET BASED BUSINESS MODELS AND THE CASE OF STREAMING

Aiming for a better understanding of internet based business models coherent, formalized and holistic representation is required. In order to receive a representation fulfilling these requirements the "Business Model Ontology" (BMO) by Osterwalder (2004) is chosen to achieve the desired outcome. As stated by Zolnowski and Böhmann (Zolnowski & Böhmann, 2014), a broad group of approaches to choose from exists, though, the BMO "comprises however, a system-level holistic view on the business logic of an economic entity or offering" (Zolnowski & Böhmann, 2014; Zott, Amit, & Massa, 2010). As also stated by Zolnowski and Böhmann (Zolnowski & Böhmann, 2014), the "Business Model Canvas" (Osterwalder, 2010) is the implementation of the business model ontology, as its theoretical foundation, and is the "most prominent example" (Zolnowski & Böhmann, 2014) for the stream identified by Zott et al. (Zott et al., 2010). In addition the authors proclaim that the model is adopted widely in practice (Zolnowski & Böhmann, 2014).

There are many examples of existing businesses and eBusinesses that have a business model that allow them to collect money from two or even more sources. An example of such a field is the internet based online streaming industry. Both audio and visual content is streamed; e.g, in the contemporary streaming industry Netflix (https://www.netflix.com/de/) and Spotify (https://www.spotify.com/de/) are the glaring examples of audio and visual content, respectively. Most of streaming businesses operate under the freemium model (basic services are free, while additional features are offered via paid subscriptions), e.g., in case of Spotify. The Netflix business model allows subscribers to pay very low subscription fees. Streaming businesses make their revenues by selling streaming subscriptions to premium users and advertising placements to third parties following the two sided market principle.

As part of this representation paradigm, the business model canvas explains the creation and capturing of value within a business model (Zott et al., 2010). This is carried out by depicting a business model based on its nine main value-related components (Osterwalder, 2010). In particular these are key partners, key activities, key resources, cost structure, relationships, customer segments, channels and value propositions as well as revenue streams (Osterwalder, 2010). For the entire description of the business model ontology and canvas we refer to the aforementioned publications by Osterwalder et al. (Osterwalder, Pigneur, & Tucci, 2005; Osterwalder, 2004, 2010). In the following we present the business model canvas of a fictional social networking site. We choose this example since social networking sites illustrate a well-known example of internet based business models, as discussed in this research.

The business model canvas, as shown in Figure 1, is based upon the reversed engineered business model of Facebook by Osterwalder (2011), complemented by own research focusing on the two sided market situation and Facebook's specific business model layout (Friedrichsen & Mühl-Benninghaus, 2014; Graw, 2001; Taulli, 2012). In addition to the provided sources, an in-depth research within the original sources mentioned by Osterwalder (2011) was conducted. In order to carve out the implications of two sided market influences, a threeway color-coding was integrated to emphasize the existing participants/market sides (see "Customer Segments"). Here, the different participants' elements are easily distinguished and the interconnections within the different elements are documented. In addition, the pervasive influence of technology onto business models like these becomes evident.

Figure 1. Social networking site business model canvas

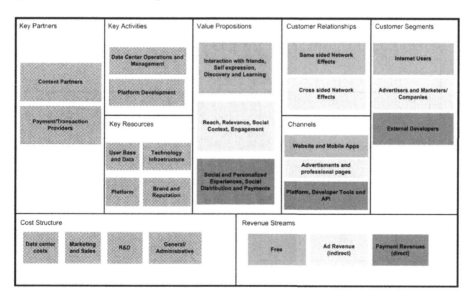

6. BUSINESS/IT ALIGNMENT IN THE CASE OF MEDIA STREAMING

In this section we discuss the business goals and their mapping to the IT processes with respect to the online streaming industry. In Section 6.1, we describe the bi-directional business and IT alignment for internet-based business models. In Section 6.2, the COBIT 5 framework is analyzed, keeping in focus the bi-directional elements of the online streaming technology with respect to the business model.

6.1. Bidirectional Business/ IT Alignment for Internet Based Business Models

As discussed, we acknowledge the contiguity of technology, business, business operations and the customer, and describe this as a merger of the (usually) physically and logically separated business and IT side.

In Figure 2 we apply the framework from previous work (Bartens et al., 2014a, 2014b) to the presented business model canvas of social networking sites from Figure 1. We propose a sound understanding of the interactions between the underlying business model and the novel approach to business/IT alignment.

Figure 2. Bi-directional business/it alignment in internet based business models

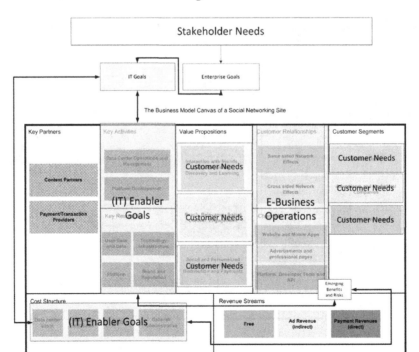

At this juncture we utilize the analysis function of the business model canvas, as postulated by Osterwalder et al. (2005), in order to depict the influence of information technology on these business models and the implications regarding a different approach towards business/IT alignment. While "classic" business/IT alignment procedures arise from the top, technology driven requirements by the customer enter the IT governance organization from the bottom through the business operations, which in internet based business models are likely to close ranks or be merged with the IT side of the business. In addition, IT is asked to be more customer-centric due to the stressed role and importance of the customer within internet based business models. To further align the resulting different inputs, bi-directional interfaces on the side of generic IT governance are needed, this correspondingly can be seen in the multiple interface within the overarching (IT) Enabler Goals.

The implications of identified characteristics in combination with a two sided market situation, become visible and obviously raise the complexity compared to an elementary top-down alignment approach. This supports the assumptions by Bartens et al. (2014a), so that the described merger, indeed, seems to be a viable approach. On the flipside, the issued requirements emerge out of the operational context. We see distinct customer groups issuing needs within different elements of the business model, all jointly influencing the business model's operations. For a successful pursuit of the strategic goals, to perform economically successful the fulfilment of these diverse classes of requirements can be considered as key elements.

The combination of these findings calls for a redirection in IT governance of internet based business models (Bartens et al., 2014a). One could argue that in scenarios like depicted above in Figure 2, different alignment paradigms have to be adopted in order to address the goals of different (customer) segments (internally as well as externally) properly.

6.2. Cobit 5 Analysis of the Media Streaming Business Model

If we look at the online streaming model in particular, there are certain technology based aspects of the internet based business models that cannot be ignored. These aspects include: Compliance of user generated content that is streamed with local laws, adaptation of systems as a result of technological change and achieving a balance between business partners. In Tables 1, 2 and 3, we analyze these aspects and map them to Cobit 5 framework's enterprise goals, IT-related goals and the relevant processes.

Table 1 illustrates in detail how the Cobit 5 framework can handle the compliance issue with local laws in case of the streaming industry.

Similarly, Table 2 elucidates in detail the processes, IT goals and business goals that the Cobit 5 framework recommends to form cooperation between a streaming

Table 1. Aspect analysis of compliance of user generated content with local laws

User Content as a Product for Customers/Users	
Aspect: User content integration, availability and access	
Issue: Controversial user content may be illegal in a particular jurisdiction jeopardize business models at risk When an audio-visual content displays controversial concepts such as, e.g., a song about the glory of National Socialism ideology is sensitive to some societies and the law in Germany, Austria and some other countries. The law of these countries may not allow the content streaming or to be sold etc. within their national borders. Such type of content can be easily abrogated by legal bodies using blocking systems. Broadcast, streaming or sale of such material may lead to business hazard in the form of a strict legal action that may cause great loss in financial terms or otherwise. Another example in Germany is that GEMA does not allow copyrighted content to be shown within its borders in YouTube for instance.	
Enterprise Goals	
3	Managed business risks (safeguarding of assets)
4	Compliance with external laws and regulations
8	Agile responses to a changing business environment
9	Information-based strategic decision making
15	Compliance with internal policies [or change / amendment of internal policies]
IT-Related Goals	
2	IT compliance and support for business compliance with external laws and regulations
4	Manage IT-related business risks
6	Transparency of IT costs, benefits and risk
9	IT agility
14	Availability of reliable and useful information for decision making
15	IT compliance with internal policies
17	Knowledge, expertise and initiatives for business innovation
Processes	
EDM03	Ensure Risk Optimization
EDM04	Ensure Resource Optimization
APO04	Manage Innovation
APO08	Manage Relationships
APO12	Manage Risk
BAI03	Manage Solution Identification and Build
BAI05	Manage Organizational Change Enablement
BAI06	Manage Changes
BAI08	Manage Knowledge
DSS03	Manage Problems
MEA03	Monitor, Evaluate and Assess Compliance With External Requirements

Table 2. Aspect analysis of adaptation of systems and business process to gain market share (on the basis of a technological change)

Indirect Revenue Streams	
Aspect: Adaptation of systems and business processes as a result of technological change.	
Issue: Cooperation of two technology-oriented companies to share business market. A new billing model became part of the business model to share revenue stream. Music streaming leads to large amount of data usage, provided by mobile internet service provider e.g. T-Mobile. The trend of the extensive use of streaming in the society lead T-Mobile to set-up a flexible new business model that introduced music option in cooperation with music streaming company: Spotify. For instance: If a customer has a T-Mobile connection and a Spotify account then s/he can listen to songs without utilizing the data packet offered by T-Mobile. In a nutshell, this lead to adaptation of systems offered by both of the service providers as well as their business processes as a result of technological change.	
Enterprise Goals	
1	Stakeholder value of business investments
2	Portfolio of competitive products and services
6	Customer-oriented service culture
8	Agile responses to a changing business environment
13	Managed business change programmes
IT-Related Goals	
1	Alignment of IT and business strategy
5	Realised benefits from IT-enabled investments and services portfolio
8	Adequate use of applications, information and technology solutions
9	IT agility
11	Optimisation of IT assets, resources and capabilities
12	Enablement and support of business processes by integrating applications and technology into business processes
Processes	
EDM02	Ensure Benefits Delivery
EDM04	Ensure Resource Optimization
APO04	Manage Innovation
APO08	Manage Relationships
APO09	Manage Service Agreements
BAI04	Manage Availability and Capacity
BAI05	Manage Organizational Change Enablement
BAI06	Manage Changes
DSS01	Manage Operations

Table 3. Aspect analysis of sustainable business between partners

Winner Takes It All	
Aspect: Sustainable business between partners.	
Issue: Some partners are the main beneficiaries of services while others´ benefits are compromised leading to an imbalance of partners. Spotify collects revenue from customers who are listeners of music tracks but there is a criticism that the other end, that is the studios or artists, are not compensated with their fair share. Some artists in response to non-justified revenue shared decided to pull out their albums. In another case Spotify pulled out some artists due to their protest against Spotify.	
Enterprise Goals	
1	Stakeholder value of business investments
2	Portfolio of competitive products and services
5	Financial transparency
8	Agile responses to a changing business environment
9	Information-based strategic decision making
IT-Related Goals	
6	Transparency of IT costs, benefits and risk
8	Adequate use of applications, information and technology solutions
9	IT agility
14	Availability of reliable and useful information for decision making
17	Knowledge, expertise and initiatives for business innovation
Processes	
EDM02	Ensure Benefits Delivery
EDM05	Ensure Stakeholder Transparency
APO02	Manage Strategy
APO04	Manage Innovation
APO08	Manage Relationships
BAI03	Manage Solution Identification and Build
BAI05	Manage Organizational Change Enablement
BAI06	Manage Changes
BAI08	Manage Knowledge

industry and the internet service provider. Example of cooperation between Spotify and T-Mobile is provided here.

In Table 3, the detailed mapping of the processes, IT goals and business goals of Cobit 5 framework to solve the problem of balancing the business partners of streaming industry is given.

From Tables 1, 2 and 3, it is evident that there are processes prescribed in Cobit 5 framework that support the bi-directional business alignment to meet enterprise goals as well as technological issues. However, the support from bottom-up alignment where technological innovation drives the change in a business model yet needs to be enhanced in Cobit 5. If we look at the aspect of exchange of digital goods which is elaborated in Table 5 (see the Appendix), in online streaming business, Spotify came up with an innovative technological solution to encode the downloaded music streams as files that can only be played as long as a subscriber remains the premium member of Spotify. Moreover, this solution also managed the problem of bad or no online streaming conditions / possibilities that is in case of no availability of Internet (WiFi or LAN). In this particular example there are more processes or change of current processes to incorporate bottom-up Business/IT alignment. In essence, the technological innovation can alter the business model and new processes may be required to make the bi-directional alignment smoother. Additional tables: Tables 4 and 5 are provided in Appendix.

7. CONCLUSION

Referring to the growing importance of business/IT alignment in two sided markets and internet based business models, we have examined requirements for IT governance frameworks to support business/IT alignment for internet based business models. We have identified and described specific characteristics and success factors in internet based business models. We have analyzed their representation within COBIT 5 using specific characteristics of media business models. Based on that, we provided requirements and solution proposals for internet business compliant frameworks of IT governance.

With this work we clearly illustrate why internet based business models require a bottom-up business/IT alignment in IT governance. The technologic drive and its integration into internet business operations are enriching the current approaches with another dimension, making business/IT alignment bi-directional. This confirms work for a modified perspective on the alignment process in IT governance (Bartens et al., 2014a, 2014b). In order to achieve the intended coverage within COBIT or other IT governance frameworks, a full description and cascade of their relation to bottom-up impacts would have to be integrated. We suggest modifications to CO-BIT 5 to effectively support business/IT alignment in two-sided markets. Thus, this work provides support in the challenge of business/IT alignment for internet based business models and illustrates how IT governance frameworks could appropriately integrate a bi-directional alignment.

Future research will cover an empirical evaluation of the COBIT 5 framework with respect to its ability to support business/IT alignment in two sided markets as well as the design of an appropriate extension of the framework. Furthermore, it has to be examined whether similar findings can also be observed in business models other than internet business.

REFERENCES

Armstrong, M. (2006). Competition in two-sided markets. *The Rand Journal of Economics, 37*(3), 668–691. doi:10.1111/j.1756-2171.2006.tb00037.x

Asdemir, K. (2004). *Essays on pricing in e-commerce: Dynamic pricing and performance based pricing*. The University of Texas at Dallas.

Bartens, Y., De Haes, S., Eggert, L., Heilig, L., Maes, K., Schulte, F., & Voß, S. (2014). A visualization approach for reducing the perceived complexity of COBIT 5. In M. C. Tremblay, D. VanderMeer, M. Rothenberger, A. Gupta, & V. Yoon (Eds.), *Advancing the Impact of Design Science: Moving from Theory to Practice* (pp. 403–407). Springer. doi:10.1007/978-3-319-06701-8_34

Bartens, Y., De Haes, S., Lamoen, Y., Schulte, F., & Voss, S. (2015). On the Way to a Minimum Baseline in IT Governance: Using Expert Views for Selective Implementation of COBIT 5. In *Proceedings of the 47th Hawaii International Conference on System Sciences (HICSS)* (pp. 4554-4563). Kauai, HI: IEEE. doi:10.1109/HICSS.2015.543

Bartens, Y., Schulte, F., & Voß, S. (2014a). E-business IT governance revisited: An attempt towards outlining a Novel Bi-directional business/IT alignment in COBIT5. In *Proceedings of the 47th Hawaii International Conference on System Sciences (HICSS)* (pp. 4356–4365). Waikaloa, HI: IEEE. doi:10.1109/HICSS.2014.538

Bartens, Y., Schulte, F., & Voß, S. (2014b). Business/IT Alignment in Two Sided Markets: A Study of COBIT 5 for Internet Based Business Models. *International Journal of IT/Business Alignment and Governance, 5*(2), 27-43.

Biggs, M. (2000). E-commerce success requires commitment to building a proper customer "community". *InfoWorld, 22*(14), 68.

Booz, Allen, & Hamilton. (Eds.). (2000). *10 Erfolgsfaktoren im e-Business*. Frankfurt am Main: FAZ.

Breuer, S. (2004). *Beschreibung von Geschäftsmodellen internetbasierter Unternehmen Konzeption-Umsetzung-Anwendung.* St. Gallen, Switzerland: Universität St. Gallen.

Chen, H.-M. (2008). Towards service engineering: Service orientation and business-IT alignment. In *Proceedings of the 41st Hawaii International Conference on System Sciences (HICSS)* (pp. 114c1–114c10). Waikaloa, HI: IEEE. doi:10.1109/HICSS.2008.462

Cochran, M. (2010). Proposal of an operations department model to provide IT governance in organizations that don't have IT c-level executives. In *Proceedings of the 43rd Hawaii International Conference on System Sciences (HICSS)* (pp. 1–10). Poipu, HI: IEEE.

Darby, R., Jones, J., & Madani, G. A. (2003). E-commerce marketing: Fad or fiction? Management competency in mastering emerging technology. An international case analysis in the UAE. *Logistics Information Management, 16*(2), 106–113. doi:10.1108/09576050310467241

De Haes, S., & Van Grembergen, W. (2005). IT governance structures, processes and relational mechanisms: Achieving IT/business alignment in a major Belgian financial group. In *Proceedings of the 38th Annual Hawaii International Conference on System Sciences.* doi:10.1109/HICSS.2005.362

Dutta, S., & Biren, B. (2001). Business transformation on the internet. *European Management Journal, 19*(5), 449–462. doi:10.1016/S0263-2373(01)00061-5

Eisenmann, T., Parker, G., & Van Alstyne, M. W. (2006). Strategies for two-sided markets. *Harvard Business Review, 84*(10), 92. PMID:16649701

Evans, P. B., & Wurster, T. S. (1996). Strategy and the new economics of information. *Harvard Business Review, 75*(5), 70–82. PMID:10170332

Fingar, P., & Aronica, R. (2001). *The death of "e" and the birth of the real new economy.* Tampa, FL: Meghan-Kiffer Press.

Friedrichsen, M., & Mühl-Benninghaus, W. (Eds.). (2014). *Handbook of Social Media Management - Value Chain and Business Models in Changing Media Markets.* Berlin: Springer.

Goeken, M., & Alter, S. (2009). Towards conceptual metamodeling of IT governance frameworks approach. In *Proceedings of the 42nd Hawaii International Conference on System Sciences (HICSS)* (pp. 1–10). IEEE.

Graw, E.-M. (2001). Lockrufe auf den Felsen und ins Netz. *FOCUS Online*. Retrieved June 29, 2014, from http://www.focus.de/politik/deutschland/profile-lockrufe-auf-den-felsen-und-ins-netz_aid_190858.html

Harkness, M. D., & Green, B. P. (2004). E-commerce's impact on audit practices. *Internal Auditing, 19*(2), 28–36.

Henderson, J. C., & Venkatraman, N. (1993). Strategic alignment: Leveraging information technology for transforming organizations. *IBM Systems Journal, 32*(1), 4–16. doi:10.1147/sj.382.0472

Hevner, A. R., March, S. T., Park, J., & Ram, S. (2004). Design science in information systems research. *Management Information Systems Quarterly, 28*(1), 75–105.

Hildebrand, T. (2011). *Two-sided markets in the online world: an empirical analysis.* (Dissertation). Humboldt-Universität zu Berlin, Berlin.

IDC. (2009). *Global revenue from internet-based applications and associated hardware from 2009 to 2014.* Retrieved May 10, 2013, from http://www.statista com/statistics/282730/global-revenue-from-internet-based-application-since-2009/

ISACA. (Ed.). (2012a). *COBIT 5 Framework.* Rolling Meadows, IL: ISACA.

ISACA. (Ed.). (2012b). *COBIT 5: Enabling processes.* Rolling Meadows, IL: ISACA.

ISACA. (Ed.). (2012c). *COBIT 5: Implementation.* Rolling Meadows, IL: ISACA.

ISACA. (2014). *COBIT 5 - A Business Framework for the Governance and Management of Enterprise IT | ISACA.* Retrieved June 12, 2014, from http://www.isaca.org/COBIT/Pages/default.aspx?cid=1003566&Appeal=PR

Iskandar, M., & Salleh, N. A. M. (2010). IT governance in e-commerce environment: Cases from airline industry. *Proceedings of ICITST, 2010*, 1–6.

Kalakota, R., & Robinson, M. (2001). *E-business 2.0: Roadmap for success.* Addison-Wesley.

Kearns, G. S., & Sabherwal, R. (2007). Strategic alignment between business and information technology: A knowledge-based view of behaviors, outcome, and consequences. *Journal of Management Information Systems, 23*(3), 129–162. doi:10.2753/MIS0742-1222230306

Kooper, M. N., Maes, R., & Lindgreen, E. E. O. R. (2011). On the governance of information: Introducing a new concept of governance to support the management of information. *International Journal of Information Management, 31*(3), 195–200. doi:10.1016/j.ijinfomgt.2010.05.009

Lainhart, J. W. IV. (2001). Why IT governance is a top management issue. *Journal of Corporate Accounting & Finance*, *11*(5), 33–40. doi:10.1002/1097-0053(200007/08)11:5<33::AID-JCAF6>3.0.CO;2-U

Langer, A. M., & Yorks, L. (2013). *Strategic IT: Best practices for managers and executives*. Academic Press.

Lin, M., Li, S., & Whinston, A. B. (2011). Innovation and Price Competition in a Two-Sided Market. *Journal of Management Information Systems*, *28*(2), 171–202. doi:10.2753/MIS0742-1222280207

Liu, X., Wu, L., Yu, J., & Lei, X. (2010). A holistic governance framework for e-business success. In *2010 Fourth International Conference on Management of e-Commerce and e-Government (ICMeCG)* (pp. 142–146). doi:10.1109/IC-MeCG.2010.36

Madureira, A., Baken, N., & Bouwman, H. (2011). Value of digital information networks: A holonic framework. *NETNOMICS: Economic Research and Electronic Networking*, *12*(1), 1–30. doi:10.1007/s11066-011-9057-6

Mahadevan, B. (2000). Business models for internet based e-commerce. *California Management Review*, *42*(4), 55–69. doi:10.2307/41166053

McFadden, C. (2012). Are textbooks dead? Making sense of the digital transition. *Publishing Research Quarterly*, *28*(2), 93–99. doi:10.1007/s12109-012-9266-3

Mirza, A. A., & Chan, S. S. (2004). Challenges for managing IT skills portfolio for e-business. In M. Nakayama & N. Sutcliffe (Eds.), *Managing IT skills portfolios: planning, acquisition, and performance evaluation* (pp. 55–82). Hershey, PA: IGI. doi:10.4018/978-1-59140-515-3.ch003

Oestreich, N. (2012). "Feels like free": Details zum Spotify-Tarif der Telekom – Vergleich aller Streaming-Anbieter. *iPhone-Ticker*. Retrieved January 19, 2014, from http://www.iphone-ticker.de/telekom-spotify-tarif-vergleich-38485/

Orr, A. (2000). Convergence: The next big issue. *Target Marketing*, *23*(11), 5.

Osterwalder, A. (2004). The business model ontology: A proposition in a design science approach. Institut d'Informatique et Organisation. Lausanne, Switzerland, University of Lausanne, Ecole Des Hautes Etudes Commerciales HEC, 173.

Osterwalder, A. (2010). *Business model generation: a handbook for visionaries, game changers, and challengers*. Hoboken, NJ: Wiley.

Osterwalder, A. (2011). Reverse Engineering Facebook's Business Model with Ballpark Figures. *Business Model Alchemist*. Retrieved June 27, 2014, from http://businessmodelalchemist.com/blog/2011/01/reverse-engineering-facebooks-business-model-with-ballpark-figures.html

Osterwalder, A., Pigneur, Y., & Tucci, C. L. (2005). Clarifying business models: Origins, present, and future of the concept. *Communications of the Association for Information Systems*, *16*(1), 1.

Patel, K., & McCarthy, M. P. (2000). *Digital Transformation: The Essentials of E-Business Leadership*. McGraw-Hill Professional.

Patel, N. V. (2002). Emergent forms of IT governance to support global e-business models. *Journal of Information Technology Theory and Application*, *4*(2), 33–48.

Patel, N. V. (2004). An emerging strategy for e-business IT governance. In W. Van Grembergen (Ed.), *Strategies for information technology governance* (pp. 81–97). Hershey, PA: IGI. doi:10.4018/978-1-59140-140-7.ch003

Pathak, J. (2003). Internal audit and e-commerce controls. *Internal Auditing*, *18*(2), 30–34.

Portuese, D. (2006). *E-commerce and the internet: A study on the impact of relationship marketing opportunities for better online consumer intentional relationship*. Capella University.

Rochet, J.-C., & Tirole, J. (2003). Platform competition in two-sided markets. *Journal of the European Economic Association*, *1*(4), 990–1029. doi:10.1162/154247603322493212

Rochet, J.-C., & Tirole, J. (2004). *Two-sided markets: An overview*. IDEI working paper. Retrieved from https://frbatlanta.org/filelegacydocs/ep_rochetover.pdf

Romm, C. T., & Sudweeks, F. (1998). *Doing business electronically*. London: Springer. doi:10.1007/978-1-4471-0591-6

Rysman, M. (2009). The economics of two-sided markets. *The Journal of Economic Perspectives*, *23*(3), 125–143. doi:10.1257/jep.23.3.125

Schepers, T. G. J., Iacob, M. E., & Van Eck, P. A. T. (2008). A lifecycle approach to SOA governance. In *Proceedings of the 2008 ACM Symposium on Applied Computing* (pp. 1055–1061). New York, NY: ACM. doi:10.1145/1363686.1363932

Schmidtke, R. (2006). *Two-sided markets with pecuniary and participation externalities*. Munich: Univ., Center for Economic Studies.

Smith, W. K., Binns, A., & Tushman, M. L. (2010). Complex business models: Managing strategic paradoxes simultaneously. *Long Range Planning*, *43*(2–3), 448–461. doi:10.1016/j.lrp.2009.12.003

Soomro, T. R., & Hesson, M. (2012). Supporting best practices and standards for information technology infrastructure library. *Journal of Computer Science*, *8*(2), 272–276. doi:10.3844/jcssp.2012.272.276

Taulli, T. (2012). *How to create the next Facebook seeing your startup through, from idea to IPO*. New York: Springer. doi:10.1007/978-1-4302-4648-0

Timmers, P. (1999). *Electronic commerce*. New York: Wiley.

Van Grembergen, W., & De Haes, S. (2009). *Enterprise governance of information technology: Achieving strategic alignment and value*. New York: Springer.

Van Grembergen, W., De Haes, S., & Guldentops, E. (2004). Structures, processes and relational mechanisms for IT governance. In W. Van Grembergen (Ed.), *Strategies for Information Technology Governance* (pp. 1–36). Hershey, PA. IGI. doi:10.4018/978-1-59140-140-7.ch001

Weill, P., & Ross, J. W. (2004). *IT governance: How top performers manage IT decision rights for superior results*. Harvard Business Press.

Wirtz, B. W. (2011). *Business model management*. Wiesbaden, Germany: Gabler.

Wirtz, B. W. (2013). *Electronic Business* (4th ed.). Wiesbaden, Germany: Springer Gabler. doi:10.1007/978-3-8349-4240-1

Zolnowski, A., & Böhmann, T. (2014). Formative evaluation of business model representations - The service business model canvas. *ECIS 2014 Proceedings*.

Zott, C., Amit, R., & Massa, L. (2010). *The business model: Theoretical roots, recent developments, and future research*. IESE Business School-University of Navarra.

APPENDIX

Table 4. Aspect analysis for ancillary services commercialization

Indirect Revenue Streams	
Aspect: Ancillary services commercialization.	
Issue: Special browser settings, e.g., ad-blockers may put business models at risk. Online advertisements are a source of income for internet based businesses, mostly as an indirect revenue stream. For instance, in case of free Spotify online streaming online ads may be easily abrogated by listeners using ad-blocking systems. Customer actions can be considered an immediate influence, business hazard or an extreme risk.	
Enterprise Goals	
3	Manage business risks
6	Customer-oriented service culture
8	Agile responses to a changing business environment
9	Information-based strategic decision making
IT-Related Goals	
4	Manage IT-related business risks
6	Transparency of IT costs, benefits and risk
8	Adequate use of applications, information and technology solutions
9	IT agility
14	Availability of reliable and useful information for decision making
17	Knowledge, expertise and initiatives for business innovation
Processes	
EDM03	Ensure Risk Optimization
APO04	Manage Innovation
APO08	Manage Relationships
APO12	Manage Risk
BAI03	Manage Solution Identification and Build
BAI05	Manage Organizational Change Enablement
BAI06	Manage Changes
BAI08	Manage Knowledge

Table 5. Aspect analysis for exchange of digital goods

Indirect Revenue Streams	
Aspect: Exchange of digital goods in case of problematic network (WiFi).	
Issue: Problem in exchange of digital goods. When operating an online streaming service, it is important that the internet (LAN/WiFi) is available to play music streams. Therefore, online streaming such as Spotify depends on the continuation of WiFi service as well as its quality. However, at times WiFi is weak or at times the service can be dismantled. As an alternate solution to this problem, Spotify came up with downloaded version of music streams that can be played by the Spotify player even when WiFi is unavailable or there are other disruptions in its quality. However, these downloaded music streams can only be played by Spotify player if the subscriber is a valid member of Spotify-premium package. If the membership of the subscriber has been expired then the downloaded music files cannot be played anymore. The downloaded Spotify files are encoded and can only be played if a subscriber has a membership. This is a technology innovation to solve the problem.	
Enterprise Goals	
3	Manage business risks
6	Customer-oriented service culture
8	Agile responses to a changing business environment
9	Information-based strategic decision making
IT-Related Goals	
4	Manage IT-related business risks
6	Transparency of IT costs, benefits and risk
8	Adequate use of applications, information, and technology solutions
9	IT agility
14	Availability of reliable and useful information for decision making
17	Knowledge, expertise and initiatives for business innovation
Processes	
EDM03	Ensure Risk Optimization
APO04	Manage Innovation
APO08	Manage Relationships
APO12	Manage Risk
BAI03	Manage Solution Identification and Build
BAI05	Manage Organizational Change Enablement
BAI06	Manage Changes
BAI08	Manage Knowledge

Chapter 5
Aligning Information Systems and Technology with Benefit Management and Balanced Scorecard

Jorge Gomes
Instituto Superior de Economia e Gestão, Portugal & Universidade de Lisboa, Portugal

Mário Romão
Instituto Superior de Economia e Gestão, Portugal & Universidade de Lisboa, Portugal

ABSTRACT

Investments in Information Systems and Technology (IS/IT) have not always generated the business value or the financial revenue that should be expected. Some authors argue that the result of those studies that related investments in IS/IT to increased organisational performance over the last thirty years were far from true. Others say that the amount spent on IS/IT and business success has no direct connection. The relationship between IS/IT and performance is widely discussed, but is little understood. Organizations today need to deliver more complex products and demanding services in a better, faster, and cheaper way. The challenges that companies address today require enterprise-wide solutions that call for an integrated approach and the effective management of organizational resources in order to achieve business objectives. Benefits Management (BM) approach proposes a continuous mapping of the benefits of IS/IT investments, implementing and monitoring intermediate results. Balanced Scorecard (BSC) is an innovative approach that considers the financial and

DOI: 10.4018/978-1-5225-0861-8.ch005

non-financial perspectives in determining the performance level of an organization. Not only does it represent a measurement tool, but it is also a multi-dimensional system of performance management which focusses on the alignment of all business initiatives with the strategy. In this paper, the authors propose a link between these two approaches to improve the management of business benefits and to ensure that actions taken along the investment life-cycle lead to foreseen benefits realization. The goal of this integration is to propose a framework that combines the "best of" the both methods. A key issue of this combination lies in the fact that all involved stakeholders must understand more clearly what is required, what is realistically expected, and what is possible to achieve from these investments.

1. INTRODUCTION

Since the 1980s, IS/IT has positioned itself as a strategic tool, which, through agility and innovative ways of conducting business can produce superior performance (McFarland, 1984; Farbey et al., 1993; Porter, 2001). As a result, the relationship between investments in IS/IT and improved organizational performance has been the subject of many studies (Melville et al., 2004). The issue remains controversial, as evidenced by articles in major journals and business magazines (Ashurst & Doherty, 2003; Carr, 2003; Doherty, Ashurst & Peppard, 2012; Farrell, 2003, Serra & Kunc, 2015; Ward & Daniel, 2006). The difficulties in implementing IS/IT solutions, as well as in assessing their performance, have been acknowledged in academic literature (Ashurst &Doherty, 2003; Doherty, Ashurst, & Peppard, 2012; Lueg & Lu, 2012, 2013; Martinsons et al, 1999; Serra & Kunc, 2015; Ward & Daniel, 2006).

At present, firms compete in a complex and challenging context that is being transformed by many factors, ranging from globalization to frequent and uncertain changes in the growing use of information technologies (DeNisi, Hitt, & Jackson, 2003). In order to survive and thrive in this competitive business environment, every business needs to possess a certain level of strategic capability. In response to these new business constrains, as they become better, faster and cheaper, successful organizations have developed three broad strategies (Gomes & Romão, 2013a):

- Hired, trained and empowered employees to use information skills, in order that the organization will become more knowledgeable and responsive to pressures for change;
- Collaborate more fully with key stakeholders, particularly customers, suppliers, and employees, to design more effective and efficient process;

- Begun to better understand what creates success, and the way to effectively manage and achieve it.

In spite of organizations learning from their past IS/IT investments successes and failures, the pattern of perceived failures continues. The following list identifies the common problems that face many organizations:

- Improper alignment of the organizations' objectives with IS/IT investments, leading to inappropriate project selection (Henderson & Venkatraman, 1999; Peppard, 2003; Teo & Ang, 1999; Thorp, 1999);
- Unrealistic or overly high expectations of benefits from IS/IT investments (Ashurst & Doherty, 2003; Doherty, Ashurst, & Peppard, 2012; Teo & Ang, 1999; Ward & Daniel, 2006);
- Uncertainty of expected benefits delivery (Ashurst & Doherty, 2003; Doherty, Ashurst, & Peppard, 2012; Farbey et al.,1999; Shang & Seddom, 2002; Ward & Daniel, 2006);
- Organizations planning to wait for long term and yet-to-be-realized IS/IT benefits (Lin and Pervan, 2003; Ward and Daniel, 2006);
- Use of financial techniques to evaluate IS/IT returns. These techniques only consider the monetary return from projects (Coleman, 1994; Milis & Mercken, 2004);
- Failure to quantify the intangible benefits of IS/IT (Gunasekaran, et al., 2001; Ward & Peppard, 2002; Ward & Daniel, 2006).

Organizations seek benefits and value only in monetary terms, which have resulted in a lot of wasted energy, time and money. It is very common that organizations place their focus on the technical aspects such as 'does it work?', rather than the social aspects such as 'is this adopted successfully?', or from a business perspective 'is this delivering value'? One of the reasons why the benefits do not always succeed results from the social aspects not being taken into consideration (Jones & Hughes, 2001).

Recognition of the importance of BM appeared in 1995 in different industries. Various approaches and models have been developed and help organizations identify, monitor, and ultimately obtain the benefits previously identified (Sapountzis et al., 2007). The basic assumption in BM literature is that benefits can be realized if they are managed appropriately. It is unlikely that benefits will simply emerge, as if by magic, from the introduction of a new technology (Gomes, Romão & Caldeira, 2013b). The perception of the continuously unsuccessful IS/IT investments led to a new way and approach for how projects are undertaken. The focus should be on the realization of the benefits, as this is an organization's main reason for the investment (Ward and Daniel, 2006). Benefits realization is emerging as being one of the methods to assist organizations manage the whole life cycle of programmes and projects (Glynne, 2007). The benefits for an organization from IS/IT-enabled change are essentially a result of three main actions (Peppard & Ward, 2005):

1. Stop doing wrong or inefficient activities;
2. Do things better than we did before;
3. Doing things completely new.

According to Peppard et al., (2007) there are five principles for accomplishing benefits through IS/IT investments:

1. Just having technology does not bring any benefit, neither create value;
2. Benefits arise when IS/IT enables people to do things differently;
3. Benefits result from changes and innovations in ways of working. Only involving people can make these changes;
4. All IS/IT projects have outcomes, but not all outcomes are benefits;
5. Benefits must be actively managed if they are to be obtained.

The success of IS/IT investments depends on the specific characteristics of each industry and their particular practices.

2. BALANCED SCORECARD AND STRATEGY MAPS

In an article published in the Harvard Business Review, Kaplan and Norton (1992) introduced BSC in response to the growing dissatisfaction of the inadequacy of traditional performance measurement systems and its dependence on being exclusively financial. The authors proposed an integrated framework for the implementation of financial and nonfinancial performance measures to help organizations align their initiatives with their strategy. The BSC is recognized as a being a comprehensive system of strategically aligned performance measures (Decoene & Bruggeman, 2006), and is used extensively in business and industry, government, and nonprofit organizations worldwide. BSC suggests that as well as financial measures of performance, attention should be paid to the requirements of customers, business processes, learning and growth and longer-term sustainability. The BSC focusses on measuring the performance from four perspectives: financial, customers, internal processes, and learning and growth initiatives. A major strength of the BSC approach is the emphasis it places on linking performance measures with business units' strategy (Otley, 1999). According to Ahn (2001), the BSC bridges the gap between the development of a strategy and its realization, by supporting and linking four critical management processes:

1. Clarifying and translating vision and strategy;
2. Communicating and linking strategic objectives and measures;
3. Planning, setting targets, and aligning strategic initiatives;
4. Enhancing strategic feedback and learning.

A well-designed BSC should be able to describe the strategies through the objectives and measures previously chosen (Niven, 2002). In modern business models, intangible assets, such as employees' skills and knowledge levels, customers and suppliers relationships, and an innovative culture are all critical in providing the much-needed cutting-edge for the organization (Margarita, 2008).

By reshaping the BSC it can also be applied to IS/IT in four specific domains (Van Grembergen & Steven, 2005; Van Grembergen et al, 2003):

1. The business contribution perspective capturing the business value created from IS/IT investments;
2. The user perspective representing the user evaluation of IS/IT;
3. The operational excellence perspective that evaluated the IS/IT processes employed to develop and deliver applications;
4. The future perspective representing the human and technology resources needed by IS/IT to deliver its services over time.

The first step in creating the management processes for the implementation of a strategy relying on the construction of a reliable and consistent framework for describing strategy, known as a Strategy Map (SM). The SM outlines all the cause-and-effect linkages between what an organization's strategy is, and what everyone does on a day-to-day basis (Kaplan and Norton, 2000). The SM identifies how to get to destinations, the strategic objectives, how tangible and intangible assets are involved, outlines how assets of all types are combined to create customer value propositions, specifies how the desired financial outcomes will be realized and details the relationships between shareholders, customers, business processes and skills (Kaplan and Norton, 2000).

3. BENEFITS MANAGEMENT AND BENEFITS DEPENDENCY NETWORK

Ward et al, (1996) developed an approach for identifying, structuring, planning, monitoring and delivery benefits. The model introduced the idea of a distinct process, targeted towards managing the benefits realization of IS/IT projects, in order to improve the results. The process of BM based on the management model of strategic change, developed by Pettigrew and Whipp (1991), recognizes that the process by which a major change is managed needs to be relevant to the content of the change involved both internal and external. The process model of BM includes the following set of steps:

1. **Identifying and Structuring Benefits:** The proposed benefits are identified and, for each proposed benefit, business measures are developed, both financial and non-financial. The benefits are structured in order to understand the linkages between technology effects, business changes and business objectives.
2. **Planning Benefits Realization:** For each benefit, specific responsibility for realizing the benefits are allocated amongst the stakeholders. The required business benefits and changes are also assessed and planned for, and a Benefits Realization Plan (BRP) is produced.
3. **Executing the Benefits Realization Plan:** Alongside the implementation of the proposed IS/IT investments, the necessary business changes as detailed in the benefits realization plan are carried out.
4. **Evaluating and Reviewing Results:** Following the full implementation of IS/IT and business changes, the previously-developed business measures are used to evaluate the effects of the project.
5. **Potential for Further Benefits:** As a result of the post-project review, it may become apparent that further benefits are now achievable

Several authors recognized the importance of the BM initial phases. Bennington and Baccarini (2004) suggest that benefits identification should be a combined approach of interviews and workshops involving key stakeholders. Best practice is to involve key stakeholders to identify and agree desired benefits, maximizing the likelihood of commitment to realize these benefits across a range of levels in the business or the organization (Glynne, 2007). The key tool of this approach is the Benefits Dependency Network (BDN), which was introduced for the first time by Ward and Elvin (1999), and was designed to enable the investment objectives and their resulting benefits to be linked in a structured way for the business, organization and IS/IT changes required to realize these benefits.

4. BALANCED SCORECARD AND BENEFITS MANAGEMENT LIMITATIONS

Kaplan and Norton (1996) assume the casual relationship between perspectives. In other words, the measures of the precedent perspective are the drivers for the measures of the following perspective. The assumption that there is a cause-effect relationship is essential, as it allows the measurements in non-financial areas to predicted future financial performance. NØrreklit (2000) argues that there is no cause-and-effect relationship between some of the suggested measurements in the BSC. The lack of a cause-effect relationship is crucial, as invalid assumptions in a feed-forward control system will cause individual organizations to anticipate performance indicators which are actually faulty, resulting in dysfunctional organizational behaviour and sub-optimized performance (de Haas & Kleingeld, 1999). The influence between measures is not unidirectional, in the sense that learning and growth are the drivers of internal business processes, which are the drivers of customer satisfaction, which in turn is the driver of financial results. Therefore, instead of a cause-effect relationship, the relationship between the areas is more likely to be one of interdependence (NØrreklit, 2000). BSC aims to solve the problems related to strategy implementation (Kaplan and Norton, 1996). However, the control model is a hierarchical top-down model, which is not rooted in the environment, neither in the organization, which makes it questionable as a strategic management tool (NØrreklit, 2000). Consequently, a gap must be expected between the strategy expressed in the actions actually undertaken, and the strategy planned. In BSC, not all stakeholders have been included, some of the excluded ones being suppliers and public authorities, which may be important for several organisations. Similarly, institutional stakeholders have been left out, as has the importance of business networks (NØrreklit, 2000). Kaplan and Norton (1996) explicitly state that the BSC is not a stakeholder approach. More recently, Gomes and Romão (2013a) and Voelpel (2005) highlighted important shortcomings of BSC in responding to the dynamic changing business world and in dealing with the corporate network environment.

The purpose of the BM process is to improve the identification of achievable benefits and to ensure that decisions and actions taken over the IS/IT investment life-cycle can lead to them being realized. The majority of value from IS/IT comes from the business changes that it enables the organization to make. The achievement of benefits obviously depends on the effective implementation of the technology, but evidence from projects success and failure suggests that organizations' inability to accommodate and exploit the capabilities of technology causes the poor return from many IS/IT investments (Ward and Daniel, 2006). The BRP and the BDN are means of ensuring these links are made and they and are the basis for the business case, as this includes not only the intended benefits, but also how each one can be achieved.

Remenyi et al., (2000) point out four causes of the difficulties of benefits identification and management:

- All benefits should be identified and quantified before the project starts;
- Due to the complexity of IS/IT investments, it is not easy to predict the development processes;
- The dichotomy tangible/intangible and quantifiable/not-quantifiable has different organizational effects;
- The benefits are not stable along the investment.

In essence, the most obvious difference in both the BSC and BM approaches is in the way benefits management plays its role in 'governing' the investment process. BSC does not show evidence of having a process to manage benefits, although benefits are distributed through the perspectives ruled by the short and long-term objectives. Ward et al. (1996) note that without a plan, it is difficult to predict how an organization might effectively realise business benefits. Assessing benefits should not be a one-off task carried out during the phase only the early stages of implementation, but persistently monitored over lifecycle investment. Benefits monitoring compares projects result with the benefits realization plan during the project and assesses whether any internal or external changes have occurred that will affect the delivery of planned benefits (Ward & Daniel, 2006). Benefits monitoring is a long cycle, starting with benefits planning and ending with benefits realization (Bartlett, 2006). Benefits review is the process by which the success of the project in terms of benefits delivery is addressed, opportunities for the realization of further benefits are identified, and lessons learned, and opportunities of improvement in future projects are identified (Ashurst & Doherty, 2003).

5. FUTURE RESEARCH DIRECTIONS

BSC through SM became a powerful tool, allowing organizations to convert their initiatives and resources – including intangible assets, such as corporate cultures and employee knowledge, into more tangible outcomes. Although the BSC emphasis primarily the financial dimension, it can integrate other sustainability aspects, such as social and environmental issues. According to Gomes and Romão (2014), several studies reveal the vitality of BSC developments, keeping it updated and suited to today´s organization needs. Subsequently show some examples:

- Formulating the BSC sustainability which integrated environmental and social issues with the management of business units (Biker & Waxenberger,

2002; Figge et al, 2002; Epstein & Wisner 2001; Schaltegger & Wagner, 2006).

- Introducing the perspective of employee satisfaction and the importance of customer perspective prioritization (McAdam and Walker, 2003).
- Combining BSC with product development and innovation (Jiménez-Zarco et al, 2006).
- Aligning IS/IT capabilities and activities with business objectives and business requirements (Huang & Hu, 2007).
- Exploring the relationship between BSC and Six Sigma, pointing out the critical issues for implementing a BSC programme (Pan & Cheng, 2008).
- Linking the use of the BSC with Scenario Planning, to reinforce the process of strategy formulation and implementation (Othman, 2008).
- Developing the quality improvement in patient care and outcomes (Aidemark & Funck, 2009).
- Studying the impact on managers' job satisfaction (Burney & Swanson, 2010).
- Proposing the BSC to assign the attribute weight by an expert group in mul tiple decision making (Yang, et al, 2010).
- Developing the design of an IS/IT BSC, mixing together business environment and IS/IT strategy to enhance IS/IT´s role in obtaining and measuring its contribution to business value (Marcos et al, 2012).
- Exploring the linkage between BDN and SM (Gomes et al, 2013b).

Since the 1990s, BM has evolved to be an independent research discipline that investigates the successful realization of IS/IT project benefits as a response to organizations' dissatisfaction with the results of IS/IT investments (Hesselmann, Ahlemann & Böhl, 2015). From a large number of published studies, we consistently found that BM is a highly effective management approach, although researchers generally still consider the BM adoption rate to be very low (Braun et al., 2010; Lin et al., 2004; Päivärinta & Dertz, 2008; Ward et al., 2007). Ward et al (2007) noticed that the adoption of BM has increased from 12% to 25% in the participating organizations of a study. Braun et al (2009) identified only 74 research papers as being highly relevant for BM. Päivärinta and Dertz (2008) highlighted that the elements that might enable the diffusion and adoption of BM practices, such as employee needs, governance mechanisms or organizational culture, are mostly underrepresented in research (Päivärinta & Dertz, 2008). Studies conducted in Australia, which provide empirical insights into local BM practices, found that only a few organizations have implemented a formal BM process (Bennington & Baccarini, 2004; Baccarini & Bateup, 2008). The same result was found in Germany, through a comprehensive approach to BM (Braun et al., 2010), and also in exploratory studies on BM practices in the Norwegian public sector (Flak et al., 2008; Hellang, et al., 2013). An interesting research conducted six case studies and found that strategic alignment and BM positively affected the increase of IS/IT outsourcing success (van Lier & Dohmen, 2007). Some research in the field of BM has drawn on the resource-based view (RBV) to address the question of how organizations can increase the likelihood of their projected benefits of IS/IT investments' being realized (Ashurst et al., 2008). Ashurst et al. (2008) developed a benefits realization capability model that is enacted through a coherent set of benefits realization skills. Each skill is underpinned by a closely-related suite of benefits realization practices. Doherty et al. (2012) stress that organizational change is needed for successful BM. No matter how effective and efficient the BM methodology is, it will be of no use if those employees expected to use and apply such practices do not really embrace and adopt them, and if contextual or governance mechanisms are neglected (Hesselmann & Kunal, 2014).

6. VIAPAV CASE STUDY

Concerning the BDN and VIAPAV specific stream, (Gomes, 2011) highlighted on Figure 1, the BDN elements are fully integrated into SM, using O2 as an example.

Figure 1. Benefits dependency network
Gomes, 2011.

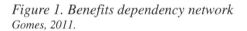
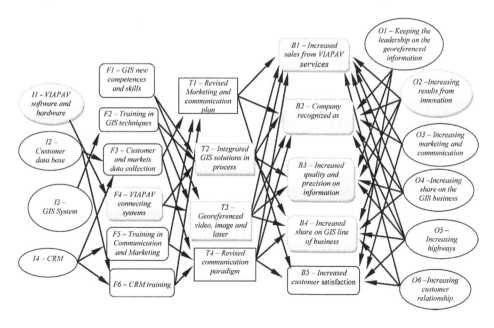

Organizations have chosen the investments to perform and have identified the business objectives (short-term) and benefits (long-term) to be realized through the business changes enabled by IS/IT investments. The linkage to the strategic objectives (BSC) should be supported by the business case. The business case includes the benefits realization plan with the routes to the objectives mapped, those responsible nominated and the establishment of metrics and targets.

7. BENEFITS DISCUSSION

In the BSC customer perspective, managers identify the clients and the market segment in which the business will compete. The core of the business strategy is the customer value proposition, which describes the unique set of products and service attributes, customer relations, corporate image and how the organization differentiates itself from competitors. The internal process and learning and growth perspectives are located in an area where the benefits are more intangible. These two perspectives are directly linked to enabling changes and business changes from the BM approach. In this approach, business changes have been described as being new ways of working that will be required by the organization in the near future. There is also a wide range of enabling changes that may be required in order to ensure that the business changes really occur and that they promote the realization of the identified benefits. The internal process reminds us that the organizational background activity is driven by objectives and goals to ensure that the customer and financial objectives are achieved. Once an organization has a clear picture of its customer and financial perspectives, it can then determine the means by which it will achieve the differentiated value proposition for customers and productivity improvements and the business changes required to reach the objectives and realize the business benefits. The foundation of any strategy map is the learning and growth perspective, which defines the core competencies and skills, the technologies, and the corporate culture. These topics enable the organization to align its human resources and information technology with its strategy. Table 1 shows the project outcomes and also highlights the benefits results tracked annually for the years 2008 to 2010. According this business information we can confirm that the expected benefits were achieved with different levels of realization.

Table 2 shows the integration table, with the full conversion of the BDN elements on the company SM.

Figure 2 shows the integration of the benefits on the SM.

Table 1. Investments outcomes

B1	VIAPAV Revenue (€)	Annual Revenue (M€)	Objective	Perform	Deviation
2008	95.000	6,750	1.0%	1.4%	0.4%
2009	206.300	6,570	2.0%	3.1%	1.1%
2010	409.644	6,120	3.0%	6.7%	3.7%
B2	Inquiries	Answers	%	Score	Rate
2008	25	15	60%	72%	Good
2009	28	17	61%	80%	Good
2010	25	16	64%	75%	Good
B3	Revenue (€)	Estimated Hours	Performed	Reduction	Deviation
2008	95.000	6.000	4.200	30%	0%
2009	203.300	10.200	6.280	38%	+ 8%
2010	409.640	20.120	12.320	39%	+ 9%
B4	Revenue (€)	Annual Revenue (M€)	Objective	Perform	Deviation
2008	200.000	6,750	3.0%	3.0%	0.0%
2009	302.000	6,570	3.0%	4.5%	1.5%
2010	20.000	6,120	3.0%	0.3%	-2.7%

Gomes, 2011.

Table 2. Integration table

Benefits Management	Balanced Scorecard	Metrics
Objective: **O2:** Increase results from innovation	Strategic Objective: **O1:** Increase results from innovation	Customer Satisfaction
Output Benefits: **B1:** Increased sales from VIAPAV **B3:** Increased quality and precision	Financial: **F1:** Increased sales from VIAPAV **F3:** Increased quality and precision	Sales Time reduction
Output Benefits: **B2:** Recognized as innovative **B4:** Increased share on GIS	Customer Perspective: **C2:** Recognized as innovative **C4:** Increased share on GIS	Customer Satisfaction/ Sales
Change Enablers SI/TI	Learning and Growth: **N1:** Align strategy **N2:** Team building **N3:** Change management **L1:** VIAPAV software and hardware	

Gomes, 2011.

Figure 2. Strategy Map

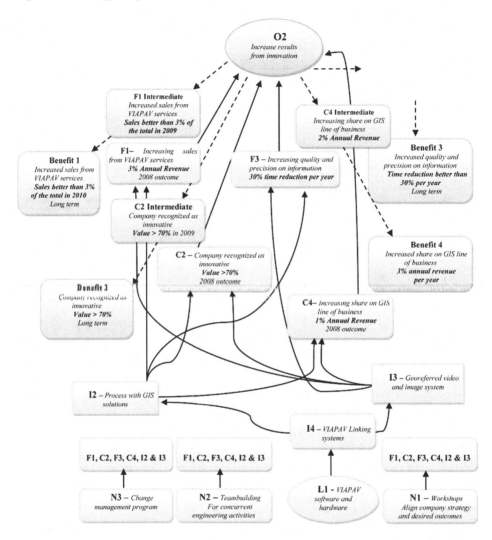

8. CONCLUSION

In this paper, the authors proposed an integration between two management approaches, Benefits Management (BM) and Balanced Scorecard (BSC), to improve the management of business benefits and to ensure that actions taken along investments' life-cycle lead to forecasted benefits realization. The proposed framework intended to capture and combine the *"best of"* both approaches. The main recognized advantage of the BSC is the alignment of management processes and the focus of the entire organization on implementing its long-term strategy. The BM approach brings to the Strategic Map (SM) the process of identifying and structuring benefits, establishing the ownership, and determining whether benefits can be managed and measured along their realization life-cycle. Using the results of a benefits mapping from a case-study, we show how a SM can be enriched with the concepts that are usually mapped in a Benefits Dependency Network (BDN).

We claimed that this framework can reinforce how a company can achieve its desired outcomes, including the value proposition (customer perspective), the innovation proposal (internal process perspective), the employee skills and the information technology capabilities (learning and growth perspective), which all combine ensure that the identified benefits will be realized according to the planned expectations.

REFERENCES

Ahn, H. (2001). Applying the Balanced Scorecard Concept: An Experience Report. *Long Range Planning, 34*(4), 441–461. doi:10.1016/S0024-6301(01)00057-7

Aidemark, L., & Funck, E. (2009). Measurement and health care management. *Financial Accountability & Management, 25*(2), 253–276. doi:10.1111/j.1468-0408.2009.00476.x

Ashurst, C., & Doherty, N. F. (2003). Towards the formulation of "a best practice" framework for benefits realization in IT projects. *Electronic Journal of Information Systems Evaluation, 6*, 1–10.

Ashurst, C., Doherty, N. F., & Peppard, J. (2008). Improving the Impact of It Development Projects: The Benefits Realization Capability Model. *European Journal of Information Systems, 17*(4), 352–370. doi:10.1057/ejis.2008.33

Baccarini, D., & Bateup, G. (2008). Benefits Management in Office Fit-out Projects. *Facilities, 26*(7/8), 310–320. doi:10.1108/02632770810877958

Bartlett, J. (2006). Managing Programmes of Business Change. Hampshire.

Bennington, P., & Baccarini, D. (2004, June). Project benefits management in IT projects – An Australian perspective. *Project Management Journal*.

Bieker, T., & Waxenberger, B. (2002). *Sustainability Balanced Scorecard and Business Ethics – using the BSC for integrity management. 10th International Conference of the Greening of Industry Network*, Göteborg, Sweden.

Braun, J., Ahlemann, F., & Mohan, K. (2010). Understanding Benefits Management Success: Results of a Field Study. ECIS 2010 Proceedings.

Burney, L. L., & Swanson, N. J. (2010). The Relationship between Balanced Scorecard Characteristics and Manager's Job Satisfaction. *Journal of Managerial Issues*, *22*(2), 166–181. doi: http://www.jstor.org/stable/20798903

Carr, N. G. (2003). IT doesn't matter. *Harvard Business Review*, *81*(5), 41–49. PMID:12747161

Coleman, T. (1994, March). Investment Appraisal: Total IT. *Accountancy*, 68-70.

de Haas, M., & Kleingeld, A. (1999). Multilevel design of performance measurement systems: Enhancing strategic dialogue throughout the organization. *Management Accounting Research*, *10*(3), 233–261. doi:10.1006/mare.1998.0098

Decoene, V., & Bruggeman, W. (2006). Strategic alignment and middle-level managers' motivation in a Balanced Scorecard setting. *International Journal of Operations & Production Management*, *26*(4), 3–4, 429–448. doi:10.1108/01443570610650576

DeNisi, A. S., Hitt, M. A., & Jackson, S. E. (2003). *The Knowledge Based Approach to Sustainable Competitive Advantage*. New York: Oxford University Press.

Doherty, N. F., Ashurst, C., & Peppard, J. (2012). Factors Affecting the Successful Realisation of Benefits from Systems Development Projects: Findings from Three Case Studies. *Journal of Information Technology*, *27*(1), 1–16. doi:10.1057/jit.2011.8

Epstein, M. J., & Wisner, P. S. (2001). Good Neighbors: Implementing Social and Environmental Strategies with the BSC. *Balanced Scorecard Report*, *3*(3), 8-11.

Farbey, B., Land, F., & Targett, D. (1993). *IT investment: A study of methods and practice*. Oxford, UK: Butterworth Heinemann.

Farbey, B., Land, F., & Targett, D. (1999). The moving staircase – problems of appraisal and evaluation in a turbulent environment. *Information Technology and People Journal*, *12*(3), 238–252. doi:10.1108/09593849910278196

Farrell, D. (2003). The real new economy. *Harvard Business Review*, *81*(9), 105–112. PMID:14521102

Figge, F., Hahn, T., Schaltegger, S., & Wagner, M. (2002). The Sustainability Balanced Scorecard: Linking Sustainability Management to Business Strategy. *Business Strategy and the Environment*, *11*(5), 269–284. doi:10.1002/bse.339

Flak, L. S., Eikebrokk, T. R., & Dertz, W. (2008). An Exploratory Approach for Benefits Management in E-Government: Insights from 48 Norwegian Government Funded Projects. In *Proceedings of the 41st Hawaii International Conference on System Sciences*. doi:10.1109/HICSS.2008.55

Glynne, P. (2007). *Benefits Management-changing the focus of delivery*. Association for Progress Management. *Yearbook, 2006/2007*, 45–49.

Gomes, J. (2011). *Gestão de benefícios numa empresa de Geoengenharia*. (MSc Thesis in Management). ISCTE-IUL, Lisboa. accessed from http://hdl.handle.net/10071/4702

Gomes, J., & Romão, M. (2013a). How benefits management helps balanced scorecard to deal with business dynamic environments. *Tourism and Management Studies, 9*(1), 129–138. ISSN 2182-8458

Gomes, J., & Romão, M. (2014). Advantages and Limitations of Performance Measurement Tools: The Balanced Scorecard. In *Proceedings of IS2014 - 7th IADIS International Conference*. IADIS Press.

Gomes, J., Romão, M., & Caldeira, M. (2013b). The Benefits Management and Balanced Scorecard Strategy Map: How They Match. *International Journal of IT/Business Alignment and Governance, 4*(1), 44–54. doi:10.4018/jitbag.2013010104

Gunasekaran, A., Love, P., Rahimic, F., & Miele, R. (2001). A model for investment justification in information technology projects. *International Journal of Information Management, 21*(5), 349–364. doi:10.1016/S0268-4012(01)00024-X

Hellang, Ø., Flak, L. S., & Päivärinta, T. (2012). *Methods for Realizing Benefits from ICT in the Norwegian Public Sector: A Comparison. In Proceedings of the Transforming Government Workshop 2012: tGov 2012*. London: Brunel University Business School.

Henderson, J. C., & Venkatraman, N. (1999). Strategic alignment: Leveraging information technology for transforming organizations. *IBM Systems Journal, 38*(2.3), 472–484. doi:10.1147/SJ.1999.5387096

Hesselmann, F., Ahlemann, F., & Böhl, D. (2015). Not Everybody's Darling - Investigating the Acceptance of Benefits Management and Moderating Organizational Characteristics. In O. Thomas & F. Teuteberg (Eds.), *Proceedings der 12. Internationalen Tagung Wirtschaftsinformatik (WI 2015)* (pp. 585–599). Osnabrück.

Hesselmann, F., & Kunal, M. (2014). Where Are We headed with Benefits Management Research? Current Shortcomings and Avenues for Future Research. *ECIS 2014 Proceedings*.

Huang, C. D., & Hu, Q. (2007). Achieving IT-business strategic alignment via enterprise-wide implementation of Balanced Scorecards. *Information Systems Management, 24*(2), 173–184. doi:10.1080/10580530701239314

Jiménez-Zarco, A. I., & Martinez-Ruiz, M. P., & Gonzalez-Benito, O. (2006). Performance Measurement System (PMS) Integration into new Product Innovation: A Literature Review and Conceptual Framework. *Academy of Marketing Science Review*, 9.

Jones, S., & Hughes, J. (2001). Understanding IS evaluation as complex social process: A case study of a UK local authority. *European Journal of Information Systems*, *10*(4), 189–203. doi:10.1057/palgrave.ejis.3000405

Kaplan, R. S., & Norton, D. P. (1992). The Balanced Scorecard: Measures that drive performance. *Harvard Business Review*, *70*(1), 71–79. PMID:10119714

Kaplan, R. S., & Norton, D. P. (1996). *The Balanced Scorecard: Translating Strategy into Action*. Harvard Business School Press.

Kaplan, R. S., & Norton, D. P. (2000). *The Strategy-Focused Organization: How Balanced Scorecard companies thrive in the new business environment*. Boston: Harvard Business School Press.

Lin, C., & Pervan, G. (2003). The practice of IS/IT benefits management in large Australian organizations. *Information & Management*, *41*(1), 31–44. doi:10.1016/S0378-7206(03)00002-8

Lin, C., Pervan, G., & Lin, K. H. C. (2004). A Survey on Evaluating and Realizing IS/IT Benefits in Taiwanese B2bEC Companies. In *Proceedings of ECIS 2004*.

Lueg, R., & Lu, S. (2012). Improving efficiency in budgeting – An interventionist approach to spreadsheet accuracy testing. *Problems and Perspectives in Management*, *10*(1), 32–41.

Lueg, R., & Lu, S. (2013). How to improve efficiency in budgeting: The case of business intelligence in SMEs. *European Journal of Management*, *13*(2), 109–120. doi:10.18374/EJM-13-2.13

Marcos, A. F., Rouyet, J. I., & Bosch, A. (2012). An IT Balanced Scorecard Design under Service Management Philosophy. In *Proceedings of the 45th Hawaii International Conference on System Sciences*.

Margarita, I. (2008). The Balanced Scorecard Method, From Theory to Practice. *Intellectual Economics.*, *1*(3), 18–28.

Martinsons, M. G., Davison, R., & Tse, D. (1999). The balanced scorecard: A foundation for the strategic management of information systems. *Decision Support Systems*, *25*(1), 71–88. doi:10.1016/S0167-9236(98)00086-4

McAdam, R., & Walker, T. (2003). An inquiry into Balanced Scorecards within best value implementation in UK local government. *Public Administration*, *81*(4), 873–892. doi:10.1111/j.0033-3298.2003.00375.x

McFarlan, W. (1984). Information Technology changes the way you compete. *Harvard Business Review*, (May-June), 93–103.

Melville, N., Kraemer, K., & Gurbaxani, V. (2004). Information technology and organizational performance: An integrative model of IT business value. *Management Information Systems Quarterly*, *28*(2), 283–322.

Milis, K., & Mercken, R. (2004). The use of the balanced scorecard for the evaluation of information and communication technology projects. *International Journal of Project Management*, *22*(2), 87–97. doi:10.1016/S0263-7863(03)00060-7

Niven, P. R. (2002). *Balanced scorecard step-by-step: Maximizing performance and maintaining results*. New York: Wiley and Sons.

Nørreklit, H. (2000). The Balanced Scorecard - a critical analysis of some of its assumptions. *Management Accounting Research*, *11*(1), 65–88. doi:10.1006/mare.1999.0121

Othman, R. (2008). Enhancing the effectiveness of Balanced Scorecard with Scenario Planning. *International Journal of Productivity and Performance Management*, *57*(3), 259–266. doi:10.1108/17410400810857266

Otley, D. (1999). Performance management: A framework for management control systems research. *Management Accounting Research*, *10*(4), 363–382. doi:10.1006/mare.1999.0115

Päivärinta, T., & Dertz, W. (2008). Pre-Determinants of Implementing II Benefits Management in Norwegian Municipalities: Cultivate the Context. In M. A. Wimmer, H. J. Scholl, & E. Ferro (Eds.), *Electronic Government* (pp. 111–123). Springer Berlin Heidelberg. doi:10.1007/978-3-540-85204-9_10

Pan, J., & Cheng, M. (2008). An Empirical Study for Exploring the Relationship between Balanced Scorecard and Six Sigma Programs. *Asia Pacific Management Review*, *13*(2), 481–496.

Peppard, J. (2003). Managing IT as a portfolio of services. *European Management Journal*, *21*(4), 467–483. doi:10.1016/S0263-2373(03)00074-4

Peppard, P., Ward, J., & Daniel, E. (2007, March). Managing the Realization of Business Benefits from IT Investments. *MIS Quarterly Executive*.

Pettigrew, A., & Whipp, R. (1991). *Managing change for competitive success.* Oxford, UK: Blackwell Publishers.

Porter, M. E. (2001). Strategy and the internet. *Harvard Business Review*, (March), 63–78. PMID:11246925

Remenyi, D., Money, A., & Sherwood-Smith, M. (2000). *The Effective Measurement and Management of IT Costs and Benefits.* Oxford, UK: Butterworth-Heinemann.

Sapountzis, S., Harris, K., & Kagioglou, M. (2007). Benefits Realisation Process for Healthcare.*International SCRI Symposium*, Salford, UK.

Schaltegger, S., & Wagner, M. (2006). Integrative Management of Sustainability Performance, Measurement and Reporting, International Journal of Accounting. *Auditing and Performance Evaluation*, *3*(1), 1–19. doi:10.1504/IJAAPE.2006.010098

Serra, C. E. M., & Kunc, M. (2015). Benefits Realisation Management and its influence on project success and on the execution of business strategies. *International Journal of Project Management, 33*(1), 53–66. doi:10.1016/j.ijproman.2014.03.011

Shang, S., & Seddon, P. (2002). Assessing and Managing the Benefits of Enterprise Systems: The Business Manager's Perspective. *Information Systems Journal*, *12*(4), 271–299. doi:10.1046/j.1365-2575.2002.00132.x

Teo, T. S. H., & Ang, J. S. K. (1999). Critical success factors in the alignment of IS plans with business plans. *International Journal of Information Management*, *19*(2), 173–185. doi:10.1016/S0268-4012(99)00007-9

Thorp, J. (1999). Computing the payoff from IT. *The Journal of Business Strategy*, *20*(3), 35–39. doi:10.1108/eb040005

Van Grembergen, W., & De Haes, S. (2005). Measuring and improving information technology governance through the balanced scorecard. *Information Systems Control Journal, 2.*

Van Grembergen, W., Saull, R., & De Haes, S. (2003). Linking the IT balanced scorecard to the business objectives at a major Canadian financial group. *Journal of Information Technology Cases and Applications.*

van Lier, J., & Dohmen, T. (2007). Benefits Management and Strategic Alignment in an IT Outsourcing Context. In *Proceedings of the 40th Hawaii International Conference on System Sciences.*

Voelpel, S. C., Leibold, M., Eckhoff, R. A., & Davenport, T. H. (2005). The Tyranny of Balanced Scorecard in the Innovation Economy. In *Proceedings of 4th International Critical Management Studies Conference-Intellectual Capital Stream*. Cambridge University.

Ward, J., & Daniel, E. (2006). *Benefits Management, Delivering Value from IS and IT Investments*. Chichester, UK: John Wiley & Sons Inc.

Ward, J., De Hertogh, S., & Viaene, S. (2007). Managing Benefits from IS/IT Investments: An Empirical Investigation into Current Practice. In *Proceedings of the HICSS 2007- 40th Annual Hawaii International Conference on System Sciences*.

Ward, J., & Elvin, R. (1999). A new framework for managing IT-enabled business change. *Information Systems Journal*, 9(3), 197–221. doi:10.1046/j.1365-2575.1999.00059.x

Ward, J., & Peppard, J. (2002). *Strategic Planning for Information Systems* (3rd ed.). Chichester, UK: John Wiley & Sons Inc.

Ward, J. M., Taylor, P., & Bond, P. (1996). Evaluation and realisation of IS/IT benefits: An empirical study of current practice. *European Journal of Information Systems*, 4(4), 214–225. doi:10.1057/ejis.1996.3

Yang, K. M., Cho, Y. W., Choi, S. H., Park, J. H., & Kang, K. S. (2010). A study on development of Balanced Scorecard using multiple attribute decision making. *Journal of Software Engineering & Applications*, 3, 286–272. doi:10.4236/jsea.2010.33032

Chapter 6
Contemporary Demands on Business and IT Alignment:
How Can Enterprise Modeling Help?

Julia Kaidalova
Jönköping University, Sweden & University of Skövde, Sweden

Ulf Seigerroth
Jönköping University, Sweden

ABSTRACT

The call for Business and IT Alignment (BITA) is an everlasting and increasing concern for today's enterprises. BITA is no longer just a technical or local concern. Instead we need to embrace various dimensions in the concept of BITA, for instance strategic, structural, social and cultural. In addition to this, the development of concepts like Digital Innovation (DI), Internet of Things (IoT), Cyber Physical Systems (CPS) has further challenged the success of BITA. As one approach to deal with the multi-dimensional BITA problem and to move the BITA positions forward, Enterprise Modeling (EM) has been acknowledged as a helpful practice. Particularly, EM provides the opportunity to facilitate the creation of integrated models that capture and represent different focal areas of an enterprise, and allows representing the numerous points of view of the key stakeholders. In order to consider the points of view of different stakeholders and create a shared understanding between them the participative character of EM sessions can play an important role. This chapter presents various challenges that EM practitioners face during participative EM sessions, and a number of recommendations that can help to overcome these challenges.

DOI: 10.4018/978-1-5225-0861-8.ch006

1. INTRODUCTION

Today's dynamic business environment – entwined as it is with rapidly advancing IT capability through digital innovation, internet of things (IoT), cyber physical systems (CPS) etc. – presents enterprises that wish to stay competitive with a great challenge. This is further complicated by the special role that IT now plays in most enterprises, i.e. as a communication backbone for realizing visions, goals, and business models. Indeed, IT can be used to change the way enterprises organize their business processes, how they communicate with their customers and the means by which they deliver their services (Silvius, 2009). However while it is undeniable that suitable IT solutions are required in order to achieve organizational goals, the effective support of business operations with appropriate IT is complicated due to the dynamic nature of business and IT (Luftman, 2003). In early studies Business and IT Alignment (BITA) implied linking the business plan and the IT plan, or alternatively the business strategy and the IT strategy. Later, considerations of BITA started to require consideration of the fit between business needs and information system priorities. These expanded over time and current research recognizes many dimensions of alignment between business and IT (Schlosser, Wagner, & Coltman, 2012). This has also been manifested in other contexts through development of concepts like European Interoperability Framework (European Commission, 2010) and the socio-technical Systems Stack (STS) (Baxter & Sommerville, 2011).

In general, it is possible to differentiate between the strategic, structural, social and cultural dimensions of BITA (Chan & Reich, 2007a). The strategic dimension refers to the degree to which the business strategy and plans, and the IT strategy and plans, complement each other. The structural dimension refers to the degree of structural fit between IT and the business that is influenced by the location of IT decision-making rights, reporting relationships, decentralization of IT, and the deployment of IT personnel. The social dimension refers to how much business and IT executives within an organizational unit understand and are committed to the business and IT mission, objectives, and plans. The cultural dimension refers to the need of IT planning to be aligned with cultural elements such as the business planning style and the top management communication style. Of these, the strategic dimension currently receives significantly more attention (ibid). However, both strategic alignment and structural alignment influence organization performance. In addition, BITA is closely linked to many of the social and cultural aspects of an organization. Improving alignment within these four dimensions permits the increase of IS effectiveness and efficiency, the enhancement of business and IT flexibility, the improvement of business performance and other positive effects (Vargas, 2011; Schlosser et al., 2012). Given that these significant benefits are matched by a number of unresolved issues, it is no surprise that attention to BITA continues to grow (Silvius, 2009).

BITA is often tightly linked to enterprise transformation, i.e. the action of taking an enterprise from one state to an improved state (Seigerroth, 2011). Some enterprises need to deal with transformation reactively while others have the possibility to be more proactive in the planning, design and implementation of changes. Regardless of type of change (reactive or proactive) there appears to be a need to agree on future vision and strategy among the stakeholders and to have a common understanding about the current praxis in the enterprise (Seigerroth, 2015). Therefore, if BITA is to be achieved, there needs to be a clear and up-to-date representation of the enterprise AS-IS and TO-BE states that accurately reflects – for the different stakeholders within the enterprise – the various aspects that these states imply.

The various aspects of an enterprise can include organizational structure, business processes, information systems, and infrastructure, which together form an Enterprise Architecture. Jonkers, Lankhorst, van Buuren, Hoppenbrouwers, Bonsangue, and van der Torre (2004) describe Enterprise Architecture (EA) and Enterprise Architecture Management (EAM), where EA is a coherent set of principles, methods and models that are used in the design and realization of these various aspects of an enterprise. Coherent description of various components of EA is able to provide insights, enable communication among stakeholders and guide complicated transformation processes (Jonkers et al. 2004). The unambiguous description of EA components and their relationships requires a coherent modeling language (Jonkers et al., 2004). The recent developments within digital innovation, CPS, and IoT has though pointed out a big challenge for EA and EAM. This development has challenged both the adaptation of products and processes, and the adaptation of enterprise-IT. In particular enterprises in manufacturing industries or in sectors where a lot of value creation is represented by IT-components built into the products find a lot of new opportunities created by seamless and real-time integration of physical systems and IT. However, these new products and services require a tight integration of what often is separated in many enterprises into enterprise-IT (i.e. the IT supporting business and administrative parts) and product-IT (i.e., what is built into the products or supporting industrial automation). EA and EAM is a means to support both, continuous alignment of business and IT, and the integration of product-IT and enterprise-IT to make innovations triggered by CPS and IoT to come true.

Enterprise Modeling (EM) has in this context been described as one of the acknowledged and widely used practices (Chen, Kazman, & Garg, 2005; Stirna & Persson, 2009). EM facilitates the creation a number of integrated models which capture and represent different aspects (focal areas) of an enterprise, for example business processes, business rules, concepts, information, data, vision, goals and actors (Stirna & Persson, 2009). Chen, Kazman, and Garg (2005) define enterprise models as visual structures, which represent the key components of the business that needs to be understood. The inherent power of enterprise models is their ability to depict and represent an enterprise from a number of perspectives (Chen, Kasman & Garg, 2005). Therefore, EM can foster a multidimensional understanding of an enterprise and it can integrate these dimensions into a coherent structure where different parts (focal areas) contribute to the whole structure (Frank, 2002). These capabilities of enterprise models provide a powerful mechanism for dealing with the strategic and structural dimensions of BITA.

On the other hand, solving BITA problem requires dealing with the numerous points of view of the stakeholders and creating a shared understanding between them, which refers to the social and cultural dimensions of BITA (Jonkers et al., 2004; Kearns & Lederer, 2003; Reich & Benbasat, 2000). In this regard EM is also able to provide solid support, as it is often used to develop a common understanding of the current multidimensional praxis and an agreement on future vision and strategies (Stirna & Persson, 2009). EM can be used for a broad range of purposes that require consensus-driven collaboration between stakeholders and decision makers; for example, development of business vision and strategies, redesign of business practice, development of supporting information systems, knowledge sharing about business or decision-making (Strirna & Persson, 2009).

The potential of EM to facilitate BITA has been recognized by number of researchers (e.g., Chan & Reich, 2007a; Gregor, Hart, & Martin, 2007; Wegmann et al., 2007; Seigerroth, 2011; Christiner, Lantow, Sandkuhl, & Wissotzki, 2012). However, according to McGinnis (2007), despite the contribution that EM can offer in supporting BITA, the creation of shared understanding between business and IT people receives scant attention in studies considering the role of EM in BITA. Clearly, the collaborative nature of EM and its usefulness for BITA achievement requires further investigation.

This study therefore focuses on participative EM, which is a highly collaborative process, where various stakeholders' interests and perspectives are considered and consolidated (Stirna & Kirikova, 2008) (e.g., the process of developing/creating models of different views on the whole enterprise as well as specific parts of the enterprise). The aim of modeling sessions is to collect required information about the enterprise (domain knowledge) and transform this information into models. The models usually evolve through discussion that enables their incremental refinement. There are usually two parties involved in such collaborative EM efforts:

1. Participants from the enterprise who have domain knowledge (domain experts), and

2. An EM practitioner (also called modeling expert, modeling facilitator or modeler) who leads and coordinates the modeling session(s).

The role of the EM practitioner is vital for the success of modeling initiatives and for managing the collaborative dimensions of EM (Rosemann, Lind, Hjalmarsson, & Recker, 2011). EM practitioners therefore need to have a broad range of knowledge about collaborative EM techniques and considerable experience of EM execution, since various problems and challenges can occur during the actual EM sessions and during the follow-up activities (Stirna & Persson, 2009). EM practitioners express a need for structured recommendations, a requirement that has been highlighted by several scholars (i.e. cf. Bandara, Gable, & Rosemann, 2005; Stirna & Persson, 2009; Mendling, Reijers, & van der Aalst, 2010). Identification of EM challenges can be used in this context as a base for generating such recommendations. There is a number of studies available that present different modeling challenges and recommendations (Bandara, Gable, & Rosemann, 2005; Mendling, Reijers, & van der Aalst, 2010). However, most of these studies do not focus on collaborative nature of EM, but rather focus on the characteristics of the resulting enterprise models. There are only a few EM studies that investigate the collaborative aspect of EM (e.g., c.f. Stirna, Persson, & Sandkuhl, 2007). Ensuring sufficient quality in the collaboration between various stakeholders involved in EM is also important in order to succeed with the intended enterprise change. Therefore, the purpose with this chapter is to investigate challenges that EM practitioners are facing during EM sessions, and in the conduct of related EM activities, considering both:

1. The collaborative nature of EM, which can help to deal with social and cultural dimensions of BITA, and
2. The required characteristics of the created enterprise models, which can help to deal with strategic and structural dimensions of BITA.

Furthermore, EM practitioners require recommendations on how to deal with these challenges. Based on the above, the following overall research question have been formulated:

How Can BITA Be Facilitated through EM?

The rest of the chapter is structured in the following way: Section 2 presents related research. Section 3 then describes the research method. In Section 4 the results are introduced, including EM challenges and recommendations structured into an integrated framework. The chapter ends with conclusions and future research in Section 5.

2. RELATED RESEARCH

Several scholars have emphasized the need to capture both organization (business) and technology during design and implementation of Information System (IS) (i.e. cf. Orlikowski & Hofman, 1997; Gibson, 2003). Enterprise models are abstractions of complex enterprises and serve to support communication, dissemination and reuse of knowledge (Frank, 2014). Enterprise models are able to capture different aspects (focal areas) of an enterprise´s practices in terms of procedures, operations, and management. In this respect EM has a strong capability to facilitate BITA (Seigerroth, 2011).

EM, sometimes also referred to as "business modeling", is a practice for developing, obtaining, and communicating enterprise knowledge (like strategies, goals and requirements) to different stakeholders (Stirna & Kirikova, 2008). Sandkuhl, Stirna, Persson, and Wissotzki (2014) define EM as:

EM is the process of creating an integrated enterprise model which captures the aspects of the enterprise required for the modeling purpose at hand. An enterprise in this context can be a private company, government department, academic institution, other kind of organization, or part thereof. An enterprise model consists of a number of related sub-models, each focusing on a particular aspect of the enterprise, e.g. processes, business rules, concepts/information, vision/goals, and actors. An enterprise model describes the current or future state of an enterprise and contains the commonly shared enterprise knowledge of the stakeholders involved in the modeling process. (Sandkuhl et al., 2014, p.29)

An EM activity usually comprises both intra-organizational and inter-organizational processes (Barjis, 2011). In order to analyze these processes a large number of stakeholders have to be involved in EM, which makes the traditional consultative approach (i.e. fact gathering, analysis, and delivering an expert opinion) hardly applicable when dealing with so called "wicked" problems (Persson, 2001; Stirna et al., 2007). As a result, participative or collaborative EM, where modeling sessions in groups are led by EM practitioners, has been established as an approach to deal with organizational design problems. The idea of collaboration and interaction has earlier also been described and formalized as non-interactive and interactive modeling where the purpose is to expand the shared knowledge through EM. Lind and Seigerroth (2003) have presented a framework where they divided the modeling process into four generic modeling phases:

1.   Interactive collection,
2.   Interactive modeling,

3.   Non interactive modeling, and

4.   Interactive validation.

Interactive collection is the phase where the modeling experts together with the business people set the scope for the upcoming modeling sessions in order to agree upon what to focus on and what not to focus on. The two next phases are the actual modeling phases where answers interactively are expressed and structured using of different model types. Interactive modeling is where answers are expressed and structured together with the respondent(s). Non-interactive modeling is a phase where answers are further structured and refined in models without any involvement of the respondent(s). This phase usually also involve the transformation of models into some IT-based tool. The last phase, Interactive validation includes a mutual agreement about the structured answers that are manifested in models being developed between the respondent(s) and the modeling experts (c.f. Lind & Seigerroth, 2003). This process is one way to conceptualize the transformation of information into enterprise models.

Generally stakeholders who are involved in participative EM can be divided into two parties - participants from the enterprise itself and an EM practitioner (or facilitator) that leads the modeling activities. The first group of stakeholders consists of enterprise employees who have the role to share and exchange their knowledge about enterprise operations (domain knowledge). There are various factors that can hinder the process of sharing knowledge between enterprise employees. For example, as the project progresses the enterprise becomes less interested to allocate their most knowledgeable human resources to modeling sessions, since it can be considered as a waste of time (Barjis, 2009). The second party of EM is an EM practitioner – a person who facilitates and drives the EM project process (partly or fully) towards effectively achieving its goals (Persson & Stirna, 2010). This role is responsible for making sure that the project resources are used properly in order to achieve the goals of the project and to complete the project on time (Persson & Stirna, 2010; Rosemann et al., 2011).

Performing collaborative EM successfully is not a trivial task that requires considerable skills and experience, since the EM practitioner needs to manage the intricate act of discovering and capturing domain knowledge, negotiating and consolidating different stakeholder views, and transforming this knowledge in coherent and comprehensive models (Stirna, Persson, & Sandkuhl, 2007). Among the core challenges of EM Barjis (2009) has highlighted the complex socio-technical nature of an enterprise and conflicting descriptions of the business given by different actors (c.f. Baxter & Sommerville 2011).

The role of the EM practitioner therefore becomes vital for the success of any modeling initiative (Rosemann et al., 2011). One dimension of improving the practice of EM would be to create a clearer understanding about EM challenges and to take the advantage of existing EM recommendations, best practices and patterns. Aimed on investigating challenges and guidelines of EM, this study also takes into account existing studies in such areas as business process modeling and business modeling, since they can provide some useful insights regarding modeling practice in a broad sense.

The Enterprise Modeling Process

It is important to have a conceptual understanding of the processes and activities that EM usually involves. One way to view EM projects in terms of involved activities was presented by Persson and Stirna (2012). According to them, a stereotypical EM process involves the following steps: (1) Define scope and objectives of the project, (2) Plan for project activities and resources, (3) Plan for modeling session, (4) Gather and analyze background information, (5) Interview modeling participants, (6) Prepare modeling session, (7) Conduct modeling session, (8) Write meeting minutes, (9) Analyze and refine models, and (10) Present the results to stakeholders. Similar to this but on a more general level Lind and Seigerroth (2003) discuss the process of team-based collaborative knowledge reconstruction based on modeling and identify four basic activities: interactive collection, interactive modeling, non-interactive modeling, and interactive validation. Another more generic view on EM is presented by Kaidalova et al. (2014) where according to this model, EM processes include three basic activities that are usually performed in sequential order, but in some cases can roll back (see Figure 1).

In this framework the first activity of EM is to collect information about the enterprise in focus. During participative EM, where domain experts play an important role the main source for getting information are modeling sessions or workshops. During such sessions the EM practitioner is supposed to have a leading role and collect opinions about various aspects of the enterprise. The ability of the EM practitioner to facilitate open discussions is crucial in order to extract the necessary

Figure 1. EM activities

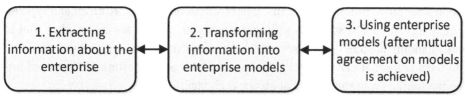

information and then to transform this information into enterprise models, i.e. to visualize the obtained information in a structured way in the form of enterprise models (activity 2 in Figure 1). Most often models are created during modeling sessions together with domain experts to make sure that existing viewpoints are considered and consolidated. It is a common practice to iterate between the first and the second activity several times when creating models to make sure that all the needed information has been captured and documented.

However, in some cases the manifestation or actual visualization of models can be done after the modeling sessions. It is important to emphasize that documentation of models is a continuous process, which will continue until a common agreement on the created models is achieved among the involved participants. There are various challenges that are specific for these two activities of EM - extracting enterprise-related information and documenting it into models. Common agreement among the stakeholders on creating enterprise models is crucial in order to use the created enterprise models for any purpose (activity 3). The objectives to achieve consensus and get a shared understanding about different enterprise aspects (focal areas) can play a central role in EM initiative, but often enterprise models serve as a visualization and blueprints for the required change process.

This model is quite generic and provides a high-level overview of EM process. It will later in this chapter be used as a ground for structuring EM challenges and recommendations.

Business and IT Alignment and Enterprise Modeling

One of the reasons contributing to the misalignment between business and IT is the lack of a common understanding between the business and information systems worlds (Singh & Woo, 2009). The achievement of BITA requires the alignment of the representations of the multiple viewpoints that an enterprise embodies. Many studies have acknowledged EM as a potential means to resolve this misalignment and facilitate BITA. Gregor et al. (2007) regard EM as one of catalyzing mechanisms for aligning the business and IT dimensions of an enterprise. According to Christiner et al. (2012) EM can support BITA by providing means for capturing, visualizing and improving different perspectives of an enterprise, including processes, organization structures, products, systems, and business objectives. Karlsen and Opdahl (2012) argue that EM supports strategic alignment, since it serves as a key tool in understanding business processes and as a prerequisite for business improvements, and what is more it can be used as a tool in conversation, communication and understanding in programs aimed at business change.

One of the most common reasons to use EM is the development or refinement of enterprise information systems (IS). In this context it is important for enterprise success that information technology (IT) supports business needs, processes and strategies (Silvius, 2009). Nowadays, with a rich variety of tools and IT solutions available for businesses, it has become increasingly difficult to manage the ever more frenetic pace of their continuous development and transformation. The problem is made more challenging by the dynamic nature of both business and IT (Vargas, 2011). Research has shown that alignment of business with IT is often addressed as a top concern of IT and business practitioners (Luftman & McLean, 2004; Chan & Reich, 2007). This is possibly caused by the organizational impact that successful BITA can achieve and its positive influence on business performance (De Haes & Van Grembergen, 2010; Vargas, 2011). There are numerous practices that aim at improving BITA and each of them has different methods and tools at their disposal. De Haes and Van Grembergen (2010) discuss various practice-oriented frameworks such as Enterprise Governance of IT (EGIT), and COBIT and Val IT. They argue, in particular, that implementation of EGIT impacts the achievement of specific IT goals, which in turn impacts the achievement of business goals. One way to classify these methods and tools was proposed by Aversano, Grasso, & Tortorella (2012), who propose BITA process model that includes three steps:

1.   Modeling of alignment-related elements,
2.   Alignment evaluation, and
3.   Evolution execution (see Figure 2).

This process model recommends that first all elements that are involved in the alignment analysis should be modeled. Thereafter it is possible to evaluate the degree of current alignment. It is obvious that EM is mostly applicable during (1)

Figure 2. Business and IT alignment process model
Aversano, Grasso, & Tortorella, 2012.

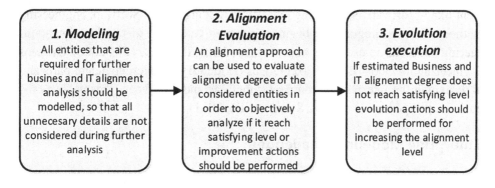

modeling phase, but it is also of help during (2) alignment evaluation and (3) evolution execution phases, since it provides a solid basis for discussions and actions.

Another challenge in the area of BITA is the emergent importance of digital innovation, IoT, and CPS in relation to EA and EAM. The areas of EA, EAM, and product-IT both have attracted a lot of research during the last 10 years. However, not much work has been spent on their integration, i.e. to position product-IT into EAM considerations. EA and EAM has received a lot of attention in industry as it is considered as one of the key activities to keep the IT of an organization aligned with the business challenges (Ahlemann et al., 2012). In general, an EA captures and structures all relevant components for describing an enterprise, including the processes used for development of the EA as such (Lankhorst, 2013). Research activities in EAM are manifold. The literature analysis included in Wißotzki Sandkuhl, 2015 shows that elements of EAM (Buckl et al. 2011) process and principles (Sandkuhl et al., 2015), and implementation drivers and strategies (Keuntje & Barkow, 2010) are among the frequently researched subjects. However, there is not much work on practices of EAM implementation.

There is a huge body of knowledge in the field of engineering embedded systems, industrial automation solutions or hardware/software systems, but a lack of work in integration of this product-IT into EA. Most product-IT developments seem to assume that development of the actual system and the integration of this system into operational processes in the enterprise are different activities, which can be supported by different methods. Not only is the internal communication between physical system and IT system affected by real-time communication but also the related enterprise systems and possibly even actors in the enterprise other than the users and operators of the actual CPS. Thus, we need a much more integrated method support for system development and system integration into business. The state-of-research in development of CPS shows that there is no dedicated CPS development methodology, instead we are using systems engineering methods (e.g. Bassi et al. 2011), pragmatic approaches (e.g. Hackmann et al., 2014) or incremental development like in software engineering (e.g. Ringert et al., 2014). Software engineering methods usually integrate the business perspective as part of requirements engineering but focus on use-cases or process modeling (Sommerville, 2006). Systems engineering methods (Buede, 2011) focus on identifying interdependent parts and in designing the internal environment, functions and interfaces. This neglects the business perspective (Baxter & Sommerville, 2011).

Enterprise Modeling Challenges

Kaidalova, Seigerroth, Kaczmarek & Shilov (2012) has identified a set of EM challenges. These challenges are related to essential characteristics of the resulting enterprise models and to the process of EM considering its collaborative nature. The first challenge is the degree of formalism. The degree of formalism is closely related to notation and notation rules for different enterprise models. There are different modeling notations that are used depending on enterprise perspectives (focal areas) that are in focus. The degree of formalism in enterprise models can vary from formal machine interpretable languages to more informal rich pictures. The expressiveness of the selected formalism will have impact on the final models. The second challenge is related to the degree of detail. In practice it is usually a challenge to decide how much information a model should contain in order to describe a certain situation. The third challenge includes the accuracy of the view related to the chosen modeling perspective. It is a challenge to select the suitable point of view(s) during modeling and stay focused on the chosen point of view, i.e. the selection of suitable focal areas like process, problem, goal, resources etc. The fourth challenge is the change and model dependencies. This challenge refers to the fact that modeling is usually done in a dynamic and constantly changing environment. Models should usually be used as a support during enterprise change. In a dynamic and changing environment this means that models also need to continuously undergo changes. It is common that modeling is performed at different levels at the same time (i.e. business model, process, IS/IT infrastructure) where one or several focal areas can be modeled within or between different levels. This multilayered modeling and change means that one model or layer of the models might have consequences for other models within or between different layers. The fifth challenge is scope of the area for investigation, which is related to the need to limit the area for investigation depending on the modeling goals and intentions. Another group of challenges related to the collaborative nature of EM includes the challenges of capturing the right information, dealing with group dynamics and human behaviors, sharing language and terminology with the participants of a modeling session, clarification of the purpose of EM and roles of stakeholders within it. These challenges have served as the most significant part of the theoretical basis when generating the EM framework.

Rexhepi (2012) identifies a number of EM challenges and divides them in three groups:

1. Challenges that can occur before modeling sessions;
2. Challenges that occur during modeling sessions;
3. Challenges that occur after modeling session.

The first group includes conducting EM without given guidelines, to anchor EM, to identify the purpose of EM, to gain access to the resources, to deal with "everyone is participating", to identify the key stakeholders and make them participate, to identify the right method according to the purpose and participants. The second group of challenges includes dealing with special interests, achieving consensus between various professional, to avoid taking the leading role, to identify "slow-doers". The third group includes the challenge of making models reused.

Delen et al. (2005) investigate the challenges of EM and identify four with regard to the decision maker's point of view: heterogeneous methods and tools, model correlation, representation extensibility, and enterprise model compiling.

Raduescu et al. (2006) identify a framework of issues related to large-scale process modeling projects that are relevant for various involved stakeholders (e.g. business analysts, modelers, vendors and managers). They divide identified is-sues into three groups:

1. Strategy-level related issues;
2. Process modeling lifecycle issues;
3. Resource-level related issues.

The first group includes the following issues: lack of top management support, lack of governance, doubts about the economic value. The second group includes the following issues during the setup phase: lack of project setup guidelines, lack of modeling objectives, lack of modeling procedures (Standards/Policy), lack of common modeling methodology (Standardization), lack of supporting infrastructure, during the design phase: model aspects and levels of granularity, model quality assurance, during the maintenance phase: rework and update of models, variant management, consolidation and integration. The third group includes a number of issues for each of the involved roles. Modeler related issues are related to the skill set of a modeler and familiarity with the application domain. It is also important to remember that the quality of a model depends on both the ability of the modeler to extract relevant information from business experts and on the modeler's own knowledge of the business context.

Persson and Stirna (2010) have presented an analysis that elucidates the competence needs for EM practitioners with regard to different steps in the EM process. They consider that the EM process consists of the following activities: project inception and planning, conducting modeling sessions, delivering a result that can be used for subsequent implementation. Two main competence areas that Stirna and Persson (2010) have identified are competences related to modeling (ability to model and ability to facilitate a modeling session) and competences related to managing EM projects. Among abilities that belong to the second group they mention the ability to select an appropriate EM approach and tailor it in order to fit the situation at hand; the ability to interview involved domain experts; the ability to define a relevant problem; the ability to define requirements on the results; the ability to establish a modeling project; the ability to adjust a presentation of project results and issues related to them to various stakeholders; the ability to navigate between the wishes of various stakeholders while upholding the EM project goal; the ability to assess the impact of the modeling result and the modeling process in the organization.

Another view on the required competence of EM practitioner is presented by Rosemann et al. (2011) where they argue that the roles of the modeling facilitator has not been researched enough and they therefore present a framework that describes four roles that the EM practitioners can play. There are ten styles of facilitation behavior, which can characterize these four roles: communication style (talking vs. listening), power style (assertive vs. empathic), adaption style (static vs. flexible), disagreement style (embraces conflict vs. avoids conflict), control style (central-ized vs. decentralized), model behavior (does model vs. al-lows model), facilitation behavior (do facilitation vs. allow facilitation), involvement style (involving vs. ignoring), work style (structured vs. unstructured), domain knowledge style (domain agnostic vs. domain expert).

Yet another topic related to EM challenges is EM critical success factors (Bandara et al., 2005, Rosemann et al., 2001). Bandara et al. (2005) divide these critical suc-cess factors of business process modeling into two groups: project-specific factors (stakeholder participation, management support, information resources, project management, modeler experience) and modeling-related factors (modeling meth-odology, modeling language, modeling tool). Rosemann et al. (2001) identifies the factors that influence process modeling success: modeling methodology, modeling language, modeling tool, modelers' expertise, modeling team orientation, project management, user participation, and management support. The overview of these theories is presented in Table 1.

Recommendations for Enterprise Modeling

There are several studies, which introduce different kinds of guidelines for carrying out modeling. A significant part of these guidelines are non-procedural and they often deal with various quality aspects of modeling, (Becker, Rosemann, & von Uthmann, 2000; Koehler & Vanhatalo, 2007; Muehlen, Wisnosky, & Kindrick, 2010; Sandkuhl et al., 2014). Persson (2001) introduces a number of guidelines for six types of situational factors that are specific for participative EM: organizational factors, project definition, resources factors, problem factors, competency factors, and human factors. Stirna et al. (2007) describe a set of experiences related to applying EM in different organizational contexts. They present a set of generic principles for applying participative EM. Their principles mark out five high-level recommenda-tions of using participative EM: assess the organizational context, assess the problem

Table 1. Studies framing EM challenges

Concept in Focus	Study	Content
EM challenges	Kaidalova, Seigerroth, Kaczmarek & Shilov (2012)	• Degree of formalism • Degree of details • Modeling perspective • Change and model dependencies • Scope of the area for investigation • The right information • Group dynamics and human behavior • Shared language and terminology • The purpose of EM and roles of stakeholders within it
	Rexhepi (2012)	• Challenges that can occur before modeling sessions: conducting EM without given guidelines; to anchor EM; to identify the purpose of EM; to gain access to the resources; to deal with "everyone is participating"; to identify the key stakeholders and make them participate; to identify the right method according to the purpose and participants. • Challenges that occur during modeling sessions: dealing with special interests; achieving consensus between various professional; to avoid taking the leading role; to identify "slow-doers". • Challenges that occur after modeling session: the challenge of making models re-used
	Delen, Dalal, & Benjamin (2005)	• Heterogeneous methods and tools • Model correlation • Representation extensibility • Enterprise model compiling
Issues in process modeling projects	Raduescu, Tan, Jayaganesh, Bandara, zur Muehlen, & Lippe (2006)	• Strategy-level related issues: lack of top management support; lack of governance; doubts about the economic value. • Process modeling lifecycle issues: lack of project setup guidelines, lack of modeling objectives, lack of modeling procedures, lack of common modeling methodology, lack of supporting infra-structure; model aspects and levels of granularity, model quality assurance; rework and update of models, variant management, consolidation and integration. • Resources-level related issues: modeler-related issues include skills of a modeler and familiarity with the application domain. The quality of a model depends on both the ability of the modeler to extract relevant information from business experts and on the modeler's own knowledge of the business context.
The competence of EM practitioner	Persson and Stirna (2010)	• Competences related to modeling (ability to model and ability to facilitate a modeling session) • Competences related to managing EM projects
	Rosemann et al. (2011)	• Communication style (talking vs. listening) • Power style (assertive vs. empathic) • Adaption style (static vs. flexible) • Disagreement style (embraces conflict vs. avoids conflict) • Control style (centralized vs. decentralized) • Model behavior (does model vs. allows model) • Facilitation behavior (do facilitation vs. allow facilitation) • Involvement style (involving vs. ignoring) • Work style (structured vs. unstructured) • Domain knowledge style (domain agnostic vs. domain expert)

continued on following page

Table 1. Continued

Concept in Focus	Study	Content
Business process modeling critical success factors	Bandara, Gable, & Rosemann (2005)	• Project-specific factors: stakeholder participation, management support, information resources, project management, modeler experience; • Modeling-related factors: modeling methodology, modeling language, modeling tool
	Rosemann, Sedera, Gable (2001)	• Modeling methodology • Modeling language • Modeling tool • Modelers' expertise • Modeling team orientation • Project management • User participation • Management support

at hand, assign roles in the modeling process, acquire re-sources for the project in general and for preparation efforts in particular, and conduct modeling sessions.

Stirna and Persson (2009) introduce guidelines for carrying out EM in the form of anti-patterns that reflect common and reoccurring pitfalls of EM projects. The presented anti-patterns address three aspects of EM: the modeling product, the modeling process, and the modeling tool support. These three groups include a number of anti-patterns – solutions that are quite commonly used, but that are wrong. For example, among anti-patterns related to the modeling process the following can be mentioned: everybody acts as a facilitator, the facilitator acts as a domain expert. Anti-patterns related to modeling tool support include the following issues: models keep themselves "alive", professionals use only computerized tools, everyone embraces a new tool. These guidelines are mostly related to dealing with collaborative nature of EM, but not focusing on the desired characteristics of models.

A set of guidelines that aiming to create sound process models has been presented by Mendling et al. (2010). These guidelines focus on certain characteristics of models such as the number of elements (it should be minimized), their structure (one start and end element), routes between elements (it should be minimized), etc. This set of guidelines provides support for creating models, but it does not focus on dealing with the collaborative nature of EM. The overview of these theories is presented in Table 2.

These theories can be considered as parts contributing to a broader picture of EM challenges and recommendations for BITA.

Table 2. Studies framing EM recommendations

Concept in Focus	Study	Content
Situational factors that influence the applicability and application of participative EM	Persson (2001)	• Organizational factor • Project definition • Resources factor • Problem factor • Competency factor • Human factor
Generic principles for applying participative EM	Stirna et al. (2007)	• Assess the organizational context • Assess the problem at hand • Assign roles in the modeling process • Acquire resources for the project in general and for preparation efforts in particular • Conduct modeling sessions
Anti-patterns for participative EM	Stirna and Persson (2009)	• Anti-patterns for the modeling product • Anti-patterns for the modeling process • Anti-patterns for the modeling tool support
Process modeling guidelines	Mendling, Reijers, van der Aalst (2010)	• Number of elements should be minimized • The structure of elements (one start and end element) • The routes between elements should be minimized and others

3. RESEARCH APPROACH

A general overview of the applied research approach is presented in Figure 3 below. This research was performed using an iterative and cumulative approach with a focus on identifying EM challenges and deriving recommendations, which were then structured into an EM framework.

From the research motivation and research questions presented in the introduction it follows that the main aim of this study is to investigate EM practice in terms of challenges and recommendations that are relevant for the context of BITA. Together, the EM challenges and recommendations form an EM framework, which plays a central role in the study. The research approach includes three iterations that are aimed to refine the EM framework. There are three versions of the framework: the initial EM framework, the intermediate EM framework and the final EM framework. Both theoretical and empirical foundations have been used to generate and validate the results iteratively, so that the aim of this study could be achieved. The theoretical foundation includes relevant theories from EM, BITA and other related domains. Empirical foundation includes empirical material on the practice of EM collected via interviews. These foundations help to generate and validate the EM framework in each of the iterations of the research process.

Figure 3. The overview of the iterative research process

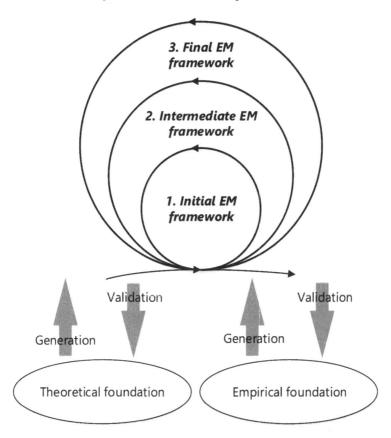

The main idea in following the cumulative research approach was to refine and present an EM framework that utilized the results from previously performed research steps. The content of the EM framework is related to the three EM activities presented in Figure 1, i.e. extracting information about the enterprise, transforming information into enterprise models, and using enterprise models. The research started by generating an initial framework that included a structured set of EM challenges. In the next step (2) the initial framework was validated and refined, which resulted in generation of an Intermediate EM Framework (Kaidalova et al., 2012). In the final step (3) the Intermediate EM Framework was validated and refined. This enabled the Final EM Framework to be generated, incorporating EM challenges and recommendations for all three EM activities.

The empirical data for validation of the EM Framework and its refinement has been captured through interviews. Interview as a data collection technique is widely used in information systems research. Interviews are especially useful for collecting qualitative data and for the purpose of understanding people's points of view regarding a certain phenomenon (Williamson, 2002). In order to collect the empirical material the following steps were taken: interview design, selection of respondents, conduct of interviews, analysis of interview data and result generation, which are described below.

Interview Design

Empirical data has been collected through semi-structured interviews. This technique was chosen because semi-structured interviews enable a flexible dialog with respondents that cover both predefined areas for investigation and allows the interviewer to follow up with additional questions (Saunders, Lewis, & Thornhill, 2006). Performing semi-structured interviews has allowed the capture of in-depth, rich, and purposeful data. Given that the interview questions were designed to investigate EM challenges and possible recommendations, the resulting responses have made a coherent and comprehensive contribution to the knowledge about EM itself, and about the applicability of EM for BITA.

Selection of Respondents

In order to capture relevant empirical data specific selection criteria were established to find suitable respondents. The main selection criterion was significant experience in EM, including both the management of modeling sessions and the usage of created models for various purposes. Based on these criteria four business development consultants were chosen for interviews, each having 5 and more years of active EM experience. The respondents' details are presented in Table 3.

Conduct of Interviews

In order to get started with the interviews the respondents were provided with a brief description of the purpose of the interviews in advance, together with the previously identified EM challenges and recommendations. This initial stage had the goal to give the respondents suitable background information. A prepared interview guide was used during all interviews.

Analysis of Interview Data and Result Generation

All interviews were recorded and then transcribed as a base for subsequent analysis. Having the interviews transcribed into textual format allowed a systematic qualitative analysis with categorization and unitizing of the data (Saunders, Lewis, & Thornhill,

Table 3. Chosen respondents

Respondent	Information about a Respondent
Respondent 1	Employed at consultancy firm working with business development. Senior Management Consultant with more than 10 years of experience within: • Business transformation; • Business process design; • Project management.
Respondent 2	Employed at consultancy firm working with business development, process improvement and education (execution of EM workshops). Consultant with more than 15 years of experience within: • Business development; • Product development and structuring; • Strategic competence analysis and management; • EM workshop facilitation; • Education for EM workshops facilitation, EM and business process modeling.
Respondent 3	Employed at consultancy firm working with business development, process improvement and broad range of EM education. At the moment of interview employed at Jönköping University. Consultant with more than 5 years of experience within: • Business development; • EM workshop facilitation; • Requirement engineering and project management for IT support.
Respondent 4	Employed at consultancy firm working with business development, process improvement and broad range of EM education. Consultant with more than 10 years of experience within: • Business development; • Process improvement; • Requirement engineering and project management for IT support; • EM workshop facilitation.

2006). Validity claims raised for our scientific contribution are in accordance with multi-grounded theory (MGT) (Goldkuhl & Cronholm, 2003), which was used for categorization and unitization of the interviews. The validity claims are that the Final EM Framework is internally, externally, and empirically justified. In this work such claims are raised for categorical knowledge about challenges and recommendations related to EM in the context of BITA. These categories have been derived from the interviews as well as from theoretical standpoints. MGT has thus been adopted in a combined inductive and deductive research approach for the analysis. MGT was originally a reaction to grounded theory and its purer inductive approach. MGT is a process for theory development in three integrated steps, all of these steps might include theory-informed open coding, axial and selective coding. The first step is theory generation, the second step is explicit grounding and the final step is research interest, reflection and revision (cf. Goldkuhl & Cronholm, 2003).

Categorization implies classifying data into meaningful categories by adding codes and labels to data to provide them with an emergent structure. Names for labels that were used for codifying the data in the research originated both from the names used in theoretical standpoints (assigning interpretation) and the terms used in the interviews by the respondents (uncovering interpretation). Following the coding steps in MGT the set of assigned labels were then evolved into the set of categories. After that it was possible to unitize the data. Unitizing data is designed as attaching relevant units of data to the corresponding categories, where units of data are lines or paragraphs of transcribed data (Saunders, Lewis, & Thornhill, 2006). This approach was used to generate both EM challenges and recommendations.

4. RESULTS

According to the research method described above, the role of EM in BITA context has been investigated and analyzed. The respondents' views at the relationship between EM and BITA support the analysis. Also, the Final EM Framework with a refined conceptual structure of Enterprise Modeling challenges (see Figure 4) has been generated.

The study resulted in formulation of recommendations that can serve as support for EM practitioners when dealing with specified challenges. The analysis of the interviews confirmed the conceptual distinction between challenges specific to each of for the three EM activities presented earlier in Figure 1. Identified EM challenges and recommendations are related to the three EM activities:

1. Extracting information about the enterprise,
2. Transforming this information into enterprise models, and
3. Using enterprise models.

Business and IT Alignment and Enterprise Modeling

The analysis of the interviews shows that the respondents have acknowledged the applicability of EM to achieving BITA. The interview analysis has also shown that the respondents have often used EM in projects that are aiming at the development and/or improvement of Information System (IS) as support for enterprise actions.

Enterprise modeling can be used either to capture opportunities in market place or to adjust something that does not operate properly. In most cases it implies changes in Information System." (Respondent 2)

Figure 4. Final conceptual structure of EM challenges

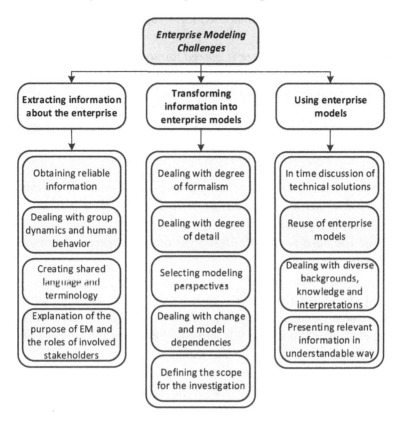

One starting point – there is a need to change the system. Another starting point is the need to develop business processes in order to become more efficient, where certain IT support is needed to make that happen. (Respondent 3)

The respondents supported the widely held view that enterprise models are used throughout all phases of IS development. They further endorsed the use of enterprise models as a base for evolutionary specification and contextualization, which depict the requirements for certain IS/IT structures.

Mostly you use enterprise models to show smarter ways of working that enterprise can realize. Often implementation of new IT system is one way of fulfilling these changes. (Respondent 4)

Alternatively, enterprise models are able to deal with the already existing IS (legacy systems) and show how new requirements can be integrated with existing

IS structures. After that specific enterprise models (i.e. process models and use cases) can be used to elaborate on needed IS/IT functionality.

I used EM a lot to identify if there is a need for some type of IT solution. If there is such a need then I have to create functionality descriptions based on business processes to get business use cases (Respondent 3)

An important advantage that is advocated with the usage of enterprise models is their visualization capabilities.

You need to visualize things – show those parts of information systems that are useful and those which are not. Then it is possible to take actions related to the parts that are not useful anymore. You have to model the actual situation - make nice pictures of it! You need to visualize the status of the systems within the company. (Respondent 1)

Often enterprise models provide a basis for discussing the requirements for IT systems functionality, but do not contain software requirements as such. The benefit of applying enterprise models for this purpose is evident, as business needs can be discussed without too early digging into technical details.

I did the business side of requirements, whereas software requirements were defined by someone else based on processes models, concept model, goal model that I have done. (Respondent 3)

In addition, enterprise models often also serve as a mean for maintenance of IS/IT structures that exist in enterprises.

Usually we need to use enterprise models to create or maintain some kind of IT application. (Respondent 4)

However, an ability of enterprise models that can be considered as the most crucial and beneficial in relation to BITA problem is the ability to slice enterprise reality into comprehensible chunks, i.e. focal areas, and then link several focal areas together into a coherent whole.

The power of enterprise models is the opportunity to see different perspectives of an enterprise. You can see all these different perspectives and based on that you can use the results for different purposes. (Respondent 1)

Focal areas or perspectives that should be considered during EM are contextually situated and will vary between different projects. For example, a set of focal areas that has been considered and analyzed for IS development described by Respondent 3 included the following perspectives: information, concept, organization, and business rules.

It never works with only one perspective! There is usually some sort of information model in the bottom, which is related to conceptual models and organizational models. Also business rules can be quite big part of the system. (Respondent 3)

From the analysis of the interviews it has also become evident that the respondents have a limited enterprise focus during EM. Even when BITA is the expressed purpose for the EM activities we have found evidence for that it still is a limited scope of the modeling that has been applied. For instance if we relate to the socio-technical stack (STS) it is usually a limited number of adherent layers that are addressed, preferably the lower layers of the STS. The same result can be seen in relation to the different layers in the European interoperability framework. In terms of BITA it is also evident that the alignment ambition in all interviews have excluded the call for integration of enterprise-IT and product-IT, which is one of the bigger BITA challenge that now is entering the scene.

Challenges and Recommendations in Extracting Information about the Enterprise

This section presents challenges that EM practitioners face while extracting information about the enterprise during EM workshops and other information capturing activities.

Obtaining Reliable Information

This challenge is related to the fact that it is usually quite problematic to get information that is relevant for solving a particular problem. EM practitioners often need to be very persistent while communicating with workshop participants in order to harvest their domain knowledge. The interviews also indicated the problem of fuzziness of information, due to domain knowledge "blank spots" among the participants. One dimension of this is when the information is valid from a local or isolated individual perspective but not from a shared inter-subjective perspective.

It is difficult to separate facts from opinions.(Respondent 4)

Recommendations:

- Capture what stakeholders know for sure, not what they believe is true. Cross-check with available company documentation regarding the subject matter, but be aware that corporate documents themselves may not be entirely valid.
- Put together a group of participants for the modeling sessions with relevant knowledge and suitable social skills.
- Make sure that the key stakeholders are involved. Stakeholder diagram can be helpful.

Dealing with Group Dynamics and Human Behavior

Another challenge is that EM practitioners have to deal with people that have varied tempers, behavior, and inter-personal skills. Group dynamics and human behavior are competence areas not directly related to EM but still issues, with which the EM practitioner needs to be capable to manage. This can be tricky in some cases, for example, when people are involved in EM sessions together with their managers.

If managers are attending modeling sessions then you should treat them in a special way to make other participants express their true opinions about things. Also if someone has dominant personality then you should treat them differently in order to get the best possible contribution from all participants. (Respondent 4)

Recommendations:

- Make sure all modeling session participants are involved and committed to the results.
- Make sure the modeling sessions are attended by participants who can contribute to the modeling purpose.
- Work with the participants as a group taking into account their different personalities.
- Avoid working with too large groups, 4 - 8 participants per session are recommended.
- Make sure that you are solving the right task that is given by the right people. Root-cause analysis can be helpful.

Creating Shared Language and Terminology

EM stakeholders usually have different frame of references and different understanding of various concepts and their relations. This can result in stakeholders using different names to address the same phenomenon or the same names when talking about different phenomenon. In addition, employees can use some unique terminology, with which the EM practitioner is not familiar, so there is a need to learn and adapt on the fly. Therefore there is a need to develop shared terminology and a common understanding in order to create a solid ground for efficient communication.

Day by day we stumble on the fact that we have different perceptions of some terminology. What is a customer? What is a product? If there is a word list available for modeled enterprise then use it to answer such questions! (Respondent 4)

A shared terminology is vital in three dimensions:

1. During the modeling sessions,
2. The enterprise as a whole, and
3. The produced models.

It is good to start with conceptual modeling, as it can help you to settle the language for the group of participants. (Respondent 4)

In this context the aim ought to be to create a common understanding that is "good enough" given the situation and the purposes at hand.

Recommendations:

*   Make sure all modeling participants have clear understanding of the key concepts used throughout the EM project. Conceptual modeling in the beginning of modeling can be helpful.
*   In case certain concepts require special attention it is helpful to use explanations from literature, previous projects or even examples from everyday operations.
*   Consider specific terminology that is used by employees in the enterprise. Use an enterprise word list or "enterprise glossary" with definitions of key concepts if available, otherwise create it.

Explanation of the Purpose of EM and the Roles of Involved Stakeholders

One challenging issue during an EM project is to make project stakeholders understand the idea and potential power of EM.

It was hard to make people understand why we use models at all! If you do not have this clarified then you will never get to the rest. (Respondent 3)

Clarification of EM might include different aspects like general explanation of purposes and goals of EM project, description of roles and responsibilities that stakeholders (including the role of EM practitioner) have during EM, and explanation of key capabilities of the enterprise.

Recommendations:

- Make participants understand what a model is, explain limitations and strengths of using models.
- Clarify the different rules during modeling sessions and the roles of participants involved, including the leading role of EM practitioner.
- Express the expectations from the EM project and each modeling session in a clear way.

Challenges and Recommendations in Transforming Information into Enterprise Models

Transforming information about the enterprise into models is a process of model creation using different tools such as plastic sheets, post-it-notes, whiteboards and/or computerized tools. This has been described earlier as interactive and non-interactive modeling where the purpose is to expand the shared knowledge through EM (Lind & Seigerroth, 2003). In this study we have acknowledged these process phases for transformation of information into enterprise models.

Dealing with Degree of Formalism

The notation of enterprise models can vary in formalism from formal machine interpretable languages to informal models like "rich pictures". From one point of view, it is preferable to conform to formal notational rules in the models, since this would make it easier to reuse enterprise models in other EM projects.

Being consistent and formal with modeling notation is very important, since created enterprise models then can be used in the long-run, in future projects. (Respondent 3)

However, formal notation can also restrain the modeling process as some participants might become overloaded and stressed by describing the enterprise in a way that is unfamiliar to them.

Too formal modeling notation that is difficult to understand can hinder modeling progress, since the energy of invited participants will be consumed by understanding the models instead of contributing with their knowledge. (Respondent 2)
Be careful with following your modeling method "by the book" instead of adjusting it to the situation. You can skip one or several steps in order to become more practical and flexible. (Respondent 1)

Opinions regarding the degree of formalism are diverse. Deciding upon the right level of formalism will be a challenging task for the EM practitioner to handle. In this case another challenge emerges in terms of how to maintain the alignment between models that have different degree of formalism.

Recommendations:

- Be consistent with chosen modeling notation throughout the project and conditions for adjustment of the degree of formalism.
- Avoid being too formal in early stages of EM, since it can make the modeling process too complex for the participants.
- Keep a balance between readability and functionality of the models given the specific modeling task and audience. Decomposing complex parts of models can be helpful.

Dealing with Degree of Detail

Models can include many or few details. From one point of view it might be beneficial to describe an enterprise with a high degree of detail to allow seeing as many elements and relations as possible. This should not be an end in itself, as it decreases the readability of enterprise models.

Sometimes models become too large, so in order to get good visualization of things you need to simplify a lot. (Respondent 4)
If you need to have detailed view on only one sub-process then you should not add details to the whole process model! We tend to detail too much, which sometimes just makes us busy. (Respondent 2)
We are often wasting time if we dig into details that are not required. Discussions on unnecessary details should be stopped! (Respondent 4)

The rationale in the modeling sessions is to reach a level that is "detailed enough" for the specific situation. Degree of detail is usually dependent on two things

1. What is being communicated, and

2.   The audience.

The respondents also stated that it is often hard to guide modeling session participants to a suitable level of detail in their discussions.

Recommendations:

- It is reasonable to work with different degrees of detail, since it is often important to see businesses on different levels of abstractions.
- Raise the level of abstraction if the models are too detailed. This can be done through stepping up from current level of detail and start asking WHY questions instead of HOW questions.
- Define a suitable degree of detail in the initial stage of the EM session taking into account the goals and purpose of the project.

Selecting Modeling Perspectives

Selecting modeling perspectives involves selecting suitable point of the view(s) (focal areas) for the actual EM situation. In addition to choosing such perspectives, this also includes selection and tailoring of suitable method(s).

However, it can also be problematic to understand the consequences of adopting certain perspectives on one layer of modeling when models need to be aligned both within the specific layer and between different layers. Therefore it might not be easy to see how certain perspectives (focal areas) on one layer will affect models on other layers or within a certain layer.

Some methodologies are fine to make changes in interconnected focal areas, but some are not that flexible. (Respondent 1)

Recommendations:

- Modeling perspectives need to be defined and clarified for involved stakeholders on the initial stage of EM.
- Simple examples illustrating required perspectives (focal areas) and clarifying difference between AS-IS and TO-BE perspectives can be helpful.

Dealing with Change and Model Dependencies

This challenge relates to the reality that EM is usually undertaken in a constantly changing environment, creating the need to keep track of changes and updates to the models. During multi-layered EM it can be quite challenging to keep track of how models influence models on other layers or within the same layer, it becomes even more challenging when there are different versions of the models. Some tools have partially automatic mechanisms for this purpose and the respondents suggested that these issues can be handled by using the capabilities of existing CASE tools.

If you have a good tool like [tool A], you can work with all models that you have loaded into that tool and see how models are related to each other. (Respondent 2)

It is even more beneficial if the perspectives that are supported by the tool are specified through some kind of meta-model or ontology; unfortunately such a feature is absent in many of the existing tools.

Recommendations:

- Capabilities of CASE-tools can be used to keep track of relationship and changes between models.
- As modeling progresses document enterprise models, so that the extracted information does not become outdated. It is important though that models are of sufficient quality and stakeholders have agreed on models versions as they evolve.

Defining the Scope for the Investigation

Scoping the area of investigation needs to satisfy two, sometimes conflicting, criteria:

1. It is important to have a rather broad overview of the enterprise, since it can provide comprehensive view of all actors, actions, and cause-effect relationships in the enterprise; and
2. There is also a need to stay focused and to delimit the area of investigation in order to be efficient.

In some cases you retrieve a lot of information, but you are not really focused on what information you need. If you do not know what question you are asking then you will not get the fundamental work done. (Respondent 3)

It is usually recommended to find a balanced mix between delimitation and focus, and to remember that there is also a need for the broad view (so called "helicopter view").

Recommendations:

- In the initial stage EM ought to address a larger area than the stakeholders are describing to identify the most problematic areas. Root-cause analysis can be helpful as a means of scoping the investigation.

Challenges and Recommendations in Using Enterprise Models

In this research challenges related to the usage of enterprise models have been classified according to the purposes behind an EM initiative. The respondents referred to the purposes for using enterprise models presented by Persson and Stirna (2001). Table 4 presents these purposes of using EM in two categories, general purpose and specific purpose, together with the corresponding challenges. In the table there is one challenge – in time discussion of technical solutions – that relates only to enterprise model usage for developing the business. This challenge is not specific to the other EM intentions, as it is mostly related to the situations when certain IS/IT solution should be implemented. Other challenges are relevant for both intentions of EM.

In Time Discussion of Technical Solutions

During EM there is a tendency to involve technical people in the discussion process to early, which can divert the discussions and create a risk of getting stuck in implementation details instead of discussing alternative solutions.

In many cases IT representatives want to take over the analysis too early. First experts from operations should make models explaining how operations are running

Table 4. EM challenges and recommendations related to using EM for certain purposes

General Purpose	For Developing the Business			To Ensure the Quality of the Business	
Specific purpose	Developing business vision or strategy	Designing or redesigning business operations	Developing supporting IS	Sharing knowledge about the business	Supporting decision making
Challenge	1. In time discussion of technical solutions				
	2. Reuse of enterprise models				
	3. Dealing with diverse stakeholders backgrounds, knowledge and interpretations				
	4. Presenting relevant information in an understandable way				

(process models, concept model, etc.). If that is ready then we start the dialog with IT representatives. (Respondent 2)

It is hard to get beyond discussion of particular IT solutions. People representing different part of the business end up talking about IT solutions. It is really hard to make people say what they want to achieve in the business, and only after this look at what type of IT support is needed. (Respondent 3)

The analysis of the interviews have shown that an EM practitioners recommend to start the modeling efforts with a smaller group with strong domain knowledge that can identify key areas for the continuing work.

Experts in operations should create models about how operations are running. When we are done with that we can involve IT representatives in the dialogue. (Respondent 2)

It is good to have technical details, but not before enterprise models are ready and have good quality. This is the best basis that you could have in order to set demands for the IT. (Respondent 2)

Recommendations:

- Start modeling with a group of participants who have strong domain knowledge of problematic areas.
- Make sure that IT experts are involved in the process only after the key areas have been identified and a general understanding of WHAT should be changed has been created.

Reuse of Enterprise Models

This challenge is related to the fact that enterprise models are mainly only used once for a specific purpose and the project for which they were created.

Resulting enterprise models might be hard to reuse. They can be too specific or incomplete, since they were aimed to be used for developing one particular IT system. (Respondent 4)

It requires quite considerable efforts to ensure the continuous value of enterprise models over time. One way to deal with this could be to appoint someone responsible for model maintenance and reuse through model repositories. Enterprise models maintenance is an important task due to the dynamic nature of today's business environment, especially if the enterprise is captured and described in models that represent different parts and states of the enterprise.

Explain people what is the value of models maintenance! (Respondent 4)
What is really needed is repository that is used in the whole company, so that all new models can be related to old ones. (Respondent 4)
For one company (sometimes for a business unit) you need to select modeling technic, notation and tool to document and store models and put them into place. Then you can use enterprise models efficiently. (Respondent 4)

Recommendations:

- Make sure the existing models are maintained in a repository and that they kept up to date.
- The benefit of models maintenance should be clarified for enterprise management.

Dealing with Diverse Backgrounds, Knowledge, and Interpretations

Stakeholders that are involved in EM project usually have different backgrounds and knowledge. Creating mutual agreements about different enterprise aspects is therefore crucial during any EM effort.

If you have a workshop with people with different backgrounds - financial persons, engineers, HR department, operations, product development - they are looking at reality differently. They often have different solutions depending based on their preferences, backgrounds and knowledge. (Respondent 1)
One very important thing is to have a common understanding of the vision, to really interpret it in the same way and have the same understanding of what the vision is about. (Respondent 1)

Diverse backgrounds and interpretations among stakeholders might restrain EM. To deal with this diversity it is therefore suggested to explain what the models really represent in the enterprise. However, the respondents have emphasized that at the stage of using enterprise models (both for developing the business and for ensuring the quality of the business) it is reasonable to keep such introduction quite short.

Some participants might know how to read models, others might not. If you mix them together you have to do a "warm-up" – a short method introduction, so that all know how to understand the models. (Respondent 2)

Recommendations:

- Provide the participants with a brief reminder of the particular purpose of the models being presented and with a summary of the notation.
- When using models as a basis for explanation and discussions, the diverse backgrounds and knowledge of the involved stakeholders should be considered and consolidated.

Presenting Relevant Information in Understandable Way

This challenge is closely related to the previous one. It emphasizes the need for EM practitioners to represent and deliver relevant information to involved stakeholders and to decision makers in a clear and understandable way.

It is hard to implement a model, since first people need to really understand it. (Respondent 1)
We are more likely to make decisions to act if we have clear understanding about the subject matter. If we do not understand then we resist making decisions. It is important to make the situation clear for key decision makers. (Respondent 2)
If you are really into the model you can fail to explain it. People are not here to learn the model, but to solve the problem. (Respondent 3)

The interviews have shown that it is important that enterprise models can be used for decision making. It was also suggested by the respondents to use models as a foundation for explanation. However, textual and verbal explanations are still important, since models themselves also need to be explained.

Good visualizations might work as a self-playing piano, since you will not need to give instructions – people can act by themselves if they have clear directions (regarding how to implement models). (Respondent 1)
Use their language and talk their talks! Try to see, feel and understand their perspectives of the company and environment. Then you can have a dialog and communicate. (Respondent 1)
Ask yourself: How would I communicate this to [management position X]? What is the suitable language? What is on the agenda? How do I translate things into the [management position X] situation? (Respondent 1)

You need to explain in other words! (Respondent 3)

Recommendations:

- Take benefit from the power of a good visualization when using models for different purposes.
- Make sure that the targeted audience can understand the models.

An Enterprise Modeling Framework with Challenges and Recommendations

The EM challenges and corresponding recommendations for the three activities of EM are summarized in Table 5.

Table 5. EM challenges and recommendations related to the three EM activities

EM Activity	Challenges	Recommendations
Extracting information about the enterprise	Obtaining reliable information	• Capture what stakeholders know for sure, not what they believe is true. Cross-check with available company documentation regarding the subject matter, but be aware that corporate documents themselves may not be entirely valid. • Put together a group of participants for the modeling sessions with relevant knowledge and suitable social skills. • Make sure that the key stakeholders are involved. Stakeholder diagram can be helpful.
	Dealing with group dynamics and human behavior	• Make sure all modeling session participants are involved and committed to the results. • Make sure participants who can contribute to the modeling purpose attend the modeling sessions. • Work with the participants as a group taking into account their different personalities. • Avoid working with too large groups, 4 - 8 participants per session are recommended. • Make sure that you are solving the right task that is given by the right people. Root-cause analysis can be helpful.
	Creating shared language and terminology	• Make sure all modeling participants have clear understanding of the key concepts used throughout the EM project. Conceptual modeling in the beginning of modeling can be helpful. • In case certain concepts require special attention it is helpful to use explanations from literature, previous projects or even examples from everyday operations. • Consider specific terminology that is used by employees in the enterprise. Use an enterprise word list or "enterprise glossary" with definitions of key concepts if available, otherwise try to create it.
	Explanation of the purpose of EM and the roles of involved stakeholders	• Make participants understand what a model is, explain limitations and strengths of using models. • Clarify the different rules during modeling sessions and the roles of participants involved, including the leading role of EM practitioner. • Express the expectations from the EM project and each modeling session in a clear way.

continued on following page

Table 5. Continued

EM Activity	Challenges	Recommendations
Transforming information into enterprise models	Dealing with degree of formalism	• Be consistent with chosen modeling notation throughout the project and conditions for adjustment of the degree of formalism. • Avoid being too formal in early stages of EM, since it can make modeling process too complex for the participants. • Keep a balance between readability and functionality of the models given the specific modeling task and audience. Decomposing complex parts of models can be helpful.
	Dealing with degree of detail	• It is reasonable to work with different degrees of detail, since it is often important to see businesses on different levels of abstractions. • Raise the level of abstraction if the models are too detailed. This can be done through stepping up from current level of detail and start asking WHY questions instead of HOW questions. • Define a suitable degree of detail in the initial stage of the EM session taking into account the goals and purpose of the project.
	Selecting modeling perspectives	• Modeling perspectives need to be defined and clarified for involved stakeholders on the initial stage of EM. • Simple examples illustrating required perspectives (focal areas) and clarifying difference between AS-IS and TO-BE perspectives can be helpful.
	Dealing with change and model dependencies	• Capabilities of CASE-tools can be used to keep track of relationship and changes between models. • As modelling progresses document enterprise models, so that the extracted information does not become outdated. It is important though that models are of sufficient quality and stakeholders have agreed on models versions as they evolve.
	Defining the scope for the investigation	In the initial stage EM ought to address a larger area than the stakeholders are describing to identify the most problematic areas. Root-cause analysis can be helpful as a means of scoping the investigation.
Using enterprise models	In time discussion of technical solutions	• Start modeling with a group of participants who have strong domain knowledge of problematic areas. • Make sure that IT experts are involved in the process only after the key areas have been identified and a general understanding of WHAT should be changed has been created.
	Reuse of enterprise models	• Make sure the existing models are maintained in a repository and that they kept up to date. • The benefit of models maintenance should be clarified for enterprise management.
	Dealing with diverse backgrounds, knowledge and interpretations	• Provide the participants with a brief reminder of the particular purpose of the models being presented and with a summary of the notation. • When using models as a basis for explanation and discussions, the diverse backgrounds and knowledge of the involved stakeholders should be considered and consolidated.
	Presenting relevant information in understandable way	• Take benefit from the power of a good visualization when using models for different purposes. • Make sure that the targeted audience can understand the models.

5. CONCLUSION AND FUTURE RESEARCH

The main purpose with this study has been to address contemporary challenges for business and IT alignment and to identify and structure challenges that EM practitioners face during EM and to suggest recommendations to deal with these challenges in the context BITA. Consequently, the main contribution is a framework with a set of conceptually structured EM challenges and corresponding recommendations. EM challenges can be grouped according to the three activities:

1.   Extracting the information that is related to enterprise operation,
2.   Transforming the information into models, and
3.   Using enterprise models for certain purposes.

Challenges that have been described within the first activity are: obtaining reliable information, dealing with group dynamic and human behavior, creating shared language and terminology, explaining the purpose of EM and the roles of stakeholders within it. The second group involves the following challenges: dealing with degree of formalism, dealing with degree of detail, selecting modeling perspective, dealing with change and model dependencies, and defining the scope for the investigation. The third group includes such challenges as: in time discussion of technical solutions, reuse of enterprise models, dealing with diverse backgrounds and knowledge of involved stakeholders leading to a diversity in interpretations, and presenting relevant information for decision makers in understandable way. Moreover, the presented framework introduces a number of recommendations that aim to help EM practitioners to deal with the identified challenges.

An important characteristic of the study is related to the aspects of EM being considered. Most contemporary studies on EM challenges and recommendations focus on either:

1.   The collaborative nature of EM, or
2.   The required characteristics of created enterprise models, whereas only a few provide a combined view.

Consideration of both of these aspects gives an opportunity to get a broader view on EM practice and to generate more comprehensive support for EM practitioners. This study considered both. Various aspects of collaboration in EM were analyzed when investigating the extraction of information about the enterprise in participative settings and the creation and the usage of enterprise models. The desired characteristics of enterprise models have been taken into account when investigating how extracted enterprise-related information is usually transformed into enterprise models and how created models can be used for various purposes. The main result of the study, the EM framework, contains challenges and recommendations for using enterprise models for various intentions, which imply both of the aforementioned aspects.

From a practical point of view presented challenges and recommendations can serve as a support for EM practitioners, which in turn can facilitate the successful execution of EM to achieve BITA. However, several of the identified challenges do not have explicit solutions at the moment. The proposed recommendations can serve as a set of best practices to deal with the identified challenges, but they should not be considered as instruction that can solve the identified problems completely. Still, identification and structuring of EM challenges are important steps on the way towards suggesting solutions for them. In addition, discussing EM challenges with EM practitioners has served as a trigger for analysis and explanation of the challenges they face and it has provided an opportunity to conceptualize EM practice.

From research point of view the identified challenges and recommendations can serve as a contribution to the area of EM best practices that contribute to more successful EM executions, and best practices that are related to EM and BITA. Evidently, there is a need for continuous research related to the role of EM in the context of BITA.

Having EM challenges and recommendations in the presented framework is a fundamental part to assist EM practitioners, but for further validation it will be important to investigate the applicability of this framework for the purpose of BITA. Such investigation will require a conceptual positioning of EM in the context of BITA, which will be able to provide a ground for applying identified challenges and recommendations in more justified way. This chapter presents an illustration of the

Figure 5. EM and integration of product-IT and enterprise-IT

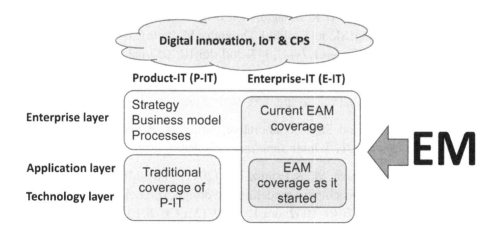

role of EM in the context of BITA and shows that EM is widely used for IS development and redesign according to the needs from the business side of the enterprise. EM is applied during most of the stages of the IS development life cycle including requirements elicitation and analysis, design and specification and to some extent during further implementation-related stages. Apart from IS development, EM is also useful for creating shared understanding in an enterprise business-related units and IT-related units. These findings provide an initial idea regarding the applicability of EM for the purpose of BITA.

A promising focus for future research related to BITA and EM is to continue to address the development traditionally EM strong areas like EA and EAM in the quest to be able to cope with the integration of enterprise-IT and product-IT in a structured and coherent way according to Figure 5.

Given the emerging trends like digital innovation, CPS and IoT the future will require interaction in real time and closer integration of product-IT and enterprise-IT. Traditionally product-IT is analyzed, designed, constructed, and maintained separately from enterprise-IT due to reliability requirements, different lifecycle, different funding strategy.

REFERENCES

Ahlemann, F., Stettiner, E., Messerschmidt, M., & Legner, C. (2012). *Strategic enterprise architecture management: Challenges, best practices, and future developments*. Berlin: Springer. doi:10.1007/978-3-642-24223-6

Aversano, L., Grasso, C., & Tortorella, M. (2012). A literature review of Business/IT Alignment Strategies. *Procedia Technology*, *5*, 462–474. doi:10.1016/j.protcy.2012.09.051

Bandara, W., Gable, G. G., & Rosemann, M. (2005). Factors and Measures of Business Process Modelling: Model Building Through a Multiple Case Study. *European Journal of Information Systems*, *14*(4), 347–360. doi:10.1057/palgrave.ejis.3000546

Barjis, J. (2009). Collaborative, Participative and Interactive Enterprise Modeling. In ICEIS 2009 (LNBIP), (vol. 24, pp. 651–662). Springer.

Barjis, J. (2011). CPI Modeling: Collaborative, Participative, Interactive Modeling. In *Proceedings of the 2011 Winter Simulation Conference* (pp. 3099-3108). IEEE.

Bassi, L., Secchi, C., Bonfé, M., & Fantuzzi, C. (2011). A SysML-based methodology for manufacturing machinery modeling and design. *IEEE/ASME Transactions on Mechatronics*, *6*(6), 1049–1062. doi:10.1109/TMECH.2010.2073480

Baxter, G., & Sommerville, I. (2011). Socio-technical systems: From design methods to systems engineering. *Interacting with Computers*, *23*(1), 4–17. doi:10.1016/j.intcom.2010.07.003

Becker, J., Rosemann, M., & von Uthmann, C. (2000). Guidelines of Business Process Modeling. In W. M. P. van der Aalst, J. Desel, & A. Oberweis (Eds.), *Business Pro-cess Management. Models, Techniques, and Empirical Studies* (pp. 30–49). Springer Berlin Heidelberg.

Buckl, S., Dierl, T., Matthes, F., & Schweda, C. M. (2010). Building Blocks for Enterprise Architecture Management Solutions. In Practice-Driven Research on Enterprise Transformation (LNBIP), (Vol. 69, pp. 17–46). Springer. doi:10.1007/978-3-642-16770-6_2

Buede, D. M. (2011). *The engineering design of systems: models and methods* (Vol. 55). John Wiley & Sons.

Chan, Y. E., & Reich, B. H. (2007). IT alignment: What have we learned? *Journal of Information Technology*, *22*(4), 297–315. doi:10.1057/palgrave.jit.2000109

Chen, H. M., Kazman, R., & Garg, G. (2005). BITAM: An engineering principled method for managing misalignments between business and IT architectures. *Science of Computer Programming*, *57*(1), 5–26. doi:10.1016/j.scico.2004.10.002

Christiner, F., Lantow, B., Sandkuhl, K., & Wissotzki, M. (2012). Multi-dimensional Visualization in Enterprise Modeling. In *Proceedings of International Conference on Business Information Systems, Workshops* (LNBIP), (vol. 127, pp. 139–152). Springer. doi:10.1007/978-3-642-34228-8_14

De Haes, S., & Van Grembergen, W. (2010). Analyzing the impact of enterprise governance of IT practices on business performance. *International Journal of IT/Business Alignment and Governance*, *1*(1), 14–38. doi:10.4018/jitbag.2010120402

Delen, D., Dalal, N. P., & Benjamin, P. C. (2005). Integrated modeling: The key to holistic understanding of the enterprise. *Communications of the ACM*, *48*(4), 107–112. doi:10.1145/1053291.1053296

European Commission. (2010). European Interoperability Framework (EIF) for European public services, isa -Interoperability Solutions for European Public Administration. Bruxelles, le 16.12.2010 COM(2010) 744 final. Author.

Frank, U. (2002). Multi-Perspective Enterprise Modeling (MEMO) – Conceptual Framework and Modeling Languages.*Proceedings of the 35th Annual Hawaii International Conference on System Sciences*. doi:10.1109/HICSS.2002.993989

Frank, U. (2014). Multi-perspective enterprise modeling: Foundational concepts, prospects and future research challenges. *Software & Systems Modeling, 13*(3), 941–962. doi:10.1007/s10270-012-0273-9

Gibson, C. F. (2003). IT-enabled Business Change - An Approach to Understanding and Managing Risk. *MIS Quarterly Executive, 2*(2), 104–115.

Gregor, S., Hart, D., & Martin, N. (2007). Enterprise architectures: Enablers of business strategy and IS/IT alignment in government. *Information Technology & People, 20*(2), 96–120. doi:10.1108/09593840710758031

Hackmann, G., Guo, W., Yan, G., Sun, Z., Lu, C., & Dyke, S. (2014). Cyber-physical codesign of distributed structural health monitoring with wireless sensor networks. Parallel and Distributed Systems. *IEEE Transactions on, 25*(1), 63–72.

Jonkers, H., Lankhorst, M., van Buuren, R., Hoppenbrouwers, S., Bonsangue, M., & van der Torre, L. (2004). Concepts for modelling enterprise architectures. *International Journal of Cooperative Information Systems, 13*(3), 257–287. doi:10.1142/S0218843004000985

Kaidalova, J., Seigerroth, U., Bukowska, E., & Shilov, N. (2014). Enterprise Modeling for Business and IT Alignment: Challenges and Recommendations. *International Journal of IT/Business Alignment and Governance, 5*(2), 43–68.

Kaidalova, J., Seigerroth, U., Kaczmarek, T., & Shilov, N. (2012). Practical challenges of Enterprise Modeling in Business and IT Alignment. In Sandkuhl et al. (Ed.), The Practice of Enterprise Modeling (LNBIP), (vol. 134, pp. 31-45). Springer Berlin Heidelberg. doi:10.1007/978-3-642-34549-4_3

Karlsen, A., & Opdahl, A. L. (2012). Enterprise modeling practice in a turnaround project. In Norsk konferanse for organisasjoners bruk av informasjonsteknologi NO-KOBIT.

Kearns, G. S., & Lederer, A. L. (2003). A resource-based view of strategic IT alignment: How knowledge sharing creates competitive advantage. *Decision Sciences, 34*(1), 1–29. doi:10.1111/1540-5915.02289

Keuntje, J., & Barkow, R. (2010). *Enterprise Architecture Management in der Praxis. Wandel, Komplexität und IT-Kosten im Unternehmen beherrschen.* Symposion Publishing GmbH.

Koehler, J., & Vanhatalo, J. (2007). Process Anti-Patterns: How to Avoid the Common Traps of Business Process Modeling. *IBM WebSphere Developer Technical Journal, 10*(4).

Lankhorst, M. (2013). *Enterprise architecture at work: Modelling, communication and analysis* (3rd ed.). Heidelberg, Germany: Springer. doi:10.1007/978-3-642-29651-2

Lind, M., & Seigerroth, U. (2003). Team-based reconstruction for expanding organizational ability. *The Journal of the Operational Research Society, 54*(2), 119–129. doi:10.1057/palgrave.jors.2601474

Luftman, J. (2003). Assessing IT-Business Alignment. *Information Systems Management, 20*(4), 9–15. doi:10.1201/1078/43647.20.4.20030901/77287.2

Luftman, J., & McLean, E. R. (2004). Key issues for IT executives. *MIS Quarterly Executive, 3*(2), 89–104.

McGinnis, L. F. (2007). Enterprise modeling and enterprise transformation. *Information, Knowledge, Systems Management, 6*(1-2), 123–143.

Mendling, J., Reijers, H. A., & van der Aalst, W. M. P. (2010). Seven process modeling guidelines (7PMG). *Information and Software Technology, 52*(2), 127–136. doi:10.1016/j.infsof.2009.08.004

Orlikowski, W. J., & Hofman, J. D. (1997). An improvisational model for change management: The case of groupware. *Sloan Management Science, 38*(2), 11–21.

Persson, A. (2001). *Enterprise Modelling in Practice: Situational Factors and their Influence on Adopting a Participative Approach.* (Doctoral Dissertation). Department of Computer and Systems Sciences, Stockholm University, Stockholm, Sweden.

Persson, A., & Stirna, J. (2001). Why Enterprise Modelling? An Explorative Study into Current Practice. In *Proceedings of 13th Conference on Advanced Information Systems Engineering.* Interlaken, Switzerland: Springer. doi:10.1007/3-540-45341-5_31

Persson, A., & Stirna, J. (2010). Towards Defining a Competence Profile for the Enterprise Modeling Practitioner. PoEM 2010. *LNBIP, 68,* 232–245.

Raduescu, C., Tan, H. M., Jayaganesh, M., Bandara, W., zur Muehlen, M., & Lippe, S. (2006). A framework of issues in large process modeling projects. In *Proceedings of the 14th European Conference on Information Systems.*

Reich, B. H., & Benbasat, I. (2000). Factors That Influence the Social Dimension of Alignment between Business and Information Technology Objectives. *Management Information Systems Quarterly, 24*(1), 81–113. doi:10.2307/3250980

Rexhepi, M. (2012). *En studie om utmaningar som kan hindra utvecklingen av mod-eller av hög kvalitet vid tillämpning av verksamhetsmodellering.* (Bachelor Thesis, In Swedish). Department of Information Systems, Skövde University.

Ringert, J. O., Rumpe, B., & Wortmann, A. (2014). *From Software Architecture Structure and Behavior Modeling to Implementations of Cyber-Physical Systems.* arXiv preprint arXiv:1408.5690

Rosemann, M., Lind, M., Hjalmarsson, A., & Recker, J. (2011). *Four facets of a process modeling facilitator.Thirty Second International Conference on Information Systems*, Shanghai, China.

Rosemann, M., Sedera, W., & Gable, G. (2001). Critical Success Factors of Process Modeling for Enterprise Systems.*Proceedings of the Americas Conference of Information Systems (AMCIS '01).*

Sandkuhl, K., Simon, D., Wißotzki, M., & Starke, C. (2015) The Nature and a Process for Development of Enterprise Architecture Principles. *18th International Conference BIS 2015* (LNBIP), (vol. 208, pp. 260-272). Springer.

Sandkuhl, K., Stirna, J., Persson, A., & Wissotzki, M. (2014). *Enterprise Modeling – Tackling Business challenges with the 4EM method.* Berlin: Springer Verlag.

Saunders, M., Lewis, P., & Thornhill, A. (2006). *Research methods for business students* (4th ed.). Harlow: Prentice Hall.

Schlosser, F., Wagner, H.-T., & Coltman, T. (2012). Reconsidering the Dimensions of Business-IT Alignment. In *Proceedings of the 45th Hawaii International Conference on System Science.* doi:10.1109/HICSS.2012.497

Seigerroth, U. (2011). Enterprise Modeling and Enterprise Architecture: the constituents of transformation and alignment of Business and IT. *International Journal of IT/Business Alignment and Governance, 2*(1), 16-34.

Seigerroth, U. (2015). The Diversity of Enterprise Modeling – a taxonomy for enterprise modeling actions. *International Complex Systems Informatics and Modeling Quarterly*, (4), 12-31. Retrieved from https://csimq-journals.rtu.lv

Silvius, A. J. G. (2009). Business and IT Alignment: What We Know and What We Don't Know. In *Proceedings of International Conference on Information Management and Engineering.* IEEE.

Singh, S. N., & Woo, C. (2009). Investigating business-IT alignment through multi-disciplinary goal concepts.*Requirements Engineering, 14*(3), 177–207. doi:10.1007/s00766-009-0081-0

Sommerville, I. (2006). *Software Engineering* (8th ed.). Addison-Wesley.

Stirna, J., & Kirikova, M. (2008). Integrating Agile Modeling with Participative Enterprise Modeling. In *Proceedings of the CAiSE workshop EMMSAD*, (pp. 171-184).

Stirna, J., & Persson, A. (2009). Anti-patterns as a Means of Focusing on Critical Quality Aspects in Enterprise Modeling. In T. Halpin, J. Krogstie, S. Nurcan, E. Proper, R. Schmidt, P. Soffer, & R. Ukor (Eds.), *BPMDS 2009 and EMMSAD 2009 (LNBIP)*, (vol. 29, pp. 407–418). Heidelberg, Germany: Springer. doi:10.1007/978-3-642-01862-6_33

Stirna, J., Persson, A., & Sandkuhl, K. (2007). Participative Enterprise Modeling: Experiences and Recommendations. CAiSE 2007. *LNCS, 4495*, 546–560.

Vargas, J. O. (2011). *A Framework of Practices Influencing IS/Business Alignment and IT Governance*. (Doctoral thesis). School of Information Systems, Computing and Mathematics in Brunel University.

Wegmann, A., Regev, G., Rychkova, I., Le, L.-S., de la Cruz, J. G., & Julia, P. (2007). Business-IT Alignment with SEAM for Enterprise Architecture. *Proceedings of the 11th IEEE International EDOC Conference*. doi:10.1109/EDOC.2007.54

Williamson, K. (2002). *Research methods for students, academics and professionals: Information management and systems* (2nd ed.). Wagga Wagga, NSW: Centre for Information Studies, Charles Sturt University. doi:10.1533/9781780634203

Wißotzki, M., & Sandkuhl, K. (2015) Elements and Characteristics of Enterprise Architecture Capabilities. *14th International Conference BIR 2015* (LNBIP), (pp. 82-96). Springer.

Chapter 7
IT Investment Consistency and Other Factors Influencing the Success of IT Performance

Tomi Dahlberg
Åbo Akademi University, Finland & University of Turku, Finland

Hannu Kivijärvi
Aalto University, Finland

Timo Saarinen
Aalto University, Finland

ABSTRACT

IT Business Value (ITBV) research generally proposes that various "good" IT governance and management practices influence positively IT performance. Yet, this claim has proved hard to verify with empirical data. In this study we first identified and analyzed factors that are seen to influence IT deployment success, then hypothesized about the relationships among and between these factors and finally integrated the hypotheses into a research model. We then empirically evaluated the hypotheses and the entire research model. The consistency of IT investments as the response to the cyclical behavior of the economy is a novel factor introduced in this

DOI: 10.4018/978-1-5225-0861-8.ch007

study to the ITBV research. Special attention was also placed on the perceived importance of IT to business, business-IT alignment and IT management. We used survey data of 212 responses collected from CxOs during an economic recession to test the hypotheses and the model for path coefficients and indirect effects. Empirical results confirmed that all research model factors influenced positively IT deployment success. Moreover, high values in the perceived importance of IT, business-IT alignment and the quality of IT management were discovered to be antecedents to the consistency of IT investments, and when that was achieved, the impact was positive on IT deployment success.

1. INTRODUCTION

During the recent decades the relationship between information technology (IT), IT performance and organizational performance has been studied extensively. There appears to be several reasons for this. In addition to the ever-expanding deployment of IT in organizational activities, IT-related investments are seen to account for a major and growing proportion of an organization's investments. For example, Gartner Inc. estimated recently that the proportion of IT investments outside of IT would grow to 90% of all investments in technology by the year 2020 from the proportion of 20% thirty years earlier (Gartner Inc., 2012). According to Gartner Inc. much of this change "is being driven by the digitization of companies' revenue and services". Moreover, direct and especially indirect IT and digital data related costs are seen to represent a growing proportion of an organization's total costs (e.g. Cha, Pingry, & Thatcher, 2009). With IT we understand anything related to computing and data processing technologies, information systems (IS) and digital data processed with these technologies and systems, such as hardware, software, networks, the Internet, data storages and data analytics, as well as the facilities, people, processes and organizational structures needed to deploy, use, manage and govern these technologies and systems as well as digital data processed with them.

There are arguments according to which IT does not provide value to organizations (Carr, 2003) or fails to offer positive competitive advantages to them (Porter, 2001; Pollalis, 2003). Yet, most practitioners as well as economists and strategy researchers agree with statements that, on average, IT deployment is able to improve organizational performance and to increase the relative competiveness of an organization (e.g. Brynjolfsson, & Brown, 2005; Wiengarten, Humphreys, Cao & McHugh, 2013). This view is also inherent in research traditions, which investigate how IT investments, IT assets as well as their deployment and management impact IT success and organizational performance. The mentioned research traditions are often labeled as IT business value (ITBV) research (e.g. Kohli & Grover, 2008;

Schreyen, 2013) and as IS success research (e.g. Petter, DeLone & McClean, 2013). For simplicity we refer to both with the term ITBV research. "Good" adherence of so-called "best" IT management practices resulting, for example, in business-IT alignment with active business management involvement and in IT governance arrangements with clear accountabilities for IT decisions and processes are seen to contribute both to the success of IT deployment and to the achievement organizational performance benefits (e.g. Weill & Ross, 2005; Van Grembergen & De Haes, 2008).

Researchers' and practitioners' propositions that good IT management/governance practices provide benefits to an organization appear intuitively sound. IT management/governance can be regarded as a specific management/governance context. Moreover, when IT is deployed growingly outside of the traditional IT domain and (co-)managed/governed more by other than the IT function professionals, it is logical to expect that good IT management/governance becomes more important to the organization, that IT is better aligned with its (business) activities and delivers more value. These expectations have proven hard to verify empirically, especially when the impacts of several constructs have been investigated simultaneously. For example, the proportion of IT project success has risen from the average of 20 - 25% between 1985 and 1994s to the average of 30 - 35% between 2003 and 2012 (Standish Group, 2013). Practitioners tend to consider this 10% rise disappointing (e.g. Eveleens & Verhoef, 2010) in comparison to their hard efforts to improve (IT) project success through more advanced (IT) project management practices such as PMBOK (2015) and Prince2 (2015). Similarly, the authors of state-of-the art ITBV research summaries, such as Kohli & Grover (2008) and Schreyen (2013), claim that we know much about the mechanisms how IT investments and IT assets impact IT success and organizational performance. Yet, at the same time they also acknowledge that research has left many issues unanswered. For example, Schreyen (2013) concludes:

While the vast majority of research papers on IS business value find empirical evidence in favour of both the operational and strategic relevance of IS, the fundamental question of the causal relationship … remains partly unexplained.

Our objective is to contribute to the ITBV research by investigating how several constructs separately and jointly influence IT deployment success as well as how the consistency of IT investments – a new theoretical construct introduced to the ITBV research – does the same. The hypothesized causal relationships between the research model constructs depict direct and indirect path dependencies between the constructs with their influence on the success of IT deployment. We used survey data of 212 responses collected from business and IT executives to test our hypotheses and the research model.

The phase of the economic cycle at the time of the survey data collection provided motivation to introduce the IT investment consistency construct. Previous research (e.g. Kohli & Grover, 2008; Schreyen, 2013) suggests that changes in an organization's environment impact IT investments and IT assets. The phase of an economic cycle is one such environmental change. The country of the survey (Finland) experienced an economic recession at the time of the survey data collection. During a recession, there could be pressures to cut IT costs, to postpone IT investments, and to limit IT development activities in order to have cost savings and to improve efficiency in the short run. On the other hand, there could also be efforts to create new business, to consolidate IT assets, to improve data quality, or to develop IT management competencies. The motive is to be better prepared for economic recovery and for the next bull market [Cha, Pingry & Thatcher, 2009]. The reactions of organizations to economic cycles probably differ. Organizations that continue to invest into IT in line to their current plans show high consistency of IT investment. They may still postpone IT investments, cut costs and have more focused IT development activities but that is done in an orderly way with little ad-hoc postponement and cut down decisions on IT investments. Our objective is to examine how the consistency of IT investment during a recession affects the success of IT deployment.

In summary, we investigate two research questions:

1.	What constructs act as enablers for the success of IT deployment?
2.	How is the consistency of IT investment related to the success of IT deployment and other constructs that act as enablers for the success of IT deployment?

To answer these research questions we review the theoretical background of the present research in Section 2. We then depict the proposed research model with related hypotheses and discuss the methods of empirical data collection and analysis in the following Section. Results from the empirical hypotheses and model testing are presented in Section 4. Finally, Section 5 ends the article with a discussion on the theoretical and empirical findings of our study and on conclusions.

2. THEORETICAL BACKGROUND

Cumulatively, the impacts of multiple factors have been investigated within the broad umbrella of the ITBV research. Constructs studied include IT capabilities (e.g. Mithas, Ramasubbu, & Sambamurthy, 2011), business-IT alignment (e.g. Kearns & Sabherwal, 2007), IT management and IT governance (e.g. Drnevich & Croson, 2013), technology strategies and their deployment (e.g. Goh & Kauffman, 2013), the execution of IT investments and projects (e.g. Kohli, Devaraj, & Ow, 2012), data and information management (e.g. Tallon, Ramirez, & Short, 2013), and enterprise architecture including integrations (e.g. Ward & Zhou, 2012). Similarly, over the years several measures for IS/IT success have been crafted (e.g. Schreyen, 2013; Petter, DeLone, & McLean, 2013), that is, to describe IT deployment success and its impacts on organizational performance and effectiveness. The generic proposition of the ITBV research is that "good" IT deployment, management and/or governance of IT capabilities, business-IT alignment and other investigated constructs influence positively IT deployment success and, when that happens, organizational performance and effectiveness.

Given the vast and diverse theoretical background of the ITBV research, we made three decisions to focus our research. First, to propose and to empirically test causal relationships between theoretical constructs, we raised the question: Are various constructs investigated within ITBV related to each other and, if so, do they separately and as a whole influence the success of IT deployment? More specifically, is it possible to design a holistic model with specified relationships between several theory-based constructs and their influences on IT deployment success and to empirically verify the influence of each construct and the entire model? Our objective is to design and test such a model.

Second, we decided to explore the success of IT deployment as a whole at the level of an organization. Thus, in the present research IT deployment success includes both the success of IT projects, (that is, IT investments and development activities) and the overall success of IT deployment (that is, IT legacy and IT operations as well as their maintenance activities). For the same reason, the statistical analysis of empirical data includes both business executive and IT executive responses. We reasoned that IT deployment decisions in organizations usually involve both business and IT executives - actually that is even in the core of the IT governance concept (e.g. Weill & Ross, 2005; Van Grembergen & De Haes, 2008). Therefore the responses of both business and IT executives should be included to determine IT deployment success. We also reasoned that due to the nature of executive work they are inclined to evaluate the success of entire IT deployment instead of just IT investments/projects' or IT legacy/operations' success, even though individual investments/projects and/or legacy IS/services could be important to an executive especially in her/his responsibility area.

Third, in our model the outcome variables depicting IT deployment success are primarily operational performance measures, or process performance measures as Schreyen (2013) calls them. Two reasons motivated us to take this decision. Firstly, both practitioners and researchers – us included - would prefer to understand how IT impacts organizational performance and effectiveness (e.g. Kohli & Grover, 2008;

Schreyen, 2013) rather than how IT affects IT deployment success. Yet, there are often significant time delays from:

1. IT investment/project launch, legacy IT maintenance and development, enterprise architecture activity and/or other key IT management/governance decisions;
2. To the implementation of those decisions and through that;
3. To the actual impacts of decisions and their implementations on organizational performance and effectiveness.

Furthermore, there are also intervening factors resulting from other organizational activities and decisions as well as from changes in the organizations environment, which all moderate the influence of IT on organizational performance and effectiveness (e.g. Kivijärvi & Saarinen, 1995; Kohli & Grover, 2008). Secondly, we propose that the success of IT deployment is related to organizational performance and effectiveness, although the empirical proof of that proposition is beyond the scope of this research. As IT has become an enabler for most organizational activities and an integral part of them, we reason it to be unlikely that IT would improve organizational performance unless it is deployed successfully. This is actually how the ITBV research describes the relationship between IT and organizational performance. Some of the survey items discussed later on in the present article, most notably overall satisfaction with IT deployment and the ability of IT projects to reach their business objectives, probably reflect respondents' perceptions about the organizational performance induced by IT.

2.1. Perceived Importance of IT

We reviewed literature on the strategic role of IT, especially the resource-based view (RBV) (e.g. Wiengarten, Humphreys, Cao & McHugh 2013). RBV considers each organization unique (Barney, 1991). An organization is equivalent to the broad set of tangible and intangible assets, resources and capabilities that it owns semipermanently or permanently, such as IT. Organization's (IT) assets, resources and capabilities as a whole, and especially imperfectly mobile, imitable and substitutable assets, resources and capabilities, with their usage arrangements and usage expectations determine the value creation potential of the organization (Barney, 1991). The findings of prior research suggest that if (IT) assets, resources and capabilities are seen to offer a competitive advantage to an organization, the organization will take necessary actions to realize that potential. We call this factor perceived importance of IT. Senior business and IT executives' education, experiences, attitudes, beliefs and emotions about the role of IT in business influence how important IT is perceived for business planning, execution and control (e.g. Liu, Zhang, Keil, & Chen, 2010) and what kind of actions executives then deem appropriate to deploy IT.

We reasoned that when executives in an organization consider IT as a strategic asset, resource or capability, then the organization are likely to put greater emphasis and to devote more efforts on the alignment of business and IT (discussed in Section 2.2.), on the management of IT (discussed in Section 2.3), and on technology usage (discussed in Section 2.4). Another possible outcome is that the organization is more consistent with IT investments (discussed in Section 2.5) and uses more money on IT in comparison to revenues (e.g. Brynjolfsson & Hitt, 1998; Brynjolfsson and Brown, 2005; Cha, Pingry and Thatcher, 2009). In addition to beliefs that IT's role is significant for an organization's current and future competitive advantages (e.g. Melville, Kraemer, & Gurbaxani, 2004; Barney 1991), the perceived importance of IT may manifest itself also in other concrete measurable ways. IT could be seen as a partner to business (Aral & Weill, 2007). IT could also be regarded to provide value to business by facilitating new innovations and/or by increasing the efficiency of business processes (e.g. Mithas, Ramasubbu, & Sambamurthy, 2011). These are the operationalized survey items of the present study for the perceived importance of IT construct.

2.2. Business–IT Alignment

Rich literature and research traditions (e.g. Chan & Reich, 2007) characterize the business–IT alignment construct. Henderson and Venkatraman (1993) divided business–IT alignment into two levels: strategic and operational. They called the former "strategic fit" and the latter "operational integration." The proposition that strategically and operatively well-aligned business and IT positively influence IT deployment is not only intuitively sound but receives also strong support from prior research. Empirical business-IT alignment studies show consistently that the quality of alignment has positive impacts on IT deployment success (e.g. Ward & Zhou, 2006; Chan & Reich, 2007; Van Grembergen & DeHaes, 2008). If the quality of alignment is high, then the organization knows also better how IT impacts its business operations and performance (Weill & Ross, 2005; Petter, DeLone & McLean, 2013). We concluded that when business and IT are well aligned on strategic and operational levels, it is likely that this positively influences IT management (section 2.3) as well as it increases the consistency of IT investments (section 2.5). The proposition regarding IT-investment consistency means that it is less likely that IT investments would be cut down during a recession as they are considered integral to business. As a consequence, IT investments and IT costs would be scaled down in line with other activities, should such needs arise. Prior business–IT alignment research also led us to expect that the quality of alignment will have a direct impact on the success of IT deployment since prior research findings suggested this (Ward & Zhou, 2006).

To operationalize the business-IT alignment construct to measurable survey items we divided business-IT alignment into strategic and operational levels in line with Henderson & Venkatraman (1993). In the present research, strategic level business-IT alignment is measured with the survey item, how comprehensively senior executives, other business executives and IT executives have agreed the accountabilities and responsibilities of IT management, IT processes and IT decisions (Weill & Ross, 2005; International Organization for Standardization, 2008). In other words, good business-IT alignment is seen to mean that the organization has established and implemented a clearly defined IT governance system, which cascades accountabilities top-down from the organizational level to unit, process and task level, and includes both IT development and operations (Van Grembergen & De Haes, 2008, International Organization for Standardization, 2008). We measure the operational level of business-IT alignment with two survey items: Do IT-infrastructure, applications, data, and processes create a well-integrated whole (e.g. Boh & Yellin, 2006; Tallon, Ramirez & Short, 2013)? Does the organization know on the basis of reliable metrics, how IT impacts its business (e.g. Petter, DeLone & McLean, 2013)? Please note that business-IT alignment construct, as discussed above, includes the establishment of an organization's IT governance system, typically accepted by the organization's governing body. According to the ISO/IEC 38500 international standards family an IT governance system is used to evaluate, monitor and control that IT is deployed responsibly in an organization and that the impacts of IT deployment are measured (International Organization for Standardization, 2008). The establishment of the IT governance system is thus separated from IT management, which is the construct we discuss next.

2.3. IT Management

We proposed above that IT management — consisting of strategic and operative IT management — is influenced both by the perceived importance of IT and by business—IT alignment. Our reasoning is that IT is managed better, when an organization considers IT important for the execution of its business, and that business-IT alignment guides IT management to focus on issues that the governing body deems important for the organization. The generic task of IT management is to transform IT-related business needs evaluated and directed by the governing body in combination with user, customer and other stakeholders' requests and needs, and other IT management issues into plans with clear measurable objectives. After planning IT management needs to execute activities to implement the plans, and to compare achieved results to plans and to IT deployment objectives. Reporting is used to ensure that IT management decisions, plans and actions lead to the achievement of organizational objectives, that corrective actions are taken if necessary, and that the governing body is able to control that IT is deployed and managed responsibly (International Organization for Standardization, 2008).

Daily strategic IT management is sometimes called (corporate) governance of IT or simply IT governance. It is seen to be the responsibility of an organization's governance body (International Organization for Standardization, 2008). The governance body typically consists of board and/or executive committee members. In more practical terms, daily strategic IT management is seen as a shared responsibility between business and IT executives. For business executives this means that they are expected to guide the deployment of technology and related IT management activities. Business executives are also expected to secure the availability of sufficient technology understanding so that the organization is capable to deploy IT in line with its measurable business objectives (International Organization for Standardization, 2008). Since the establishment of IT governance system was discussed above as one part of business-IT alignment, it is necessary to distinguish these two aspects of IT governance. IT governance means the extension of corporate governance to IT (Weill & Ross, 2005; International Organization for Standardization, 2008). Corporate governance refers to arrangements through which the suppliers of funds assure returns on their investments (Schleifer & Vishny, 1997). According to Schleifer and Vishny that means ideally that the financiers and the management sign a contract that specifies how the management uses the provided funds and how the returns are divided between the financiers and the management. In real life, due to the uncertainties of an organizations environment, the financiers and the management agree objectives, organizational structures, processes and controls, and those cooperation mechanisms that constitute the corporate – and the IT - governance system. This system establishes the basis for (IT) management (Schleifer & Vishny, 1997; Van Gremberg & De Haes, 2008) as IT management describes activities, which turn the IT governance system into practice.

In addition to articles cited above our research builds also on Henderson & Venkatraman (1993), as well as that of Boynton, Zmud & Jacobs (1994) and Petter, DeLone & McLean (2013) for the IT management construct. Cumulatively studies cited so far describe what needs to be managed, how IT management decisions and other similar IT management actions should be taken, and with what measures the outcomes of IT management should be evaluated. We concluded that well managed IT has a positive impact on technology usage (section 2.5), on the consistency of IT investments (section 2.6) and on the success of IT deployment (section 2.7). The first proposition suggests that good IT management is likely to result in clearer and more business justified objectives for novel technology usage, in higher usage of technologies considered business justified, and in better integration between various technologies deployed by an organization. The second proposition reflects reasoning according to which IT investments are likely to be continued unless an IT investment shows poor results and need reconsideration for this reason, or unless there are compelling business related reasons to cut down (IT) investments and costs overall. The final proposition states that better IT management leads in better IT deployment. Cumulatively these propositions inquire, why bother with IT management unless activities taken improve what is managed?

At survey item level we measured the impact of IT management by considering does an organization manage IT as a strategic means currently (e.g. Kearns & Sabherwal, 2007) and develop IT management competencies as a strategic means for the future success of the organization (e.g. Melville, Kraemer & Gurbaxani, 2004). We also measured the impact of IT management by looking at does an organization align the objectives of IT activities with business objectives in such a way that the organization is able to evaluate how IT impacts the achievement of those business objectives (e.g. Drnevich & Croson, 2013). Furthermore, good IT management practices are considered to result in knowing the outcomes of IT management decisions, plans, and activities on the basis of reliable metrics (e.g. Melville, Kraemer & Gurbaxani, 2004; Petter, DeLone & McLean, 2013).

2.4. Technology Usage

In sections 2.1 – 2.3 we reviewed literature only briefly although the literature is voluminous. However, discussed constructs and concepts are rather well known, and the propositions are fairly obvious to the researchers in the field. What is, however, less obvious is, how the constructs together and with those constructs discussed in sections 2.4 – 2.5 are linked to each other and how they as a whole impact the success of IT deployment. So far, we have proposed that the perceived importance of IT positively influences technology usage since technology usage is seen to offer more benefits when such an attitude prevails. We also suggested that good IT management favorably affects technology usage since technology usage has clearer objectives and measures when that is the case. These propositions are drawn from theoretical literature but they also appear to be intuitively sound.

Some people may expect that technology usage is an important, if not the most important determinant for the success of IT deployment. As researchers, we also expect that technology usage will be detected to impact the success of IT deployment. Yet, the importance of the construct needs to be empirically determined. At the same time, technology usage is a challenging theoretical construct. We reason that the impact of legacy technology deployment is, at least partly, embedded into the business – IT alignment construct. More specifically, legacy technologies probably have already delivered most of their technology usage impacts – that is, their technological potential - on IT deployment success, whereas this has not happened to the same extent with newer technologies (Cecez-Kecmanovic, Kautz & Abrahall, 2014). It may also be easier to adjust the usage volume of legacy IT. An organization knows better what the business and other outcomes are, should the volume of legacy IT usage be modified (e.g. Bergeron, Raymond & Rivard, 2001). Another challenge with the technology usage construct is to determine what technologies to include. By definition a new technology cannot be legacy. At the same time, the adoption of a new technology needs to have reached such a level that business and IT executives are able to evaluate the business potential and IT management needs of the technology on the basis of personal and organizational experiences.

For these reasons we investigated the following technologies as the survey items of the technology usage construct: e-business (e.g. Coltman, Devinney & Midgley, 2007), social media (e.g. Luo & Zhang, 2013), cloud services (e.g. Choudhary & Vithayathil, 2013), and bring-your-own device (BYOD) (e.g. Harris, Ives & Junglas, 2012). BYOD is sometimes called IT consumerization. In addition to devices, the BYOD concept also means the use of applications and services originally and/or primarily developed to consumer markets such as Dropbox and Skype. All of the technologies mentioned above have been available for several years. Executives and organizations have thus had plenty of opportunities to consider the deployment of these technologies and to learn from their own and other persons' and organizations' experiences. For the same reasons we excluded some newer technologies, such as big data and Internet of things. In addition to what was written above, the logic of these decisions is similar to that explained in Section 1 about the decision to focus on IT performance instead of organizational performance. After a decision is made to deploy a particular new technology, it takes time to implement necessary IT solutions and services and to gain experience about the technology. Thus, the success of IT deployment does not happen immediately and could be mediated by intervening factors. We examined the impacts of technology usage by measuring: Do organizations have a clear strategy and implementation plan for the business deployment of a new technology? Do organizations have an objective to increase the usage of a new technology in business? Is a new technology acknowledged in an organization's IT strategy (e.g. Harris, Ives & Junglas, 2012) and/or architecture plan (Boh & Yellin, 2006)? Better technology usage is expected to positively influence the success of IT deployment.

2.5. IT Investment Consistency

Investment behavior is a topical issue in economic and finance literature. IT and IS investments have received attention also in the ITBV research (e.g. Melville, Kraemer & Gurbaxani, 2004; Schreyen, 2013). Yet, how IT investments and IT expenditures react to the cyclical behavior of the economy has received little attention in the ITBV research. We introduce the IT investment consistency construct to the ITBV research to describe, how organizations adjust their IT investments, IT costs and IT development activities to economic cycles, especially to recessions. The IT investment consistency construct is also useful to investigate, how such adjustments relate to other ITBV constructs, most notably to IT deployment success. The underlying idea of the present research is that changes in an organization's environment, such as the change of an economic cycle, will impact the organization's IT investments, IT costs and IT development activities. In general, changes in the environment may either create incentives to increase IT investments, IT costs and/or IT development activities, or lead to the postponements, scale downs or discontinuations of the same.

Our survey data was collected during an economic recession, which continued for the second year at the time of the survey data collection. We deemed it to be more likely that organizations try to find ways to postpone and cut down IT investments rather than to increase them. Likewise we considered it possible that the recession could influence expectations regarding the financial returns on investments as well as risk-return ratios. An organization could, for example, prefer short-return times on investments combined with low risks. On the other hand, we also expect that organizations respond in different ways to economic cycles / recessions, i.e., that the consistency of their IT investment behavior varies. The question is, how to investigate IT investment consistency? We consider those organizations to show higher IT investment consistency, which continue IT investments and other IT development activities as planned and/or which avoid unplanned IT investment postponements or cut downs. Postponements, cut downs and discontinuations of IT investments, IT costs and/or IT development activities could still happen, but they are conducted in a pre-planned way and aligned to related business activities (e.g. Bergeron, Raymond & Rivard, 2001). In summary, the assumption of the present study is that less IT investment and IT costs cuts or postponement as well as more IT development activities reflect higher IT investment consistency. In Sections 2.2 and 2.3, we proposed that, if business is better aligned with IT and if IT is managed better, then it is more likely that IT investments are conducted more consistently. We now also propose that higher consistency of IT investment positively influences the success of IT deployment.

We reasoned that within the above-described generic response scenario there could be two more specific complementary approaches during a recession (Bergeron, Raymond & Rivard, 2001). First, an organization may cut down IT costs (e.g. Cha, Pingry & Thatcher, 2009), postpone IT investments (e.g. Kohli, Deweral & Ow, 2012) and other cost-inducing IT development activities in order to increase the efficiency of the organization in the short run. Similar cost cutting and efficiency improvement activities could be carried out in other activities, such as marketing, business development or legal expenses. The organization could also focus risk-bearing (IT) investments into (new) businesses (e.g. Mithas, Ramasubbu & Sambamurthy, 2011), which are believed to be important for the organization's future after the recession. Second, short and long term efficiency could be enhanced by improving the quality of data (Tallon, Ramirez & Short, 2013), by educating users to deploy IT better (Mithas, Ramasubbu & Sambamurthy, 2011), by developing IT management capabilities (e.g. Aral & Weill, 2007), or by standardizing and consolidating IT to reduce the IT complexity and to remove overlapping IT assets through architecture work (e.g. Pollalis, 2003). At least a part of these activities could be implemented with no or little out-of-the pocket costs by utilizing available internal organizational resources. Such activities could have positive long-term effects after the recession similar to (IT) investments with new business focus.

2.6. The Success of IT Deployment

The ultimate goal of organizations is to increase the success of IT deployment and through that, organizational performance. Our research proposes that the perceived significance of IT, business–IT alignment, IT management, technology usage, and IT-investment consistency influence positively the success of IT deployment. The linkages between the theoretical constructs discussed in sections 2.1–2.5 are seen to have strong causalities and also path-mediated impacts between some of the constructs. For example, the perceived significance of IT is not deemed to directly impact the success of IT deployment but to do that path-mediated through business–IT alignment, IT management and technology usage, that is, as indirect effects.

For reasons given at in the beginning of this section, the present research addresses the influence of ITBV research constructs on the success of IT deployment instead of how IT impacts organizational performance. We drew on user satisfaction research (e.g. Cecez-Kecmanovic, Kautz & Abrahall, 2014) and on IT project performance research (e.g. Nelson, 2007) when dependent variables were defined. The survey items of this research build on the user satisfaction measure (e.g. Aladwani, 2002; Cecez-Kecmanovic, Kautz & Abrahall, 2014) and on the IS success measure studies (e.g. Petter, DeLone and McLean, 2013) for the success of IT deployment in an organization as a whole. The survey items build also IT project success and performance studies (e.g. Nelson, 2007; Liu, Zhang, Keil & Chen, 2010) for the success of IT projects.

It is noteworthy that the following three outcome survey items (of five survey items in total) reflect organizational performance:

What elementary school grading (4-10) would you give to the deployment of IT as a whole within your organization? The outcomes of IT projects correspond in general with our plans. IT projects achieved the business objectives defined for them.

3. RESEARCH MODEL AND METHODOLOGY

3.1. Research Model and Hypotheses

The theoretical research model used in this study is shown in Figure 1. The model builds on the theoretical background discussed in Section 2 and consists of six main constructs. The research model suggests that there is a relatively complex structure of direct and indirect relationships behind the success of IT deployment. We hypothesize that the outcomes of IT – the measures of IT deployment success - are not solely dependent on the technology usage, the IT management, IT investments, or the business-IT alignment, but are a right combination of these determinants and an antecedent to them – the perceived importance of IT.

Thus, the hypotheses for this research are as follows:

H1: Perceived importance of IT positively affects technology usage.
H2: Perceived importance of IT positively affects IT management.
H3: Perceived importance of IT positively affects business-IT alignment.
H4: Business-IT alignment positively affects IT management.
H5: Business-IT alignment positively affects the success of IT deployment.

Figure 1. Research model

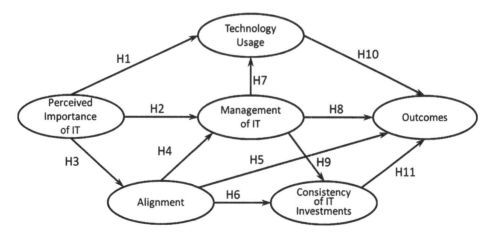

H6: Business-IT alignment positively affects the consistency of IT investments.
H7: Management of IT positively affects technology usage.
H8: Management of IT positively affects the success of IT deployment.
H9: Management of IT positively affects the consistency of IT investments.
H10: Technology usage positively affects the success of IT deployment.
H11: Business-IT alignment positively affects the success of IT deployment.

One may notice that all eleven hypotheses are expected to have positive effects, direct or indirect, on the success of IT deployment. In addition to the direct causal effects we consider the indirect effects important, since they answer such questions as: How does the perceived importance of IT influence outcomes, that is, the success of IT deployment, and what are the most significant path dependencies between the constructs of the model

3.2. Research Method

To validate these research hypotheses, we adopted survey research as the data collection method. In the study, we used a relatively large, existing data set called IT-Barometer 2013, which includes data that was collected by a National Data Processing Association in mid-2013. The data was collected from the Business Executives, the CIOs and other IT Managers, mainly of organizations with over 500 employees. In this study, we used only that part of the available data (survey items) that concentrated on the hypothesized issues. The operationalization of the constructs, that is, the respective measurement items with appropriate references, are given in Table 2 in the Appendix. The listed references served as the theoretical background of our study and as a source and/or motivation for the survey question items. Each construct and concept/measurement item was reviewed in Section 2 to show the link between the constructs of the theoretical background and their measurement items. The number of measurement items per construct varies between three and eleven items.

Invitation to participate in the survey along with one reminder was sent to 2,128 people. The response rate was 10% with 212 responses, which we regard as normal for IS management studies. Of the respondents, 53% (n=115) were CIOs and other IT managers, 19% were business executives, and 28% were senior business experts. Twenty-seven percent of them worked in industry, 12% in commerce, 46% in services, and 14% in public sector organizations. Forty-nine percent of the CIOs in the data reported to CEOs, 26% to CFOs, and 25% to other CxOs.

The relevance of the study's theoretical findings was empirically assessed using one form of confirmatory factor analysis (CFA), namely structural equations modeling (SEM). The variance-based SEM - more often referred to as partial least squares (PLS) - was used instead of covariance based SEM (CBSEM).

This choice was based on three arguments that limit the usage of CBSEM in certain circumstances: First, CBSEM aims to estimate a set of given parameters in a way that the theorized covariance matrix corresponds as closely as possible to the empirically discovered covariance matrix. This notion fundamentally limits the usability of CBSEM for predicting the future, as the objective is to achieve a fit for the status quo rather than to open ways for alternative solutions (Hair, Ringle & Sarstedt, 2011). Furthermore, due to its purely confirmatory nature, CBSEM might prove to be problematic specifically in situations where the theoretical fundaments for the proposition are still developing.

Second, because CBSEM uses either maximum likelihood or generalized-least-squares regression methods in calculations, it requires that the empirically gathered dataset be normally distributed. Moreover, the sample size requirements significantly increase, requiring at least 200 observations as a minimum for the research to be valid (Hair, Ringle & Sarstedt, 2011). The small sample size is perhaps the most pervasive argument for using PLS (Ringle, Sarstedt & Straub, 2012). It is generally accepted that the minimum sample size is only 10 times the number of indicators in the most complex formative construct, added to by the number of paths directed at the construct. In this case, the highest number of constructs is thirteen, directed to technology usage, and thus the minimum sample size would be 130, which our number of useful responses (212) clearly exceeds. Although the rule is questioned (Goodhue, Lewis & Thompson, 2006; Marcoulides & Saunders, 2006), it is commonly proposed and applied (Braunscheidel & Suresh, 2009; Hair, Ringle & Sarstedt, 2011). Contrasting to CBSEM, PLS does not provide overall fit indices for the evaluation of the model quality but there are different measures to evaluate the measurement and the structural models.

A PLS-model of the success of enterprise IT deployment was created using SmartPLS 2.0M3 to evaluate the measurement quality and to verify the structural hypotheses of the research model (Ringle, Wende & Alexander, 2012).

4. ANALYSIS AND RESULTS

In the analysis of the data, we adopted a two-step analysis, in which the measurement model and the structural model were validated separately.

Table 1. Reliability measures of the model

Construct	# of Items	Mean	Std	Loading (t-Value)	AVE	CR	CA	A	C	PI	M	O	TU
Alignment, A	3	4.47	1.27	0.77, 0.88, 0.78 / 16.66, 39.39, 24.80	0.66	0.85	0.75	**0.81**					
Consistency, C	5	4.53	1.10	0.59, 0.75, 0.83, 0.74, 0.84 / 9.61, 16.40, 31.99, 15.29, 36.83	0.57	0.87	0.81	0.51	**0.76**				
Perceived Importance, PI	4	5.52	0.97	0.74, 0.79, 0.86, 0.75 / 18.33, 25.31, 48.17, 15.37	0.62	0.87	0.79	0.52	0.54	**0.79**			
Management, M	4	4.42	1.25	0.86, 0.66, 0.87, 0.84 / 37.42, 10.68, 44.39, 34.87	0.66	0.89	0.83	0.63	0.64	0.69	**0.81**		
Outcomes, O	5	5.26	1.05	0.86, 0.75, 0.72, 0.84, 0.68 / 39.58, 16.60, 14.99, 31.75, 18.79	0.60	0.88	0.83	0.62	0.48	0.54	0.51	**0.77**	
Technology Usage, TU	5	3.75	1.26	0.76, 0.65, 0.77, 0.74, 0.61 / 12.34, 8.10, 16.44, 12.29, 6.61	0.50	0.82	0.77	0.37	0.32	0.34	0.41	0.32	**0.71**

AVE=Average Variance Extracted, CR=Composite Reliability, CA=Cronbach's Alpha.

4.1. Measurement Model

First, the reliability of the full PLS model was analyzed. It soon became clear that the reliability of some constructs (composite reliability) as well as their average variances extracted (AVE) were much too low and that modifications to the original model had to be made. For this purpose, some badly behaving indicators (X15, X21, X22, X23, X24, X26, X29, X51, and X52) behind the latent constructs were identified for possible exclusion. The indicator cross-loadings for the full PLS model were used to find the proper indicator candidates for the exclusion. The overview of the quality indicators of the final model is summarized in Table 1. Please, note that in Section 2 we first discussed each theoretical construct in general to cover the entire construct, and then discussed the measurement items that constitute the indicators of the initial and the final research models.

Because all AVE, composite reliability, and Cronbach's alpha values were greater than the recommended threshold values (0.50, 0.70, and 0.70) in the final model, the variance caused by error terms no longer gave reasons to doubt the validity of the model, and the analysis of the measurement model suggested acceptable convergent validity. In addition, the items significantly loaded on their constructs, showing satisfactory discriminant and convergent validities.

The discriminant validity was evaluated by comparing the square root of the AVE for each construct with the correlations between it and all other constructs. Bolded elements in the diagonal (Table 1, last six columns) are square roots of AVE and off-diagonal elements are interconstruct correlations. Because the bolded elements on the diagonal are greater than the elements in the respective row or column, the results indicate that the particular construct differs from all other constructs. That is, no indicator loaded higher on any other construct that on the "right" construct.

Since the PLS models were firmly backed up by reliability and validity statements, the assessment of the structural model and the respective hypotheses could be conducted in order to meet the objectives of the study and to answer the research questions.

4.2. Structural Model

After the refinement and validation of the measurement model, we proceeded to test the hypotheses described by the research model by assessing the structural (inner) model. After some experiments with a different number of bootstrap samples, we decided to use a bootstrapping procedure with 212 cases and 1000 resamples to test the significance of all paths in the research model (Hair, Ringle & Sarstedt. 2011). The results of the analysis are summarized in Figure 2 and Table 3 in the Appendix, which show the explained variances (R^2), the path coefficients, indirect, and total effects, and the respective significance levels (t-tests). The analysis indicates that Hypotheses H2 – H7, H9, and H11 were supported by the data, whereas Hypotheses H1, H8, and H10 were not.

In addition to the expected direct effects there were some significant indirect effects between the constructs. The perceived importance of IT had the most significant indirect effect on the consistence of IT investments thru three routes $(0.494*0.517 + 0.519*0.187 + 0.519*0.378*0.517 = 0.454)$. The importance of IT had also significant indirect effects on the outcomes of IT deployment (0.395) and on the management of IT (0.196) through business-IT alignment in addition to the direct effect 0.494. Similarly, also business-IT alignment and IT management had significant indirect effects on the other constructs of the model. For the evaluation of the research models predictive power it is important to notice that all indirect effects follow the logic of the model derived from the theoretical background. For example, the management of IT did not influence the outcomes of IT deployment in a statistically significant way – which was probably the biggest surprise of data analysis – but had an indirect effect (0.108) through the consistency of IT investments. In Table 3 (appendix) the total effects are calculated by summing up the

Figure 2. Results of the PLS analysis

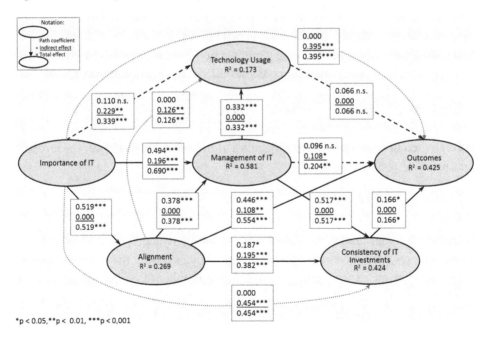

*p < 0.05,**p < 0.01, ***p < 0,001

direct and indirect effects in line with Sattler et al., 2010. Generally, the results indicate a good predicting power of the model, such as

- The perceived importance of IT has a significant impact on the business–IT alignment and on the management of IT. The perceived importance of IT has also several indirect influences and appears an important construct.
- Almost 60% of the quality of IT management is determined by the importance of IT and by the business-IT alignment.
- Consistency of IT investments depends on the quality of IT management together with the level of business-IT alignment. The usage of new technology (e-commerce, social media, cloud computing, BYOD) is affected by the quality of IT management, but the technology usage alone seem to have only a minor effect on the outcomes of IT deployment. In contrast to that, the consistency of IT investments and the level of business-IT alignment have strong effects on the outcomes of IT deployment. The quality of IT management seems to be perceived through the consistency of IT investments.
- The proposed model determines 42.5% of the outcomes of IT deployment.

Because there are no negative relationships in the model, one can expect a kind of cumulative process behind the outcomes of IT deployment. Success in one area leads to success in another area and finally to the success of IT deployment in general. And vice versa - if one area fails, there is a big risk that the other areas in the path will also fail. The relationships within the model can be further analyzed in details. Probably the most important result of the model testing is that no construct alone is able to explain the success of IT deployment. For example, the positive impact of the business-IT alignment alone on the outcomes of IT deployment is illustrated in Figure 3.

5. DISCUSSION AND CONCLUSION

In the present study, we investigated multiple constructs potentially impacting an organization's IT performance. Many interesting and some even obvious results were discovered. In summary, several things have to succeed at the same time to achieve desired good outcomes from IT deployment. IT needs to be considered important, aligned with business, managed properly, IT investments need to show consistency, and IT used responsibly. In other words, we discovered that no single ITBV construct alone is able to explain the outcomes of IT deployment. That appears to be possible only with causal multi-construct models, such as the model we crafted and tested. Our model was able to explain a large proportion of IT performance success

Figure 3. The impact of business: IT alignment on IT outcomes

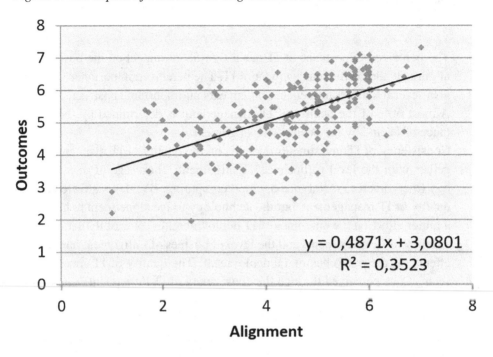

$y = 0,4871x + 3,0801$
$R^2 = 0,3523$

(R^2=0.425). These sentences constitute our answer to the first research question presented in Section one. We were especially interested in finding out, if the consistency of IT investments during a recession helps organizations to deploy IT better. Consistent IT investments were detected to result from proper alignment between business and IT as well as from good IT management. Data collected during an economic recession indicated clearly that organizations, which showed consistency in their IT investments - that in other words followed their original plans to deploy IT - performed better in terms of IT deployment during a bear market. This is our answer to the second research question.

Although our research was able to explain 43% of IT performance success, the constructs of our model, of course, do not represent a complete list of possible success factors that influence IT deployment outcomes. The key question is, how theoretically exhaustive is our model and are some important constructs missing from the model? In the beginning of Section two we listed constructs studied in prior ITBV research. State-of-the-art articles such as Kohli & Grover (2008) and Schreyen (2013) also summarize relevant constructs. We have explained that our research is limited to IT performance and hence organizational performance is excluded. Of the other constructs listed our model does not include IT capabilities and competencies (e.g. Mithas, Ramasubbu, & Sambamurthy, 2011), which are also depicted in the mentioned state-of-the-art articles. Given the vast volume and diversity of ITBV literature it is evident that the survey items in the analyzed data do not capture all concepts of an ITBV construct discussed cumulatively in literature. Adding capabilities and competencies as a construct to the model as well as individual concepts as survey items offer possibilities for further research.

We were forced to leave out the possible effects of business and IT executive competencies in general and their competencies in the governance of IT in particular due to limitations in the data. The survey data we were allowed to use included 182 survey questions. The national information processing association (FIPA) responsible for the survey had not included questions on respondents' personal capabilities and competencies, management culture of the organization and the composition of IT budgets to avoid survey fatigues and to ensure the receiving of as many responses as possible from the busy business and IT executives of primarily large organizations. On the other hand, respondent's industry, size of organization, position either in business or IT, to whom the CIO reported, whether or not IT costs included "traditional" or also business IT costs were included in the survey. They had limited amount of non-systematic dependencies with the survey items shown in Table 2 (appendix). Dependencies were measured with Pearson's correlation coefficient and/or with the Student's t-test. Due to the randomness of dependencies we omitted the reporting of these statistical test results. On the other hand we encouraged FIPA to add competencies as new survey items into their annual survey, which they have recently done. In a more recent study on IT project performance (Dahlberg & Kivijärvi, 2016) we discovered that management competencies had a statistically significant effect on IT project outcomes. Adding the competencies construct to the research model of the present article is another possibility for future studies.

The relationship between IT investments and organizational performance has received a lot of attention in research. The famous productivity paradox claims that IT investments may not contribute to better performance, i.e. higher productivity (Brynjolfsson, 1993). Many factors have been put forward to explain the paradox. Long-term immaterial benefits with delays and intervening factors, as discussed previously, and poor management of IT assets were often proposed as the reasons for the paradox. (Brynjolfsson & Hitt, 1998) showed in a later study that organizations do actually gain productivity benefits, but a big part of the benefits eventually leak to their customers in the form of lower prices and/or better quality. Consider the definition of productivity. Economists calculate productivity as the value of produced goods and services during a certain period of time divided by their production costs, that is, as the ratio of outputs over inputs (Pritchard, 1995). The deployment of IT is typically expected to increase productivity through cost reductions by replacing labor with IT (e.g. Cardona, Kretschmer, & Strobel, 2013), or to increase output (per invested capital) by facilitating higher production volumes per

Table 2. Operational definitions of the measures

Construct	Question Item: Evaluate How Well the Following Statements Apply to Your Organization		Reference: Theoretical Background and/or Idea Source and/or Motivation of Survey Item
Perceived Importance of IT	IT as a Source of Competitive Advantage and Improved Organizational Performance		
	X11	The role of IT as a future competitive advantage increases	Barney, 1991; Melville, Kraemer & Gurbaxani, 2004
	X12	IT serves our business as a partner	Boynton, Zmud & Jacobs, 1994; Aral & Weill, 2007; Wiengarten, Humphreys, Cao & McHugh, 2013
	The Capability of IT to Support Innovations and to Provide Value to Business in this Way		
	X13	IT provides value to our business by facilitating the development of new innovations and by increasing the efficiency of our business processes	Boynton, Zmud & Jacobs, 1994; Mithas, Ramasubbu & Sambamurthy, 2012
	X14	It is extremely important to our future success that IT provide value to our business by facilitating the development of new innovations and by increasing the efficiency of our business processes in the future	Mithas, Ramasubbu & Sambamurthy, 2012
	How Big Is the Proportion of IT Costs from the Revenues of Your Organization or from the Total Budget?		
	X15	Percent (%) of revenues	Brynjolfsson & Hitt, 1998; Brynjolfsson & Brown, 2005; Cha, Pingry & Thatcher, 2009; Mithas, Ramasubbu & Sambamurthy, 2012
Technology Usage	Strategic Role and Deployment of Electronic Business, Social Media, and Innovation IT		
	X21	My organization has a clear strategy and implementation plan for e-commerce as a part of business operations	Coltman, Devinney & Midgley, 2007; Goh & Kauffman, 2013
	X22	The goal of my organization is to significantly increase the use of e-business as a part of business operations	Coltman, Devinney & Midgley, 2007; Goh & Kauffman, 2013
	X23	My organization has a clear strategy and implementation plan for social media as a part of business operations	Luo & Zhang, 2013
	X24	The goal of my organization is to significantly increase the use of social media as a part of business operations	Luo & Zhang, 2013

continued on following page

Table 2. Continued

Construct	Question Item: Evaluate How Well the Following Statements Apply to Your Organization		Reference: Theoretical Background and/or Idea Source and/or Motivation of Survey Item
Technology Usage	**Strategic Role and Deployment of Cloud Services**		
	X25	My organization has a clear strategy and implementation plan for cloud services as a part of business operations	Choudhary & Vithayathil, 2013
	X26	The goal of my organization is to significantly increase the use of cloud services	Choudhary & Vithayathil, 2013
	Strategic Role and Deployment of BYOD (Bring Your Own Device)/IT Consumerization		
	X27	My organization has a clear strategy and implementation plan for BYOD/IT consumerization as a part of business operations	Harris, Ives & Junglas, 2012
	X28	The goal of my organization is to enable the use of same devices at work and for leisure time	Harris, Ives & Junglas, 2012
	X29	The goal of my organization is to enable the use of the same applications and services at work as for leisure time	Harris, Ives & Junglas, 2012
	X210	In my organization, BYOD/IT consumerization is acknowledged in our IT strategy and implementation plan as well as in the development of IT services	Harris, Ives & Junglas, 2012
	X211	The current enterprise architecture of my organizations enables the inclusion of BYOD devices, applications, and services into enterprise architecture	Boh & Yellin, 2006; Harris, Ives & Junglas, 2012

invested capital / used inputs (e.g. Colecchia, & Schreyer, 2001). But what happens if the prices – that is the value - of products and services are also reduced? Superior IT deployment may mean to some companies that they have lower production costs per produced unit. This may appear as a tempting opportunity to increase market share with lower prices. Alternatively, should these companies not reduce prices, their margins and hence profitability will increase. Other companies in the industry will probably take actions to copy the new superior operating way. Also companies from other industries and start-ups may consider the industry lucrative and enter the market should superior IT deployment lead to exceptionally high profitability. If that happens increased capacity and competition could lower prices. In summary, either way, productivity benefits could in the long run leak to customers and the productivity increase may appear small or nonexistent in economic statistics. As an example, consider how IT capacity has improved in relation to its price.

Brynjolfsson and Hitt (1998) actually speculated that a new way of operating gradually becomes a new standard in an industry and no longer offers a competitive advantage. The new way of operating becomes gradually even a strategic necessity to survive. Porter put forward similar argumentation on the strategic impact of Internet (Porter, 2001). However, if IT investments are made consistently and wisely over a long period of time – for example to establish high-performance IT infrastructure and sound application portfolios - organizational performance benefits could be achieved through improved IT performance (Kivijärvi & Saarinen, 1995). The results of our study support such a conclusion. IT investment consistency was detected to result in better ICT deployment success. Thus in the short run an organization will benefit comparatively from consistent IT investments although the benefits may in the long run leak to their customers.

Investment literature on production investments typically assumes that investments are unique one-time transactions into fixed assets with the objective to maximize the utility of a firm over the life-time of an investment until the investment is eventually put to rest with a replacement investment (e.g. Jorgenson, 1963). This approach is typical also in the ITBV research. For example, both Kohli & Grover (2008) and Schreyen (2013) describe IT investments as antecedents to mediating factors (e.g. IT-strategy alignment in Kohli and Grover) and to performance. Schreyen, however, also proposes that the conceptual and empirical disaggregation of IT/IS investments is a research gap in the ITBV research. Our article takes a different approach to IT investments in two ways. First, we proposed and empirically verified that the perceived importance of IT, business-IT alignment and IT management influence IT investment behavior. The theoretical implication is that IT investments should not be seen only as an isolated fixed asset type starting point for IT value delivery but also as a dynamic construct, which is influenced by IT deployment constructs.

Second, in our research the IT investment (consistency) construct includes also IT development activities and their costs, for example user education, improvement of data quality or development of IT management competencies. In financial accounting such items are most often booked into costs instead to investments. Yet, the purpose of application maintenance, user education, data quality and IT management competence improvements is to increase the efficiency and the effectiveness of IT asset utilization. Thus the logic of these costs is similar to IT investments, value is expected after their implementations. Furthermore, over the lifecycle of an IT asset the cumulative maintenance costs can be significantly higher than the initial investment expenditure. This is especially true for information systems and databases. Annual maintenance fee for an IS if often between 15 to 25% of the initial one-time license fee. The maintenance fee typically covers software bug fixes, smaller and larger improvements and adaptations to evolving technologies. If the life-cycle of an IS would be 10 years, then the organization would pay 1.5 to 2.5 times the amount of the initial (license) investment as maintenance fees. The theoretical implication is that IT investments should not be seen only as unique one-time transactions but also as a series of one major initial and several consecutive smaller investments, or disaggregated as Schreyen (2013) notes. We believe that our model captures this feature of IT investments with its consistency effect.

Our findings provide evidence that consistent IT investments are especially important to organizations that perceive IT to have great importance for their business. If IT is seen to have only a support and non-enabling role, it could be easier to cut IT costs during a recession. On the other hand, one might ask if IT could be used to cut other costs in these organizations, and if IT investments should still be continued in order to achieve that. Furthermore, what happens to organizations that did not invest into IT, if the new standard of their industry will more IT-dependent? Longitudinal studies on the consistency of IT investment are needed in the future to properly address these issues and to give organizations better contextual advice on how to manage their IT investments.

Our advice to practitioners is to ensure the existence of a smooth and continuous IT budget, to develop and to realize the plans based on a well-aligned investment portfolio. This pays off when the economic situation changes. It offers opportunities to realize identified benefits and to cash them in when the economy turns again to a bull market. Even though cost cutting and IT-investment postponement sound like an easy way to save funds during a recession, the consequences can be very harmful in the long run.

REFERENCES

Aladwani, A. M. (2002). Organizational Actions, Computer Attitudes, and End-User Satisfaction in Public Organizations: An Empirical Study. *Journal of End User Computing*, *14*(1), 42–49. doi:10.4018/joeuc.2002010104

Aral, S., & Weill, P. (2007). IT Assets, Organizational Capabilities, and Firm Performance: How Resource Allocations and Organizational Differences Explain Performance Variation. *Organization Science*, *18*(5), 763–780. doi:10.1287/orsc.1070.0306

Barney, J. B. (1991). Firm Resources and Sustained Competitive Advantage. *Journal of Management*, *17*(1), 109–120. doi:10.1177/014920639101700108

Bergeron, F., Raymond, L., & Rivard, S. (2001). Fit in Strategic Information Technology Management Research: An Empirical Comparison of Perspectives. *Omega*, *29*(2), 125–142. doi:10.1016/S0305-0483(00)00034-7

Boh, W. F., & Yellin, D. (2006). Using Enterprise Architecture Standards in Managing Information Technology. *Journal of Management Information Systems*, *23*(3), 163–207. doi:10.2753/MIS0742-1222230307

Boynton, A. C., Zmud, R. W., & Jacobs, G. C. (1994). The Influence of IT Management Practice on IT Use in Large Organizations. *Management Information Systems Quarterly*, *18*(3), 299–318. doi:10.2307/249620

Braunscheidel, M. J., & Suresh, N. C. (2009). The organizational antecedents of a firm's supply chain agility for risk mitigation and response. *Journal of Operations Management*, *27*(2), 119–140. doi:10.1016/j.jom.2008.09.006

Brynjolfsson, E. (1993). The productivity paradox of information technology. *Communications of the ACM*, *36*(12), 66–77. doi:10.1145/163298.163309

Brynjolfsson, E., & Brown, P. (2005). VII pillars of IT Productivity. *Optimize*, *4*(5), 26–35.

Brynjolfsson, E., & Hitt, L. M. (1998). Beyond the Productivity Paradox. *Communications of the ACM*, *41*(8), 49–55. doi:10.1145/280324.280332

Cardona, M., Kretschmer, T., & Strobel, T. (2013). ICT and productivity: Conclusions from the empirical literature. *Information Economics and Policy*, *25*(3), 109–125. doi:10.1016/j.infoecopol.2012.12.002

Carr, N. G. (2003). *IT Doesn't Matter*. Harvard Business School Publishing Corporation.

Cecez-Kecmanovic, D., Kautz, K., & Abrahall, R. (2014). Reframing Success and Failure of Information Systems: A Performative Perspective. *Management Information Systems Quarterly*, *38*(2), 561–588.

Cha, H. S., Pingry, D. E., & Thatcher, M. E. (2009). What determines IT spending priorities? *Communications of the ACM*, *52*(8), 105–110. doi:10.1145/1536616.1536644

Chan, Y., & Reich, B. (2007). IT Alignment: What Have We Learned? *Journal of Information Technology*, *22*(4), 297–315. doi:10.1057/palgrave.jit.2000109

Choudhary, V., & Vithayathil, J. (2013). The Impact of Cloud Computing: Should the IT Department Be Organized as a Cost Center or a Profit Center? *Journal of Management Information Systems*, *30*(2), 67–100. doi:10.2753/MIS0742-1222300203

Colecchia, A., & Schreyer, P. (2001). *ICT Investment and Economic Growth in the 1990s: Is the United States a Unique Case? A Comparative Study of Nine OECD Countries.* Organisation for Economic Co-operation and Development (OECD), Directorate for Science, Technology and Industry (DSTI), STI Working papers 7/2001.

Coltman, T. R., Devinney, T. M., & Midgley, D. F. (2007). EBusiness Strategy and Firm Performance: A Latent Class Assessment of the Drivers and Impediments to Success. *Journal of Information Technology, 22*(2), 87–101. doi:10.1057/palgrave.jit.2000073

Dahlberg, T., & Kivijärvi, H. (2016). Towards an Integrative, Multilevel Theory for Managing the Direct and Indirect Impacts of IT Project Success Factors.*Proceedings of the 49th Annual Hawaii International Conference.* doi:10.1109/HICSS.2016.616

Drnevich, P. L., & Croson, D. C. (2013). Information Technology and Business-Level Strategy: Toward an Integrated Theoretical Perspective. *Management Information Systems Quarterly, 37*(2), 484–509.

Eveleens, J. L., & Verhoef, C. (2010). The Rise and Fall of the Chaos Report Figures. *IEEE Software, 27*(1), 30–36. doi:10.1109/MS.2009.154

Gartner Inc. (2012). *Gartner Market Databook, 2Q12 Update.* Available from https://www.gartner.com/doc/2070316/gartner-market-databook-q-update

Goh, K. H., & Kauffman, R. J. (2013). Firm Strategy and the Internet in U.S. Commercial Banking. *Journal of Management Information Systems, 30*(2), 9–40. doi:10.2753/MIS0742-1222300201

Goodhue, D., Lewis, W., & Thompson, R. (2006). PLS, Small Sample Size and Statistical Power in MIS Research.*Proceedings of the 39th Annual Hawaii International Conference.* doi:10.1109/HICSS.2006.381

Hair, J. F. C., Ringle, C. M., & Sarstedt, M. (2011). PLS_SEM: Indeed a Silver Bullet. *Journal of Marketing Theory and Practice, 19*(2), 139–151. doi:10.2753/MTP1069-6679190202

Harris, J., Ives, B., & Junglas, I. (2012). IT Consumerization: When Gadgets Turn Into Enterprise IT Tools. *MIS Quarterly Executive, 11*(3), 90–112.

Henderson, J. C., & Venkatraman, N. (1993). Strategic Alignment: Leveraging Information Technology for Transforming Organizations. *IBM Systems Journal, 32*(1), 4–16. doi:10.1147/sj.382.0472

International Organization for Standardization and the International Electrotechnical Commission. (n.d.). *ISO/IEC 35800:2008Corporate Governance of Information Technology standard.* Downloaded from http://www.iso.org

Jorgenson, D. W. (1963). Capital Theory and Investment Behavior. *The American Economic Review, 53*(2), 247–259.

Kearns, G., & Sabherwal, R. (2007). Strategic Alignment between Business and Information Technology: A KnowledgeBased View of Behaviors, Outcome, and Consequences. *Journal of Management Information Systems, 23*(1), 129–162. doi:10.2753/MIS0742-1222230306

Kivijärvi, H., & Saarinen, T. (1995). Investment in Information Systems and the Financial Performance of the Firm. *Information & Management, 28*(2), 143–163. doi:10.1016/0378-7206(95)94022-5

Kohli, R., Devaraj, S., & Ow, T. T. (2012). Does Information Technology Investment Influence a Firm's market Value? A Case of Non-Publicly Traded Healthcare Firms. *Management Information Systems Quarterly, 36*(4), 1145–1163.

Kohli, R., & Grover, V. (2008). Business Value of IT: An Essay on Expanding Research Directions to Keep up with the Times. *Journal of the Association for Information Systems, 9*(1), 23–39.

Liu, S., Zhang, J., Keil, M., & Chen, T. (2010). Comparing Senior Executive and Project Manager Perceptions of IT Project Risk: A Chinese Delphi Study. *Information Systems Journal, 20*(4), 319–355. doi:10.1111/j.1365-2575.2009.00333.x

Luo, X., & Zhang, J. (2013). How Do Consumer Buzz and Traffic in Social Media Marketing Predict the Value of the Firm? *Journal of Management Information Systems, 30*(2), 213–238. doi:10.2753/MIS0742-1222300208

Marcoulides, G. A., & Saunders, C. (2006). PLS: A Silver Bullet? *Management Information Systems Quarterly, 30*(2), iii–ix.

Melville, N., Kraemer, K., & Gurbaxani, V. (2004). Information Technology and Organizational Performance: An Integrative Model of IT Business Value. *Management Information Systems Quarterly, 28*(2), 283–322.

Mithas, S., Ramasubbu, N., & Sambamurthy, V. (2011). How Information Management Capability Influences Firm Performance. *Management Information Systems Quarterly, 3*(1), 237–256.

Nelson, R. R. (2007). IT Project Management: Infamous Failures, Classic Mistakes, and Best Practices. *MIS Quarterly Executive, 6*(2), 163–183.

Petter, S., DeLone, W., & McLean, E. R. (2013). Information Systems Success: The Quest for the Independent Variables. *Journal of Management Information Systems*, *29*(4), 7–61. doi:10.2753/MIS0742-1222290401

PMBOK. (2015). Data retrieved June 1, 2015 from https://www.pmi.org/PMBOK-Guide-and-Standards.aspx

Pollalis, Y. (2003). Patterns of Co-alignment in Informationintensive Organizations: Business Performance Through Integration Strategies. *International Journal of Information Management*, *23*(6), 469–492. doi:10.1016/S0268-4012(03)00063-X

Porter, M. E. (2001). Strategy and the Internet. *Harvard Business Review*, *79*(3), 62–78. PMID:11246925

PRINCE2. (2015). Data retrieved June 1, 2015 from https://www.prince2.com/prince2-methodology

Pritchard, R. D. (Ed.). (1995). *Productivity Measurement and Improvement – Organizational Case Studies*. Westport, CT: Praeger Publishers.

Ringle, C., Sarstedt, M., & Straub, D. W. (2012). A Critical Look at the Use of PLS-SEM in MIS Quarterly. *Management Information Systems Quarterly*, *36*(1), iii–xiv.

Ringle, C., Wende, S., & Alexander, W. (2012). *SmartPLS Version: 2.0.M3*. Retrieved from http://www.smartpls.de

Sattler, H., Völckner, F., Riediger, C., & Ringle, C. M. (2010). The Impact of Brand Extension Success Factors on Brand Extension Price Premium. *International Journal of Research in Marketing*, *27*(4), 319–328. doi:10.1016/j.ijresmar.2010.08.005

Schreyen, G. (2013). Revisiting IS Business Value Research: What We Already Know, What We Still Need to Know, and How We Can Get There. *European Journal of Information Systems*, *22*(2), 139–169. doi:10.1057/ejis.2012.45

Shleifer, A., & Vishny, R. W. (1997). A survey of Corporate Governance. *The Journal of Finance*, *52*(2), 737–783. doi:10.1111/j.1540-6261.1997.tb04820.x

Standish Group. (2013). *CHAOS Manifesto 2013: Think Big, Act Small*. Retrieved June 1, 2015 from http://versionone.com/assets/img/files/ChaosManifesto2013.pdf

Tallon, P. P., Ramirez, V., & Short, J. E. (2013). The Information Artifact in IT Governance: Toward a Theory of Information Governance. *Journal of Management Information Systems*, *30*(3), 141–177. doi:10.2753/MIS0742-1222300306

Van Grembergen, W., & De Haes, S. (2008). *Implementing Information Technology Governance: Models, Practices and Cases*. Hershey, PA: Idea Group Global. doi:10.4018/978-1-59904-924-3

Ward, P., & Zhou, H. (2006). Impact of Information Technology Integration and Lean/Just-In-Time Practices on Lead-Time Performance. *Decision Sciences*, *37*(2), 177–203. doi:10.1111/j.1540-5915.2006.00121.x

Weill, P., & Ross, J. (2005). A Matrixed Approach to Designing IT Governance. *Sloan Management Review*, *40*(2), 26–34.

Wiengarten, F., Humphreys, P., Cao, G., & McHugh, M. (2013). Exploring the Important Role of Organizational Factors in IT Business Value: Taking a Contingency Perspective on the Resource-Based View. *International Journal of Management Reviews*, *15*(1), 30–463. doi:10.1111/j.1468-2370.2012.00332.x

APPENDIX

Table 3. Direct, indirect, and total effects

Construct	Question Item - Evaluate How Well the Following Statements Apply to Your Organization		Reference - Theoretical Background and/or Idea Source and/or Motivation of Survey Item
IT Management	**The Strategic Management of IT**		
	X31	We manage IT and develop its management as a strategic means	Boynton, Zmud & Jacobs, 1994; Melville, Kraemer & Gurbaxani, 2004; Chan & Reich, 2007; Kearns & Sabherval, 2007)
	X32	It is extremely important to our future success that we manage IT and develop its management as a strategic means in the future	Melville, Kraemer & Gurbaxani, 2004
	X33	We align the objectives of our IT activities with our business objectives so that we are able to evaluate how IT impacts the achievement of our business objectives	Henderson & Venkatraman, 1993; Weil & Ross, 2005; Chan & Reich, 2007; Drnevich & Croson, 2013
	X34	Based on reliable metrics, we know well the benefits of IT management and its development as a strategic means	Boynton, Zmud & Jacobs, 1994; Melville, Kraemer & Gurbaxani, 2004; Petter, DeLone & MCLean, 2013
Business-IT Alignment	**Operative Alignment of Business and IT**		
	X41	We know well the impact of IT on our business	Boynton, Zmud & Jacobs, 1994; Melville, Kraemer & Gurbaxani, 2004; Petter, DeLone & MCLean, 2013
	X42	In our organization's IT infrastructure, applications, data, and processes create an integrated whole	Tallon, Ramirez & Short, 2013
	Strategic Alignment of Business and IT		
	X43	Senior executives, business unit executives, and IT executives share the accountabilities and responsibilities of IT management on the basis of clearly defined governance arrangement	Henderson & Venkatraman, 1993; Weil & Ross, 2005; Chan & Reich, 2007; Tallon, Ramirez & Short, 2013; Van Grembergen & De Haes, 2008

continued on following page

Table 3. Continued

Construct	Question Item - Evaluate How Well the Following Statements Apply to Your Organization		Reference - Theoretical Background and/or Idea Source and/or Motivation of Survey Item
Consistency of IT Investments	**The Impact of Economy on Business Operations during the Recent Year**		
	X51	We increased the efficiency of IT by cutting IT costs	Brynjolfsson & Hitt, 1998; Brynjolfsson & Brown, 2005; Cha, Pingry & Thatcher, 2009
	X52	We postponed IT purchases and IT investments	Brynjolfsson & Hitt, 1998; Brynjolfsson & Brown, 2005; Kohli, Deveraj & Ow, 2012
	X53	We used IT to create new business	Mithas, Ramasubbu & Sambamurthy, 2012
	X54	We increased IT benefits by educating users	Mithas, Ramasubbu & Sambamurthy, 2012
	X55	We improved the quality of IT-enabled data/ information and eliminated problems caused by broken data flows	Pollalis, 2003; Mithas, Ramasubbu & Sambamurthy, 2012; Tallon, Ramirez & Short, 2013
	X56	We integrated and consolidated our enterprise architecture	Pollalis, 2003; Boh & Yellin, 2006
	X57	We improved business driven IT management within our organization	Aral & Weill, 2007
Outcomes	**What Elementary School Grading (4-10) Would You Give to the Deployment of IT within Your Organization**		
	Y1	What elementary school grading (4-10) would you give to the deployment of IT as a whole within your organization?	Aladwani, 2002; Petter, DeLone & McLean, 2013; Cecez-Kecmanovic, Kautz & Abrahall, 2014
	Evaluate How Well IT Projects Succeeded in Your Organization		
	P1	The outcomes of IT projects correspond in general with our plans	Cecez-Kecmanovic, Kautz & Abrahall, 2014; Nelson, 2007
	P2	IT projects kept their time-tables	Nelson, 2007; Liu, Zhang, Keil & Chen, 2010
	P3	IT projects kept their agreed budgets	Nelson, 2007; Liu, Zhang, Keil & Chen, 2010
	P4	IT projects achieved the business objectives defined for them	Nelson, 2007; Liu, Zhang, Keil & Chen, 2010

Chapter 8

The Impact of IT Governance Compliance on Enhancing Organizational Performance in Abu Dhabi

Zoheir Ezziane
University of Pennsylvania – Abu Dhabi, UAE & Higher Colleges of Technology, UAE

Abdulla Al Shamisi
Al Ain Women's College, UAE

ABSTRACT

Information Technology (IT) governance is known to play a vital role in the corporate governance in terms of the accountability of the organization's Board of Executives to determine that organization's IT promotes to attain the goals and objectives of the organization, through employing various specific methods, processes and procedures for communication and relationship. In addition, IT governance focuses on how IT is delivering value, controlling risks, managing resources and increase performance. The aim of this work is to analyse IT governance practices used in Abu Dhabi public sector. It employs a quantitative research ap-

DOI: 10.4018/978-1-5225-0861-8.ch008

proach to accomplish the goals of this study. The outcomes of this work refer to important findings such as that most known and recommended international standards and IT frameworks as well as non-IT frameworks are employed by the Abu Dhabi public sector. The known frameworks and standards include ISO 9001, ITILv3, ISO 27001, ISO 20000, PMBOK, BSC, and COBIT respectively, are used as per public entities' needs to enhance the performance of public sector organizations and to comply with local, federal and governmental regulations. This work recommends many plans and best practices that can be employed by both IT governance Board and IT practitioners to leverage IT assets and improve IT governance. Ultimately, the enforcement of such recommended measures in the organizations will result in decreasing overall operational cost as well as enhancing service quality, IT governance effectiveness and interoperability between government bodies.

1. INTRODUCTION

Implementing information technology (IT) governance frameworks to public organizations is critically important for most of the countries as they need to consolidate infrastructure and IT operations, to get greater efficiencies, make technology more effective and improve information security. Also, it helps to improve the quality of the existing services to public and it assists to develop solutions to meet their needs more quickly, and cuts down on the costs of running and supporting technology.

IT has become crucial for the government agencies to serve and provide their constituents modernized services more effectively, capably, and sustainably, and making IT governance as a priority for the public organizations leaders to seek best practices of IT frameworks for their agencies. Furthermore, Lucas (2005, 5) mentioned that "the key to success with technology is not the technology per se, but the ability to manage it well".

IT is also of high relevance in public administrations and its usage in the field has increased rapidly in recent years due to its enabling capacity to adapt to change and its role as a driving force for modernization (Greger, Petra & Helmut, 2015). Moon, Lee and Roh (2014) reviewed research themes and methods used in IT in government and e-government research as well as acknowledged the differences in IT in government and e-government, which are not completely understood in public administration.

Moreover, IT is not just essential to a corporate business, but has become fundamental to public sector entities in order to deliver the necessary outcomes for the specific stakeholders. In fact IT has grown to be a vital element in the functioning of the public sector heightens the importance of proper governing of the IT environment and processes of the public sector entity (Nfuka & Rusu, 2009; Woods, 2010).

Implementing IT governance frameworks to the governmental sector help its agencies to share information and other resources as necessary to meet the needs of the citizens and the society (Rubino & Vitolla, 2014; Pardo & Burke 2008). Addition to that, IT governance frameworks are considered to be mandatory for the public sector to create interoperability between agencies and improve the capabilities of government agencies to effectively serve the needs of the citizens and the society as a whole including the private sector and other agencies (Mergel et al., 2014; Goldsmith and Eggers 2004). Due to the significance of IT systems to organizations, managing the IT risks is no more just a technical problem, but it has become a business problem that can adversely impact the whole business (Bergeron et al., 2015; Spremic, 2011; De Haes & Van Grembergen, 2010). Therefore, the strategic role of information technology in organizations has become a critical factor involving the IT governance and implementing widely applicable Information System (IS) frameworks, best practices, standards and methodologies that are reliable and ensuring smooth functioning of the information systems (ITGI, 2003; Ezziane & Al Shamisi, 2013).

The Government of Abu Dhabi is realizing the importance of IT systems in sustaining future growth, and economic development is investing considerable amount of money in IT systems that can help to transform its oil driven economy to a knowledge based economy (Shane, 2011). Over the last decade due to rapid economic development and to meet the growing IT needs, public sector organizations have adopted a number of different international standards, based on availability of expertise (Abu Talib, El Barachi, Khelifi &Ormandjieve, 2012).

Recently, many public sector organizations in Abu Dhabi have increasingly become IT driven and initiatives such as e-Government and e-Services have transformed the traditional role of IT from a support tool to a strategic tool that is driving change and transformation (Datamonitor, 2009; Ezziane & Al Shamisi, 2013). Due to the strategic nature of IT, its effective governance has become extremely important and IT decisions makers have used several frameworks to meet their IT governance needs (Abu Talib, El Barachi, Khelifi & Ormandjieve, 2012). Directly related to the complexity inherited from various frameworks IT managers may face challenges in choosing the right framework to manage their IT assets (PWC, 2009; Abu Talib, El Barachi, Khelifi & Ormandjieve, 2012).

The different standards used by government departments, pose added challenges in implementing the e-Government strategy of the Abu Dhabi Government. Towards this end Abu Dhabi Government is working to harmonize the standards since standards ensure a high level of quality, safety, reliability, and efficiency in the products and services used (Richards & Dar, 2009). Therefore Abu Dhabi government established Abu Dhabi Systems & Information Center Authority (ADSIC) to control and harmonize the standards in public sector.

The current IT environment is an intrinsic part of the Abu Dhabi public sector environment as it plays a critical role in business processes. Due to this scenario IT is expected to meet regulatory compliance, ensure availability, information security and cost control and address risk management. The overall expectations from IT are growing and the challenges of IT governance faced by IT managers become more complicated (Selig, 2008). IT managers therefore are faced with the challenge of implementing and choosing the appropriate framework that meets the expectations of internal and external IT stakeholders (Selig, 2008).

The government of Abu Dhabi in late 2005 established Abu Dhabi systems & information center department (ADSIC) to control the implementation of the e-Government program in Abu Dhabi government entities. The center is considered as the IT agenda of Abu Dhabi emirate and has the right to implement policies and standards and apply them to all the government entities. ADSIC recommend technology standards and frameworks for Abu Dhabi government and other entities to help delivering world class services and highest level of efficiency, confidentiality, and safety (ADSIC, 2013).

Mochiko (2010) states that government organizations invest significantly in IT assets but struggle with regard to their full utilization and benefit little, mainly due to the use of various frameworks and non-integrated systems. This dissertation entitled, "A Critical Analysis of the IT Governance Frameworks Employed by Public Sector Organizations in Abu Dhabi" is an attempt to investigate and find out the IT governance standards and frameworks used in the Abu Dhabi Public sector and the value brought to public sector by adopting IT frameworks and the challenges that faced by IT managers during the implementation of the respective frameworks.

This study aims to provide an insight into the common used IT frameworks in Abu Dhabi government sector, best practices of each, and major challenges faced during the implementation of IT frameworks. It highlights the importance of implementing IT governance frameworks in Abu Dhabi public sector. Specifically, this study seeks to find answers on the following questions:

- What are the IT Governance frameworks employed by Abu Dhabi public sector organizations?
- What are the values and benefits gained by adopting IT Governance frameworks in Abu Dhabi public sector organizations?
- What are the IT Governance implementation challenges faced by IT managers in Abu Dhabi public sector?

This study is an effort to find out the IT frameworks that are implemented by the Abu Dhabi public sector and to address the IT Governance challenges faced by IT managers in the Abu Dhabi public sector and provide them with thoroughly researched information that can help them in choosing the appropriate framework and cope with the new challenges. In addition to that, this study will help IT managers and practitioners to have good analysis knowledge about IT best practices and the challenges that may face during implementation. In details, the significance of this study is to provide IT managers' researched information that highlights the IT frameworks used by authorities, ministries, departments in the Abu Dhabi public sector and the values and benefits brought by adopting the IT governance frameworks.

Furthermore, this conducted study is intended to make a contribution to the academic community on the phenomenon of IT governance frameworks used in the Abu Dhabi public sector. The findings of this research will give a good view about the IT governance frameworks used in the public sector and will help the public sector agencies to promote an efficient and effective IT governance implementation. Also, due to the lack of scholarly publications around the IT governance frameworks in the Abu Dhabi public sector, this study should motivate and ensure the interest of those involved in research. However, the results and the findings will be helpful for both academics and practitioners. Last but not least, the results of this dissertation will help us in making a comparison with an international study.

The main focus of this investigation is to identify and understand the best known IT frameworks used in the Abu Dhabi public sector. Also, this dissertation concentrates on recognizing the value that IT governance frameworks bring to the Abu Dhabi government sector. On the other hand, this study attends to have knowledge about the IT governance frameworks implementation and the challenges faced by IT managers.

2. LITERATURE REVIEW

In general, governance means the way rules are set and implemented to guide direct and control the organization and constituent's actions. In other words, governance is the ability of an organization to control its actions (ITGI, 2003). Governance describes the methods an organization exercise to make sure that its constituents adhere to its agreed processes, rules and policies (Kaselowski, 2008). Organizations implement proper governance strategy systems to monitor, document and record every event, uses proper actions to ensure compliance with established policies, and offers corrective action in case policies and rules have been ignored or misunderstand (Alam, 2009).

There has been a worldwide concentration on corporate governance (CG), because of many collapses of international organizations at the beginning of this decade such as Enron and WorldCom in the United States (Gartner, 2009). Sohal and Fitzpatrick (2002, 97) defined Corporate governance as "a setting in which others can manage their tasks effectively". Later this definition was expanded by Sohal and Fitzpatrick (2002) to cover various aspects within organization and to answer the question of what must be done to add value to an organization while including activities such as administration, coordination, assessing and planning.

Koch (2002) describes the term 'Corporate governance' as what an organization must do to add value, how it must be done and what is the structure required to achieve that. This contains organizational policies, structures and management processes (Schwarz & Hirschheim, 2003). These policies, rules processes and structures assist organization to achieve its vision, values and strategies, by supporting the key decisions that are addressed by corporate governance (Weill & Ross, 2005).

The IT Governance Institute, defines Enterprise (Corporate) Governance "as a set of responsibilities and practices exercised by the Board and Executive Management with the goal of providing strategic direction, ensuring that objectives are achieved, ascertaining that risks are managed appropriately and verifying that the enterprise's resources are used responsibly" (ITGI, 2003).

IT governance is very broad topic, though no one can depict what it is exactly (Broadbent, 2003). There are many interesting definitions for IT Governance written by different practitioners, and international institutes in this area. One of these definitions is provided by IT Governance Institute, an internationally recognized authority in this area that defines IT governance as "The responsibility of the board of directors and executive management, It is an integral part of enterprise governance and consists of the leadership and organizational structures and processes that ensure that the organization's IT sustains and extends the organization's strategies and objectives" ITGI (2003, 11).

Other interesting definitions provided by Weill and Woodham (2002, 10) saying that "IT governance is specifying the decision rights and accountability framework to encourage desirable behaviour in the use of IT "; for Van Grembergen (2004, 17), "IT governance is the organizational capacity exercised by the board, executive management and IT management to control the formulation and implementation of IT strategy and in this way ensure the fusion of business and IT ".

The definitions cited above are different in most but they also agree in some fundamental parts:

- Accountability and responsibility of IT governance is the role of the board of directors and executive management.

- Aligning business strategy and IT strategy is the main objective of IT governance (ITGI, 2003).
- IT governance contains many related aspects which are strategies, policies, responsibilities, structures and processes for using IT within an organization.
- The role of IT governance is differing from the role of IT management.
- IT governance is one of the essential parts of corporate governance.

While the main aim of IT governance is to align the business strategies and Information Technology strategies all together in an effective and efficient manner. IT governance strategies are developed by the board of directors, shareholders, and other stakeholders with common interests, these IT governance policies are very important as it ensures the smooth flow of processes (Wessels & van Luggoernberg, 2006; Wu, Straub & Liang, 2015).

There are major components identified by IT Governance Institute (ITGI) and other institutes that are essential for IT governance structure and to motivate organizations to adopt IT governance practices. These main points are considered the common areas that organizations may benefit from effective IT governance practices and techniques. Managing these areas properly enhance IT governance practices and allow IT function to operate as a business enabler in an organization. In 2007 the ITGI reports that there are four major key drivers for adopting IT governance practices such as stakeholder value, setting strategy, managing risk, delivering value and measuring performance. On the other hand, Symons (2005) presented four other important objectives that motivate organizations to adopt IT governance practices. These drivers are striving for excellence; IT value alignment, risk management, accountability and performance measurement.

To align IT environment properly with the objectives of the company in order to achieve IT governance is a very challenging and complicated task (ITGI, 2003; Coltman et al, 2015). Obviously, there are two reasons behind senior management and board members are unwilling to take ownership for IT matters, even though great costs and risks are at large (Butler & Butler, 2010). One of these reasons is the uncertainty about IT requirements and the lack knowledge of the technical components (ITGI, 2003; IBM, 2010) and the second reason is about the differences between managing and governing IT. These two problems are discussed in details in the section that follow (ITGI, 2003).

However, institutions that have good governance practices get a higher return on assets, chief information officers (CIOs) believe that their executives have poor insight into IT governance (Willson & Pollard, 2009) IT governance is the same as using frameworks to support and monitor the process, but using frameworks without a guidance and good knowledge will not essentially lead to good IT governance, nor will it avoid risks and realize synergy between IT processes and business processes

(Willson & Pollard, 2009). The IT governance model chosen by the organizations should be matching the business environment and the characteristics of the social environment of the business. (Willson & Pollard, 2009)

There are many widely used IT governance frameworks that exist to govern IT in order for IT to add value to the business and to support the process of IT governance (Nfuka & Rusu, 2009). Many organizations aim to use well-known frameworks as reference for achieving IT governance principles (ITGI, 2008b; Janahi, Griffiths and Ammal, 2015). In order to implement the IT governance, organizations could formulate their own IT governance framework, or they can decide between some pre-established IT governance frameworks that are in use (ITGI, 2008b; Janahi, Griffiths and Ammal, 2015). These frameworks are standards because they have been tested by many experts in the field across many countries. There are several standards, some of these are, ITIL, COBIT, ASL, Six Sigma, SAS70, CMM/ CMMI, ISO 17799:9000, IT services CMM, SOX, IT Due Diligence, SysTrust, IT Governance Review, IT Governance Assessment, PRINCE2, IT Governance Assessment, IT Audit, IT Governance Checklist, IT Governance Assessment Process (ITGAP) Model.

According to PwC survey conducted from July 2005 till October 2005 on behalf ITGI, the population of the survey consisted of two groups of CIOs and CEOs. The population of the survey selected from ITGI's contact database and random organizations. The total number of population was 695, of which 623 were from the random sample of organizations and 72 were from ITGI's database. This survey shows the major of participants use or thinking to use an internally designed framework. The survey illustrates that use of COBIT framework has declined slightly when compared with the previous survey conducted in 2003, this is because COBIT most of the time acts as a baseline, in part or whole form (ITGI Global Status Report, 2006).

Among these frameworks some frameworks are more in existence than others, i.e. they are used by more sectors as compared to the other frameworks, and these frameworks are COBIT, ITIL, CMMI, Six Sigma and ISO 17799, 27001 as shown in Figure 1 (Spremic, 2011).

All of these frameworks are designed in order to meet the most specific needs of the companies, for instance the ITIL framework was developed in order to implement the best of IT service management, while the CMMI was formulated keeping in the mind the improvement in the processes that are used in software development, while Six Sigma also focuses on the improvement of processes, the technique that is used by the company is statistical techniques. The ISO 17799 framework is a security standard that is implemented by establishing some of the best practices in information security, whereas the ISO 9000 is a standard that was published by the ISO guiding quality management systems (Consulting-Portal Inc., 2007).

Figure 1. Most used IT governance frameworks

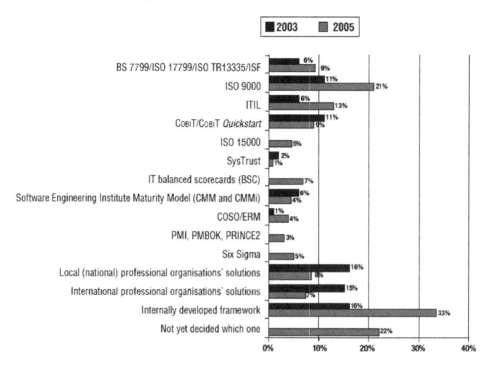

The COBIT framework i.e. Control Objectives for Information and Related Technology, is a framework that is dedicated towards the alignment of the IT control in order to achieve the business goals of the company. COBIT bridges the gap between control needs, business risks and other technical issues by placing a system of IT controls that are in relation to the business objectives (Gerke & Ridley, 2006; Janahi, Griffiths & Ammal, 2015).

The ITIL i.e. IT infrastructure library, is a set of several practices that are formulated by the office of government commerce, which is under the British Government, ITIL has formulated itself as the most preferred standard in the support of providing IT infrastructure (Iden & Eikebrokk, 2014). The main idea behind ITIL is rather amazing, as ITIL bundles the best practices that are observed in private and public firms all around the world (Consulting-Portal Inc., 2007).

The main idea behind CMMI i.e. Capability Maturity Model Integration, is to transform into a process with greater randomness, and immaturity, into a process that is rather stable, disciplined, and is mature. This framework is often used as a benchmark in the determining the level of maturity of a company towards software development. The main feature of CMMI is that it can support the entire software development lifecycle rather than just supporting developmental life cycle, CMMI can be used effectively in the entire organization and in anywhere, because it can guide improvement in projects, or in a particular organization in the company, or in the entire organization (Consulting-Portal Inc., 2007).

Some of the most widely used IT frameworks selected in this study include COBIT, ITIL and ISO as shown in Figure 1. These are considered best-practices and organizations use them as development models when coming up with their IT governance structures. COBIT is powerful in IT controls and metrics; ISO 27001 standards is more convenient for IT security and ITIL focuses on processes, especially those surrounding the IT helpdesk and used to provide improved IS service delivery and service management.

Despite the fact that frameworks are designed to be able to support IT governance, but they are too difficult to implement and too detailed. Besides that, there is no framework that gives the exact answer and when companies think to implement several frameworks in combination, they often become confused and mixed up (Calder, 2008).

On the other hand, IT governance frameworks are available and broadly used; whereas some of these frameworks and best practices are insufficient and have many deficiencies. (Hoekstra & Conradie, 2002). ITGI (2008a) and Rudman (2010) claims that COBIT is a high-level control tool, but have some deficiencies and not offering the required technical particulars and the detail needed.

Hoekstra and Conradie (2002), Arraj (2010) concluded that as ITIL focuses generally on processes, ITIL by itself is inadequate as a governance practices and should be used in combination with other frameworks to get the best governance practices. On the other hand, there is a strong connection between ITIL and COBIT and when they used in collaboration they cover high-level and low-level controls and activities (Hoekstra & Conradie, 2002; Arraj, 2010; Karkoskova, & Feuerlicht, 2015).

The implementation of different practices and frameworks does not bring success; it is all about the adoption, constant observing and improvement to these practices will help to achieve effectiveness and efficiency in IT environments that will help organization to grow (IBM, 2010). IT best practices and frameworks need to be reformed to fit the specific needs of the business processes and organizational structure (Hoekstra & Conradie, 2002; ITGI, 2008a; Bahsani, Semma & Sellam, 2015). The challenge is to manage the different frameworks and to ensure that the IT architecture and processes are assisting the business methods of the particular entity (IBM, 2010).

Abu Talib, Khelifi, and El Barachi (2011) conducted a survey about the IT frameworks used in the UAE. The study conducted between September 2010 to December 2010 The study was called " Exploratory study on innovative use of ISO standards for IT security in the UAE" the study is about setting guidelines for any organization that is concerned about applying ISO 27001 standard.

The study gives background information on IT standards in the UAE and shows the methodology that is used to get the results. The paper sum up that the most organizations in the UAE are not certified, but they use local standards (i.e. ADSIC).

Based on the results of Abu Talib, Khelifi, and El Barachi (2011) survey, it shows that organizations in the UAE are preferred to implement data management and interchange standards, IT security techniques standards, and software and systems engineering standards. The study also shows that number of organizations that are ISO certified in UAE about 8% and the rest of organizations are uncertified in both private and public sector (Abu Talib, Khelifi, & El Barachi, 2011).

3. RESEARCH METHODOLOGY

The objective of this research was to gain an understanding of IT governance and the implementation of IT practices in Abu Dhabi public sector organizations, through the identification and gathering of empirical data (Zikmund, 2003) It aims at laying down a framework to apply sort of validity and reliability to the research results. Carmines and Zeller (1979) stated that reliability is usually concerned with stability over time. Consequently, both terms are crucial to understand measurement in theoretical and applied data gathering settings.

Judgmental sampling has been adopted to determine or select the number of Abu Dhabi public sector organization of the study as this helps to control the sample size on judgment basis. This type of technique is also selected in this work due to the minimal population of the organization being selected. Such situation makes the use of nonprobability sampling procedures more convenient. In addition, it is apparent from the research topic that the goal is to look at a specific target which is IT units in Abu Dhabi government public sector. As a result, the research sample selection will be based on non-random sampling and specifically self-selection sampling. Limiting the selection to not include all Abu Dhabi government entities IT departments is due to the fact that not all entities have an IT department. Some of them only have IT help desk function and including them in the sample will be insufficient.

Two methods have been used in obtaining data in conducting the empirical research. This includes primary data obtained by formulating a set of questionnaires designed to be replied by IT managers, IT Investment decision makers working in the government departments in Abu Dhabi, to determine which IT governance framework is the most preferred framework by the respondents, to gain an understanding of IT governance and the implementation barriers of IT practices in Abu Dhabi public sector organizations. Secondary data obtained from journal papers, internal reports and documents, websites, magazines, books, which serve as a good theoretical foundation for the research.

In this study, the questionnaire is used as a tool of data collection which enables easy col- lection. The questionnaire comprised of twenty questions divided into three parts. The first part focused on the demographic details and the current IT governance framework used in Abu Dhabi. The second was on the value and benefits that the IT framework brings to an organization and the third was on the challenges and barriers of implementing IT governance framework.

The wording of the questions was open, in that it did not give clues about any desirable results. The respondent was free to choose the answers as he/she deemed fit. Furthermore, clear instructions were included in the questionnaire. This was purely to guide the respondent in answering the questions, and give a rationale for any items whose purpose was unclear. The final-product was then inspected to ensure it addressed the key issues of the research.

The questionnaire was directed and emailed to the Heads of IT departments working for Abu Dhabi Public sector organizations after contacting them to get their approval.

The questionnaire has offered the most efficient means to obtain the needed responses; however, the online Survey Monkey software was used to collect the re- sponses from the re- spondents and analyze the data collected from the questionnaire as well as an email sent to the participants containing a copy of the question- naires if they are not able to fill it online. The statistical data will be presented in tables and graphs in Microsoft excel spreadsheet. The data was then verified to eliminate non-response and data capturing mistakes.

4. RESULTS AND ANALYSIS

The data were collected using, e-mail surveys, and online surveys questionnaire. The data were collected from IT specialists within selected public organizations in Abu Dhabi to determine the most used IT framework and the values or benefits brought by adopting IT governance frameworks in the public sector. Also, a list of implementation challenges that are faced by public organizations during the imple- mentation phase of current IT frameworks introduced and evaluated. A total of 20 questionnaires are published online on "Survey Monkey" website to collect the re- spondents answer and a printed version of the same survey was sent to participants who could not fill it online. The survey Monkey is a well-known tool to enable the collection of data relating to the research and the academic needs. Email messages were sent to all IT seniors in Abu Dhabi public sector organizations to participate in the study, and follow up calls were made to the selected organizations participants to motivate them to participate in the study. The collected responses from the selected public organization show that are 18 out of 30 of the public organizations surveyed participated and completed the questionnaires online.

4.1 Data Analysis

Based on the research questions and the research objectives, the survey questionnaires are classified into three main categories that can lead to reach the answers for the research questions. In this work, the questionnaires are classified into three main categories in a logical order. Each section of the survey questionnaires is analyzed by selecting the key questions of each part and linked them to the research questions to deduce the answers based on the analysis of the data and the way the results were interpreted.

The respondents were asked to specify which department or public organization they belong. A 23 of 30 public organizations participated and the response rate of 76.7% was achieved. The collected responses from the selected public organization show that the 23 of them completed and answered all the questions in the survey. This high number of participants indicates that there is a high-level of awareness to IT governance among Abu Dhabi public organizations.

One of questions has been designed to ask participants to select which IT frameworks are used by their respective organization. The results given by the respondents are depicted in figure 2 and shows that most frequently used frameworks for IT governance in Abu Dhabi government sector are ISO 9001 as quality standard framework, ITIL v3 as service management framework, ISO 27001 as IT security standard, and others such as ADSIC, HAAD as internally developed frameworks, PMBOK, Balance scorecard, COBIT as a performance measuring method.

Based on the results given by Abu Dhabi organization respondents, there are some issues that need to be considered and brought forward. One of these issues is that many respondents have selected not just one framework; they have chosen multiple frameworks as it is allowed in this work. Mainly the three abovementioned frameworks are ISO 9001, ITIL, ISO 27001 and ISO 20000. Also, respondents with the option "others" for this question have provided ADSIC framework and HAAD framework as an answer to this question. These respective frameworks are considered as organization own developed frameworks. These frameworks are developed internally for auditing purposes and for complying with government regulations. On the other hand, the implementation of ISO 9001 and ITIL has become popular among Abu Dhabi government sector due to the support and encouragements of the Sheikh Khalifa Excellence Award, and due to the increased number of security audits performed.

Figure 2. Frameworks and standards implemented in Abu Dhabi public sector

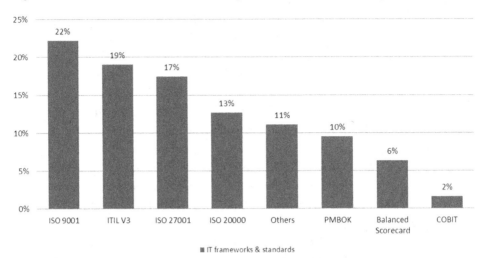

Due to the similarities in the functions of most IT frameworks, these are organized by their focus area to have a good perception of the IT governance frameworks in the public sector. As illustrated in the Table 2, the IT frameworks are organized into six areas based on their function, concentration and what areas that they can support. These areas as shown on the table below are IT governance, Service management, quality management, project management, risk management, and internally developed frameworks.

As illustrated in Figure 3, it appears that implemented frameworks which focus on IT governance practices represents only 8% of the implemented frameworks and it is noticeable that fewer of the public organizations implemented it. On the other hand, Abu Dhabi government is focusing more on quality management frameworks which they indicate 35% of the total adopted frameworks. This is can be due to wide use of quality management frameworks among public sector organizations for enhancing IT services, better control and for customer satisfaction also it can be concluded that some of the quality management frameworks may not require any special expertise, easy to implement, and not expensive compares to COBIT and Balanced Scorecard. The reasons behind designing and developing an internal framework can be referred to the nature of the organization and its structure such as health sector.

The last questions were asked to the respondents in the demographic section is to identify and select the most important drivers for IT-related governance activities to their organizations. This question can help the study to identify the motives that make Abu Dhabi government public sector implement the respective frameworks. In this question the respondents were allowed to choose from 6 different options as

Table 1. Implemented frameworks scope

Category	Type	Examples	Adoption Percentage %
IT Governance practices	Help on how to manage information, measuring performance.	COBIT, Balanced Scorecard	8%
Service Management	How to perform and organize IT management, such as service delivery & support	ITIL	19%
Quality Management	Quality standards used to support IT processes & to improve the processes performance	ISO 900x, ISO 20000	35%
Project Management	Portfolio, program & project management	PMBOK	10%
Risk Management, Security	Helps identifying & managing risk, security issues	ISO 2700x	17%
Internally Developed Framework	Developed internally by public organizations for auditing IT processes & security issues	ADSIC, SKEA, HAAD	11%

Figure 3. Frameworks and standards implemented in Abu Dhabi public sector

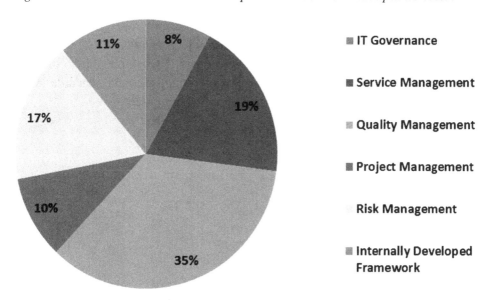

well respondents can select 2 or 3 options at the same time depend on his perception. Also, option "other reasons" allows the respondents to stimulate their own reasons or drivers for implementing IT governance frameworks. Figure 4 shows that approximately 21% of the respondents stated that complying with industry and governmental regulations is the most important driver for implementing IT governance-related practices for the public sector. The response of complying with industry and governmental regulations may be a result of governmental instructions, statute or third party demand.

The less important driver between the other drivers is increasing agility to support future changes in the business with response rate of 9%. Leaders, complexity of organization environment and fear to change are some predicted reasons behind the low response of this driver.

4.2 Values and Benefits Brought by Adopted Governance Frameworks and Standards

In this section, all the participants were questioned to specify the significance of IT governance frameworks to be, to the successful delivery of the organization strategy or vision as shown in Figure 5. The figure shows that 17.1% and 26.1% of the participants consider frameworks and standards are very important and important respectively to organization strategy and vision. Both percentages indicates that Abu Dhabi public organizations have shown a high-level of awareness towards the importance of frameworks and standards to organization strategy and vision, and it is generally seen as contributing significantly to the delivery of organization strategy. On the other hand, 43.5% of participants understand that standards and frameworks are somewhat important to the organization strategy. This can be due to the lack of knowledge and training about the international frameworks and standards. Also, small portion of participants consider them not very important.

Figure 4. IT governance drivers

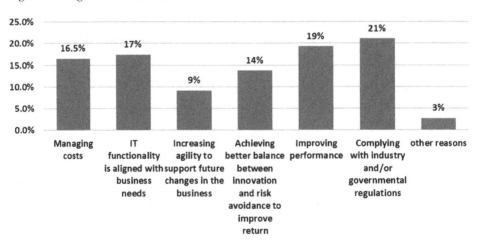

Figure 6 shows that respondents were requested to assess the effectiveness of their respective adopted IT governance frameworks in their organizations. Based on the findings from Figure 6, it's apparent that approximately 30.5% of the respondents were aware of the effectiveness of IT governance frameworks which indicates that public organizations using some measurement and assessments tools to evaluate the benefits and the values that are brought by adopting the respective frameworks. Around half of the participants considered the applied standards and frameworks in their organizations are somewhat effective. Actually the reason behind that can be due to the recent implementation of the respective standards and frameworks in Abu Dhabi public organizations and due to limitation of expertise in this field as well standards are not fully applied some parts of frameworks and standards are applied. In fact, most of Abu Dhabi public organizations implemented some of the international standards and frameworks in the late of year 2005 (ADSIC website). Therefore, to realize and assess the benefits of those frameworks it takes some time to know how they are effective for their organization. Generally, to assess the ef-

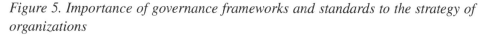

Figure 5. Importance of governance frameworks and standards to the strategy of organizations

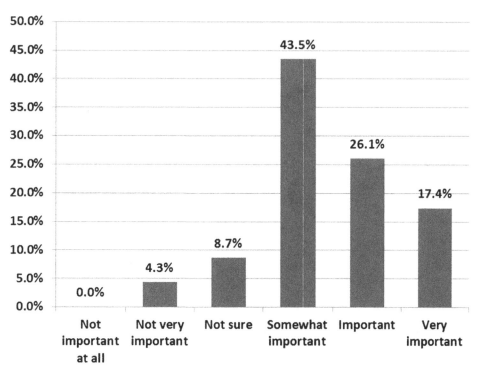

fectiveness of standards and frameworks in Abu Dhabi public sector the researchers need to consider the abovementioned reasons to reach the accurate conclusion.

In Figure 7 the respondents were asked to rate the performance of their IT governance framework used. Obviously, the respondents are satisfied with performance of the respective IT governance in their organizations with a response rate of 60%. In contrast, 22% of the respondents believed that the performance of their IT governance framework is acting below the expected standard to a certain degree. The rest of the respondents in some of the public organizations mentioned that they don't know if it is performing or underperforming, this can be due to lack of performance measurements in the respective organizations as the performance of IT investments intangible and so difficult to measure. The lessons learned from this question that the majority of the public organizations feel that IT is performing in line with their manager's expectations.

In the respect of value and benefits of IT governance, the respondents were requested to indicate the benefits that have been gained from implementing the current IT governance framework in their respective organizations. This is a general open ended question intended to identify the values of IT governance practices has brought to the public sector organisation. Again, the results of the study reveal that the operational excellence is another important benefits obtained by Abu Dhabi public organization with a response rate of 13% as shown in Figure 8.

Figure 6. Effectiveness of governance frameworks and standards

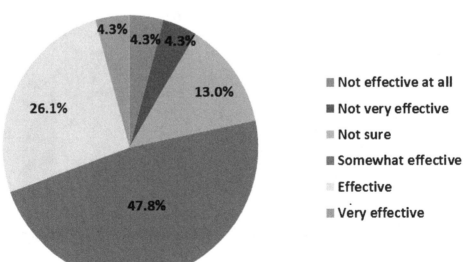

Figure 7. Performance of governance frameworks and standards

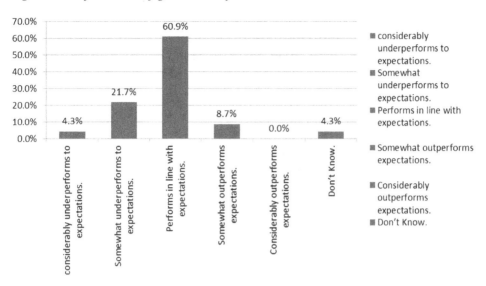

Figure 8. Benefits of adopting governance frameworks and standards

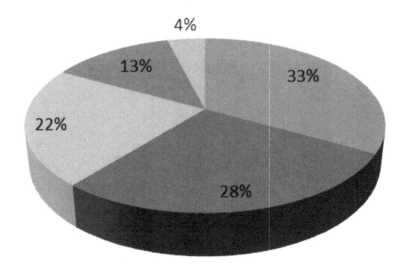

4.3. IT Governance Framework's Challenges and Barriers

Implementation of IT governance frameworks is similar to any other projects, face obstacles and challenges that prevent attainment of full value. Therefore, IT governance frameworks adoption needs to be approached and managed in the same way of managing projects. The implementation of IT governance frameworks, in public organizations or private sector, requires access to the organization's scarce resources to ensure the effective formulation and implementation of IT governance standards. Based on the foregoing, this part of results analysis is considered the last section of the survey questionnaires and there is four questions are presented and analyzed to tackle the research questions and objectives.

The first question on this part was designed to identify and determine the barriers that preventing organization from realizing the full value of IT governance framework. Figure 9 illustrates the three previously stated challenges are very close in the regard of the response rate and this can be due to some deficiencies in the database system in the respondent's organizations. These obstacles identified by respondents are related to planning issues, top management commitment, and no clear goals.

Figure 9. Barriers preventing full return of IT governance framework

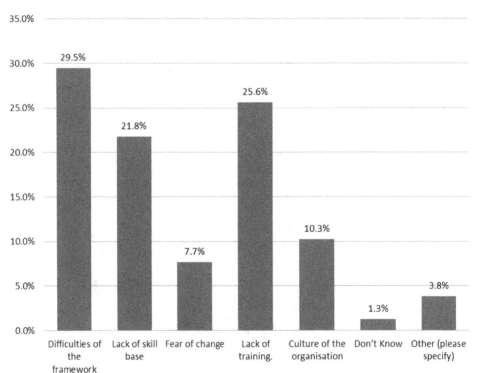

Figure 9 shows that during the implementation of frameworks and standards in public entities different barriers were identified that limit public entities from getting the full value of the framework. Respondents of 30% said that difficulties of the used framework made it difficult for public entities to get the expected value of the framework. Also, 22% of participants recognized lack of skill base as another important barrier that prevents public entities from realizing the estimated benefits of the respective framework. Lack of training is considered another barrier by 25.6% of respondents which limit public organizations from getting the full value of the used framework. These barriers identified in figure 9 shows that there are some deficiencies during the implementation of the frameworks in the public sector that prevent them from realizing the full value of the employed frameworks. These deficiencies in the implementation are a result of the framework structure and public organization themselves since they didn't provide their users by the knowledge needed and training.

The implementation experience of IT governance frameworks in Abu Dhabi public sector organizations went through different phases like any other projects and faces many challenges. Therefore, the respondents were requested to identify and list the challenges they confronted with the implementation of the IT governance framework. Based on the data collected shown on figure 10, 37% of the respondents reported that one of the main challenges is no clear communicating policies applied through IT governance framework implementation. Figure 10 indicates that Abu Dhabi public entities are recommended to focus more during the implementation of the framework and should have proper planning for each phase of the implementation as well develop a communication plan policy and define the roles and the responsibilities.

Figure 10. Implementation challenges of IT governance frameworks

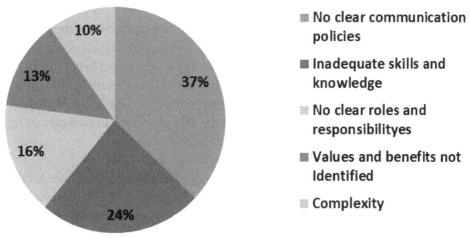

- No clear communication policies
- Inadequate skills and knowledge
- No clear roles and responsibilityes
- Values and benefits not Identified
- Complexity

5. DISCUSSION

This study among others are all revealing that centralized IT governance structure leads to achieve effective governance practices, and it induces the decision-making process which in turn encapsulates IT/business alignment. In addition, in business–performance metrics environment, the effectiveness of IT governance usually catalyzes the role of IT as an enabler for overall enterprise strategy.

The results indicated that Abu Dhabi public organization focuses more on quality management frameworks that are applied by public entities to improve the efficiency of services provided. The implementation of quality frameworks in public sector influenced by governmental regulations, statutes, and compliance with international standards and to enhance services provided to the society. IT service management frameworks such as ITIL is coming the second preferred framework by Abu Dhabi public entities this is due to the transformation of public entities to electronic government. Addition to that, the results of the study indicated that adoption of the other IT frameworks in public sector is driven by a number of internal and external motivators such as ADSIC and SKEA organizations as external forces and managing costs, aligning IT with business operations, and increasing agility to support future change as internal forces.

The findings revealed that respondents identified and recognized many intangible ben- efits that are gained by practicing IT governance frameworks in Abu Dhabi public entities. This study also identified many challenges which are faced by IT managers and IT practitioners through their experience in the implementation of IT governance frameworks in Abu Dhabi public sector. The implementation of IT gov- ernance frameworks, in public organizations as elsewhere, requires skill and knowledge and this knowledge should be shared and communicated to other stakeholders by applying effective communication plan. Also, public organizations must define roles and responsibilities during the implementation of IT governance framework in order to avoid conflict between stakeholders. It is very important for IT managers to understand their organization environments and its culture during the implementation processes. This will aid in avoid many obstacles during the imple- mentation of IT governance frameworks and will promote better practices.

First of all, the research project has been limited to issues related to the knowledge of IT managers and IT practitioners within public organizations in Abu Dhabi. Also, lack of scholarly publications around the IT governance frameworks in the Abu Dhabi public sector made collecting data very challenging.

Secondly, the method applied in this study to collect data was not suitable to a certain degree; a face to face and semi-structure interview would be suitable for this kind of research since it helped to have a better understanding of different practices by surveying more questions. Lastly, the progress, strength and weaknesses of IT governance in Abu Dhabi public sector were not measured in this study. Assessing IT governance progress is considered a very important issue for public organizations to address the status of the IT governance in their entities and to measure the strengths and the weaknesses of the applied frameworks based on a set of agreed upon criteria.

5. CONCLUSION

It is clear that exploring this critical research domain leads to establishing knowledge about IT governance and best practices, recommending a framework to understand how organizational value is generated using IT governance mechanisms, and setting out additional support on how strategic alignment can better improve the effectiveness of IT governance mechanisms on organizational performance.

The significance of IT governance practices and its contexts has emerged during the last five years in Abu Dhabi public sector. The need for ongoing standardization of IT products and services brought to the surface the concept of IT governance and the control of IT assets. As it discussed previously, the main goal of IT governance is to align the IT with the business needs and processes and to increase the value delivery of IT. In this work, critical analysis of IT governance framework employed in Abu Dhabi government public sector is presented and analyzed. The objective of this study is to find out the most used IT governance frameworks in Abu Dhabi public sector and the value realized from adopting IT governance practices. The results found that the most used frameworks and standards in the public organization of Abu Dhabi are ISO 9001 as a quality standard, ITILv3 as a service management framework, ISO 27001 as IT security standard, ISO 20000, PMBOK, BSC, and COBIT respectively. Also, other internally developed and designed frameworks such ADSIC and HAAD. In addition, the main benefits realized by adopting the respective frameworks are increasing the efficiency and the performance of public sector organizations as well complying with governmental regulations and statute. Also, the study found that lack of communication strategy, lack of skills and knowledge, no clear roles. Addition to that, responsibilities, values and benefits of frameworks applied not communicated to stakeholders considered the main challenges that faced managers and practitioners in Abu Dhabi public organizations during the implementations.

The analysis of the results has shown the importance of IT governance and its positive impact on the public sector entities. Also, the analysis has further indicated that Abu Dhabi public sector is aware of adopting latest international standards. In spite of latest international standards applied but there still a need to adopt best practices and arrangements by top management to reach accepted maturity level in their entities. The study also listed the motivational and the driving forces that make public entities implement the IT governance frameworks. Some of these driving forces are complying with industry and governmental regulations, improving performance within departments, managing costs, aligning IT with business processes, quality and security.

REFERENCES

Abu Talib, M., Barachi, E. M., Alhosn, A. K., & Ormandjieva, O. (2012). Guide to ISO 27001: UAE Case Study. *Issues in Informing Science and Information Technology, 7*. Retrieved May 10, 2013, from http://iisit.org/Vol9/IISITv9p331-349Talib041.pdf

ADSIC. (2013). *ADSIC Vision*. Retrieved January 7, 2013, from http://adsic.abudhabi.ae/Sites/ADSIC/Navigation/EN/about-adsic.html

Alam. (2009). *Can governance and regulatory control ensure private higher education as business or public goods in developing countries*. Retrieved February 23, 2013 from http://www.academicjournals.org/ajbm/pdf/pdf2011/4June/Kefela.pdf

Bahsani, S., Semma, A., & Sellam, N. (2015). Towards a New Approach For Combining The IT Frameworks. *International Journal of Computer Science Issues, 12*(1), 118–123.

Bergeron, F., Croteau, A.-M., Uwizeyemungu, S., & Raymond, L. (2015). IT Governance Framework Applied to SMEs. *International Journal of IT/Business Alignment and Governance, 6*(1), 33–49. doi:10.4018/IJITBAG.2015010103

Broadbent, M. (2003). *Understanding IT Governance*. IT World Canada News. Retrieved February 16, 2013 from http://www.itworldcanada.com/article/understanding-it-governance/19174

Calder, A. (2008). *Developing an IT governance framework*. Retrieved March 2, 2013 from www.ncc.co.uk/article/?articleid=13371

Coltman, T., Tallon, P., Sharma, R., & Queiroz, M. (2015). Strategic IT alignment: Twenty-five years on. *Journal of Information Technology, 30*(2), 1–10.

Consulting-Portal Inc. (2007). *Necessary Frameworks for IT Governance: Clarifying the tangled web*. Retrieved December 5, 2012, from http://consulting-portal.com/documents/Necessary%20Frameworks%20for%20IT%20Governance.pdf

De Haes, S., & Van Grembergen, W. (2010). Analysing the impact of enterprise governance of IT practices on business performance. *International Journal of IT/Business Alignment and Governance*, *1*(1), 14–38. doi:10.4018/jitbag.2010120402

Ezziane, Z., & Al Shamisi, A. (2013, June). Improvement of the Organizational Performance through Compliance with Best Practices in Abu-Dhabi. *International Journal of IT/Business Alignment and Governance*, *4*(2), 19–36. doi:10.4018/ijitbag.2013070102

Gartner. (2009). *IT governance must be driven by corporate governance*. Retrieved on April 17, 2013 from http://www.gartner.com/it/content/1229500/1229528/it_governance_must_be_driven _corp_gov.pdf

Gerke, L., & Ridley, G. (2006). Towards an abbreviated COBIT framework for use in an Australian State Public Sector. In S. Pencer, S & A. Jenkins, A. (Eds.), *17th Australasian Conference on Information Systems* (pp. 1-10). Retrieved January 15, 2013, from http://eprints.utas.edu.au/513/1/ACIS2006.pdf

Goldsmith, S., & Eggers, W. D. (2004). *Governing by Network: The New Shape of the Public Sector*. Washington, DC: Brookings Institute Press.

Greger, V., Wolf, P., & Krcmar, H. (2015). Perception of Benefits Achieved by IT Management Accounting in the Public Sector. In *Smart Enterprise Engineering: 12. Internationale Tagung Wirtschaftsinformatik* (WI 2015). Retrieved December 21, 2015, from http://www.wi2015.uni-osnabrueck.de/Files/WI2015-D-14-00106.pdf

IBM. (2010). *IT compliance management*. Retrieved May 15, 2013 from http://www.openpages.com/solutions/IT_Compliance_38.asp

Iden, J., & Eikebrokk, T. R. (2014). Exploring the Relationship between Information Technology Infrastructure Library and Process Management: Theory Development and Empirical Testing. *Knowledge and Process Management*, *21*(4), 292–306. doi:10.1002/kpm.1437

ITGI. (2003). *Board briefing on IT Governance*. IT Governance Institute. Retrieved January 15, 2013, from http://wikimp.mp.go.gov.br/twiki/pub/EstruturaOrganica/AreaMeio/Superintendencias/SINFO/Estrategia/BibliotecaVirtual/MaterialExtra/26904_Board_Briefing_final.pdf

ITGI (IT Governance Institute). (2008). *IT governance global status report*. Retrieved on February 22, 2013 from http://www.isaca.org/Knowledge-Center/Research/Documents/ITGI-Global-Status-Report-2008.pdf

Janahi, L., Griffiths, M., & Al-Ammal, H. (2015). A conceptual model for IT governance in public sectors.*Fourth International Conference on Future Generation Communication Technology (FGCT)*. doi:10.1109/FGCT.2015.7300242

Karkoskova, S., & Feuerlicht, G. (2015). Extending MBI Model using ITIL and COBIT Processes. *Journal of Systems Integration*, *6*(4), 29–44. doi:10.20470/jsi. v6i4.244

Kaselowski, E. (2008). *Mitigating risk through effective information technology operations in local governments: Towards a best practice*. Retrieved May 16, 2013 from http://www.nmmu.ac.za/documents/theses/Mitigating%20Risk%20 Through%20Effective%20Information%20Technology%20Governance%20in%20 Local%20Government s.pdf

Leedy, P. D., & Ormrod, J. E. (Eds.). (2005). *Practical Research: Planning and Design*. Upper Saddle River, NJ: Pearson Education.

Mergel, I., Bretschneider, S. I., Louis, C., & Smith, J. (2014) The Challenges of Challenge. Gov: Adopting Private Sector Business Innovations in the Federal Government. *47th Hawaii International Conference on System Sciences* (HICSS). Retrieved December 21, 2015, from http://ieeexplore.ieee.org/stamp/stamp. jsp?tp=&arnumber=6758860

Mochiko, T. (2010). *South Africa: Public sector pays dearly for technology*. Retrieved January 7, 2013 from: http://allafrica.com/stories/201006210624.html

Moon, M. J., Lee, J., & Roh, C. Y. (2014). The Evolution of Internal IT Applications and e-Government Studies in Public Administration. *Administration & Society*, *46*(1), 3–36. doi:10.1177/0095399712459723

Nfuka, E. N., & Rusu, L. (2009). *Critical success factors for effective IT governance in the public sector organizations in a developing country: The case of Tanzania*. Retrieved May 10, 2013 from http://web.up.ac.za/ecis/ECIS2010PR/-ECIS2010/ Content/Papers/0450.R1.pdf

Pardo, T. A., & Brian Burke, G. (2008). *Improving Government Interoperability: A capability framework for government managers*. The Center for Technology in Government. The Research Foundation of State University of New York. Retrieved April 20, 2013 from http://www.ctg.albany.edu/publications/reports/improving_government_interoperability

PWC. (2009). *The governance of information technology*. Retrieved December 5, 2013, from http://www.pwc.com/za/en/king3/the-governance-of-information-technology/index.jhtml

Richards, S., & Dar, R. (2009). *Standardization & classification in the UAE.* Al Tamimi & Company. Retrieved November 14, 2012, from http://www.thyh.com/Publications/International/Standardization%20and%20Classification%20in%20the%20UAE.pdf

Rubino, M., & Vitolla, F. (2014). Corporate governance and the information system: How a framework for IT governance supports ERM. *Corporate Governance, 14*(3), 320–338. doi:10.1108/CG-06-2013-0067

Spremic, M. (2011). Standards and Frameworks for Information System Security Auditing and Assurance. In S. Athanasios (Ed.), *Proceedings of the World Congress on Engineering* (vol. 1, pp. 1-6). Retrieved February 2, 2013, from http://www.iaeng.org/publication/WCE2011/WCE2011_pp514-519.pdf

Spremic, M. (2011), Standards and frameworks for information system security auditing and assurance. *Proceedings of the World Congress on Engineering* (vol. 1). Retrieved February 20, 2013, from http://www.iaeng.org/publication/WCE2011/WCE2011_pp514-519.pdf

Spremic, M. (2012). Measuring IT Governance Performance: A Research Study on CobiT Based Regulation Framework Usage. *International Journal of Mathematics and Computers in Simulation,* 1–9.

Symons, C. (2005). *IT Governance Framework: Structures, Processes and Framework.* Retrieved March 3, 2013, from http://www.computerweekly.com/news/2240065721/IT-Governance-Framework-Structures-Processes-and-Communication

Tshinu, S. M., Botha, G., & Herselman, M. (2008). An integrated ICT management framework for commercial banking organisations in South Africa. *Interdisciplinary Journal of Information, Knowledge, and Management, 3,* 39–53.

Van Grembergen, W., De Haes, S., & Guldentops, E. (2004). *Structures, process and Relational mechanisms for IT Governance.* Retrieved on March 13, 2013 from www.itgi.org

Weill, P., & Ross, J. W. (2005). How effective are your IT Governance. *Research Briefing, 5*(1). Retrieved May 3rd 2013 from: http://web.mit.edu/cisr/www

Weill, P., & Woodham, R. (2002). *State street corporate: evolving IT Governance.* MIT Sloan Working Paper, 11-20.

Wessels, E., & van Luggoernberg, J. (2006). IT Governance: Theory and Practice. In C. de Villiers & L. Smit (Eds.), *Conference on Information Technology in Tertiary Education* (pp. 1-14). Retrieved January 10, 2013, from http://citeseerx.ist.psu.edu/viewdoc/download?doi=10.1.1.100.2838&rep=rep1&type=pdf

Willson, P., & Pollard, C. (2009). Exploring IT governance in theory and practice in a large multi-national organisation in Australia. *Information Systems Management*, *26*(2), 98–109. doi:10.1080/10580530902794760

Wu, S. P. J., Straub, D. W., & Liang, T. P. (2015). How information technology governance mechanisms and strategic alignment influence organizational performance: Insights from a matched survey of business and it managers. *Management Information Systems Quarterly*, *39*(2), 497–518.

Chapter 9
Enterprise Architecture:
A Snapshot from Practice

Michael Clarke
The Open University, UK

Jon G. Hall
The Open University, UK

Lucia Rapanotti
The Open University, UK

ABSTRACT

Enterprise Architecture (EA) has been portrayed as one of the cornerstones of modern IT Governance, with increasing numbers of organisations formally recognising an EA function and adopting EA frameworks such as TOGAF (The Open Group Architectural Framework). Many claims have been made of the benefits of EA, yet little is known as to what organisations actually do or evidence of the benefits they accrue through EA. In this paper we report on the results of a small scale survey painting a snapshot of recent EA practice in large UK organisations across the private and public sectors. A key insight from the survey is that, in practice, EA appears to have a greater effect on business-IT alignment than on technological choices.

DOI: 10.4018/978-1-5225-0861-8.ch009

1. INTRODUCTION

The discipline of Enterprise Architecture (EA) (Bernus & Nemes, 1996; Ross et al. 2006) has grown over the past twenty years to become a notable part of IT Governance, the latter described by Calder (2009) as a "framework for the leadership, organisational structures and business processes, standards and compliance to these standards, which ensure that the organisation's IT supports and enables the achievement of its strategies and objectives." EA is often portrayed at the intersection of an organisation's IT and business strategies, with its effectiveness depending upon the specification of an IT architecture able to support adequately the organisation's business model (Winter and Schelp, 2008). Indeed, many claims have been made of the benefits of EA accruing from its holistic view of the organisation, including the ability to: support business processes and deliver organisational change effectively and efficiently (Schelp & Aier, 2009), simplify and future-proof the IT infrastructure (Ross et al. 2006), optimise procurement and outsourcing, better decision making (Van den Berg, 2006), and deliver organisational change more quickly and cheaply (Aier, 2004).

Of course, business models can vary significantly and are contingent upon many factors, including organisational culture, customer type (consumer or business), product or service variety on offer, tangibility of such an offer, and geographical diversity, to name but a few. However, a common belief that there are certain shared characteristics and needs between the business models of diverse organisations has led to the development of generic EA frameworks and methodologies. In parallel, technical innovations in the nature of software development, such as Service Oriented Architecture (SOA), have enabled practical implementation of some of the key theoretical benefits of EA, such as cost savings in software development through the re-use of existing software. This has allowed a closer association of business processes with discrete pieces of software which are specifically required to perform these processes, with EA performing a key role in realising such an association and fostering corporate agility with better adaptation of IT to changing business processes (Schelp & Aier, 2009).

EA has increasingly been adopted as standard practice in many large (and some smaller) organisations, often embodied as a separate and well defined function. Yet information of what individual organisations actually do and evidence of the benefits they are accruing through EA is lacking, partly because of commercial sensitivity, but also because this remains a fragmented, practitioner-led subject area with little published academic research. Much of the literature is aimed at a practical, self-help market, often relying on anecdote and supposition to support a method's effectiveness, as evidence, for instance by (Schöenherr, 2009), which, from a comprehensive review of the literature concludes that the large majority of published EA literature discussed theoretical approaches to EA which speculate about the areas of a business that might benefit from an EA practice. More recent literature also stresses the practitioner-led nature of the subject matter and the speculative nature of related research (e.g., Abraham et al., 2012; Simon et al., 2013). Therefore, it remains the case that relatively little academic research has been carried out into the application and efficacy of EA as a discipline and to test the suppositions made about the EA's role in the achievement of organisational objectives.

The work in this paper is a step towards collecting evidence from practice to substantiate some of the claims made of EA. We conducted a survey within a practitioner network, with respondents from a number of large, mainly UK-based organisations from the private and public sectors. Although on a small scale, data from the survey provides a snapshot of EA practice, with an indication of the level of adoption of EA frameworks and approaches and perceived benefits of EA within the respondents' organisations. Findings appear to confirm claimed benefits of EA as to improving governance structures, working relationships between business and IT, enabling new business strategy or re-engineering, reducing overall IT costs and increasing IT value. However, a novel key insight from the survey is that, in practice, EA appears to have a greater effect on business-IT alignment than on technological choices.

The paper is structured as follow. Section 2 provides some background literature review. Section 3 gives an overview of the survey with the analysis of its data in Section 4. Section 5 discusses the results and Section 6 offers some conclusion and outlines possible future work.

2. BACKGROUND

IT Governance

There are two key facets to IT Governance. First, there is the need for a good alignment between IT and the business with greater transparency in the IT-related decision making process meaning that the business value of IT investments in supporting strategic objectives can be more clearly seen. Second, there is the need for the judicious treatment of business risk, and of greater accountability and control, the latter often the result of legislation and regulation (such as the Sarbanes–Oxley Act in the US or the Data Protection Act in the UK).

The first facet is much portrayed in the work of Weill and Ross (2004), which defines IT Governance as "specifying the decision rights and accountability framework to encourage desirable behaviour in using IT." This strategic perspective is mainly concerned with management and organisational design rather than with the operation of IT, and makes a clear distinction between the taking of individual decisions and the framework created to facilitate effectively that decision making.

The second facet is present, for instance in Calder (2009), which portrays risk management at the core of effective IT Governance, with IT-related risk including: interruptions to business processes and customer services (whether from project failure or unplanned disruption); IT overspend placing the company at a cost disadvantage compared to its competitors; and operational risk deriving from an organisation's failure to deliver IT services or lack of internal control. Key standards which take a risk-centric view of IT Governance include the BS ISO/IEC 20000 standard and BS ISO/IEC 27000 family of standards, addressing the principles and best practice implementation of, respectively, service management systems and information security management systems.

These two facets are closely related and effective IT Governance critically depends on both. Moreover, the focus on decision rights and accountability and risk management puts an emphasis on stakeholder involvement: effective IT Governance must incorporate formal decision making involving all relevant stakeholders in an organisation. This view is also embodied in BS ISO/IEC 38500, a standard stating the fundamental principles for the corporate governance of IT.

The complexity and wide scope of influence of IT Governance within an organisation has led to the emergence of a large number of frameworks to help organisations address various aspects of IT Governance effectively, the better known being: COBIT, for overarching IT corporate governance; ITIL, for service management; PRINCE2, for project management; and the already mentioned TOGAF, for enterprise architecture, the latter being the focus of this work. It should be noted, however, that while adoption appears to be on the rise, such frameworks are currently more finely tuned to the needs and resources of blue chip corporations, with SMEs, not-for-profits and the public sector lagging behind (Ayat et al., 2011; Begg & Caira, 2012).

Enterprise Architecture and TOGAF

An initial problem with research into EA is a recurring debate about the definition and scope of the discipline. Additionally, some advocates argue that EA's ultimate purpose is as the primary catalyst for and enabler of strategic change across an organisation. Definitional debates on the scope of EA cause problems for empirical researchers into the practical adoption of benefits of EA as they confuse the scope of any sample population.

The Zachman framework is one of the oldest tools for the analysis of EA and is essentially an ontology based on a grid of six interrogatives (types of question, such as "who', "what", "how') in one dimension and by six types of perspective across an enterprise (business, system, technology, etc.) in a second dimension. The intersections in the grid prompt practitioners to create a corresponding "view" in order to investigate an issue from one of the 36 possible perspectives. Therefore, Zachman's framework encompasses questions that range from drivers of business strategy (the intersection of "why?" and the enterprise level) to the very technical ("how?"/engineering). Zachman never intended the framework to be fully populated for any given EA initiative, only to prompt practitioners to select only those views that are of the greatest relevance to the EA issue under consideration (Zachman, 2015). Nevertheless, the Zachman Framework offers a very wide potential scope for the application of EA

From the literature and an analysis of the Zachman Framework for EA (Zachman, 1987), Lapalme (2012) identified and named three EA "schools": Enterprise IT Architecting; Enterprise Integrating; and Enterprise Ecological Adaptation. These are characterised by the increasing involvement of EA in the encompassing design of the business and its processes and contrasts with a more traditional view of EA as being primarily motivated by the IT function.

TOGAF, (The Open Group, 2011), which is the most widely adopted EA framework (see below), aligns its scope with the concerns of the IT practitioner community. It explicitly includes other IT architectural disciplines (Business, Data, Applications and Technology Architecture) as "commonly accepted […] subsets" of Enterprise Architecture whereby business strategy tends to be handled as an external "input" into TOGAF's Architecture Development Method (ADM).

From the practitioner perspective, BCS, The Chartered Institute for IT, cites Ross et. al. (2006) as the core reference work in its syllabus for its professional qualification in Enterprise Architecture. Ross defines EA as "the organising logic for core business processes and IT infrastructure, reflecting the standardisation and integration of a company's operating model." This definition, emphasising the match between IT and business processes, reflects most closely Lapalme's first "school"— that of Enterprise IT Architecting – which is described as "the glue between business and IT". These two definitions stand as the core scope for EA despite much of the literature attempting to make the case for EA's application in wider business strategy.

This view also has substantial overlap with the emphasis that Weill and Ross (2004) put on the strategic aspects of IT Governance: EA could be viewed as the conceptual result of successful IT Governance at a strategic level. It also aligns with Van den Berg's analogy of EA as a "city plan" (Van den Berg, 2006), and his view that EA "exists at a very high conceptual level, has a broad scope and serves as a support for senior management in its high-level decision making." Clearly one of the key functions of EA in supporting decision making is its role in supporting and enabling IT Governance.

Many EA frameworks and methodologies have been developed in the last twenty years, and the role of Enterprise Architect is now well understood, at least in large organisations. Early EA frameworks (Bernus & Nemes, 1997) were either proprietary tools offered by consultants, e.g. the Zachman Framework, or had grown out of best practices specified by government agencies, e.g., DoDAF, the US Department of Defense Architecture Framework. More recently, the Open Group, a consortium of over 300 academics, practitioners and suppliers, have developed TOGAF, The Open Group Architectural Framework, using the principles of open source collaboration: the core material is freely available on the internet for use by practitioners (although there are commercial restrictions on trade-marking and training). The first enterprise edition of TOGAF was released in 2002, and as a result of contributions from the Open Group's large body of practitioners, has grown since and evolved from a collection of practices into a step-by-step method – the Architecture Development Method (ADM) – on how to build, maintain, and implement an enterprise architecture. It also contains examples of content that can be adapted and reused by practitioners, such as the Enterprise Continuum and the Technical Reference Model.

The Open Group has also developed an Enterprise Architecture modelling standard, Archimate, [cite] designed to complement TOGAF's ADM. Archimate provides a classification and taxonomy for modelling entities within an organisation and describing the relationships between them. Archimate 2.0, introduced in 2012, has three core layers: business, application and technology (Lankhorst et.al.2013). These three layers suggest the designers of Archimate see EA providing the linkage between business and technology via the use of business IT applications.

Iacob et. al. (2012) validated Archimate's ability to effectively model entities in its business layer, so that Archimate is a credible tool for modelling the relationship between business and IT, where lies the focus of industry practitioners who make up the membership of the Open Group. Archimate has developed a set of "motivation extensions" which can be used to capture concepts relevant to business strategy, such as stakeholder goals. However, these are explicitly described as optional and not part of the core specification. More generally, it provides a language designed to be used for the creation of lasting models of an enterprise, and the persistent use of Archimate within an organisation may point to a securely established EA function. This would contrast with a project lifecycle-orientated methodology such as the TOGAF ADM.

Simon (2013b) provides a comprehensive bibliometric survey of the literature on Enterprise Architecture, finishing in 2011. The analysis points out areas of greatest research coverage in different dimensions, such as EA layers, methodology, management/processes and lifecycle phases. The most popular areas of research include the business and application architecture layers, modelling, IT landscape management and documentation. Governance is not strongly cited – with only 28% of research referencing the term. The author provides a multi-dimension mapping of the most cited works which clusters together the most similar research by content.

Simon discovers two distinct groupings of research. The first concentrates on the EA Frameworks themselves, notably TOGAF (The Open Group, 2011), Zachman (2015) or theoretical research closely based on EA Frameworks. The second is based around very practical analyses of implementation (e.g. Buckl (2007, 2008), Aier (2008), Matthes (2008), Kurojuweit/Winter (2007). A relatively small number of citations are located between the two clusters. However, as may be expected, these include works that attempt to provide to practitioners more general guides for EA implementation. For example, Ross et. al (2005), from whom we have taken our definition of EA, and Lankhorst's (2013) work on the application of Archimate.

While TOGAF appears to be growing in popularity among practitioners and the works by Ross (2004), Lankhorst (2013) offer advice and case studies, very little evidence or academic work has been published on the wider adoption and perceived value amongst practitioners of TOGAF or other frameworks. Of the few articles we could locate: Dietz et al. (2011) and Zadeh et al. (2012) discuss the need for a theoretical underpinning of TOGAF; Buckl et al. (2009) propose the use of Enterprise Architecture Management Patterns to tailor what they see as the "highly generic" TOGAF to specific practitioners' needs; and Chaczko et al. (2010) give a narrative account of the creation of a middleware integration model in the health sector using TOGAF.

None of these articles contains much empirical work, and we could not locate any empirical evidence that has been published as to TOGAF's actual adoption and benefits, perceived or otherwise, in practice. In fact, as already noted in the introduction, empirical evidence around EA in general remains very sparse, with few notable exceptions in the case study work of Schelp et al. (Winter and Schelp, 2008; Schelp and Ariel, 2009). Indeed, Schöenherr (2009), in his survey of the many published articles which refer to EA, concludes that they resemble "a horrible mess", with no common understanding of the term, no core topic or underlying theory and most approaches still exhibiting a low level of maturity; the paucity of best practice and empirical evidence is also noted.

3. SURVEY

With the aim of collecting empirical evidence, we conducted a small scale survey in the context of the Corporate IT Forum, an "independent organisation that brings together practitioners from large, well-established businesses to share and document their unique insights and experiences into Enterprise IT problems and solutions" based in the UK.

The Forum is a wide practitioner network with more than 320 organisations as members, including some of the largest IT user organisations in the UK, many with international operations. It runs regular "Reality Checkers", a monthly series of online questionnaires on topical subjects of relevance to the IT user community, with results made available to the Forum's members at the end of each month. Our survey was proposed as the Forum's Reality Checker in October 2010.

The survey was hosted on the Forum's website and advertised to all Corporate IT Forum members, regardless of job discipline through their monthly membership email, which had a reach of about 30,000 members. In addition, e-mails with links to the survey were sent to employees in the Forum's member companies who had registered an interest in EA in their online membership profiles. The survey was also referenced in communication with the Forum's wider membership population, such as newsletters. Therefore, although theoretically any of the 30,000 members would have been able to answer the survey, a particular effort was made to target those who had expressed an interest in EA on their profile information.

Our approach was significantly different from other practitioner surveys that we found in the literature. Two surveys with similar objectives, by Simon (2013a) and Mending (2011), selected small groups of Enterprise Architecture "expert" practitioners using personal contacts and social media networks (sample totals of 7 and 16 respectively). These small samples were examined qualitatively in the form of structured interviews with the researchers interpreting interview answers into broad categories (such as agreement with statements) to conclude their results. The sample in our survey was significantly larger and self-selected from respondents in a professional IT industry body who were interested in EA.

Among other things, the survey questions were designed to gather some evidence as to:

1. The perceived benefits of EA in practice;
2. The extent of use and adaptation of TOGAF and other EA frameworks in practice, and relative to the adoption of other IT Governance frameworks;
3. The involvement of key stakeholders within the EA function, these been widely regarded as a key success factor in IT Governance in general.

The full list of survey questions can be found in Clarke (2011). Data collected were mainly qualitative, through the use of Likert scales; free text comments were also invited.

4. DATA ANALYSIS

There were thirty-eight responses to the survey from twenty-five separate organisations (listed in Appendix A) spanning both public and private sectors and across a number of domains from finance, transport, retail, publishing to engineering. Responses to all questions can be found[1] in Clarke (2011). In this section, we summarise the results pertaining to the key issues listed above.

Benefits of EA (1)

In this part of the survey, the focus was on claimed benefits of specific EA initiatives and functions, as stated in the literature, including: improved IT Governance (e.g. Architecture board); improved working relationship between business and IT; increased IT agility; more effective introduction of new architectures (e.g. SOA); reduced complexity of IT architecture; and simplified infrastructure.

The aim of the question was to ascertain to which extent such benefits were experienced in practice by the surveyed participants. A four-point Likert scale was used in this question (Significant, Some, Little, None). Responses indicated that:

- 84% of respondents reported that EA provided at least some benefit on the overall IT Governance, with 35% reporting it had a significant impact.
- 84% of respondents also reported that EA had at least some benefit in improving the working relationship between business and IT, with nearly 50% reporting it had a significant impact.
- Respondents also reported some impact on the introduction of new architectures (35%), reducing complexity (61%), and simplifying infrastructure (48%).
- In free text comments, opinions from the whole the spectrum were expressed, including one respondent stating that EA was the focus of IT strategy alignment, and another reporting that EA was seen as a failed experiment in the company.

Benefits to the Organisation

In this part of the survey, the focus was on the claimed beneficial effects of EA to the wider organisation, including: enabling the deployment of new business strategy or re-engineering the business, reduced overall IT costs, increased IT added value, more effective purchasing practices, improved offshoring/outsourcing relationships, improved management information, enabled more effective regulatory compliance, and improved risk management.

As for the previous question, the aim was to ascertain to which extent such benefits were experienced in practice by the surveyed participants. The same four-point Likert scale was used in this question. Responses indicated that:

- The top three benefits (when Significant and Some responses were combined) were: increasing IT's added value (83%); enabling new business strategy or re-engineering (73%); reducing overall IT costs (70%).
- 57% respondents believed that EA has some benefits in enabling better risk management, while 27% thought it had little effect, and only 7% thought it had a significant impact.
- The factors where the majority of respondents believed EA had little effect were: more effective purchasing practices and improving offshoring/out-sourcing relationships.

In free text comments: one respondent indicated that EA had a beneficial effect on "Shaping projects so that they better fit longer term requirements rather than immediate imperatives.". Another added that, while the role of Enterprise Architect was common, a separate EA function was less so, with organisations not having that specific function or only in the process of introducing one.

EA Frameworks Adoption (2)

In this part of the survey, the focus was on gaining an understanding of EA frameworks adoption, also considering the combination of EA frameworks with other IT Governance frameworks or standards adopted by the organisation. A list of the main frameworks and standards was provided to participants, who could also add others not included in the list. As before, a four-point Likert scale was used (Mandatory Use, Widespread Use, Ad hoc use, No Use). Responses indicated:

- There was widespread experience of TOGAF: 27% of respondents were using TOGAF successfully, and 46% had used it in the past. Only 27% of the respondents said they had not used TOGAF at all.
- Comparably to TOGAF adoption, ad-hoc in-house approaches had been successfully used by 31% of the respondents, and a further 31% of them had used them in the past. From the free text comments it emerged that some of those ad-hoc approaches included some elements of TOGAF in combination with elements of other frameworks or ad-hoc organisational practices.
- The Zachman Framework was not currently used by the respondents, but had been used in the past by 40% of them.
- 62% said that they had adapted an adopted framework.
- Combined with EA frameworks, the only other IT Governance framework that had significant (i.e., widespread or mandatory) use was ITIL (57%), while CoBIT was used significantly only by 16% of the respondents. PRINCE2 was

used by most respondents – with 60% reporting significant use, and BS ISO/IEC 27001 was used by many – with 42% reporting significant use. There was little knowledge of BS ISO/IEC 38500 – only 16% respondents had used it at all.

From the free text comments, it emerged that most organisations were taking a pragmatic approach, adopting elements of frameworks and standards in a pick-and-mix fashion and tailoring them to the needs of their organisation. One respondent stated that TOGAF was only used because there was nothing better around.

Stakeholders (3)

As discussed previously, IT Governance emphasises stakeholder involvement as a key success factor. Hence, this part of the survey aimed to ascertain stakeholder participation in EA practice. A list of fourteen stakeholder roles across the organisation, informed by TOGAF recommendations, from business to technical, were provided to participants, who were asked to estimate how frequently the EA function interacted with each of them on a five-point Likert scale (Very Frequently, Often, Occasionally, Rarely, Never).

Responses indicated:

- The stakeholders with most frequent interaction, with over half respondents reporting it as Very frequently, were Enterprise Architects and Solution Architects, followed by CIO/IT Director and IT Project Management.
- Less frequent but still substantial interaction was reported with some stakeholders outside the IT organisation. When Very frequently and Often responses are combined, a significant level of interaction includes Senior Business Management (65%) and Business End Users (70%). 30% of respondents reported interacting often with Board Members although a similar level of interaction with the CEO was rare (10% when Very frequent and Often responses are combined).

5. DISCUSSION

The survey results confirm that, by and large, practitioners perceive a number of benefits of EA. Amongst these, EA scored the highest impact on: IT Governance structures; improving the working relationship between business and IT; enabling new business strategy and/or re-engineering; and reducing overall IT costs and increasing IT value. It is notable that these are all generic benefits claimed of IT Governance. In terms of risk management, although some beneficial effects of EA were recognised, their impact was not seen as particularly significant.

On the other hand, and perhaps surprisingly, EA appeared to have a lesser impact on the introduction of new technical architectures and in simplifying and reducing complexity of infrastructure. In other words, EA appears to have a greater effect on business-IT alignment, and a lesser one on technological choices. This seems to indicate that, in practice, the relation between EA and technology is weaker than, for instance, what has been portrayed for EA and SOA (Schelp and Ariel, 2009).

However, the relative success of EA in aligning IT with business and enabling new business strategy reinforces the conclusions of other research, mainly carried out using qualitative methods, such as interviews. For example, Mending's (2011) survey of EA "experts" defined a number of EA goals. Those which were found to be strongly supported were: transparency; complexity management; governance or transformation/IT management; and business/IT alignment. By contrast, EA had little influence on: agility; innovation; risk management; and regulatory alignment. These findings correspond strongly to our quantitative survey.

There was also a sense that EA is still immature in organisations, despite the notion having being around for a quarter of a century, with many only just starting to implement a separate EA function. This confirms similar observations by Schöen-herr (2009). (This is also supported by the number of respondents claiming to have experimented with frameworks that were not actively used for governance purposes.)

In terms of framework adoption, the survey results indicate that TOGAF is the most widely known and used framework, rivalled only by ad-hoc, in-house approaches. The Zachman Framework appears to have been significant historically, but its adoption has declined. Significantly, only certain parts of TOGAF were often adopted by the surveyed organisations and much adaptation was going on, which seems to point to a lack of maturity of the existing framework and some level of dissonance from the needs of practice. More striking yet, the rate of successful use was only 27% for TOGAF and 31% for ad-hoc, in house approaches. Mending (ibid) discovered that 66.7% of organisations sampled also used TOGAF. However, 75% of those using TOGAF expressed dissatisfaction either with its ability to be customised or in the support available for implementation. Taken in combinations these findings might also support our result of a 27% successful use of TOGAF.

EA frameworks were commonly applied in organisations in combination with other IT Governance frameworks, primarily ITIL, PRINCE2 and BS ISO/IEC 27001. This begs the question as to whether it is actually sensible or possible to single out the impact and benefits deriving from one specific framework application from the combined effect of applying them all within an organisation.

Finally, the survey results indicated that in EA functions projects, interaction was most common with stakeholders within the IT department as well as with business specialist stakeholders, while access to strategic business stakeholders (e.g., CEO, board members) was reported as being much less frequent. As board-level buy-in and involvement is cited as a critical success factor and recommended by most frameworks and standards, this begs the question of how problematic it is in practice to consult regularly with all key stakeholders.

The level of interaction with key stakeholders could also be viewed as one objective measure of the influence of EA within an organisation. Our sample reported relatively frequent engagement with operational business stakeholders (for example those with whom the Enterprise Architect is engaged on project work). However, the lower level of engagement with CEOs and board members, the shapers and gatekeepers of corporate strategy, suggests that the practitioners we surveyed have more success engaging in the school of EA that pursues business-IT alignment than, for example, Lapalme's Enterprise Integrating and Enterprise Ecological Adaptation.

The types of stakeholders with which our EA practitioner sample interacted could also give some indication of which of the squares in the Zachman Framework grid are likely to be most often addressed by Enterprise Architects. For example, the high level of interaction with solution architects suggests that the system and technical levels of the grid (used by "designers" and "builders" are more commonly referenced, along with referencing the enterprise layer when consulting with business stakeholders. However, the very infrequent interaction with CEOs suggests that questions addressing the intersections on highest level of the Zachman grid (the "scope" view) are unlikely to be answered by direct stakeholder contact with information being obtained indirectly (e.g. organisation's published strategies, mission statements, etc.).

Threats to Validity

The survey was made available to the members of an IT professional network, the Corporate IT Forum, regardless of job discipline, although members who had registered an interest in EA in their profile information were explicitly targeted by e-mail. The Corporate IT Forum draws its membership from organisations with more traditional corporate IT departments or which are more likely to follow methodological processes, such as TOGAF. The survey was completed by a self-selecting sample of those practitioners and it is possible that there could be an inbuilt bias in the sample of the population that responded. In particular, although there was no intention to target EA practitioners exclusively, it is likely that only respondents with an interest in EA would have chosen to participate. It is also quite possible that EA sceptics could have contributed their views.

Moreover, although the response level was good for a survey of this kind, the sample size is relatively small. However, looking at the spread of the respondents' organisations, key UK players are well represented across a wide variety of industries, hence providing some level of confidence that the data collected paint a realistic snapshot of UK EA practice. The survey appears to be rare within the literature in collecting quantitative data direct from practitioners rather than using qualitative data interpreted by researchers from structured interviews.

6. CONCLUSION AND FUTURE WORK

The work in this paper provides some evidence from practice in the area of EA in general, and the adoption of specific EA frameworks in particular.

Empirical data from this study seems to confirm claimed benefits of EA as to improving governance structures, working relationships between business and IT, enabling new business strategy or re-engineering, reducing overall IT costs and increasing IT value. However, a key insight from the survey is that, in practice, EA appears to have a greater effect on business-IT alignment than on technological choices. This seems to reinforce the findings of Mending (2011) and Simon (2013a) and to support claims in some of the literature that in current practice the relation between EA and technological choices remains weak. It would be interesting to investigate the root causes of such a disconnect. For instance, we may speculate that legacy technological practices and infrastructures within an organisation might prevent EA from having a transformative effect, when compared for instance to more modern SOA-based systems. It may also be possible that technology suppliers with vested interests in maintaining vendor lock-in to a product set have worked outside the influence of weak IT governance structures. A much more in-depth study of organisations would be required to address this, and this remains the subject of future work.

Although respondents appear generally supportive of EA's worth, the survey data appears to confirm Schöenherr's opinion (2009) that, despite two decades of EA effort, its adoption in practice is still patchy and that current frameworks and approaches remains immature and often inadequate, leading organisations to take more pragmatic and ad-hoc approaches to EA. In particular, the data indicate that ad-hoc, in-house approaches remain widespread and that TOGAF is the most widely known and adopted EA framework, although this is often adapted to suit the needs of the organisation. It would be interesting to track whether increased standardisation of EA methods will be witnessed in the future. For example, it would be worthwhile investigating whether the use of Archimate as a modelling language has achieved any wide traction in establishing EA as a function with longevity within a similar sample of organisations.

Despite an acknowledged improved working relationship between business and IT as a result of EA practices, the survey results indicate that interactions remain confined primarily to IT and business specialist stakeholders, with only limited access to strategic business stakeholders. Given the critical IT Governance role of these stakeholders it might be time to rethink stakeholder participations in EA initiatives and functions, to ensure that what is recommended in theory is also effective and practically feasible.

Finally, while the results start to paint a picture of current EA practice in large UK organisations, more and much larger scale studies are required to build a much more comprehensive picture and for surveys to be repeated at periodic intervals to track rates of adoption, etc. Such studies should look beyond qualitative data, which may be subject of bias, and introduce and apply more objective quantitative measures. This is, however, not a trivial task, both because of the intrinsic complexity of what needs to be measured and because of possible resistance in organisations to disclose potentially commercially sensitive information.

REFERENCES

Abraham, R., Aier, S., & Labusch, N. (2012). Enterprise Architecture as a Means for Coordination–An Empirical Study on Actual and Potential Practice. *MCIS Proceedings*.

Aier, S. (2004). Sustainability of enterprise architecture and EAI. *Proceedings of the 2004 International Business Information Management Conference Information Technology and Organizations in the 21st Century: Challenges & Solutions* (IBIMA2004).

Ayat, M., Masrom, M., Sahibuddin, S., & Sharifi, M. (2011). Issues in implementing IT Governance in Small and Medium Enterprises. *Proceeding of the Second International Conference on Intelligent Systems, Modelling and Simulation*. doi:10.1109/ISMS.2011.40

BCS. (2010). *The Chartered Institute for IT*. Retrieved from: http://bcs.org/upload/pdf/syllabus-enterprise-solution-architecture.pdf

Begg, C., & Caira, T. (2012). Exploring the SME quandary: Data governance in practise in the small to medium-sized enterprise sector. *Electronic Journal of Information Systems Evaluation, 15*(1), 1–12.

Bernus, P. L., & Nemes, L. (1996). A framework to define a generic enterprise reference architecture and methodology. *Computer Integrated Manufacturing Systems*, *9*(3), 179–191. doi:10.1016/S0951-5240(96)00001-8

Buckl, S., Ernst, A. M., Matthes, F., Ramacher, R., & Schweda, C. (2009). Using enterprise architecture management patterns to complement TOGAF. *Proceedings of the 13th IEEE International Enterprise Distributed Object Computing Conference (EDOC 2009)*. doi:10.1109/EDOC.2009.30

Calder, A. (2009). *IT Governance: Implementing Frameworks and Standards for the Corporate Governance of IT*. IT Governance Publishing, Ely.

Calder, A., & Watkins, S. (2008). *'IT Governance: A Manager's Guide to Data Security and ISO 27001 / ISO 27002: A Manager's Guide to Data Security and ISO 27001/ISO 27002*. Kogan Page.

Chaczko, Z., Kohli, A. S., Klempous, R., & Nikodem, J. (2010). Middleware integration model for Smart Hospital System using the open group architecture framework (TOGAF). *Proceedings of the 14th IEEE International Conference on Intelligent Engineering Systems (INES 2010)*. doi:10.1109/INES.2010.5483846

Clarke, M. (2011). *IT Governance Design: An Application of Problem Oriented Engineering to Enterprise Architecture, TOGAF and SOA Development*. (MSc Dissertation). The Open University.

CoBIT. (n.d.). Retrieved from: http://www.isaca.org/cobit/pages/default.aspx

Corporate I. T. Forum. (n.d.) Retrieved from http://www.corporateitforum.com

Data Protection Act of 1998. (1998). Retrieved from: http://www.legislation.gov.uk/ukpga/1998/29/contents

Dietz, J. L., & Hoogervorst, J. A. P. (2011). A critical investigation of TOGAF - Based on the enterprise engineering theory and practice. *Proceedings of the First Enterprise Engineering Working Conference (EEWC 2011)*. doi:10.1007/978-3-642-21058-7_6

DODAF. (n.d.). Retrieved from: http://dodcio.defense.gov/dodaf20.aspx

Iacob, M. E., Meertens, L. O., Jonkers, H., Quartel, D. A., Nieuwenhuis, L. J., & Van Sinderen, M. J. (2014). From enterprise architecture to business models and back. *Software & Systems Modeling*, *13*(3), 1059–1083.

ITIL. (n.d.). Retrieved from: http://www.itil-officialsite.com/home/home.asp

Lankhorst, M. (2013). *Enterprise Architecture at Work* (3rd ed.). Berlin: Springer. doi:10.1007/978-3-642-29651-2

Lapalme, J. (2012). Three schools of thought on enterprise architecture. *IT Professional*, *14*(6), 37–43. doi:10.1109/MITP.2011.109

PRINCE2. (n.d.). Retrieved from http://www.prince-officialsite.com/

Ross, J. W., Weill, P., & Robertson, D. C. (2006). *Enterprise Architecture as Strategy*. Boston: Harvard Business School Press.

Sarbannes-Oxley Act of 2002. (n.d.). Retrieved from: https://www.sec.gov/about/laws/soa2002.pdf

Schelp, J., & Aier, S. (2009). SOA and EA-sustainable contributions for increasing corporate agility. *Proceedings of the 42nd Hawaii International Conference on System Sciences (HICSS 2009)*. IEEE.

Schoenherr, M. M. (2008). Towards a common terminology in the discipline of enterprise architecture. *Proceeding of the International Conference on Service-Oriented Computing (ICSOC 2008)*.

Simon, D., Fischbach, K., & Schoder, D. (2013). An exploration of enterprise architecture research. *Communications of the Association for Information Systems*, *32*(1), 1–72.

Simon, D., Fischbach, K., & Schoder, D. (2014). Enterprise architecture management and its role in corporate strategic management. *Information Systems and e-Business Management, 12*(1), 5-42.

The Open Group. (2011). *TOGAF Version 9.1*. Zaltbommel, The Netherlands: Van Haren Publishing.

The Zachman Framework. (n.d.). Retrieved from: https://www.zachman.com/about-the-zachman-framework

TOGAF. (n.d.). Retrieved from: http://www.opengroup.org/togaf/

Van den Berg, M. (2006). *Building an Enterprise Architecture Practice: Tools, Best Practices, Ready-to-Use Insights*. Dordrecht, The Netherlands: Springer. doi:10.1007/978-1-4020-5606-2

Web References, B. S. ISO/IEC Standards. (n.d.) Retrieved from: http://shop.bsigroup.com/Navigate-by/Standards/Standards-LP/

Weill, P., & Ross, J. W. (2004). *IT Governance*. Boston: Harvard Business School Press.

Winter, R., & Schelp, J. (2008). Enterprise architecture governance: the need for a business-to-it approach. *Proceedings of the 23rd Annual ACM Symposium on Applied Computing (SAC2008)*. doi:10.1145/1363686.1363820

Zachman, J. A. (1987). A framework for information systems architecture. *IBM Systems Journal, 26*(3), 276–292. doi:10.1147/sj.263.0276

Zachman, J. A. (2015). *IRM Enterprise Architecture Conference*. Retrieved from http://www.irmuk.co.uk/eac2015/day1.cfm#Day1S28

Zadeh, M. E., Millar, G., & Lewis, E. (2012). Mapping the Enterprise Architecture Principles in TOGAF to the Cybernetic Concepts--An Exploratory Study. *Proceedings of the 45th Hawaii International Conference on System Science (HICSS)*. doi:10.1109/HICSS.2012.422

ENDNOTE

[1]   Available from http://computing-reports.open.ac.uk/2010/TR2010-25.pdf

APPENDIX: RESPONDENTS' ORGANISATIONS

- Aviva Plc
- BAE Systems Plc
- Balfour Beatty plc
- Cambridge Assessment
- Centrica plc
- European Bank for Reconstruction Development
- Friends Provident
- GlaxoSmithKline plc
- HM Land Registry
- HM Revenue and Customs
- J D Williams and Co Ltd.
- John Lewis Partnership
- Leicestershire County Council
- National Grid
- National Policing Improvement Agency
- Network Rail
- Office for National Statistics
- Ordnance Survey
- Reed Elsevier Technology Services
- SABIC UK Petrochemicals Limited
- Severn Trent Water
- Syngenta Crop Protection AG
- TUI Travel plc
- Virgin Atlantic Airways Limited

Compilation of References

Abor, J., & Adjasi, C. K. D. (2007). Corporate governance and the small and medium enterprises sector: Theory and implications. *Corporate Governance*, *7*(2), 111–122. doi:10.1108/14720700710739769

Abor, J., & Biekpe, N. (2007). Corporate governance, ownership structure and performance of SMEs in Ghana: Implications for financing opportunities. *Corporate Governance*, *7*(3), 288–300. doi:10.1108/14720700710756562

Abraham, R., Aier, S., & Labusch, N. (2012). Enterprise Architecture as a Means for Coordination–An Empirical Study on Actual and Potential Practice. *MCIS Proceedings*.

Abraham, S. E. (2012). Information technology, an enabler in corporate governance. *Corporate Governance*, *12*(3), 281–291. doi:10.1108/14720701211234555

Abu Talib, M., Barachi, E. M., Alhosn, A. K., & Ormandjieva, O. (2012). Guide to ISO 27001: UAE Case Study. *Issues in Informing Science and Information Technology*, *7*. Retrieved May 10, 2013, from http://iisit.org/Vol9/IISITv9p331-349Talib041.pdf

ADSIC. (2013). *ADSIC Vision*. Retrieved January 7, 2013, from http://adsic.abudhabi.ae/Sites/ADSIC/Navigation/EN/about-adsic.html

Ahlemann, F., Stettiner, E., Messerschmidt, M., & Legner, C. (2012). *Strategic enterprise architecture management: Challenges, best practices, and future developments*. Berlin: Springer. doi:10.1007/978-3-642-24223-6

Ahn, H. (2001). Applying the Balanced Scorecard Concept: An Experience Report. *Long Range Planning*, *34*(4), 441–461. doi:10.1016/S0024-6301(01)00057-7

Aidemark, L., & Funck, E. (2009). Measurement and health care management. *Financial Accountability & Management*, *25*(2), 253–276. doi:10.1111/j.1468-0408.2009.00476.x

Aier, S. (2004). Sustainability of enterprise architecture and EAI. *Proceedings of the 2004 International Business Information Management Conference Information Technology and Organizations in the 21st Century: Challenges & Solutions* (IBIMA2004).

Compilation of References

Akhlaghpour, S., Wu, J., Lapointe, L., & Pinsonneault, A. (2013). The ongoing quest for the IT artifact: Looking back, moving forward. *Journal of Information Technology*, *28*(S2), 150–166. doi:10.1057/jit.2013.10

Al Mamun, A., Yasser, Q. R., & Rahman, M. A. (2013). A discussion of the suitability of only one vs. more than one theory for depicting corporate governance. *Modern Economy*, *4*(1), 37–48. doi:10.4236/me.2013.41005

Aladwani, A. M. (2002). Organizational Actions, Computer Attitudes, and End-User Satisfaction in Public Organizations: An Empirical Study. *Journal of End User Computing*, *14*(1), 42–49. doi:10.4018/joeuc.2002010104

Alam. (2009). *Can governance and regulatory control ensure private higher education as business or public goods in developing countries*. Retrieved February 23, 2013 from http://www.academicjournals.org/ajbm/pdf/pdf2011/4June/Kefela.pdf

Almeida, R., Pereira, R., & Mira da Silva, M. (2013). IT Governance Mechanisms: A Literature Review. In J.F. Cunha, M. Snene, & H. Nóvoa, (Eds.), *International Conference in Exploring Services Science 1.3* (vol. 143, pp. 186-199). Berlin, Germany: Springer-Verlag. doi:10.1007/978-3-642-36356-6_14

Al-Mudimigh, A., Zairi, M., & Al-Mashari, M. et al. (2001). ERP software implementation: An integrative framework. *European Journal of Information Systems*, *10*(4), 216–226. doi:10.1057/palgrave.ejis.3000406

Altinkemer, K., Ozcelik, Y., & Ozdemir, Z. (2011). Productivity and Performance Effects of Business Process Reengineering: A Firm-Level Analysis. *Journal of Management Information Systems*, *27*(4), 129–162. doi:10.2753/MIS0742-1222270405

Alves, C. R. C., Riekstin, A. C., Carvalho, T. C. M. B., & Vidal, A. G. R. (2013). IT governance frameworks: A literature review of Brazilian publications. *Proceedings of the International Conference on Information Resources Management* (CONF-IRM).

Aral, S., & Weill, P. (2007). IT Assets, Organizational Capabilities, and Firm Performance: How Resource Allocations and Organizational Differences Explain Performance Variation. *Organization Science*, *18*(5), 763–780. doi:10.1287/orsc.1070.0306

Armstrong, M. (2006). Competition in two-sided markets. *The Rand Journal of Economics*, *37*(3), 668–691. doi:10.1111/j.1756-2171.2006.tb00037.x

Asdemir, K. (2004). *Essays on pricing in e-commerce: Dynamic pricing and performance based pricing*. The University of Texas at Dallas.

Ashurst, C., & Doherty, N. F. (2003). Towards the formulation of "a best practice" framework for benefits realization in IT projects. *Electronic Journal of Information Systems Evaluation*, *6*, 1–10.

Ashurst, C., Doherty, N. F., & Peppard, J. (2008). Improving the Impact of It Development Projects: The Benefits Realization Capability Model. *European Journal of Information Systems*, *17*(4), 352–370. doi:10.1057/ejis.2008.33

Aversano, L., Grasso, C., & Tortorella, M. (2012). A literature review of Business/IT Alignment Strategies. *Procedia Technology, 5,* 462–474. doi:10.1016/j.protcy.2012.09.051

Avison, D., Gregor, S., & Wilson, D. (2006). Managerial IT unconsciousness. *Communications of the ACM, 49*(7), 89–93. doi:10.1145/1139922.1139923

Ayat, M., Masrom, M., Sahibuddin, S., & Sharifi, M. (2011). Issues in implementing IT Governance in Small and Medium Enterprises. *Proceeding of the Second International Conference on Intelligent Systems, Modelling and Simulation.* doi:10.1109/ISMS.2011.40

Baccarini, D., & Bateup, G. (2008). Benefits Management in Office Fit-out Projects. *Facilities, 26*(7/8), 310–320. doi:10.1108/02632770810877958

Bahsani, S., Semma, A., & Sellam, N. (2015). Towards a New Approach For Combining The IT Frameworks. *International Journal of Computer Science Issues, 12*(1), 118–123.

Bandara, W., Gable, G. G., & Rosemann, M. (2005). Factors and Measures of Business Process Modelling: Model Building Through a Multiple Case Study. *European Journal of Information Systems, 14*(4), 347–360. doi:10.1057/palgrave.ejis.3000546

Banham, H., & He, Y. (2010). SME governance: Converging definitions and expanding expectations. *International Business & Economics Research Journal, 9*(2), 77–82.

Barjis, J. (2009). Collaborative, Participative and Interactive Enterprise Modeling. In ICEIS 2009 (LNBIP), (vol. 24, pp. 651–662). Springer.

Barjis, J. (2011). CPI Modeling: Collaborative, Participative, Interactive Modeling. In *Proceedings of the 2011 Winter Simulation Conference* (pp. 3099-3108). IEEE.

Barney, J. B. (1991). Firm Resources and Sustained Competitive Advantage. *Journal of Management, 17*(1), 109–120. doi:10.1177/014920639101700108

Baron, R. M., & Kenny, D. A. (1986). The moderator mediator variable distinction in social psychological research: Conceptual, strategic, and statistical considerations. *Journal of Personality and Social Psychology, 51*(6), 1173–1182. doi:10.1037/0022-3514.51.6.1173 PMID:3806354

Bartens, Y., Schulte, F., & Voß, S. (2014a). E-business IT governance revisited: An attempt towards outlining a Novel Bi-directional business/IT alignment in COBIT5. In *Proceedings of the 47th Hawaii International Conference on System Sciences (HICSS)* (pp. 4356–4365). Waikaloa, HI: IEEE. doi:10.1109/HICSS.2014.538

Bartens, Y., Schulte, F., & Voß, S. (2014b). Business/IT Alignment in Two Sided Markets: A Study of COBIT 5 for Internet Based Business Models. *International Journal of IT/Business Alignment and Governance, 5*(2), 27-43.

Bartens, Y., De Haes, S., Eggert, L., Heilig, L., Maes, K., Schulte, F., & Voß, S. (2014). A visualization approach for reducing the perceived complexity of COBIT 5. In M. C. Tremblay, D. VanderMeer, M. Rothenberger, A. Gupta, & V. Yoon (Eds.), *Advancing the Impact of Design Science: Moving from Theory to Practice* (pp. 403–407). Springer. doi:10.1007/978-3-319-06701-8_34

Compilation of References

Bartens, Y., De Haes, S., Lamoen, Y., Schulte, F., & Voss, S. (2015). On the Way to a Minimum Baseline in IT Governance: Using Expert Views for Selective Implementation of COBIT 5. In *Proceedings of the 47th Hawaii International Conference on System Sciences (HICSS)* (pp. 4554-4563). Kauai, HI: IEEE. doi:10.1109/HICSS.2015.543

Barthon, P., & Jepsen, B. (1997). How time affects transaction costs and relational governance in the distribution channel: A review and research proposition. *Management Research News*, *20*(6), 14–29. doi:10.1108/eb028566

Bartlett, J. (2006). Managing Programmes of Business Change. Hampshire.

Bassellier, G., & Benbasat, I. (2004). Business competence of information technology professionals: Conceptual development and influence on IT-business partnership. *Management Information Systems Quarterly*, *28*(4), 673–694.

Bassellier, G., Benbasat, I., & Reich, B. H. (2003). The influence of business managers' IT competence on championing IT. *Information Systems Research*, *14*(4), 317–336. doi:10.1287/isre.14.4.317.24899

Bassi, L., Secchi, C., Bonfé, M., & Fantuzzi, C. (2011). A SysML-based methodology for manufacturing machinery modeling and design. *IEEE/ASME Transactions on Mechatronics*, *6*(6), 1049–1062. doi:10.1109/TMECH.2010.2073480

Baxter, G., & Sommerville, I. (2011). Socio-technical systems: From design methods to systems engineering. *Interacting with Computers*, *23*(1), 4–17. doi:10.1016/j.intcom.2010.07.003

BCS. (2010). *The Chartered Institute for IT*. Retrieved from: http://bcs.org/upload/pdf/syllabus-enterprise-solution-architecture.pdf

Beatty, C., & Gordon, J. (1991). Preaching the Gospel: The Evangelists of New Technology. *California Management Review*, *33*(3), 73–94. doi:10.2307/41166662

Becker, J., Rosemann, M., & von Uthmann, C. (2000). Guidelines of Business Process Modeling. In W. M. P. van der Aalst, J. Desel, & A. Oberweis (Eds.), *Business Pro-cess Management. Models, Techniques, and Empirical Studies* (pp. 30–49). Springer Berlin Heidelberg.

Begg, C., & Caira, T. (2012). Exploring the SME quandary: Data governance in practise in the small to medium-sized enterprise sector. *Electronic Journal of Information Systems Evaluation*, *15*(1), 1–12.

Bennington, P., & Baccarini, D. (2004, June). Project benefits management in IT projects – An Australian perspective. *Project Management Journal*.

Bergeron, F., Croteau, A.-M., Uwizeyemungu, S., & Raymond, L. (2015). IT Governance Framework Applied to SMEs. *International Journal of IT/Business Alignment and Governance*, *6*(1), 33–49. doi:10.4018/IJITBAG.2015010103

Bergeron, F., Raymond, L., & Rivard, S. (2001). Fit in Strategic Information Technology Management Research: An Empirical Comparison of Perspectives. *Omega, 29*(2), 125–142. doi:10.1016/S0305-0483(00)00034-7

Bergeron, F., Raymond, L., & Rivard, S. (2004). Ideal patterns of strategic alignment and business performance. *Information & Management, 41*(8), 1003–1020. doi:10.1016/j.im.2003.10.004

Bernus, P. L., & Nemes, L. (1996). A framework to define a generic enterprise reference architecture and methodology. *Computer Integrated Manufacturing Systems, 9*(3), 179–191. doi:10.1016/S0951-5240(96)00001-8

Bharadwaj, A. S., Bharadwaj, S. G., & Konsynski, B. R. 1995. The moderator role of information technology in firm performance: A conceptual model and research propositions.*Proceedings of the Sixteenth International Conference on Information Systems.*

Bieker, T., & Waxenberger, B. (2002). *Sustainability Balanced Scorecard and Business Ethics – using the BSC for integrity management.10th International Conference of the Greening of Industry Network*, Göteborg, Sweden.

Biggs, M. (2000). E-commerce success requires commitment to building a proper customer "community". *InfoWorld, 22*(14), 68.

Blili, S., & Raymond, L. (1993). Information technology: Threats and opportunities for small and medium-sized enterprises. *International Journal of Information Management, 13*(6), 439–448. doi:10.1016/0268-4012(93)90060-H

Boh, W. F., & Yellin, D. (2006). Using Enterprise Architecture Standards in Managing Information Technology. *Journal of Management Information Systems, 23*(3), 163–207. doi:10.2753/MIS0742-1222230307

Booz, Allen, & Hamilton. (Eds.). (2000). *10 Erfolgsfaktoren im e-Business*. Frankfurt am Main: FAZ.

Boynton, A. C., Zmud, R. W., & Jacobs, G. C. (1994). The Influence of IT Management Practice on IT Use in Large Organizations. *Management Information Systems Quarterly, 18*(3), 299–318. doi:10.2307/249620

Bradley, R. V., Byrd, T. A., Pridmore, J. L., Thrasher, E., Pratt, R. M., & Mbarika, V. W. (2012). An empirical examination of antecedents and consequences of IT governance in US hospitals. *Journal of Information Technology, 27*(2), 156–177. doi:10.1057/jit.2012.3

Braun, J., Ahlemann, F., & Mohan, K. (2010). Understanding Benefits Management Success: Results of a Field Study. ECIS 2010 Proceedings.

Braunscheidel, M. J., & Suresh, N. C. (2009). The organizational antecedents of a firm's supply chain agility for risk mitigation and response. *Journal of Operations Management, 27*(2), 119–140. doi:10.1016/j.jom.2008.09.006

Compilation of References

Breuer, S. (2004). *Beschreibung von Geschäftsmodellen internetbasierter Unternehmen Konzeption-Umsetzung-Anwendung*. St. Gallen, Switzerland: Universität St. Gallen.

Broadbent, M. (2003). *Understanding IT Governance*. IT World Canada News. Retrieved February 16, 2013 from http://www.itworldcanada.com/article/understanding-it-governance/19174

Brouard, F., & Di Vito, J. (2008). Identification des mécanismes de gouvernance applicables aux PME. *9ème Congrès International Francophone en Entrepreneuriat et PME*. Université Louvain-La-Neuve.

Brown, D., & Lockett, N. (2004). Potential of critical e-applications for engaging SMEs in e-business: A provider perspective. *European Journal of Information Systems*, *13*(1), 21–34. doi:10.1057/palgrave.ejis.3000480

Brown, S., & Eisenhardt, K. (1997). The art of continuous change: Linking complexity theory and time-paced evolution in relentlessly shifting organizations. *Administrative Science Quarterly*, *42*(1), 1–34. doi:10.2307/2393807

Brunninge, O., Nordqvist, M., & Wiklund, J. (2007). Corporate governance and strategic change in SMEs: The effects of ownership, board composition and top management teams. *Small Business Economics*, *29*(3), 295–308. doi:10.1007/s11187-006-9021-2

Bryman, A. (2012). *Social Research Methods*. Oxford University Press.

Brynjolfsson, E. (1993). The productivity paradox of information technology. *Communications of the ACM*, *36*(12), 66–77. doi:10.1145/163298.163309

Brynjolfsson, E., & Brown, P. (2005). VII pillars of IT Productivity. *Optimize*, *4*(5), 26–35.

Brynjolfsson, E., & Hitt, L. M. (1998). Beyond the Productivity Paradox. *Communications of the ACM*, *41*(8), 49–55. doi:10.1145/280324.280332

Buckl, S., Dierl, T., Matthes, F., & Schweda, C. M. (2010). Building Blocks for Enterprise Architecture Management Solutions. In Practice-Driven Research on Enterprise Transformation (LNBIP), (Vol. 69, pp. 17–46). Springer. doi:10.1007/978-3-642-16770-6_2

Buckl, S., Ernst, A. M., Matthes, F., Ramacher, R., & Schweda, C. (2009). Using enterprise architecture management patterns to complement TOGAF. *Proceedings of the 13th IEEE International Enterprise Distributed Object Computing Conference (EDOC 2009)*. doi:10.1109/EDOC.2009.30

Buede, D. M. (2011). *The engineering design of systems: models and methods* (Vol. 55). John Wiley & Sons.

Burney, L. L., & Swanson, N. J. (2010). The Relationship between Balanced Scorecard Characteristics and Manager's Job Satisfaction. *Journal of Managerial Issues*, *22*(2), 166–181. doi: http://www.jstor.org/stable/20798903

Caldeira, M. M., & Ward, J. M. (2003). Using resource-based theory to interpret the successful adoption and use of information systems and technology in manufacturing small and medium sized enterprises. *European Journal of Information Systems*, *12*(2), 127–141. doi:10.1057/palgrave.ejis.3000454

Calder, A. (2008). *Developing an IT governance framework*. Retrieved March 2, 2013 from www.ncc.co.uk/article/?articleid=13371

Calder, A. (2009). *IT Governance: Implementing Frameworks and Standards for the Corporate Governance of IT*. IT Governance Publishing, Ely.

Calder, A., & Watkins, S. (2008). *'IT Governance: A Manager's Guide to Data Security and ISO 27001 / ISO 27002: A Manager's Guide to Data Security and ISO 27001/ISO 27002*. Kogan Page.

Cardona, M., Kretschmer, T., & Strobel, T. (2013). ICT and productivity: Conclusions from the empirical literature. *Information Economics and Policy*, *25*(3), 109–125. doi:10.1016/j.infoecopol.2012.12.002

Carr, N. G. (2003). *IT Doesn't Matter*. Harvard Business School Publishing Corporation.

Carr, N. G. (2003). IT doesn't matter. *Harvard Business Review*, *81*(3), 41–49. PMID.12747161

Cecez-Kecmanovic, D., Kautz, K., & Abrahall, R. (2014). Reframing Success and Failure of Information Systems: A Performative Perspective. *Management Information Systems Quarterly*, *38*(2), 561–588.

Chaczko, Z., Kohli, A. S., Klempous, R., & Nikodem, J. (2010). Middleware integration model for Smart Hospital System using the open group architecture framework (TOGAF). *Proceedings of the 14th IEEE International Conference on Intelligent Engineering Systems (INES 2010)*. doi:10.1109/INES.2010.5483846

Cha, H. S., Pingry, D. E., & Thatcher, M. E. (2009). What determines IT spending priorities? *Communications of the ACM*, *52*(8), 105–110. doi:10.1145/1536616.1536644

Chan, Y. E., & Reich, B. H. (2007). IT alignment: What have we learned? *Journal of Information Technology*, *22*(4), 297–315. doi:10.1057/palgrave.jit.2000109

Chen, H.-M. (2008). Towards service engineering: Service orientation and business-IT alignment. In *Proceedings of the 41st Hawaii International Conference on System Sciences (HICSS)* (pp. 114c1–114c10). Waikaloa, HI: IEEE. doi:10.1109/HICSS.2008.462

Chen, D. (2007). The behavioral consequences of CEO-board trust and power relationships in corporate governance. *Business Renaissance Quarterly*, *2*(4), 59–75.

Chen, H. M., Kazman, R., & Garg, G. (2005). BITAM: An engineering principled method for managing misalignments between business and IT architectures. *Science of Computer Programming*, *57*(1), 5–26. doi:10.1016/j.scico.2004.10.002

Compilation of References

Choudhary, V., & Vithayathil, J. (2013). The Impact of Cloud Computing: Should the IT Department Be Organized as a Cost Center or a Profit Center? *Journal of Management Information Systems*, *30*(2), 67–100. doi:10.2753/MIS0742-1222300203

Christiner, F., Lantow, B., Sandkuhl, K., & Wissotzki, M. (2012). Multi-dimensional Visualization in Enterprise Modeling. In *Proceedings of International Conference on Business Information Systems, Workshops* (LNBIP), (vol. 127, pp. 139–152). Springer. doi:10.1007/978-3-642-34228-8_14

Chwelos, P., Benbasat, I., & Dexter, A. S. (2001). Research report: Empirical test of an EDI adoption model. *Information Systems Research*, *12*(3), 304–321. doi:10.1287/isre.12.3.304.9708

Clarke, M. (2011). *IT Governance Design: An Application of Problem Oriented Engineering to Enterprise Architecture, TOGAF and SOA Development*. (MSc Dissertation). The Open University.

CoBIT. (n.d.). Retrieved from: http://www.isaca.org/cobit/pages/default.aspx

Cochran, M. (2010). Proposal of an operations department model to provide IT governance in organizations that don't have IT c-level executives. In *Proceedings of the 43rd Hawaii International Conference on System Sciences (HICSS)* (pp. 1–10). Poipu, HI: IEEE.

Colecchia, A., & Schreyer, P. (2001). *ICT Investment and Economic Growth in the 1990s: Is the United States a Unique Case? A Comparative Study of Nine OECD Countries*. Organisation for Economic Co-operation and Development (OECD), Directorate for Science, Technology and Industry (DSTI), STI Working papers 7/2001.

Coleman, T. (1994, March). Investment Appraisal: Total IT. *Accountancy*, 68-70.

Coltman, T. R., Devinney, T. M., & Midgley, D. F. (2007). EBusiness Strategy and Firm Performance: A Latent Class Assessment of the Drivers and Impediments to Success. *Journal of Information Technology*, *22*(2), 87–101. doi:10.1057/palgrave.jit.2000073

Coltman, T., Tallon, P., Sharma, R., & Queiroz, M. (2015). Strategic IT alignment: Twenty-five years on. *Journal of Information Technology*, *30*(2), 1–10.

Consulting-Portal Inc. (2007). *Necessary Frameworks for IT Governance: Clarifying the tangled web*. Retrieved December 5, 2012, from http://consulting-portal.com/documents/Necessary%20 Frameworks%20for%20IT%20Governance.pdf

Corporate I. T. Forum. (n.d.) Retrieved from http://www.corporateitforum.com

Cragg, P., Caldeira, M., & Ward, J. (2011). Organizational information systems competences in small and medium-sized enterprises. *Information & Management*, *48*(8), 353–363. doi:10.1016/j. im.2011.08.003

Croteau, A.-M., & Bergeron, F. (2009). Interorganizational governance of information technology. *42nd Hawaii International Conference on System Sciences*.

Croteau, A.-M., Bergeron, F., & Dubsky, J. (2013). Contractual and consensual profiles for an interorganizational governance of information technology. *International Business Research, 6*(9), 30–43. doi:10.5539/ibr.v6n9p30

Dahlberg, T., & Kivijärvi, H. (2016). Towards an Integrative, Multilevel Theory for Managing the Direct and Indirect Impacts of IT Project Success Factors.*Proceedings of the 49th Annual Hawaii International Conference.* doi:10.1109/HICSS.2016.616

Daily, C. M., Dalton, D. R., & Cannella, A. A. Jr. (2003). Corporate governance: Decades of dialogue and data. *Academy of Management Review, 28*(3), 371–382.

Dalkey, N. (1969).*The Delphi Method: An Experimental Study of Group Opinion (No. RM-5888-PR).* The Rand Corporation.

Darby, R., Jones, J., & Madani, G. A. (2003). E-commerce marketing: Fad or fiction? Management competency in mastering emerging technology. An international case analysis in the UAE. *Logistics Information Management, 16*(2), 106–113. doi:10.1108/09576050310467241

Data Protection Act of 1998. (1998). Retrieved from: http://www.legislation.gov.uk/ukpga/1998/29/contents

Davenport, T., Harris, J., De Long, D., & Jacobson, A. (2001). Data to Knowledge to Results: Building an Analytic Capability. *California Management Review, 43*(2), 117–138. doi:10.2307/41166078

Davenport, T., Harris, J., & Shapiro, J. (2010). Competing on Talent Analytics. *Harvard Business Review, 88*(10), 52–58. PMID:20929194

Davenport, T., & Short, J. (1990). The New Industrial Engineering: Information Technology and Business Process Redesign. *Sloan Management Review, 31*(4), 11–27.

de Haas, M., & Kleingeld, A. (1999). Multilevel design of performance measurement systems: Enhancing strategic dialogue throughout the organization. *Management Accounting Research, 10*(3), 233–261. doi:10.1006/mare.1998.0098

De Haes, S., & Grembergen, W. (2004). IT Governance and Its Mechanisms. *Information Systems Control Journal, 1.*

De Haes, S., & Van Grembergen, W. (2013). Improving enterprise governance of IT in a major airline: a teaching case. *Journal of Information Technology Teaching Cases.*

De Haes, S., & Grembergen, W. (2008). Analysing the Relationship Between IT Governance and Business/IT Alignment Maturity.*Proceedings of the 41st Hawaii International Conference on System Sciences,* 428. doi:10.1109/HICSS.2008.66

De Haes, S., & Grembergen, W. (2008a). An exploratory study into the design of an IT Governance minimum baseline through Delphi research. *Communications of the Association for Information Systems, 22,* 24.

Compilation of References

De Haes, S., & Van Grembergen, W. (2005). IT governance structures, processes and relational mechanisms: Achieving IT/business alignment in a major Belgian financial group. In *Proceedings of the 38th Annual Hawaii International Conference on System Sciences.* doi:10.1109/HICSS.2005.362

De Haes, S., & Van Grembergen, W. (2006). Information technology governance best practices in Belgian organizations.*39th Hawaii International Conference on System Sciences.*

De Haes, S., & Van Grembergen, W. (2008). An exploratory study into the design of an IT governance minimum baseline through Delphi research. *Communications of the Association for Information Systems, 22,* 443–458.

De Haes, S., & Van Grembergen, W. (2010). Analyzing the impact of enterprise governance of IT practices on business performance. *International Journal of IT/Business Alignment and Governance, 1*(1), 14–38. doi:10.4018/jitbag.2010120402

De Haes, S., Van Grembergen, W., & Debreceny, R. S. (2013). COBIT 5 and enterprise governance of information technology: Building blocks and research opportunities. *Journal of Information Systems, 27*(1), 307–324. doi:10.2308/isys-50422

Decoene, V., & Bruggeman, W. (2006). Strategic alignment and middle-level managers' motivation in a Balanced Scorecard setting. *International Journal of Operations & Production Management, 26*(4), 3–4, 429–448. doi:10.1108/01443570610650576

Del Baldo, M. (2012). Corporate social responsibility and corporate governance in Italian SMEs: The experience of some spirited businesses. *Journal of Management & Governance, 16*(1), 1–36. doi:10.1007/s10997-009-9127-4

Delen, D., Dalal, N. P., & Benjamin, P. C. (2005). Integrated modeling: The key to holistic understanding of the enterprise. *Communications of the ACM, 48*(4), 107–112. doi:10.1145/1053291.1053296

DeNisi, A. S., Hitt, M. A., & Jackson, S. E. (2003). *The Knowledge Based Approach to Sustainable Competitive Advantage.* New York: Oxford University Press.

Devos, J., Van Landeghem, H., & Deschoolmeester, D. (2012). Rethinking IT governance for SMEs. *Industrial Management & Data Systems, 112*(2), 206–223. doi:10.1108/02635571211204263

Dietz, J. L., & Hoogervorst, J. A. P. (2011). A critical investigation of TOGAF - Based on the enterprise engineering theory and practice. *Proceedings of the First Enterprise Engineering Working Conference (EEWC 2011).* doi:10.1007/978-3-642-21058-7_6

DiMaggio, P. J., & Powell, W. W. (1983). The iron cage re-visited: Institutional isomorphism and collective rationality in organizational fields. *American Sociological Review, 48*(2), 147–160. doi:10.2307/2095101

DODAF. (n.d.). Retrieved from: http://dodcio.defense.gov/dodaf20.aspx

Doherty, N. F., Ashurst, C., & Peppard, J. (2012). Factors Affecting the Successful Realisation of Benefits from Systems Development Projects: Findings from Three Case Studies. *Journal of Information Technology, 27*(1), 1–16. doi:10.1057/jit.2011.8

Drnevich, P. L., & Croson, D. C. (2013). Information Technology and Business-Level Strategy: Toward an Integrated Theoretical Perspective. *Management Information Systems Quarterly, 37*(2), 484–509.

Dutot, V., Bergeron, F., & Raymond, L. (2014). Information management for the internationalization of SMEs: An exploratory study based on a strategic alignment perspective. *International Journal of Information Management, 34*(5), 672–681. doi:10.1016/j.ijinfomgt.2014.06.006

Dutta, S., & Biren, B. (2001). Business transformation on the internet. *European Management Journal, 19*(5), 449–462. doi:10.1016/S0263-2373(01)00061-5

Eisenmann, T., Parker, G., & Van Alstyne, M. W. (2006). Strategies for two-sided markets. *Harvard Business Review, 84*(10), 92. PMID:16649701

Epstein, M. J., & Wisner, P. S. (2001). Good Neighbors: Implementing Social and Environmental Strategies with the BSC. *Balanced Scorecard Report, 3*(3), 8-11.

European Commission. (2010). European Interoperability Framework (EIF) for European public services, isa -Interoperability Solutions for European Public Administration. Bruxelles, le 16.12.2010 COM(2010) 744 final. Author.

Evans, P. B., & Wurster, T. S. (1996). Strategy and the new economics of information. *Harvard Business Review, 75*(5), 70–82. PMID:10170332

Eveleens, J. L., & Verhoef, C. (2010). The Rise and Fall of the Chaos Report Figures. *IEEE Software, 27*(1), 30–36. doi:10.1109/MS.2009.154

Ezziane, Z., & Al Shamisi, A. (2013, June). Improvement of the Organizational Performance through Compliance with Best Practices in Abu-Dhabi. *International Journal of IT/Business Alignment and Governance, 4*(2), 19–36. doi:10.4018/ijitbag.2013070102

Farbey, B., Land, F., & Targett, D. (1993). *IT investment: A study of methods and practice.* Oxford, UK: Butterworth Heinemann.

Farbey, B., Land, F., & Targett, D. (1999). The moving staircase – problems of appraisal and evaluation in a turbulent environment. *Information Technology and People Journal, 12*(3), 238–252. doi:10.1108/09593849910278196

Farrell, D. (2003). The real new economy. *Harvard Business Review, 81*(9), 105–112. PMID:14521102

Ferguson, C., Green, P., Vaswani, R., & Wu, G. (2013). Determinants of effective information technology governance. *International Journal of Auditing, 17*(1), 75–99. doi:10.1111/j.1099-1123.2012.00458.x

Compilation of References

Fiegener, M. K., Brown, B. M., Dreux, D. R., & Dennis, W. J. (2004). CEO stakes and board composition in small private firms. *Entrepreneurship Theory and Practice, 28*(4), 5–24.

Figge, F., Hahn, T., Schaltegger, S., & Wagner, M. (2002). The Sustainability Balanced Scorecard: Linking Sustainability Management to Business Strategy. *Business Strategy and the Environment, 11*(5), 269–284. doi:10.1002/bse.339

Fingar, P., & Aronica, R. (2001). *The death of "e" and the birth of the real new economy.* Tampa, FL: Meghan-Kiffer Press.

Flak, L. S., Eikebrokk, T. R., & Dertz, W. (2008). An Exploratory Approach for Benefits Management in E-Government: Insights from 48 Norwegian Government Funded Projects. In *Proceedings of the 41st Hawaii International Conference on System Sciences.* doi:10.1109/HICSS.2008.55

Flynn, D., Pan, G., Keil, M., & Mähring, M. (2009). De-escalating IT projects: The DMM model. *Communications of the ACM, 52*(10), 131–134. doi:10.1145/1562764.1562797

Franken, A., Edwards, C., & Lambert, R. (2009). Executing Strategic Change: Understanding the Critical Management Elements That Lead to Success. *California Management Review, 51*(3), 49–73. doi:10.2307/41166493

Frank, U. (2002). Multi-Perspective Enterprise Modeling (MEMO) – Conceptual Framework and Modeling Languages.*Proceedings of the 35th Annual Hawaii International Conference on System Sciences.* doi:10.1109/HICSS.2002.993989

Frank, U. (2014). Multi-perspective enterprise modeling: Foundational concepts, prospects and future research challenges. *Software & Systems Modeling, 13*(3), 941–962. doi:10.1007/s10270-012-0273-9

Friedrichsen, M., & Mühl-Benninghaus, W. (Eds.). (2014). *Handbook of Social Media Management - Value Chain and Business Models in Changing Media Markets.* Berlin: Springer.

Gartner Inc. (2012). *Gartner Market Databook, 2Q12 Update.* Available from https://www.gartner.com/doc/2070316/gartner-market-databook-q-update

Gartner. (2009). *IT governance must be driven by corporate governance.* Retrieved on April 17, 2013 from http://www.gartner.com/it/content/1229500/1229528/it_governance_must_be_driven_corp_gov.pdf

Gartner. (2013, September 26). *Gartner Worldwide IT Spending Forecast.* Retrieved December 6, 2013, from http://www.gartner.com/technology/research/it-spending-forecast/

Gattiker, T. F., & Goodhue, D. L. (2004). Understanding the local-level costs and benefits of ERP through organizational information processing theory. *Information & Management, 41*(4), 431–443. doi:10.1016/S0378-7206(03)00082-X

Gerke, L., & Ridley, G. (2006). Towards an abbreviated COBIT framework for use in an Australian State Public Sector. In S. Pencer, S & A. Jenkins, A. (Eds.), *17th Australasian Conference on Information Systems* (pp. 1-10). Retrieved January 15, 2013, from http://eprints.utas.edu.au/513/1/ACIS2006.pdf

Gerrard, M. (2009). *IT Governance, a Flawed Concept: It's Time for Business Change Governance*. Stamford: Gartner Research.

Gibson, C. F. (2003). IT-enabled Business Change - An Approach to Understanding and Managing Risk. *MIS Quarterly Executive*, *2*(2), 104–115.

Glynne, P. (2007). *Benefits Management-changing the focus of delivery*. Association for Progress Management. *Yearbook*, *2006/2007*, 45–49.

Goeken, M., & Alter, S. (2009). Towards conceptual metamodeling of IT governance frameworks approach. In *Proceedings of the 42nd Hawaii International Conference on System Sciences (HICSS)* (pp. 1–10). IEEE.

Goh, K. H., & Kauffman, R. J. (2013). Firm Strategy and the Internet in U.S. Commercial Banking. *Journal of Management Information Systems*, *30*(2), 9–40. doi:10.2753/MIS0742-1222300201

Goldsmith, S., & Eggers, W. D. (2004). *Governing by Network: The New Shape of the Public Sector*. Washington, DC: Brookings Institute Press.

Gomes, J. (2011). *Gestão de benefícios numa empresa de Geoengenharia*. (MSc Thesis in Management). ISCTE-IUL, Lisboa. accessed from http://hdl.handle.net/10071/4702

Gomes, J., & Romão, M. (2014). Advantages and Limitations of Performance Measurement Tools: The Balanced Scorecard. In *Proceedings of IS2014 - 7th IADIS International Conference*. IADIS Press.

Gomes, J., & Romão, M. (2013a). How benefits management helps balanced scorecard to deal with business dynamic environments. *Tourism and Management Studies*, *9*(1), 129–138. ISSN 2182-8458

Gomes, J., Romão, M., & Caldeira, M. (2013b). The Benefits Management and Balanced Scorecard Strategy Map: How They Match. *International Journal of IT/Business Alignment and Governance*, *4*(1), 44–54. doi:10.4018/jitbag.2013010104

Goodhue, D., Lewis, W., & Thompson, R. (2006). PLS, Small Sample Size and Statistical Power in MIS Research.*Proceedings of the 39th Annual Hawaii International Conference*. doi:10.1109/HICSS.2006.381

Graw, E.-M. (2001). Lockrufe auf den Felsen und ins Netz. *FOCUS Online*. Retrieved June 29, 2014, from http://www.focus.de/politik/deutschland/profile-lockrufe-auf-den-felsen-und-ins-netz_aid_190858.html

Compilation of References

Greger, V., Wolf, P., & Krcmar, H. (2015). Perception of Benefits Achieved by IT Management Accounting in the Public Sector. In *Smart Enterprise Engineering: 12. Internationale Tagung Wirtschaftsinformatik* (WI 2015). Retrieved December 21, 2015, from http://www.wi2015.uni-osnabrueck.de/Files/WI2015-D-14-00106.pdf

Gregor, S., Hart, D., & Martin, N. (2007). Enterprise architectures: Enablers of business strategy and IS/IT alignment in government. *Information Technology & People, 20*(2), 96–120. doi:10.1108/09593840710758031

Grembergen, W., & De Haes, S. (2008). *Implementing Information Technology Governance: Models, Practices, and Cases*. Hershey, PA: IGI Publishing. doi:10.4018/978-1-59904-924-3

Grembergen, W., & De Haes, S. (2009). *Enterprise Governance of Information Technology: Achieving Strategic Alignment and Value*. Heidelberg, Germany: Springer-Verlag.

Grembergen, W., De Haes, S., & Guldentops, E. (2003). Structures, Processes and Relational Mechanisms for IT Governance. In W. Grembergen (Ed.), *Strategies for information technology governance* (pp. 1–36). Hershey, PA: IGI Publishing.

Guillemette, M. G., & Paré, G. (2012). Towards a new theory of the contribution of the IT function in organizations. *Management Information Systems Quarterly, 36*(2), 529–551.

Guldentops, E. (2003). Governing information technology through COBIT. In W. Grembergen (Ed.), *Strategies for information technology governance* (pp. 269–309). Hershey, PA: IGI Publishing.

Gunasekaran, A., Love, P., Rahimic, F., & Miele, R. (2001). A model for investment justification in information technology projects. *International Journal of Information Management, 21*(5), 349–364. doi:10.1016/S0268-4012(01)00024-X

Hackmann, G., Guo, W., Yan, G., Sun, Z., Lu, C., & Dyke, S. (2014). Cyber-physical codesign of distributed structural health monitoring with wireless sensor networks. Parallel and Distributed Systems. *IEEE Transactions on, 25*(1), 63–72.

Hair, J. F. C., Ringle, C. M., & Sarstedt, M. (2011). PLS_SEM: Indeed a Silver Bullet. *Journal of Marketing Theory and Practice, 19*(2), 139–151. doi:10.2753/MTP1069-6679190202

Hambrick, D. C., & Mason, P. A. (1984). Upper echelons: The organization as a reflection of its top managers. *Academy of Management Review, 9*(2), 193–206.

Harkness, M. D., & Green, B. P. (2004). E-commerce's impact on audit practices. *Internal Auditing, 19*(2), 28–36.

Harris, J., Ives, B., & Junglas, I. (2012). IT Consumerization: When Gadgets Turn Into Enterprise IT Tools. *MIS Quarterly Executive, 11*(3), 90–112.

Hellang, Ø., Flak, L. S., & Päivärinta, T. (2012). *Methods for Realizing Benefits from ICT in the Norwegian Public Sector: A Comparison. In Proceedings of the Transforming Government Workshop 2012: tGov 2012*. London: Brunel University Business School.

Henderson, J.C., & Venkatraman, N. (1993). Strategic alignment: leveraging information technology for transforming organizations. *IBM Systems Journal, 38*(2-3), 472-484.

Henderson, J. C., & Venkatraman, N. (1993). Strategic alignment: Leveraging information technology for transforming organizations. *IBM Systems Journal, 32*(1), 4–16. doi:10.1147/sj.382.0472

Herrera, A., & Giraldo, O. (2012). IT Governance State of Art in the Colombian Health Sector Enterprises. In J. Varajão, M. M. Cruz-Cunha, & A. Trigo (Eds.), *Organizational Integration of Enterprise Systems and Resources: Advancements and Applications* (pp. 332–353). Hershey, PA: IGI Publishing. doi:10.4018/978-1-4666-1764-3.ch019

Hesselmann, F., & Kunal, M. (2014). Where Are We headed with Benefits Management Research? Current Shortcomings and Avenues for Future Research. *ECIS 2014 Proceedings*.

Hesselmann, F., Ahlemann, F., & Böhl, D. (2015). Not Everybody's Darling - Investigating the Acceptance of Benefits Management and Moderating Organizational Characteristics. In O. Thomas & F. Teuteberg (Eds.), *Proceedings der 12. Internationalen Tagung Wirtschaftsinformatik (WI 2015)* (pp. 585–599). Osnabrück.

Hevner, A. R., March, S. T., Park, J., & Ram, S. (2004). Design science in information systems research. *Management Information Systems Quarterly, 28*(1), 75–105.

Hildebrand, T. (2011). *Two-sided markets in the online world: an empirical analysis.* (Dissertation). Humboldt-Universität zu Berlin, Berlin.

Hitt, L., Wu, D., & Zhou, X. (2002). Investment in enterprise resource planning: Business impact and productivity measures. *Journal of Management Information Systems, 19*(1), 71–98.

Hsiao, R. (2008). Knowledge sharing in a global professional service firm. *MIS Quarterly Executive, 7*(3), 399–412.

Huang, C. D., & Hu, Q. (2007). Achieving IT-business strategic alignment via enterprise-wide implementation of Balanced Scorecards. *Information Systems Management, 24*(2), 173–184. doi:10.1080/10580530701239314

Huang, R., Zmud, R. W., & Price, R. L. (2010). Influencing the effectiveness of IT governance practices through steering committees and communication policies. *European Journal of Information Systems, 19*(3), 288–302. doi:10.1057/ejis.2010.16

Iacob, M. E., Meertens, L. O., Jonkers, H., Quartel, D. A., Nieuwenhuis, L. J., & Van Sinderen, M. J. (2014). From enterprise architecture to business models and back. *Software & Systems Modeling, 13*(3), 1059–1083.

Iacovou, C., & Dexter, A. (2004). Turning Around Runaway Information Technology Projects. *California Management Review, 46*(4), 68–88. doi:10.2307/41166275

IBM. (2010). *IT compliance management.* Retrieved May 15, 2013 from http://www.openpages.com/solutions/IT_Compliance_38.asp

IDC. (2009). *Global revenue from internet-based applications and associated hardware from 2009 to 2014*. Retrieved May 10, 2013, from http://www.statista.com/statistics/282730/global-revenue-from-internet-based-application-since-2009/

Iden, J., & Eikebrokk, T. R. (2014). Exploring the Relationship between Information Technology Infrastructure Library and Process Management: Theory Development and Empirical Testing. *Knowledge and Process Management*, *21*(4), 292–306. doi:10.1002/kpm.1437

International Organization for Standardization and the International Electrotechnical Commission. (n.d.). *ISO/IEC 35800:2008Corporate Governance of Information Technology standard*. Downloaded from http://www.iso.org

ISACA. (2012). *COBIT 5 Enabling Processes*. ISACA.

ISACA. (2014). *COBIT 5 - A Business Framework for the Governance and Management of Enterprise IT | ISACA*. Retrieved June 12, 2014, from http://www.isaca.org/COBIT/Pages/default.aspx?cid=1003566&Appeal=PR

ISACA. (Ed.). (2012a). *COBIT 5 Framework*. Rolling Meadows, IL: ISACA.

ISACA. (Ed.). (2012b). *COBIT 5: Enabling processes*. Rolling Meadows, IL: ISACA.

ISACA. (Ed.). (2012c). *COBIT 5: Implementation*. Rolling Meadows, IL: ISACA.

Iskandar, M., & Salleh, N. A. M. (2010). IT governance in e-commerce environment: Cases from airline industry. *Proceedings of ICITST, 2010*, 1–6.

Islamoglu, M., & Liebenau, J. (2007). Information technology, transaction costs and governance structures: Integrating an institutional approach. *Journal of Information Technology*, *22*(3), 275–283. doi:10.1057/palgrave.jit.2000107

ITGI (IT Governance Institute). (2008). *IT governance global status report*. Retrieved on February 22, 2013 from http://www.isaca.org/Knowledge-Center/Research/Documents/ITGI-Global-Status-Report-2008.pdf

ITGI. (2003). *Board briefing on IT Governance*. IT Governance Institute. Retrieved January 15, 2013, from http://wikimp.mp.go.gov.br/twiki/pub/EstruturaOrganica/AreaMeio/Superintendencias/SINFO/Estrategia/BibliotecaVirtual/MaterialExtra/26904_Board_Briefing_final.pdf

ITGI. (2008). *Enterprise Value: Governance of IT Investments: The Business Case*. IT Governance Institute. Retrieved from www.isaca.org

ITIL. (n.d.). Retrieved from: http://www.itil-officialsite.com/home/home.asp

Jackling, B., & Johl, S. (2009). Board structure and firm performance: Evidence from India's top companies. *Corporate Governance*, *17*(4), 492–509. doi:10.1111/j.1467-8683.2009.00760.x

Janahi, L., Griffiths, M., & Al-Ammal, H. (2015). A conceptual model for IT governance in public sectors.*Fourth International Conference on Future Generation Communication Technology (FGCT)*. doi:10.1109/FGCT.2015.7300242

Janowicz, M., Kenis, P., & Oerlemans, L. (2005). *Promises and pitfalls of studying process patterns of networks*. Unpublished manuscript, Tilburg University, Netherlands.

Jeffrey, M., & Leliveld, I. (2004). Best practices in IT portfolio. *MIT Sloan Management Review*, *45*(3), 41–49.

Jennings, P., & Beaver, G. (1997). The performance and competitive advantage of small firms: A management perspective. *International Small Business Journal*, *15*(2), 63–75. doi:10.1177/0266242697152004

Jiménez-Zarco, A. I., & Martinez-Ruiz, M. P., & Gonzalez-Benito, O. (2006). Performance Measurement System (PMS) Integration into new Product Innovation: A Literature Review and Conceptual Framework. *Academy of Marketing Science Review*, 9.

Jones, C., Hesterly, W. S., & Borgatti, S. (1997). A general theory of network governance: Exchange conditions, and social mechanisms. *Academy of Management Review*, *22*(4), 911–945.

Jones, S., & Hughes, J. (2001). Understanding IS evaluation as complex social process: A case study of a UK local authority. *European Journal of Information Systems*, *10*(4), 189–203. doi:10.1057/palgrave.ejis.3000405

Jonkers, H., Lankhorst, M., van Buuren, R., Hoppenbrouwers, S., Bonsangue, M., & van der Torre, L. (2004). Concepts for modelling enterprise architectures. *International Journal of Cooperative Information Systems*, *13*(3), 257–287. doi:10.1142/S0218843004000985

Jorgenson, D. W. (1963). Capital Theory and Investment Behavior. *The American Economic Review*, *53*(2), 247–259.

Kaidalova, J., Seigerroth, U., Kaczmarek, T., & Shilov, N. (2012). Practical challenges of Enterprise Modeling in Business and IT Alignment. In Sandkuhl et al. (Ed.), The Practice of Enterprise Modeling (LNBIP), (vol. 134, pp. 31-45). Springer Berlin Heidelberg. doi:10.1007/978-3-642-34549-4_3

Kaidalova, J., Seigerroth, U., Bukowska, E., & Shilov, N. (2014). Enterprise Modeling for Business and IT Alignment: Challenges and Recommendations. *International Journal of IT/Business Alignment and Governance*, *5*(2), 43–68.

Kalakota, R., & Robinson, M. (2001). *E-business 2.0: Roadmap for success*. Addison-Wesley.

Kaplan, R. S., & Norton, D. P. (1992). The Balanced Scorecard: Measures that drive performance. *Harvard Business Review*, *70*(1), 71–79. PMID:10119714

Kaplan, R. S., & Norton, D. P. (1996). *The Balanced Scorecard: Translating Strategy into Action*. Harvard Business School Press.

Kaplan, R. S., & Norton, D. P. (2000). *The Strategy-Focused Organization: How Balanced Scorecard companies thrive in the new business environment*. Boston: Harvard Business School Press.

Karake, Z. A. (1995). Information technology performance: Agency and upper echelon theories. *Management Decision*, *33*(9), 30–37. doi:10.1108/00251749510098964

Karkoskova, S., & Feuerlicht, G. (2015). Extending MBI Model using ITIL and COBIT Processes. *Journal of Systems Integration*, *6*(4), 29–44. doi:10.20470/jsi.v6i4.244

Karlsen, A., & Opdahl, A. L. (2012). Enterprise modeling practice in a turnaround project. In Norsk konferanse for organisasjoners bruk av informasjonsteknologi NO-KOBIT.

Kaselowski, E. (2008). *Mitigating risk through effective information technology operations in local governments: Towards a best practice.* Retrieved May 16, 2013 from http://www.nmmu. ac.za/documents/theses/Mitigating%20Risk%20Through%20Effective%20Information%20 Technology%20Governance%20in%20Local%20Government s.pdf

Kearns, G. S., & Lederer, A. L. (2003). A resource-based view of strategic IT alignment: How knowledge sharing creates competitive advantage. *Decision Sciences*, *34*(1), 1–29. doi:10.1111/1540-5915.02289

Kearns, G. S., & Sabherwal, R. (2007). Strategic alignment between business and information technology: A knowledge based view of behaviors, outcome, and consequences. *Journal of Management Information Systems*, *23*(3), 129–162. doi:10.2753/MIS0742-1222230306

Keuntje, J., & Barkow, R. (2010). *Enterprise Architecture Management in der Praxis. Wandel, Komplexität und IT-Kosten im Unternehmen beherrschen.* Symposion Publishing GmbH.

Kivijärvi, H., & Saarinen, T. (1995). Investment in Information Systems and the Financial Performance of the Firm. *Information & Management*, *28*(2), 143–163. doi:10.1016/0378-7206(95)94022-5

Ko, D., & Fink, D. (2010). Information technology governance: An evaluation of the theory-practice gap. *Corporate Governance*, *10*(5), 662–674. doi:10.1108/14720701011085616

Ko, E., Kim, S. H., Kim, M., & Woo, J. Y. (2008). Organizational characteristics and the CRM adoption process. *Journal of Business Research*, *61*(1), 65–74. doi:10.1016/j.jbusres.2006.05.011

Koehler, J., & Vanhatalo, J. (2007). Process Anti-Patterns: How to Avoid the Common Traps of Business Process Modeling. *IBM WebSphere Developer Technical Journal, 10*(4).

Kohli, R., Devaraj, S., & Ow, T. T. (2012). Does Information Technology Investment Influence a Firm's market Value? A Case of Non-Publicly Traded Healthcare Firms. *Management Information Systems Quarterly*, *36*(4), 1145–1163.

Kohli, R., & Grover, V. (2008). Business value of IT: An essay on expanding research directions to keep up with the times. *Journal of the Association for Information Systems*, *9*(1), 23–39.

Kohli, R., & Grover, V. (2008). Business Value of IT: An Essay on Expanding Research Directions to Keep up with the Times. *Journal of the Association for Information Systems*, *9*(1), 23–39.

Kooper, M. N., Maes, R., & Lindgreen, E. E. O. R. (2011). On the governance of information: Introducing a new concept of governance to support the management of information. *International Journal of Information Management, 31*(3), 195–200. doi:10.1016/j.ijinfomgt.2010.05.009

Kraemmergaard, P., & Rose, J. (2002). Managerial competences for ERP journeys. *Information Systems Frontiers, 4*(2), 199–211. doi:10.1023/A:1016054904008

Krell, K., & Matook, S. (2009). Competitive advantage from mandatory investments: An empirical study of Australian firms. *The Journal of Strategic Information Systems, 18*(1), 31–45. doi:10.1016/j.jsis.2008.12.001

Lainhart, J. W. IV. (2001). Why IT governance is a top management issue. *Journal of Corporate Accounting & Finance, 11*(5), 33–40. doi:10.1002/1097-0053(200007/08)11:5<33::AID-JCAF6>3.0.CO;2-U

Langer, A. M., & Yorks, L. (2013). *Strategic IT: Best practices for managers and executives.* Academic Press.

Lankhorst, M. (2013). *Enterprise architecture at work: Modelling, communication and analysis* (3rd ed.). Heidelberg, Germany: Springer. doi:10.1007/978-3-642-29651-2

Lapalme, J. (2012). Three schools of thought on enterprise architecture. *IT Professional, 14*(6), 37–43. doi:10.1109/MITP.2011.109

Lapão, L. V. (2007). Survey on the status of the hospital information systems in Portugal. *Methods of Information in Medicine, 46*(4), 493–499. PMID:17694246

Lapão, L.V., & Rebuge, A., Mira da silva, M., & Gomes, R. (2009). ITIL Assessment in a healthcare environment: The role of IT governance at Hospital São Sebastião. *Studies in Health Technology and Informatics, 150*, 76–80. PMID:19745270

Law, C., & Ngai, E. (2005). IT Business Value Research: A Critical Review and Research Agenda. *International Journal of Enterprise Information Systems, 1*(3), 35–55. doi:10.4018/jeis.2005070103

Law, C., & Ngai, E. (2007). ERP systems adoption: An exploratory study of the organizational factors and impacts of ERP success. *Information & Management, 44*(4), 418–432. doi:10.1016/j.im.2007.03.004

Leedy, P. D., & Ormrod, J. E. (Eds.). (2005). *Practical Research: Planning and Design.* Upper Saddle River, NJ: Pearson Education.

Lin, C., & Pervan, G. (2003). The practice of IS/IT benefits management in large Australian organizations. *Information & Management, 41*(1), 31–44. doi:10.1016/S0378-7206(03)00002-8

Lin, C., Pervan, G., & Lin, K. H. C. (2004). A Survey on Evaluating and Realizing IS/IT Benefits in Taiwanese B2bEC Companies. In *Proceedings of ECIS 2004.*

Compilation of References

Lind, M., & Seigerroth, U. (2003). Team-based reconstruction for expanding organizational ability. *The Journal of the Operational Research Society*, *54*(2), 119–129. doi:10.1057/palgrave. jors.2601474

Lin, M., Li, S., & Whinston, A. B. (2011). Innovation and Price Competition in a Two-Sided Market. *Journal of Management Information Systems*, *28*(2), 171–202. doi:10.2753/MIS0742-1222280207

Linstone, H., Turoff, M., & Helmer, O. (1975). The Delphi method: Techniques and applications. Addison-Wesley Publishing Company.

Liu, S., Zhang, J., Keil, M., & Chen, T. (2010). Comparing Senior Executive and Project Manager Perceptions of IT Project Risk: A Chinese Delphi Study. *Information Systems Journal*, *20*(4), 319–355. doi:10.1111/j.1365-2575.2009.00333.x

Liu, X., Wu, L., Yu, J., & Lei, X. (2010). A holistic governance framework for e-business success. In *2010 Fourth International Conference on Management of e-Commerce and e-Government (ICMeCG)* (pp. 142–146). doi:10.1109/ICMeCG.2010.36

Lueg, R., & Lu, S. (2012). Improving efficiency in budgeting – An interventionist approach to spreadsheet accuracy testing. *Problems and Perspectives in Management*, *10*(1), 32–41.

Lueg, R., & Lu, S. (2013). How to improve efficiency in budgeting: The case of business intelligence in SMEs. *European Journal of Management*, *13*(2), 109–120. doi:10.18374/EJM-13-2.13

Luftman, J. (2003). Assessing IT-Business Alignment. *Information Systems Management*, *20*(4), 9–15. doi:10.1201/1078/43647.20.4.20030901/77287.2

Luftman, J., Ben-Zvi, T., Dwivedi, R., & Rigoni, E. H. (2010). IT governance: An alignment maturity perspective. *International Journal of IT/Business Alignment and Governance*, *1*(2), 13–25.

Luftman, J., & McLean, E. (2004). Key issues for IT executives. *MIS Quarterly Executive*, *3*(2), 89–104.

Luo, X., & Zhang, J. (2013). How Do Consumer Buzz and Traffic in Social Media Marketing Predict the Value of the Firm? *Journal of Management Information Systems*, *30*(2), 213–238. doi:10.2753/MIS0742-1222300208

MacGregor, R. C. (2004). Factors associated with formal networking in regional small business: Some findings from a study of Swedish SMEs. *Journal of Small Business and Enterprise Development*, *11*(1), 60–74. doi:10.1108/14626000410519100

Madureira, A., Baken, N., & Bouwman, H. (2011). Value of digital information networks: A holonic framework. *NETNOMICS: Economic Research and Electronic Networking*, *12*(1), 1–30. doi:10.1007/s11066-011-9057-6

Maes, K., De Haes, S., & Van Grembergen, W. (2013). Investigating a Process Approach on Business Cases: An Exploratory Case Study at Barco. *International Journal of IT/Business Alignment and Governance*, *4*(2), 37–53.

Maes, K., De Haes, S., & Van Grembergen, W. (2014). An Expert View on Business Case Usage: A Delphi Study. In *Proceedings of the European Conference on Information Management and Evaluation.*

Maes, K., Van Grembergen, S., & De Haes, S. (2013). Identifying Multiple Dimensions of a Business Case: A Systematic Literature Review. *The Electronic Journal Information Systems Evaluation, 16*(4), 302–314.

Mahadevan, B. (2000). Business models for internet based e-commerce. *California Management Review, 42*(4), 55–69. doi:10.2307/41166053

March, S., & Smith, G. (1995). Design and Natural Science Research on Information Technology. *Decision Support Systems, 15*(4), 251–266. doi:10.1016/0167-9236(94)00041-2

Marcos, A. F., Rouyet, J. I., & Bosch, A. (2012). An IT Balanced Scorecard Design under Service Management Philosophy. In *Proceedings of the 45th Hawaii International Conference on System Sciences.*

Marcoulides, G. A., & Saunders, C. (2006). PLS: A Silver Bullet? *Management Information Systems Quarterly, 30*(2), iii–ix.

Mardikyan, S. (2010). Analyzing the usage of IT in SMEs. *Communications of the IBIMA,* 1-10.

Margarita, I. (2008). The Balanced Scorecard Method, From Theory to Practice. *Intellectual Economics., 1*(3), 18–28.

Martinsons, M. G., Davison, R., & Tse, D. (1999). The balanced scorecard: A foundation for the strategic management of information systems. *Decision Support Systems, 25*(1), 71–88. doi:10.1016/S0167-9236(98)00086-4

Mason, M., & O'Mahony, J. (2008). Post-traditional Corporate Governance. *Journal of Corporate Citizenship, 31*(31), 31–44. doi:10.9774/GLEAF.4700.2008.au.00007

Matthews, H. (2004). Thinking Outside "the Box": Designing a Packaging Take-Back System. *California Management Review, 46*(2), 105–119. doi:10.2307/41166213

McAdam, R., & Walker, T. (2003). An inquiry into Balanced Scorecards within best value implementation in UK local government. *Public Administration, 81*(4), 873–892. doi:10.1111/j.0033-3298.2003.00375.x

McFadden, C. (2012). Are textbooks dead? Making sense of the digital transition. *Publishing Research Quarterly, 28*(2), 93–99. doi:10.1007/s12109-012-9266-3

McFarlan, W. (1984). Information Technology changes the way you compete. *Harvard Business Review,* (May-June), 93–103.

McGinnis, L. F. (2007). Enterprise modeling and enterprise transformation. *Information, Knowledge, Systems Management, 6*(1-2), 123–143.

Compilation of References

McGinnis, S. K., Pumphrey, L., Trimmer, K., & Wiggins, C. (2004). Sustaining and extending organization strategy via information technology governance. *37th Annual Hawaii International Conference on System Sciences.* doi:10.1109/HICSS.2004.1265390

Melville, N., Kraemer, K., & Gurbaxani, V. (2004). Information technology and organizational performance: An integrative model of IT business value. *Management Information Systems Quarterly, 28*(2), 283–322.

Melville, N., Kraemer, K., & Gurbaxani, V. (2004). Information Technology and Organizational Performance: An Integrative Model of IT Business Value. *Management Information Systems Quarterly, 28*(2), 283–322.

Mendling, J., Reijers, H. A., & van der Aalst, W. M. P. (2010). Seven process modeling guidelines (7PMG). *Information and Software Technology, 52*(2), 127–136. doi:10.1016/j.infsof.2009.08.004

Mergel, I., Bretschneider, S. I., Louis, C., & Smith, J. (2014). The Challenges of Challenge. Gov: Adopting Private Sector Business Innovations in the Federal Government. *47th Hawaii International Conference on System Sciences* (HICSS). Retrieved December 21, 2015, from http://ieeexplore.ieee.org/stamp/stamp.jsp?tp=&arnumber=6758860

Messabia, N., & Elbekkali, A. (2010). Information technology governance: A stakeholder approach, *An Enterprise Odyssey. International Conference Proceedings.*

Messeghem, K. (2003). Strategic entrepreneurship and managerial activities in SMEs. *International Small Business Journal, 21*(2), 197–212. doi:10.1177/0266242603021002004

Milis, K., & Mercken, R. (2004). The use of the balanced scorecard for the evaluation of information and communication technology projects. *International Journal of Project Management, 22*(2), 87–97. doi:10.1016/S0263-7863(03)00060-7

Mirza, A. A., & Chan, S. S. (2004). Challenges for managing IT skills portfolio for e-business. In M. Nakayama & N. Sutcliffe (Eds.), *Managing IT skills portfolios: planning, acquisition, and performance evaluation* (pp. 55–82). Hershey, PA: IGI. doi:10.4018/978-1-59140-515-3.ch003

Mitchell, R. K., Agle, B. R., & Wood, D. J. (1997). Toward a theory of stakeholder identification and salience: Defining the principle of who and what really counts. *Academy of Management Review, 22*(4), 853–886.

Mithas, S., Ramasubbu, N., & Sambamurthy, V. (2011). How Information Management Capability Influences Firm Performance. *Management Information Systems Quarterly, 3*(1), 237–256.

Mochiko, T. (2010). *South Africa: Public sector pays dearly for technology.* Retrieved January 7, 2013 from: http://allafrica.com/stories/201006210624.html

Mohamed, N., & Singh, J. K. G. (2012). A conceptual framework for information technology governance effectiveness in private organizations. *Information Management & Computer Security, 20*(2), 88–106. doi:10.1108/09685221211235616

Mohnnak, K. (2007). Innovation networks and capability building in the Australian high-technology SMEs. *European Journal of Innovation Management, 10*(2), 236–251. doi:10.1108/14601060710745279

Moon, M. J., Lee, J., & Roh, C. Y. (2014). The Evolution of Internal IT Applications and e-Government Studies in Public Administration. *Administration & Society, 46*(1), 3–36. doi:10.1177/0095399712459723

Nakatsu, R., & Iacovou, C. (2009). A comparative study of important risk factors involved in offshore and domestic outsourcing of software development projects: A two-panel Delphi study. *Information & Management, 46*(1), 57–68. doi:10.1016/j.im.2008.11.005

Napoli, F. (2012). The effects of corporate governance processes of strategy change and value creation in small- or medium-sized firms: A study of family-owned firms in Italy. *International Journal of Management, 29*(3), 232–260.

Nelson, R. R. (2007). IT Project Management: Infamous Failures, Classic Mistakes, and Best Practices. *MIS Quarterly Executive, 6*(2), 163–183.

Nfuka, E. N., & Rusu, L. (2009). *Critical success factors for effective IT governance in the public sector organizations in a developing country: The case of Tanzania.* Retrieved May 10, 2013 from http://web.up.ac.za/ecis/ECIS2010PR/-ECIS2010/Content/Papers/0450.R1.pdf

Nfuka, E. N., & Rusu, L. (2011). The effect of critical success factors on IT governance performance. *Industrial Management & Data Systems, 111*(9), 1418–1448. doi:10.1108/02635571111182773

Nicholson, G. J., & Kiel, G. C. (2007). Can directors impact performance? A case-based test of three theories of corporate governance. *Corporate Governance, 15*(4), 585–608. doi:10.1111/j.1467-8683.2007.00590.x

Niven, P. R. (2002). *Balanced scorecard step-by-step: Maximizing performance and maintaining results.* New York: Wiley and Sons.

Nørreklit, H. (2000). The Balanced Scorecard - a critical analysis of some of its assumptions. *Management Accounting Research, 11*(1), 65–88. doi:10.1006/mare.1999.0121

OECD. (Ed.). (2005). *SME and Entrepreneurship Outlook.* Paris: OECD.

Oestreich, N. (2012). "Feels like free": Details zum Spotify-Tarif der Telekom – Vergleich aller Streaming-Anbieter. *iPhone-Ticker.* Retrieved January 19, 2014, from http://www.iphone-ticker.de/telekom-spotify-tarif-vergleich-38485/

Okoli, C., & Pawlowski, S. (2004). The Delphi method as a research tool: An example, design considerations and applications. *Information & Management, 42*(1), 15–29. doi:10.1016/j.im.2003.11.002

Orlikowski, W. J., & Hofman, J. D. (1997). An improvisational model for change management: The case of groupware. *Sloan Management Science, 38*(2), 11–21.

Compilation of References

Orlikowski, W. J., & Iacono, C. S. (2001). Research commentary: Desperately seeking the "IT" in IT research - A call to theorizing the IT artifact. *Information Systems Research, 12*(2), 121–134. doi:10.1287/isre.12.2.121.9700

Orr, A. (2000). Convergence: The next big issue. *Target Marketing, 23*(11), 5.

Osterle, H., Becker, J., Frank, U., Hess, T., Karagiannis, D., Krcmar, H., & Sinz, E. J. et al. (2011). Memorandum on Design-Oriented Information Systems Research. *European Journal of Information Systems, 20*(1), 7–10. doi:10.1057/ejis.2010.55

Osterwalder, A. (2004). The business model ontology: A proposition in a design science approach. Institut d'Informatique et Organisation. Lausanne, Switzerland, University of Lausanne, Ecole Des Hautes Etudes Commerciales HEC, 173.

Osterwalder, A. (2011). Reverse Engineering Facebook's Business Model with Ballpark Figures. *Business Model Alchemist*. Retrieved June 27, 2014, from http://businessmodelalchemist.com/blog/2011/01/reverse-engineering-facebooks-business-model-with-ballpark-figures.html

Osterwalder, A. (2010). *Business model generation: a handbook for visionaries, game changers, and challengers*. Hoboken, NJ: Wiley.

Osterwalder, A., Pigneur, Y., & Tucci, C. L. (2005). Clarifying business models: Origins, present, and future of the concept. *Communications of the Association for Information Systems, 16*(1), 1.

Othman, R. (2008). Enhancing the effectiveness of Balanced Scorecard with Scenario Planning. *International Journal of Productivity and Performance Management, 57*(3), 259–266. doi:10.1108/17410400810857266

Otley, D. (1999). Performance management: A framework for management control systems research. *Management Accounting Research, 10*(4), 363–382. doi:10.1006/mare.1999.0115

Päivärinta, T., & Dertz, W. (2008). Pre-Determinants of Implementing II Benefits Management in Norwegian Municipalities: Cultivate the Context. In M. A. Wimmer, H. J. Scholl, & E. Ferro (Eds.), *Electronic Government* (pp. 111–123). Springer Berlin Heidelberg. doi:10.1007/978-3-540-85204-9_10

Pan, J., & Cheng, M. (2008). An Empirical Study for Exploring the Relationship between Balanced Scorecard and Six Sigma Programs. *Asia Pacific Management Review, 13*(2), 481–496.

Pardo, T. A., & Brian Burke, G. (2008). *Improving Government Interoperability: A capability framework for government managers*. The Center for Technology in Government. The Research Foundation of State University of New York. Retrieved April 20, 2013 from http://www.ctg.albany.edu/publications/reports/improving_government_interoperability

Paré, G., & Sicotte, C. (2001). Information technology sophistication in health care: An instrument validation study among Canadian hospitals. *International Journal of Medical Informatics, 63*(3), 205–223. doi:10.1016/S1386-5056(01)00178-2 PMID:11502433

Patel, K., & McCarthy, M. P. (2000). *Digital Transformation: The Essentials of E-Business Leadership*. McGraw-Hill Professional.

Patel, N. V. (2002). Emergent forms of IT governance to support global e-business models. *Journal of Information Technology Theory and Application, 4*(2), 33–48.

Patel, N. V. (2003). An emerging strategy for e-business IT Governance. In W. Grembergen (Ed.), *Strategies for Information Technology Governance* (pp. 81–98). Hershey, PA: IGI Publishing.

Patel, N. V. (2004). An emerging strategy for e-business IT governance. In W. Van Grembergen (Ed.), *Strategies for information technology governance* (pp. 81–97). Hershey, PA: IGI. doi:10.4018/978-1-59140-140-7.ch003

Pathak, J. (2003). Internal audit and e-commerce controls. *Internal Auditing, 18*(2), 30–34.

Pekovic, S. (2010). The determinants of ISO 9000 certification: A comparison of the manufacturing and service sectors. *Journal of Economic Issues, 44*(4), 895–914. doi:10.2753/JEI0021-3624440403

Peppard, P., Ward, J., & Daniel, E. (2007, March). Managing the Realization of Business Benefits from IT Investments. *MIS Quarterly Executive*.

Peppard, J. (2003). Managing IT as a portfolio of services. *European Management Journal, 21*(4), 467–483. doi:10.1016/S0263-2373(03)00074-4

Pereira, R., Almeida, R., & Mira da Silva, M. (2013). How to Generalize an Information Technology Case Study. In J. vom Brocke, R. Hekkala, S. Ram, & M. Rossi (Eds.), *8th International Conference on Design Science Research in Information Systems and Technology* (vol. 7939, pp. 150-164). Berlin, Germany: Springer-Verlag. doi:10.1007/978-3-642-38827-9_11

Pereira, R., Almeida, R., & Mira da Silva, M. (2014). *IT Governance Patterns in the Portuguese Financial Industry*. 47th Hawaii International Conference on System Sciences, Hawaii, HI. doi:10.1109/HICSS.2014.541

Pereira, R., & Mira da Silva, M. (2012). Designing a new Integrated IT Governance and IT Management Framework Based on Both Scientific and Practitioner Viewpoint. *International Journal of Enterprise Information Systems, 8*(4), 1–43. doi:10.4018/jeis.2012100101

Pereira, R., & Mira da Silva, M. (2012a). Towards an Integrated IT Governance and IT Management Framework. *Proceedings of the 16th International Enterprise Distributed Object Computing Conference.* doi:10.1109/EDOC.2012.30

Persson, A. (2001). *Enterprise Modelling in Practice: Situational Factors and their Influence on Adopting a Participative Approach.* (Doctoral Dissertation). Department of Computer and Systems Sciences, Stockholm University, Stockholm, Sweden.

Persson, A., & Stirna, J. (2001). Why Enterprise Modelling? An Explorative Study into Current Practice. In *Proceedings of 13th Conference on Advanced Information Systems Engineering.* Interlaken, Switzerland: Springer. doi:10.1007/3-540-45341-5_31

Compilation of References

Persson, A., & Stirna, J. (2010). Towards Defining a Competence Profile for the Enterprise Modeling Practitioner. PoEM 2010. *LNBIP, 68,* 232–245.

Peterson, R. (2003). Integration Strategies and Tactics for Information Technology Governance. In W. Grembergen (Ed.), *Strategies for information technology governance* (pp. 37–80). Hershey, PA: IGI Publishing.

Peterson, R. (2004). Crafting information technology governance. *Information Systems Management, 21*(4), 7–22. doi:10.1201/1078/44705.21.4.20040901/84183.2

Petter, S., DeLone, W., & McLean, E. R. (2013). Information Systems Success: The Quest for the Independent Variables. *Journal of Management Information Systems, 29*(4), 7–61. doi:10.2753/MIS0742-1222290401

Pettigrew, A., & Whipp, R. (1991). *Managing change for competitive success.* Oxford, UK: Blackwell Publishers.

Pflughoest, K. A., Ramamurthy, K., Soofi, E. S., Yasai-Ardekani, M., & Zahedi, F. (2003). Multiple conceptualizations of small business Web use and benefit. *Decision Sciences, 34*(3), 467–512. doi:10.1111/j.1540-5414.2003.02539.x

Philip, G., & Booth, M. E. (2001). A new six 'S' framework on the relationship between the role of information systems (IS) and competencies in 'IS' management. *Journal of Business Research, 51*(3), 233–247. doi:10.1016/S0148-2963(99)00051-X

PMBOK. (2015). Data retrieved June 1, 2015 from https://www.pmi.org/PMBOK-Guide-and-Standards.aspx

Pollalis, Y. (2003). Patterns of Co-alignment in Informationintensive Organizations: Business Performance Through Integration Strategies. *International Journal of Information Management, 23*(6), 469–492. doi:10.1016/S0268-4012(03)00063-X

Pollard, C. (2003). Exploring continued and discontinued use of IT: A case study of OptionFinder, a group support system. *Group Decision and Negotiation, 12*(3), 171–193. doi:10.1023/A:1023314606762

Porter, M. E. (2001). Strategy and the internet. *Harvard Business Review,* (March), 63–78. PMID:11246925

Porter, M. E. (2001). Strategy and the Internet. *Harvard Business Review, 79*(3), 62–78. PMID:11246925

Portuese, D. (2006). *E-commerce and the internet: A study on the impact of relationship marketing opportunities for better online consumer intentional relationship.* Capella University.

Post, B. (1992). A Business Case Framework for Group Support Technology. *Journal of Management Information Systems, 9*(3), 7–26. doi:10.1080/07421222.1992.11517965

PRINCE2. (2015). Data retrieved June 1, 2015 from https://www.prince2.com/prince2-methodology

PRINCE2. (n.d.). Retrieved from http://www.prince-officialsite.com/

Pritchard, R. D. (Ed.). (1995). *Productivity Measurement and Improvement – Organizational Case Studies*. Westport, CT: Praeger Publishers.

PWC. (2009). *The governance of information technology*. Retrieved December 5, 2013, from http://www.pwc.com/za/en/king3/the-governance-of-information- technology/index.jhtml

Quershil, S., Kamal, M., & Wolcott, P. (2009). Information Technology Interventions for Growth and Competitiveness in Micro-Enterprises. *International Journal of E-Business Research*, *5*(1), 117–140. doi:10.4018/jebr.2009010106

Raduescu, C., Tan, H. M., Jayaganesh, M., Bandara, W., zur Muehlen, M., & Lippe, S. (2006). A framework of issues in large process modeling projects. In *Proceedings of the 14th European Conference on Information Systems*.

Ramdani, B., Kawalek, P., & Lorenzo, O. (2009). Knowledge management and enterprise systems adoption by SMEs: Predicting SMEs' adoption of enterprise systems. *Journal of Enterprise Information Management*, *22*(1/2), 10–24. doi:10.1108/17410390910922796

Rasheed, H. S., & Geiger, S. W. (2001). Determinants of governance structure for the electronic value chain: Resource dependency and transaction costs perspectives. *The Journal of Business Strategy*, *18*(2), 159–176.

Rau, K. G. (2004). Effective governance of IT: Design objectives, roles, and relationships. *Information Systems Management*, *21*(4), 35–42. doi:10.1201/1078/44705.21.4.20040901/84185.4

Raymond, L., Bergeron, F., & Rivard, S. (1998). Determinants of business process reengineering success in small and large enterprises: An empirical study in the Canadian context. *Journal of Small Business Management*, *36*(1), 72–85.

Raymond, L., & Croteau, A.-M. (2006). Enabling the strategic development of SMEs through advanced manufacturing systems: A configurational perspective. *Industrial Management & Data Systems*, *106*(7), 1012–1032. doi:10.1108/02635570610688904

Raymond, L., Croteau, A.-M., & Bergeron, F. (2011). The strategic role of IT as an antecedent to the IT sophistication and IT performance of manufacturing SMEs. *International Journal on Advances in Systems and Measurements*, *4*(3&4), 203–211.

Raymond, L., Paré, G., & Bergeron, F. (1995). Matching information technology and organizational structure: Implications for performance. *European Journal of Information Systems*, *4*(1), 3–16. doi:10.1057/ejis.1995.2

Raymond, L., Uwizeyemungu, S., Bergeron, F., & Gauvin, S. (2012). A framework for research on e-learning assimilation in SMEs: A strategic perspective. *European Journal of Training and Development*, *36*(6), 592–613. doi:10.1108/03090591211245503

Compilation of References

Reich, B. H., & Benbasat, I. (2000). Factors That Influence the Social Dimension of Alignment between Business and Information Technology Objectives. *Management Information Systems Quarterly*, *24*(1), 81–113. doi:10.2307/3250980

Reich, B. H., & Nelson, K. M. (2003). In their own words: CIO visions about the future of in-house IT organizations. *The Data Base for Advances in Information Systems*, *34*(4), 28–44. doi:10.1145/957758.957763

Remenyi, D., Money, A., & Sherwood-Smith, M. (2000). *The Effective Measurement and Management of IT Costs and Benefits*. Oxford, UK: Butterworth-Heinemann.

Rexhepi, M. (2012). *En studie om utmaningar som kan hindra utvecklingen av modeller av hög kvalitet vid tillämpning av verksamhetsmodellering*. (Bachelor Thesis, In Swedish). Department of Information Systems, Skövde University.

Ribbers, P., Peterson, R., & Parker, M. (2002). Designing Information Technology Governance Processes: Diagnosing Contemporary Practices and Competing Theories. *Proceedings of the 35th Hawaii International Conference on System Sciences*. doi:10.1109/HICSS.2002.994351

Richards, S., & Dar, R. (2009). *Standardization & classification in the UAE*. Al Tamimi & Company. Retrieved November 14, 2012, from http://www.thyh.com/Publications/International/Standardization%20and%20Classification%20in%20the%20UAE.pdf

Ringert, J. O., Rumpe, B., & Wortmann, A. (2014). *From Software Architecture Structure and Behavior Modeling to Implementations of Cyber-Physical Systems*. arXiv preprint arXiv:1408.5690

Ringle, C., Wende, S., & Alexander, W. (2012). *SmartPLS Version: 2.0.M3*. Retrieved from http://www.smartpls.de

Ringle, C., Sarstedt, M., & Straub, D. W. (2012). A Critical Look at the Use of PLS-SEM in MIS Quarterly. *Management Information Systems Quarterly*, *36*(1), iii–xiv.

Rochet, J.-C., & Tirole, J. (2004). *Two-sided markets: An overview*. IDEI working paper. Retrieved from https://frbatlanta.org/filelegacydocs/ep_rochetover.pdf

Rochet, J.-C., & Tirole, J. (2003). Platform competition in two-sided markets. *Journal of the European Economic Association*, *1*(4), 990–1029. doi:10.1162/154247603322493212

Romm, C. T., & Sudweeks, F. (1998). *Doing business electronically*. London: Springer. doi:10.1007/978-1-4471-0591-6

Rosemann, M., Lind, M., Hjalmarsson, A., & Recker, J. (2011). *Four facets of a process modeling facilitator*. *Thirty Second International Conference on Information Systems*, Shanghai, China.

Rosemann, M., Sedera, W., & Gable, G. (2001). Critical Success Factors of Process Modeling for Enterprise Systems. *Proceedings of the Americas Conference of Information Systems (AMCIS '01)*.

Ross, J. W. (2003). Creating a strategic IT architecture competency: Learning in stages. *MIS Quarterly Executive*, *2*(1), 31–43.

Ross, J. W., Weill, P., & Robertson, D. C. (2006). *Enterprise Architecture as Strategy*. Boston: Harvard Business School Press.

Rubino, M., & Vitolla, F. (2014). Corporate governance and the information system: How a framework for IT governance supports ERM. *Corporate Governance, 14*(3), 320–338. doi:10.1108/CG-06-2013-0067

Ruivo, P., Oliveira, T., & Neto, M. (2012). ERP use and value: Portuguese and Spanish SMEs. *Industrial Management & Data Systems, 112*(7), 1008–1025. doi:10.1108/02635571211254998

Rysman, M. (2009). The economics of two-sided markets. *The Journal of Economic Perspectives, 23*(3), 125–143. doi:10.1257/jep.23.3.125

Sambamurthy, V., & Zmud, R. W. (1999). Arrangements for Information Technology Governance: A theory of multiple contingencies. *Management Information Systems Quarterly, 23*(2), 261–290. doi:10.2307/249754

Sandkuhl, K., Simon, D., Wißotzki, M., & Starke, C. (2015) The Nature and a Process for Development of Enterprise Architecture Principles. *18th International Conference BIS 2015* (LNBIP), (vol. 208, pp. 260-272). Springer.

Sandkuhl, K., Stirna, J., Persson, A., & Wissotzki, M. (2014). *Enterprise Modeling – Tackling Business challenges with the 4EM method*. Berlin: Springer Verlag.

Sapountzis, S., Harris, K., & Kagioglou, M. (2007). Benefits Realisation Process for Healthcare. *International SCRI Symposium*, Salford, UK.

Sarbannes-Oxley Act of 2002. (n.d.). Retrieved from: https://www.sec.gov/about/laws/soa2002.pdf

Sattler, H., Völckner, F., Riediger, C., & Ringle, C. M. (2010). The Impact of Brand Extension Success Factors on Brand Extension Price Premium. *International Journal of Research in Marketing, 27*(4), 319–328. doi:10.1016/j.ijresmar.2010.08.005

Saunders, M., Lewis, P., & Thornhill, A. (2006). *Research methods for business students* (4th ed.). Harlow: Prentice Hall.

Schadewizt, N., & Timothy, J. (2007). Comparing Inductive and Deductive Methodologies for Design Patterns Identification and Articulation.*Proceedings of the International Design Research Conference*.

Schaltegger, S., & Wagner, M. (2006). Integrative Management of Sustainability Performance, Measurement and Reporting, International Journal of Accounting. *Auditing and Performance Evaluation, 3*(1), 1–19. doi:10.1504/IJAAPE.2006.010098

Schelp, J., & Aier, S. (2009). SOA and EA-sustainable contributions for increasing corporate agility. *Proceedings of the 42nd Hawaii International Conference on System Sciences (HICSS 2009)*. IEEE.

Compilation of References

Schepers, T. G. J., Iacob, M. E., & Van Eck, P. A. T. (2008). A lifecycle approach to SOA governance. In *Proceedings of the 2008 ACM Symposium on Applied Computing* (pp. 1055–1061). New York, NY: ACM. doi:10.1145/1363686.1363932

Schermann, M., B'Ohmann, T., & Krcmar, H. (2009). Explicating Design Theories with Conceptual Models: Towards a Theoretical Role of Reference Models. In J. Becker, H. Krcmar, & B. Niehaves (Eds.), Wissenschaftstheorie (pp. 175-194). Heidelberg, Germany: Springer Berlin.

Schlosser, F., Wagner, H.-T., & Coltman, T. (2012). Reconsidering the Dimensions of Business-IT Alignment. In *Proceedings of the 45th Hawaii International Conference on System Science.* doi:10.1109/HICSS.2012.497

Schmidtke, R. (2006). *Two-sided markets with pecuniary and participation externalities.* Munich: Univ., Center for Economic Studies.

Schmidt, R. (1997). Managing Delphi Surveys Using Nonparametric Statistical Techniques. *Decision Sciences, 28*(3), 763–774. doi:10.1111/j.1540-5915.1997.tb01330.x

Schmidt, R., Lyytinen, K., Keil, M., & Cule, P. (2001). Identifying software project risks: An international Delphi study. *Journal of Management Information Systems, 17*(4), 5–36.

Schoenherr, M. M. (2008). Towards a common terminology in the discipline of enterprise architecture. *Proceeding of the International Conference on Service-Oriented Computing (ICSOC 2008).*

Schreyen, G. (2013). Revisiting IS Business Value Research: What We Already Know, What We Still Need to Know, and How We Can Get There. *European Journal of Information Systems, 22*(2), 139–169. doi:10.1057/ejis.2012.45

Scupola, A. (2008). Conceptualizing competences in e-services adoption and assimilation in SMEs. *Journal of Electronic Commerce in Organizations, 6*(2), 78–91. doi:10.4018/jeco.2008040105

Seigerroth, U. (2011). Enterprise Modeling and Enterprise Architecture: the constituents of transformation and alignment of Business and IT. *International Journal of IT/Business Alignment and Governance, 2*(1), 16-34.

Seigerroth, U. (2015). The Diversity of Enterprise Modeling – a taxonomy for enterprise modeling actions. *International Complex Systems Informatics and Modeling Quarterly*, (4), 12-31. Retrieved from https://csimq-journals.rtu.lv

Serra, C. E. M., & Kunc, M. (2015). Benefits Realisation Management and its influence on project success and on the execution of business strategies. *International Journal of Project Management, 33*(1), 53–66. doi:10.1016/j.ijproman.2014.03.011

Shang, S., & Seddon, P. (2002). Assessing and Managing the Benefits of Enterprise Systems: The Business Manager's Perspective. *Information Systems Journal, 12*(4), 271–299. doi:10.1046/j.1365-2575.2002.00132.x

Sherif, K., & Vinze, A. (2002). Domain engineering for developing software repositories: A case study. *Decision Support Systems, 33*(1), 55–69. doi:10.1016/S0167-9236(01)00130-0

Shleifer, A., & Vishny, R. W. (1997). A survey of Corporate Governance. *The Journal of Finance, 52*(2), 737–783. doi:10.1111/j.1540-6261.1997.tb04820.x

Sila, I., & Dobni, D. (2012). Patterns of B2B e-commerce usage in SMEs. *Industrial Management & Data Systems, 112*(8), 1255–1271. doi:10.1108/02635571211264654

Silvius, A. J. G. (2009). Business and IT Alignment: What We Know and What We Don't Know. In *Proceedings of International Conference on Information Management and Engineering*. IEEE.

Simon, D., Fischbach, K., & Schoder, D. (2014). Enterprise architecture management and its role in corporate strategic management. *Information Systems and e-Business Management, 12*(1), 5-42.

Simon, D., Fischbach, K., & Schoder, D. (2013). An exploration of enterprise architecture research. *Communications of the Association for Information Systems, 32*(1), 1–72.

Simon, H. A. (1996). *The Sciences of the Artificial*. MIT Press.

Singh, S. N., & Woo, C. (2009). Investigating business-IT alignment through multi-disciplinary goal concepts. *Requirements Engineering, 14*(3), 177–207. doi:10.1007/s00766-009-0081-0

Smith, H., McKeen, J., Cranston, C., & Benson, M. (2010). Investment Spend Optimization: A New Approach to IT Investment at BMO Financial Group. *MIS Quarterly Executive, 9*(2), 65–81.

Smith, W. K., Binns, A., & Tushman, M. L. (2010). Complex business models: Managing strategic paradoxes simultaneously. *Long Range Planning, 43*(2–3), 448–461. doi:10.1016/j.lrp.2009.12.003

Sommerville, I. (2006). *Software Engineering* (8th ed.). Addison-Wesley.

Soomro, T. R., & Hesson, M. (2012). Supporting best practices and standards for information technology infrastructure library. *Journal of Computer Science, 8*(2), 272–276. doi:10.3844/jcssp.2012.272.276

Spremic, M. (2011), Standards and frameworks for information system security auditing and assurance. *Proceedings of the World Congress on Engineering* (vol. 1). Retrieved February 20, 2013, from http://www.iaeng.org/publication/WCE2011/WCE2011_pp514-519.pdf

Spremic, M. (2011). Standards and Frameworks for Information System Security Auditing and Assurance. In S. Athanasios (Ed.), *Proceedings of the World Congress on Engineering* (vol. 1, pp. 1-6). Retrieved February 2, 2013, from http://www.iaeng.org/publication/WCE2011/WCE2011_pp514-519.pdf

Spremic, M. (2012). Measuring IT Governance Performance: A Research Study on CobiT Based Regulation Framework Usage. *International Journal of Mathematics and Computers in Simulation*, 1–9.

Standish Group. (2013). *CHAOS Manifesto 2013: Think Big, Act Small*. Retrieved June 1, 2015 from http://versionone.com/ assets/img/files/ChaosManifesto2013. pdf

Stirna, J., & Kirikova, M. (2008). Integrating Agile Modeling with Participative Enterprise Modeling. In *Proceedings of the CAiSE workshop EMMSAD*, (pp. 171-184).

Compilation of References

Stirna, J., & Persson, A. (2009). Anti-patterns as a Means of Focusing on Critical Quality Aspects in Enterprise Modeling. In T. Halpin, J. Krogstie, S. Nurcan, E. Proper, R. Schmidt, P. Soffer, & R. Ukor (Eds.), *BPMDS 2009 and EMMSAD 2009 (LNBIP),* (vol. 29, pp. 407–418). Heidelberg, Germany: Springer. doi:10.1007/978-3-642-01862-6_33

Stirna, J., Persson, A., & Sandkuhl, K. (2007). Participative Enterprise Modeling: Experiences and Recommendations. CAiSE 2007. *LNCS, 4495,* 546–560.

Swanton, B., & Draper, L. (2010). *How do you expect to get value from ERP if you don't measure it?* AMR Research.

Symons, C. (2005). *IT Governance Framework: Structures, Processes and Framework.* Retrieved March 3, 2013, from http://www.computerweekly.com/news/2240065721/IT-Governance-Framework-Structures-Processes-and-Communication

Talaulicar, T. (2010). The concept of the balanced company and its implications for corporate governance. *Society and Business Review, 5*(3), 232–244. doi:10.1108/17465681011079464

Tallon, P. P., Ramirez, V., & Short, J. E. (2013). The Information Artifact in IT Governance: Toward a Theory of Information Governance. *Journal of Management Information Systems, 30*(3), 141–177. doi:10.2753/MIS0742-1222300306

Taudes, A., Feurstein, M., & Mild, A. (2000). Options Analysis of Software Platform Decisions: A Case Study. *Management Information Systems Quarterly, 24*(2), 227–243. doi:10.2307/3250937

Taulli, T. (2012). *How to create the next Facebook seeing your startup through, from idea to IPO.* New York: Springer. doi:10.1007/978-1-4302-4648-0

Taylor-Powell, E. (2002). *Quick Tips Collecting Group Data: Delphi Technique.* University of Wisconsin. Retrieved from http://www.uwex.edu/ces/pdande/resources/pdf/Tipsheet4.pdf

Teo, T. S. H., & Ang, J. S. K. (1999). Critical success factors in the alignment of IS plans with business plans. *International Journal of Information Management, 19*(2), 173–185. doi:10.1016/S0268-4012(99)00007-9

The Open Group. (2011). *TOGAF Version 9.1.* Zaltbommel, The Netherlands: Van Haren Publishing.

The Zachman Framework. (n.d.). Retrieved from: https://www.zachman.com/about-the-zachman-framework

Thorp, J. (1999). Computing the payoff from IT. *The Journal of Business Strategy, 20*(3), 35–39. doi:10.1108/eb040005

Timmers, P. (1999). *Electronic commerce.* New York: Wiley.

TOGAF. (n.d.). Retrieved from: http://www.opengroup.org/togaf/

Torrès, O., & Julien, P.-A. (2005). Specificity and denaturing of small business. *International Small Business Journal, 23*(4), 355–377. doi:10.1177/0266242605054049

Tshinu, S. M., Botha, G., & Herselman, M. (2008). An integrated ICT management framework for commercial banking organisations in South Africa. *Interdisciplinary Journal of Information, Knowledge, and Management*, *3*, 39–53.

Turlea, E., Mocanu, M., & Radu, C. (2010). Corporate governance in the banking industry. *Accounting and Management Information Systems*, *9*(3), 379–402.

Uhlaner, L., Wright, M., & Huse, M. (2007). Private firms and corporate governance: An integrated economic and management perspective. *Small Business Economics*, *29*(3), 225–241. doi:10.1007/s11187-006-9032-z

Van de Ven, A. (1992). Suggestions for studying strategy process: A research note. *Strategic Management Journal*, *13*(5), 169–188. doi:10.1002/smj.4250131013

Van den Berg, M. (2006). *Building an Enterprise Architecture Practice: Tools, Best Practices, Ready-to-Use Insights*. Dordrecht, The Netherlands: Springer. doi:10.1007/978-1-4020-5606-2

Van den Heede, K., Clarke, S., Vleugels, A., & Aiken, L. (2007). International experts' perspectives on the state of the nurse staffing and patient outcomes literature. *Journal of Nursing Scholarship*, *39*(4), 290–297. doi:10.1111/j.1547-5069.2007.00183.x PMID:18021127

van Gils, A. (2005). Management and governance in Dutch SMEs. *European Management Journal*, *23*(5), 583–589. doi:10.1016/j.emj.2005.09.013

Van Grembergen, W., & De Haes, S. (2005). Measuring and improving information technology governance through the balanced scorecard. *Information Systems Control Journal, 2*.

Van Grembergen, W., De Haes, S., & Guldentops, E. (2004). *Structures, process and Relational mechanisms for IT Governance*. Retrieved on March 13, 2013 from www.itgi.org

Van Grembergen, W., Saull, R., & De Haes, S. (2003). Linking the IT balanced scorecard to the business objectives at a major Canadian financial group. *Journal of Information Technology Cases and Applications*.

Van Grembergen, W., & De Haes, S. (2009). *Enterprise governance of information technology: Achieving strategic alignment and value*. New York: Springer.

Van Grembergen, W., & De Haes, S. (2010). A research journey into enterprise governance of IT, business/IT alignment and value creation. *International Journal of IT/Business Alignment and Governance*, *1*(1), 1–13. doi:10.4018/jitbag.2010120401

Van Grembergen, W., De Haes, S., & Guldentops, E. (2004). Structures, processes and relational mechanisms for IT governance. In W. Van Grembergen (Ed.), *Strategies for Information Technology Governance* (pp. 1–36). Hershey, PA: IGI. doi:10.4018/978-1-59140-140-7.ch001

van Lier, J., & Dohmen, T. (2007). Benefits Management and Strategic Alignment in an IT Outsourcing Context. In *Proceedings of the 40th Hawaii International Conference on System Sciences*.

Compilation of References

Vargas, J. O. (2011). *A Framework of Practices Influencing IS/Business Alignment and IT Governance.* (Doctoral thesis). School of Information Systems, Computing and Mathematics in Brunel University.

Venkatraman, N. (1989). The concept of fit in strategy research: Toward verbal and statistical correspondence. *Academy of Management Review, 14*(3), 423–444.

Voelpel, S. C., Leibold, M., Eckhoff, R. A., & Davenport, T. H. (2005). The Tyranny of Balanced Scorecard in the Innovation Economy. In *Proceedings of 4th International Critical Management Studies Conference-Intellectual Capital Stream.* Cambridge University.

Vogt, M., Küller, P., Hertweck, D., & Hales, K. (2011). Adapting IT governance frameworks using domain specific requirements methods: Examples from small & medium enterprises and emergency management. *Proceedings of the 17th Americas Conference on Information Systems.*

Vom Brocke, J., Simons, A., Niehaves, B., Reimer, K., Plattfaut, R., & Cleven, A. (2009). Reconstructing the Giant: On the importance of Rigour in Documenting the Literature Search Process. *Proceedings of the 17th European Conference On Information System.*

Wainwright, D., Green, G., Mitchell, E., & Yarrow, D. (2005). Towards a framework for benchmarking ICT practice, competence and performance in small firms. *Performance Measurement and Metrics, 6*(1), 39–52. doi:10.1108/14678040510588580

Ward, J., De Hertogh, S., & Viaene, S. (2007). Managing Benefits from IS/IT Investments: An Empirical Investigation into Current Practice. In *Proceedings of the HICSS 2007- 40th Annual Hawaii International Conference on System Sciences.*

Ward, J. M., Taylor, P., & Bond, P. (1996). Evaluation and realisation of IS/IT benefits: An empirical study of current practice. *European Journal of Information Systems, 4*(4), 214–225. doi:10.1057/ejis.1996.3

Ward, J., & Daniel, E. (2006). *Benefits Management, Delivering Value from IS and IT Investments.* Chichester, UK: John Wiley & Sons Inc.

Ward, J., & Daniel, E. (2006). *Benefits management: delivering value from IS and IT investments.* Wiley.

Ward, J., Daniel, E., & Peppard, J. (2008). Building better business cases for IT investments. *MIS Quarterly Executive, 7*(1), 1–15.

Ward, J., & Elvin, R. (1999). A new framework for managing IT-enabled business change. *Information Systems Journal, 9*(3), 197–221. doi:10.1046/j.1365-2575.1999.00059.x

Ward, J., & Peppard, J. (2002). *Strategic Planning for Information Systems* (3rd ed.). Chichester, UK: John Wiley & Sons Inc.

Ward, P., & Zhou, H. (2006). Impact of Information Technology Integration and Lean/Just-In-Time Practices on Lead-Time Performance. *Decision Sciences, 37*(2), 177–203. doi:10.1111/j.1540-5915.2006.00121.x

Web References, B. S.ISO/IEC Standards. (n.d.) Retrieved from: http://shop.bsigroup.com/ Navigate-by/Standards/Standards-LP/

Webb, P., Pollard, C., & Ridley, G. (2006). Attempting to Define IT Governance: Wisdom or Folly? *Proceedings of the 39th Hawaii International Conference on System Science.* doi:10.1109/ HICSS.2006.68

Webster, J., & Watson, R. T. (2002). Analyzing the past to prepare for the future: Writing a Literature Review. *Management Information Systems Quarterly, 26*(2), xiii–xxiii.

Wegmann, A., Regev, G., Rychkova, I., Le, L.-S., de la Cruz, J. G., & Julia, P. (2007). Business-IT Alignment with SEAM for Enterprise Architecture.*Proceedings of the 11th IEEE International EDOC Conference.* doi:10.1109/EDOC.2007.54

Weill, P., & Ross, J. W. (2005). How effective are your IT Governance. *Research Briefing, 5*(1). Retrieved May 3rd 2013 from: http://web.mit.edu/cisr/www

Weill, P., & Woodham, R. (2002). *State street corporate: evolving IT Governance.* MIT Sloan Working Paper, 11-20.

Weill, P. (2004). Don't Just Lead, Govern: How Top-Performing Firms Govern IT. *Management Information Systems Quarterly Executive, 3*(1), 1–17.

Weill, P., & Ross, J. (2004). *IT Governance: How Top Performers Manage IT Decision Rights for Superior Results.* Boston: Harvard Business School Press.

Weill, P., & Ross, J. (2005). A matrix approach to designing IT Governance. *Sloan Management Review, 46*(2).

Weill, P., & Ross, J. (2005). A Matrixed Approach to Designing IT Governance. *Sloan Management Review, 40*(2), 26–34.

Weill, P., & Ross, J. (2005). A matrixed approach to designing IT governance. *Sloan Management Review, 46*(2), 26–34.

Weill, P., & Ross, J. (2009). *IT Savvy: What Top Executives Must Know to Go from Pain to Gain.* Harvard Business Press Books.

Weill, P., & Ross, J. W. (2004). *IT Governance.* Boston: Harvard Business School Press.

Weill, P., & Ross, J. W. (Eds.). (2004). *IT governance: How top performers manage IT decision rights for superior results.* Boston: Harvard Business School Press.

Wessels, E., & van Luggoernberg, J. (2006). IT Governance: Theory and Practice. In C. de Villiers & L. Smit (Eds.), *Conference on Information Technology in Tertiary Education* (pp. 1-14). Retrieved January 10, 2013, from http://citeseerx.ist.psu.edu/viewdoc/download?doi=10.1.1.1 00.2838&rep=rep1&type=pdf

Compilation of References

Wiengarten, F., Humphreys, P., Cao, G., & McHugh, M. (2013). Exploring the Important Role of Organizational Factors in IT Business Value: Taking a Contingency Perspective on the Resource-Based View. *International Journal of Management Reviews, 15*(1), 30–463. doi:10.1111/j.1468-2370.2012.00332.x

Wilkin, C. L. (2012). The role of IT governance practices in creating business value in SMEs. *Journal of Organizational and End User Computing, 24*(2), 1–17. doi:10.4018/joeuc.2012040101

Wilkin, C. L., Campbell, J., & Moore, S. (2013). Creating value through governing IT deployment in a public/private-sector inter-organizational context: A human agency perspective. *European Journal of Information Systems, 22*(5), 498–511. doi:10.1057/ejis.2012.21

Wilkin, C. L., & Riddet, J. L. (2008) Issues for IT Governance in a Large Not-for-Profit Organization: A Case Study. *Proceedings of the International MCETECH Conference on e-Technologies.* doi:10.1109/MCETECH.2008.24

Willcocks, L., Feeny, D., & Olson, N. (2006). Implementing core IS capabilities: Feeny-Willcocks IT governance and management framework revisited. *European Management Journal, 24*(1), 28–37. doi:10.1016/j.emj.2005.12.005

Williamson, K. (2002). *Research methods for students, academics and professionals: Information management and systems* (2nd ed.). Wagga Wagga, NSW: Centre for Information Studies, Charles Sturt University. doi:10.1533/9781780634203

Willson, P., & Pollard, C. (2009). Exploring IT governance in theory and practice in a large multi-national organisation in Australia. *Information Systems Management, 26*(2), 98–109. doi:10.1080/10580530902794760

Winter, R., & Schelp, J. (2008). Enterprise architecture governance: the need for a business-to-it approach. *Proceedings of the 23rd Annual ACM Symposium on Applied Computing (SAC2008).* doi:10.1145/1363686.1363820

Wirtz, B. W. (2011). *Business model management.* Wiesbaden, Germany: Gabler.

Wirtz, B. W. (2013). *Electronic Business* (4th ed.). Wiesbaden, Germany: Springer Gabler. doi:10.1007/978-3-8349-4240-1

Wißotzki, M., & Sandkuhl, K. (2015) Elements and Characteristics of Enterprise Architecture Capabilities. *14th International Conference BIR 2015* (LNBIP), (pp. 82-96). Springer.

Witman, P., & Ryan, T. (2010). Think big for reuse. *Communications of the ACM, 53*(1), 142–147. doi:10.1145/1629175.1629209

Wittenburg A. & Matthes, F. (2007). Building an integrated IT governance platform at the BMW Group. *International Journal Business Process Integration and Management, 2*(4).

Wu, S. P. J., Straub, D. W., & Liang, T. P. (2015). How information technology governance mechanisms and strategic alignment influence organizational performance: Insights from a matched survey of business and it managers. *Management Information Systems Quarterly, 39*(2), 497–518.

Xiaobao, P., Wei, S., & Yuzhen, D. (2013). Framework of open innovation in SMEs in an emerging economy: Firm characteristics, network openness, and network information. *International Journal of Technology Management*, 62(2-4), 223–250. doi:10.1504/IJTM.2013.055142

Xue, Y., Liang, H., & Boulton, W. R. (2008). Information technology governance in information technology investment decision processes: The impact of investment characteristics, external environment, and internal context. *Management Information Systems Quarterly*, 32(1), 67–96.

Yang, K. M., Cho, Y. W., Choi, S. H., Park, J. H., & Kang, K. S. (2010). A study on development of Balanced Scorecard using multiple attribute decision making. *Journal of Software Engineering & Applications*, 3, 286–272. doi:10.4236/jsea.2010.33032

Zachman, J. A. (2015). *IRM Enterprise Architecture Conference*. Retrieved from http://www.irmuk.co.uk/eac2015/day1.cfm#Day1S28

Zachman, J. A. (1987). A framework for information systems architecture. *IBM Systems Journal*, 26(3), 276–292. doi:10.1147/sj.263.0276

Zadeh, M. E., Millar, G., & Lewis, E. (2012). Mapping the Enterprise Architecture Principles in TOGAF to the Cybernetic Concepts--An Exploratory Study. *Proceedings of the 45th Hawaii International Conference on System Science (HICSS)*. doi:10.1109/HICSS.2012.422

Zarvić, N., Stolze, C., Boehm, M., & Thomas, O. (2012). Dependency-based IT Governance practices in inter-organizational collaborations: A graph-driven elaboration. *International Journal of Information Management*, 32(6), 541–549. doi:10.1016/j.ijinfomgt.2012.03.004

Zolnowski, A., & Böhmann, T. (2014). Formative evaluation of business model representations - The service business model canvas. *ECIS 2014 Proceedings*.

Zott, C., Amit, R., & Massa, L. (2010). *The business model: Theoretical roots, recent developments, and future research*. IESE Business School-University of Navarra.

About the Editors

Steven De Haes, PhD, is Full Professor Information Systems Management at the University of Antwerp and the Antwerp Management School. He is actively engaged in teaching and applied research in the domains of Digital Strategies, IT Governance & Management, IT Strategy & Alignment, IT Value & Performance Management, IT Assurance & Audit and Information Risk & Security. He teaches at bachelor, master, executive and PhD level. He also acts as Academic Director for the Executive Master of IT Governance & Assurance, the Executive Master of Enterprise IT Architecture, the Executive Master of IT Management and the (full-time pre-experience) Master in Management. His research has been published in international peer-reviewed journals and leading conferences. He is co-editor-in-chief of the International Journal on IT/Business Alignment and Governance (www.igi-global.com/ijitbag) and co-authored and/or edited several books, including "Enterprise Governance of IT: Achieving Strategic Alignment and Value" (Springer, first edition - 2009; second edition – 2015). He also acts as Academic Director of the IT Alignment and Governance (ITAG) Research Institute. He held positions of Director of Research and Associate Dean Master Programs for the Antwerp Management School (2008-2012) and currently is Associate Dean of Faculty. He also acts as speaker and facilitator in academic and professional conferences and coaches organizations in their digital strategies, IT governance, alignment, value and audit/assurance efforts. He was involved in the development of the international IT governance framework COBIT as researcher and co-author.

Wim Van Grembergen is emeritus professor at the Economics and Management Faculty of the University of Antwerp, immediate past-chair of the MIS department, and executive professor at the Antwerp Management School. For many years he has been teaching information systems at bachelor, master and executive level, and researched in business transformations through information technology, audit of information systems, IT performance management, business-IT alignment and IT governance. Professor Van Grembergen is since many years engaged in the continuous development of the COBIT framework. He was also a member of the ISO Enterprise

Governance of IT workgroup and in this capacity involved in the development of the ISO 38500 standard. Dr. Van Grembergen is a frequent speaker at academic and professional meetings and conferences and has served in a consulting capacity to a number of firms. In 2003 he established the ITAG Research Institute that aims to contribute to the understanding of IT Alignment and Governance through research and dissemination of the knowledge via publications, conferences and seminars. In 2009, he started as chief-editor a new journal *International Journal on IT/Business Alignment and Governance (IJITBAG)*. Within this research institute he is currently involved in a by ISACA commissioned research project on the business case of COBIT 5. He co-authored "Enterprise Governance of IT. Achieving strategic alignment and value" (Springer, 2009 and 2015).

Index